KU-070-192

Malta & Gozo

Carolyn Bain

Contents

Gozo & Comino
p139

Northwest
Malta p98

Sliema & St
Julian's p84

Central Malta
p115

Valletta, Floriana
& The Three
Cities p57

Southeast
Malta p128

Destination: Malta & Gozo

In its long and turbulent history, the diminutive island nation of Malta (all 316 sq km of it) has often assumed an importance out of all proportion to its size. It has served as a stepping stone between Europe and Africa, a policeman of the central Mediterranean sea lanes, a guardian of imperial trade routes and a launching pad for invasions.

In recent history Malta has been regarded as an inexpensive destination for a packaged beach holiday – and why not, when the weather is sunny and hot for most of the year and the sea is clear and warm; accommodation is good value (especially in the low season); there's an abundance of high-quality, reasonably priced restaurants and decent nightlife in resort areas. Added to these selling points is some dramatic coastal scenery and excellent opportunities for snorkelling, scuba diving and other water sports.

Malta's true highlights are not its beaches, however, and this sun-and-sand image doesn't do the country enough justice. What makes Malta a unique destination is that so much of its intriguing past is visible today – from 5000-year-old temples to immense fortifications built by the Knights of St John in the 16th century. A few days off the beaches will confirm that there is much to discover: the magnificent fortified capital of Valletta ('history encased in golden stone' was how the novelist Nicholas Monsarrat described it) with its glorious harbour and bustling Mediterranean street life; stone-built towns and villages with their idiosyncratic baroque churches and exuberant annual festas; the mysterious prehistoric temples and archaeological finds that pre-date Egypt's pyramids; the elegant, medieval fortress town of Mdina; and, if you want to get away from it all, the smaller and quieter island of Gozo with its quaint landscape of flat-topped hills and towering cliffs. Good things do indeed come in small packages!

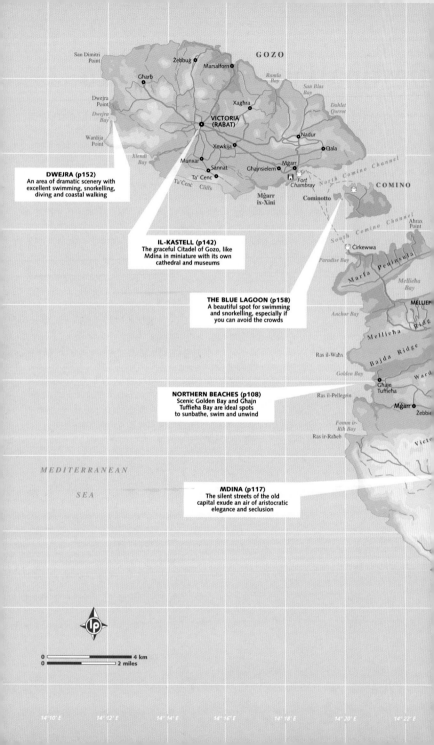

GOZO

San Dimitri Point

Żebbuġ

Gharb

Marsalforn

Ramla Bay

Dwejra Point

San Blas Bay

Dwejra Bay

Xaghra

Dahlet Qorrot

VICTORIA (RABAT)

Wardija Point

Nadur

Xlendi Bay

Xewkija

Qala

Munxar

Sannat

Ghajnsielem

Mġarr

North Comino Channel

DWEJRA (p152)
An area of dramatic scenery with excellent swimming, snorkelling, diving and coastal walking

Ta' Cenc

Ta'Cenc Cliffs

Fort Chambray

COMINO

Mġarr ix-Xini

Cominotto

Cominotto

South Comino Channel

Ahrax Point

IL-KASTELL (p142)
The graceful Citadel of Gozo, like Mdina in miniature with its own cathedral and museums

Ċirkewwa

Paradise Bay

Marfa Peninsula

Mellieha Bay

MELLIEĦA

THE BLUE LAGOON (p158)
A beautiful spot for swimming and snorkelling, especially if you can avoid the crowds

Anchor Bay

Mellieha

Bajda Ridge

Ras il-Wahx

Golden Bay

Ward

NORTHERN BEACHES (p108)
Scenic Golden Bay and Ghajn Tuffieha Bay are ideal spots to sunbathe, swim and unwind

Ghajn Tuffieha

Mġarr

Ras il-Pellegrin

Żebbie

Fomm ir-Rih Bay

Ras ir-Raheb

Victo

MEDITERRANEAN

SEA

MDINA (p117)
The silent streets of the old capital exude an air of aristocratic elegance and seclusion

N

(LP)

0 —————— 4 km
0 —————— 2 miles

14° 10' E   14° 12' E   14° 14' E   14° 16' E   14° 18' E   14° 20' E   14° 22' E

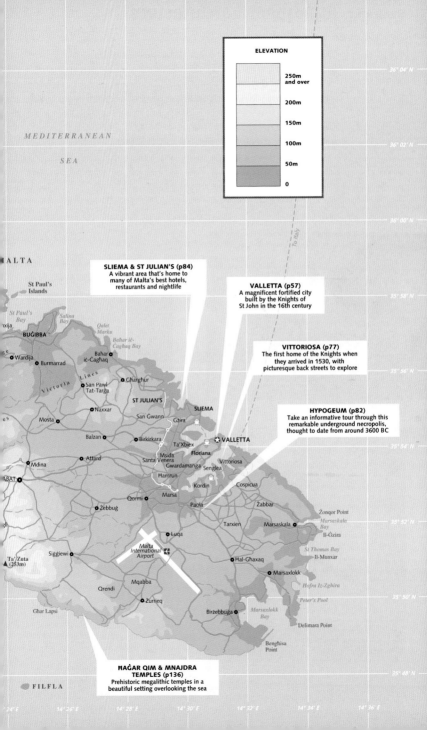

ELEVATION

250m
and over

200m

150m

100m

50m

0

MEDITERRANEAN

SEA

MALTA

To Italy

SLIEMA & ST JULIAN'S (p84)
A vibrant area that's home to
many of Malta's best hotels,
restaurants and nightlife

VALLETTA (p57)
A magnificent fortified city
built by the Knights of
St John in the 16th century

VITTORIOSA (p77)
The first home of the Knights when
they arrived in 1530, with
picturesque back streets to explore

HYPOGEUM (p82)
Take an informative tour through this
remarkable underground necropolis,
thought to date from around 3600 BC

St Paul's
Islands

St Paul's
Bay

Salina
Bay

Qalet
Marku

nxija

BUĠIBBA

Bahar ić-
Ċagħaq Bay

Wardija

Bahar
ić-Ċagħaq

Burmarrad

Lines

San Pawl
Tat-Tarġa

Għargħur

G</br>

Victoria

ST JULIAN'S

Mosta

Naxxar

San Gwann

SLIEMA

Gżira

Balzan

Birkirkara

Ta'Xbiex

VALLETTA

Msida
Santa Venera
Gwardamanga

Floriana

Mdina

Attard

Hamrun

Senglea

Vittoriosa

ABAT

Qormi

Marsa

Kordin

Cospicua

Żebbuġ

Paola

Żabbar

Żonqor Point

Tarxien

Marsaskala

Marsaskala
Bay

Il-Gżira

gli

Luqa

Malta
International
Airport

Hal-Għaxaq

St Thomas Bay

Il-Munxar

Ta' Żuta
▲ (253m)

Siggiewi

Marsaxlokk

Hofra Iz-Zghira

Qrendi

Mqabba

Peter's Pool

Żurrieq

Birżebbuġa

Marsaxlokk
Bay

Għar Lapsi

Delimara Point

Benghisa
Point

**HAĠAR QIM & MNAJDRA
TEMPLES (p136)**
Prehistoric megalithic temples in a
beautiful setting overlooking the sea

FILFLA

There's no denying that Malta is richly endowed with architectural gems. There are 359 Catholic **churches** (p38) and many of them are masterpieces. Aside from these vast temples of Catholicism, there are massive fortifications to keep out unwelcome guests – the most impressive of these surround Valletta and the **Three Cities** (p77). The graceful old towns of **Mdina** (p119) and **Il-Kastell** (p144) are home to peaceful, traffic-free alleyways hosting aristocratic palazzos – it's a treat to just wander these towns and admire the streetscapes (look for detail on door knockers, balconies and windows). The crumbling alleyways of **Vittoriosa** (p79) offer more out-of-the-way places where it's a joy to get lost and soak up the history.

EOIN CLARKE

Stroll through Mdina's Main Gate (p119), as locals have done since 1724

EOIN CLARKE

Be impressed, but undeterred, by Valletta's fortifications (p59)

Admire the restrained baroque façade of St Paul's Cathedral (p117), Mdina

PATRICK BEN LU

JULIET COOMBE

Study the richly ornamented interior of St John's Co-Cathedral (p63), Valletta

BETHUNE CARMICHAEL

Delight in the detail, Valletta (p68)

Check out the Mosta Dome (p125), site of a bona fide WWII miracle

EOIN CLARKE

Spectacular Natural Scenery

You don't expect a small and densely populated country like Malta to offer much in the way of natural beauty, and in many places it may feel like the only vistas are of built-up cities and resorts. But the coastline and rural areas provide relief from all that urban sprawl! **Dwejra** (p152) on Gozo showcases Malta's nature at its rawest – bays, a lagoon, a natural arch and other oddly shaped rock formations. Walk along the coast to the pretty swimming cove of **Għar Lapsi** (p137). Do some more cliff-top walking at **Dingli** (p124) on Malta's west coast. Enjoy a swim in pristine sea at **Ramla Bay** (p155) on Gozo, the popular beaches of **Għajn Tuffieħa Bay** and **Golden Bay** (p108) or the altogether more windswept and remote **Fomm ir-Riħ** (p123).

Take in spectacular cliff-top views at Ta'Ċenċ (p150) in Gozo's south

NEIL WILSON

VERONICA GARBUTT

Snorkel or dive around the Azure Window (p152), Gozo

Catch a boat to the Blue Grotto (p135), south Malta

SCOTT DARSNEY

Right: Swim in the crystal-clear waters of Comino (p158)

MICHAEL GEBICKI

Stock up on film, carry your camera at all times and get ready for many Kodak moments in Malta. Savour the incredible views of Grand Harbour, the historic **Three Cities** (p77) and Marsamxett harbour from the massive fortifications of **Valletta** (p68). Head over to the Three Cities or Sliema and enjoy stunning vistas of Valletta in return. High up on the walls of **Mdina** (p117) you can enjoy views over all northern and central Malta (and perhaps even Sicily on a clear day). Walking around **Comino** (p158) offers you prime viewing of Gozo to the north and Malta to the south, while from wild **Ras il-Qammieħ** (p113) your viewing pleasure is provided by the dramatic western sea-cliffs of Malta.

MICHAEL GEBICKI

Delight in the view of Grand Harbour from the vedette at Senglea (p81)

Snap the quintessential Maltese view of Marsaxlokk harbour (p133)

CRAIG F

Pinpoint all of Gozo's towns and attractions in a 360° turn on il-Kastell (p142)

EC

SCOTT DARSNEY

Pause and admire the bustling town of Sliema (p84) from Valletta

BETHUNE CARMICHAEL

Hike along the scenic coastline at Dwejra (p152)

Gaze across the water to Fort St Angelo (p79)

BETHUNE CARMICHAEL

The oldest freestanding stone structures on Earth, Malta's prehistoric temples pre-date Stonehenge and the pyramids of Egypt by 1000 years. A visit to these ancient megaliths prompts questions as to how these babies were built, who built them and why. If you can't come up with answers, just enjoy the scenery as there are certainly no answers to be found. And the most wondrous ancient wonder lies underground: the ancient necropolis **Hypogeum** (p82), where tour guides will do their best to give you some answers.

BETHUNE CARMICHAEL

Step back over 5000 years at the Ġgantija temples (p156)

Unravel the mystery of the solar alignments at the Mnajdra temple (p136)

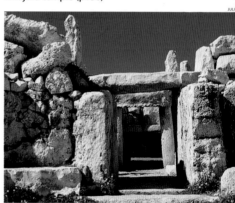

Catch the sunrise at Ħaġar Qim (p136)

Getting Started

Malta is a traveller-friendly, tourism-conscious country that provides options for people on all budgets, and allows for more than just hot-weather, beach-going holidays – there's a good deal of history, culture and tradition to explore too, so a long weekend here in the low season could constitute a cheap and fun city break (and the country is so small you could cover most of the highlights in just a few days).

Malta has a typically Mediterranean climate, with mild winters, hot, dry summers and some 300 days of sunshine. This means it's a year-round destination, so if you're planning to visit from most parts of Europe you should be able to find flights and package deals at any time of year. There are not too many alternatives to Malta if you want to stay within Europe and still be sunbathing in November! Winters are not at all unpleasant here, with an average of six hours of sunshine daily in January and daytime temperatures around 15°C. Sea temperatures around the islands range from 14.5°C in midwinter, to a balmy 25°C in August and September.

WHEN TO GO

The peak season for travel to Malta is June to September, when many resort hotels are booked solid. However, daytime temperatures in July and August can reach more than 35°C – uncomfortably hot – and it's tough to find your own patch of sand or rock at any beach (or battle the crowds at attractions). Weather-wise, the best time to visit is in spring (April to June) and autumn (September and October), though September still counts as high season in many hotels and the pleasant weather can sometimes be interrupted by a hot and humid wind.

See the climate chart (p164) for more information.

In November and December you can expect daytime temperatures of 12°C to 18°C and a fair amount of sunshine between spells of rain showers (the total annual rainfall is low, at around 580mm, and it falls mainly between October and February). January and February are the coldest months, when a strong northeasterly wind makes conditions more unpleasant. Winds are a feature of Malta's weather (see the boxed text p134). The stiff sea breeze is cooling in summer, but

---

DON'T LEAVE HOME WITHOUT...

- Double-checking the visa situation (p172)
- Sunscreen, sunglasses and a hat to protect you from the fierce summer sun
- A travel insurance policy specifically covering you for any planned 'high risk' activities (and remember that to many insurance companies, this includes scuba diving, p168)
- A copy of your diving qualifications, or a snorkel and mask to help you better investigate Malta's underwater world (p46)
- Long trousers or a long skirt and something to cover your shoulders if you plan to visit churches – too much bare flesh is frowned upon here
- A few glossy mags to keep you up-to-date on the lives of movie stars – very helpful if Russell Crowe or Brad Pitt makes a return visit to Malta, or in case any other movies are being made here during your visit (see the boxed text, p83)

in winter the northeasterly *grigal* can whip up the waves that pound across the harbour walls and occasionally disrupt the ferry service to Gozo. In spring and autumn the southeasterly *xlokk* (scirocco) sometimes blows in from North Africa, bringing humid and occasionally foggy conditions.

The main season for festas (feast days) is June to September, but if you want to catch a festa out of season, there's the Feast of St Paul's Shipwreck in Valletta on 10 February, and the Feast of the Immaculate Conception in Cospicua on 8 December. Two of the liveliest and most popular events on the islands, marked by public holidays, are the Carnival Week in early March and the L-Imnarja festival on 28 and 29 June. See Festivals & Events on p166 for more information on these events, plus details of how this nation of dedicated Catholics celebrates Christmas and Easter.

The Christmas and New Year period is a mini-high season in the middle of winter, when many Maltese emigrants return home to visit friends and family, and European tourists come looking for a spot of winter sunshine. Otherwise you can find some very cheap flight and accommodation deals from November to March.

HOW MUCH?

One night in a guest-house: Lm6-8 per person

Harbour cruise: Lm6.50

Bus trip: Lm0.15-0.20

Local newspaper: Lm0.15

Car hire: Lm6-10 per day

COSTS

By European standards, Malta is good value, although prices are increasing slowly and the authorities are behind a push to get more upscale tourism down this way (hence more five-star hotels, and cruise liners dropping in to see the sights).

If you can budget on around Lm15 per day, you'll get pleasant hostel or guesthouse accommodation, a simple restaurant meal, a decent streetside snack and enough cold drinks to keep you going. If you cook your own meals your costs will be even lower. On Lm20 to Lm25 a day you can start to live it up in a hotel with air-con and a swimming pool (especially in the low season) and enjoy meals at better restaurants. Allow extra for car rental (average about Lm8 per day).

LP INDEX

Litre of unleaded/leaded petrol: Lm0.36/0.39

Litre of bottled water: Lm0.40

Beer (in bar): Lm0.40

Souvenir T-shirt: Lm4

Street treat (*pastizzi*, pastries filled with ricotta or mushy peas): Lm0.10

TRAVEL LITERATURE

Considering how many tourists Malta receives, it's somewhat surprising that there's nothing by way of travel literature – and the genre of dissatisfied/overworked/lovelorn cityslickers finding themselves/finding love/renovating a farmhouse (or all three) in regions like Provence or Tuscany has yet to encompass Malta (although Gozo seems a logical place to set one of these stories – there are plenty of interesting characters and farmhouses to restore!).

There are, however, a few writers who have relocated to or holidayed in Malta and subsequently used the islands as a backdrop for their stories. *The Kappillan of Malta* by Nicholas Monsarrat is the best example – it's the classic English-language novel about Malta. Written in the early 1970s when the author was living in San Lawrenz, Gozo, it describes the experiences of the humble parish priest Dun Salvatore during WWII, interlaced with a potted history of Malta.

The British novelist Anthony Burgess was a tax exile in Malta for a brief spell at the end of the 1960s. He lived in a house in Lija, which became the fictional home of the 81-year-old protagonist in his masterly novel *Earthly Powers*.

Nicholas Rinaldi's novel *The Jukebox Queen of Malta* uses WWII Malta as a backdrop for his book – a love story between an American soldier

TOP TENS

FAVOURITE FESTIVALS & EVENTS

An intriguing combination of religion, music, food and fireworks constitute a festa in Malta, and every village has one. But there are plenty of other excuses to celebrate – here are our favourites (turn to p166 for more information on each).

- Carnival (February/March)
- Mediterranean Food Festival (March)
- Easter Week (March/April)
- Fireworks Festival (May)
- L'Imnarja (June)
- Malta Jazz Festival (July)
- Farsons Great Beer Festival (July)
- Historic Cities Festival (October)
- Mediterranea (November)
- Christmas (December)

TOP SWIMMING SPOTS

There are some great swimming spots scattered around Malta and Gozo – but don't expect to have them all to yourself in the high season (and remember the hat and sunscreen!).

- Blue Lagoon, Comino (p158)
- Wied il-Għasri, Gozo (p153)
- Għajn Tuffieħa Bay, Northwest Malta (p109)
- San Blas, Gozo (p158)
- Ġnejna Bay, Northwest Malta (p110)
- Ramla Bay, Gozo (p158)
- Fomm ir-Riħ, Central Malta (p123)
- Għar Lapsi, Southeast Malta (p137)
- Golden Bay, Northwest Malta (p108)
- Peter's Pool, Southeast Malta (p133)

MUST-SEE HISTORIC SITES

Many parts of Malta feel like open-air museums. The most remarkable and mysterious sites date back 5000 years, but the era of the Knights of St John is the most fascinating, and resulted in some magnificent architecture and damn good stories!

- Hypogeum, Paola – built between 3600 and 3000 BC (p82)
- Mdina – buildings from the 13th century (p117)
- Valletta's auberges and alleys – dating from the late 16th century (p68)
- Fortifications of Valletta & the Three Cities – defences from the mid-16th century (p68)
- Vittoriosa's Il Collachio – buildings from the 11th century (p79)
- Il-Kastell, Gozo – buildings from the 17th century (p142)
- St John's Co-Cathedral, Valletta – built in the 1570s (p63)
- Ħaġar Qim and Mnajdra Temples – built between 3600 and 3000 BC (p136)
- St Agatha's Catacombs, Rabat – frescoes from the 12th century (p122)
- Ġgantija Temples, Gozo – built between 3600 and 3000 BC (p156)

and a girl called Melita. The book has been compared to *Captain Corelli's Mandolin* with its juxtaposition of island romance, local history and the senseless violence of war.

The Brass Dolphin by Joanna Trollope (writing as Caroline Harvey) is another romance set in wartime Malta – with the protagonist an English woman pursued by a number of suitors. Easy beach or poolside reading.

INTERNET RESOURCES

About Malta (www.aboutmalta.com) A useful directory of Malta sites.

Gozo (www.gozo.com) Gozo-specific news and travel information.

Lonely Planet (www.lonelyplanet.com) Get started with summaries on Malta, links to Malta-related sites and travellers trading information on the Thorn Tree.

Malta Media (http://maltamedia.com) Interesting site of news, webcasts and special features from Malta.

Malta Tourism Authority (www.visitmalta.com) Huge official site available in a number of languages and full of info for travellers.

Maltese Government (www.gov.mt) Click on 'English' to access the gateway to all government departments and their sites.

Maltese Islands (www.malteseislands.com) Nicely designed site with extensive travel information.

Search Malta (www.searchmalta.com) Another comprehensive, searchable directory of links to Malta-related websites.

StarWeb Malta (www.starwebmalta.com) It bills itself as 'Malta's first online concierge' and has great listings under categories that travellers will find very useful.

Itineraries
CLASSIC ROUTES

MALTA'S MAGIC   One Week

Malta's small size (all of 27km by 15km) means that you can squeeze a lot of sightseeing into a short time if you want to. But it's more fun to take it easy – leave yourself time to absorb the sense of history that seeps from the stones of historic towns such as Valletta, Vittoriosa and Mdina, or to cool off at inviting swimming spots while you're out exploring. On the first day take in the sights of **Valletta** (p63), visiting St John's Co-Cathedral, the Grand Master's Palace and the Museum of Archaeology; and spend some time exploring the steep, narrow streets and alleys and walking around the vast fortifications. On the second day explore **Vittoriosa** (p77) and **Senglea** (p81), and on the third visit the **Tarxien Temples** and the **Hypogeum** (p82) before heading further south for a leisurely seafood lunch at **Marsaxlokk** (p133). On day four spend the morning at **Ħaġar Qim** and **Mnajdra temples** (p136) and the **Blue Grotto** (p135), and the afternoon exploring **Mdina** (p117) and **Rabat** (p121). Day five should be spent doing very little on a beach in the northwest (p108), recharging your batteries for some physical activity on day six – a long coastal or cliff-top walk, scuba diving or snorkelling perhaps. End on a high with a day trip to Comino's spectacular **Blue Lagoon** (p158).

Discover the mainland with this leisurely tour; it takes in the main towns and ancient temples, and makes time for the beach!

GOZITAN DELIGHTS

Five Days

The island of Gozo is even smaller than Malta (14km by 7km) and some might think a day here is all that's needed. But that wouldn't be doing little Gozo justice – a slower sightseeing pace is necessary in order to appreciate the more relaxed pace of rural life here. Your trip should start with a day exploring **Il-Kastell** and **Victoria** (p141), and day two could be spent at **Dwejra** (p152), swimming, snorkelling and walking along the coastline. Begin day three with a visit to the temples and other attractions of **Xagħra** (p155), then spend an afternoon reclining on a nearby beach such as **Ramla Bay** (p158). Day four could be set aside for exploring around **Ta'Ċenċ** (p149) and for seeking out a lesser-known spot for swimming and snorkelling (**Wied il-Għasri**, p153, is highly recommended). Spend day five visiting **Comino** (p158), discovering the tiny island on foot and swimming in crystal-clear water. But why not allocate a week to Gozo, rent a lovely old farmhouse and spend a few days relaxing poolside – hell, you're on holidays aren't you?!

Diminutive but delightful to explore. Take your time on Gozo and be sure to make the trip to pretty Comino.

The Author

CAROLYN BAIN

Carolyn grew up in a small country town outside Melbourne, Australia, where many of her classmates had surnames like Abela, Azzopardi, Borg, Buhagiar and Camilleri – their parents were all part of the great Maltese diaspora, although she didn't quite grasp this concept at primary school! Carolyn eagerly signed up for the chance to visit Malta for Lonely Planet and investigate this wee speck on the world map – what could be more perfect than a small, sunny island in the Med where everyone speaks English? Once there she fell in love with ricotta *pastizzi*; Gozitan farmhouses; old, bright-yellow buses and the peaceful back alleys of Vittoriosa.

MY FAVOURITE TRIP

My trip to Malta got off to a fine start on the island of **Comino** (p158), where I spent a couple of days sorting out jet lag after a 30-hour flight from Australia. Days were spent sampling the local food and wine, chatting to hotel staff and fellow travellers, and reading the local newspapers and all the Maltese history books I picked up at the hotel's souvenir shop. Walking the island was a pleasant pastime – this small, barren islet is wedged between Malta and Gozo and enjoys stunning views of both its neighbours. But the highlight was swimming in the exquisitely clear waters of the **Blue Lagoon** (p158) at about 5pm each day, after the crowds had departed and I had the area almost all to myself – especially knowing that in the rest of Europe, winter had well and truly arrived.

LAST EDITION

Neil Wilson wrote the 1st edition of this book. Born in Glasgow, Neil worked as a geologist in Australia and the North Sea and doing geological research at Oxford University. He gave up the rock business for the more precarious life of a freelance writer and photographer.

Snapshot

The hottest topic for the Maltese is obviously Malta's status as a brand-new member of the EU (as of May 2004), and what this will mean for the country. Will Europe take away Malta's hard-earned independence finally gained in 1964 after centuries of foreign rule? Money might soften the blow of a perceived loss of independence – so how much EU funding will there be and on what will it be spent? Will prices increase? Will there be pressure to legalise abortion (Ireland is the only other EU country where it is illegal) and other anti-Catholic acts like divorce, euthanasia and same-sex marriage? No less important to the gun-wielding bird-shooters: will bird hunting in Malta be outlawed? The government has attempted to answer many of these anxious questions on the website www.mic.org.mt (and some of the answers to the more controversial questions are that abortion will remain illegal in Malta, and hunting will continue). For an outline of events leading up to Malta's bid for EU membership see the History chapter, p32.

Hunting is a hot topic (see p44 in the Environment chapter for background information). Many Maltese are opposed to the shooting of birds that occurs here on such a large scale, but they are even more opposed to the EU dictating on such matters. These people justifiably point out the hypocrisy of the EU potentially telling Malta to stop bird hunting while animal cruelty continues elsewhere in Europe (for example, bullfighting in Spain and fox hunting in England).

Hunting is part of a larger issue facing Malta – the environment. Maltese authorities are waking up to the fact that because Malta's economy relies so heavily on tourism, in a post-September 11 world it must put its best foot forward to attract and retain tourists – and its bumpy, congested roads, pollution and vast urban sprawl can make a poor impression. There is a growing awareness of the need to treat environmental issues as a high priority, but it often comes down to the issue of costs, and who will pay for the necessary cleanups and enforcement of more environmentally friendly regulations.

The authorities figure that one way to place less stress on natural resources and be less at the mercy of tourist trends is to drive Malta's tourist industry upmarket, away from the old-fashioned cheap-and-cheerful package holiday image, and to develop niche markets such as conference travel, cultural and educational tours, and cruise liners. This strategy is epitomised by the new five-star hotels in the St Julian's-Paceville area, the ritzy Portomaso apartment and marina complex near Paceville (p89), and the Cottonera waterfront development in Vittoriosa (p77). But with so many cashed-up Europeans visiting and now able to purchase property in Malta should they so desire, will house prices escalate beyond the reach of the average Maltese wage-earner?

These are just some of the issues getting coverage in the media and being heatedly discussed by the Maltese at their local watering holes. One hot topic you won't have too much trouble understanding and joining in on: what's the latest blockbuster being filmed in Malta, which movie stars are in town and where are they hanging out?

FAST FACTS

Population: 400,000 (2003 estimate)

Area: 316 sq km

Population density: 1266 people per sq km

GDP growth: 2.2%

Inflation: 2.4%

Unemployment: 5.1%

Number of tourists annually: 1.2 million (around 450,000 from the UK)

Average height for women: 159.9cm (5ft 4 in) – the shortest in Europe

Average height for men: 169.4cm (5 ft 8 in) – second-shortest in Europe (after Portugal)

History

Malta has a fascinating history, and the island is crowded with physical and cultural reminders of the past, most of them easily accessible to visitors. The fossilised bones of animals found in Ghar Dalam cave (p135) in the southeast suggest that Malta was once linked by a land bridge to Sicily and southern Europe. But Malta was not big enough to support a hunting-gathering lifestyle, and the earliest evidence of human habitation – the remains of primitive farming settlements – has been dated to the period 5200 to 4000 BC. Neolithic pottery fragments unearthed at Skorba (p109) are similar to those found in Sicily.

A Concise History of Malta It's no small feat to cover a country's past in under 300 pages. This book, by Carmel Cassar, is a readable introduction to Maltese history.

THE TEMPLE BUILDERS

The Maltese Islands' oldest monuments are the beautifully preserved megalithic temples built between 3600 and 2500 BC, the oldest surviving freestanding structures in the world. About 1000 years before the construction of the Great Pyramid of Cheops in Egypt, the people of Malta were manipulating megaliths weighing up to 50 tonnes and creating elaborate buildings that appear to be oriented in relation to the winter solstice sunrise (see the boxed text, p137).

No-one knows whether the temple builders evolved from the pre-existing farming communities of Malta, or whether they arrived from elsewhere bringing their architectural skills with them. Rock-cut tombs found on a hillside near Xemxija and dated to before 4000 BC display a trefoil layout which may be a precursor to the three-lobed plan seen in the temples. The remains of around a dozen megalithic temples survive today, and some of them are remarkably well preserved. The best places to view these prehistoric marvels are at Tarxien (p82), south of Siġġiewi (p136) and on Gozo, near Xagħra (p156).

www.my-malta.com A website chock-full of interesting articles. Click on the 'Our Rich History' section for a good overview and links to more detailed history pages.

Whatever their origins, the temple people seem to have worshipped a cult of fertility. Archaeologists have found large numbers of figurines and statues of wide-hipped, well-endowed female figures – the so-called 'fat ladies' of Malta – that have been interpreted as fertility goddesses. These figures range in size from barely 10cm long to more than 1.5m, and the best examples can be seen at the National Museum of Archaeology in Valletta (p66).

The culmination of Malta's temple culture was the large temple complex at Tarxien and the subterranean burial chambers of the nearby Hypogeum (p82). These sites appear to have been abandoned some time after 2500 BC and then taken over by a noticeably different Bronze Age culture. The new inhabitants cremated their dead and used the Tarxien temple site as a cemetery.

http://web.infinito.it/ utenti/m/malta_mega _temples Everything you ever wanted to know about Malta's megalithic temples, and then some.

PHOENICIANS & ROMANS

From around 800 to 218 BC, Malta was colonised by the Phoenicians and, for the last 250 years of this period, by Phoenicia's principal North African colony, Carthage. With their watchful eyes painted on the prow,

TIMELINE	c 5200 BC	c 3600–2500 BC
	Arrival of first known habitants (from Sicily)	Megalithic temples are built on Malta and Gozo

the colourful Maltese fishing boats – the *luzzu* and the *kajjik* (check them out at Marsaxlokk, p133) – seem little changed from the Phoenician trading vessels that once plied the Mediterranean. The islands may have served as a Carthaginian naval base during the First Punic War against Rome (264–241 BC).

www.heritagemalta.org
Get acquainted with
14 major museums and
11 heritage sites in
Malta, plus find out
how to visit them.

During the Second Punic War (218–201 BC) Rome took control of Malta before finally crushing Carthage in the Third Punic War (149–146 BC). The island was then given the status of a municipium, or free town, with the power to control its own affairs and to send an ambassador to Rome. However, there is evidence that Malta retained a Punic influence. The 1st-century BC historian Diodorus Siculus described the island as a Phoenician colony, and the biblical account of St Paul's shipwreck on Malta in AD 60 (see the boxed text, p102) describes the islanders as 'barbarous' (ie they did not speak the 'civilised' languages of Latin or Greek).

St Paul's shipwreck was certainly the most influential event of this period. According to tradition, during Paul's three-month stay both the Roman governor of Malta (later to become St Publius) and many of the islanders were converted to Christianity, making the Maltese one of the oldest Christian peoples in the world.

Malta seems to have prospered under Roman rule. The main town, called Melita, occupied the hilltop of Mdina but spread over an area around three times the size of the later medieval citadel. The excavated remains of townhouses, villas, farms and baths suggest that the inhabitants enjoyed a comfortable lifestyle and occupied themselves with the production of olives, wheat, honey and grapes.

When the Roman Empire split into East and West in AD 395 Malta seems to have fallen under the sway of Constantinople. But very little is known of this period of Maltese history, when the islands seem to have been little more than a neglected Byzantine backwater.

DID YOU KNOW?

The *luzzu* (traditional Maltese fishing boat) still carries the watchful 'Eye of Osiris' on its bow, a custom thought to date back more than 2500 years.

ARABS & NORMANS

The rapid expansion of Islam in the 7th to 9th centuries saw an Arab empire extend from Spain to India. Arab armies invaded Sicily in 827 and finally conquered it in 878; Malta fell into Arab hands in 870. Both Malta and Sicily remained Muslim possessions until the end of the 11th century. The Arab rulers generally tolerated the Christian population, introduced irrigation and the cultivation of citrus fruits and cotton, and had a notable impact on Maltese customs and language. Apart from the names Malta and Gozo, which probably have Latin roots, there is not a single place name in the Maltese Islands that can be proved to pre-date the Arab occupation.

During the 11th century small groups of Norman adventurers from northern Europe arrived in Italy, formed allegiances with local leaders and set up a system of feudal lordships. One, Robert Guiscard, took over much of southern Italy and in 1060 his younger brother, Count Roger, captured Messina and used it as a base for the conquest of Sicily. It took 30 years of constant struggle, but by 1091 Count Roger had driven the Arabs out of Sicily. A year earlier, in 1090, he had captured Malta after a surprise attack. Tradition has it that, needing the support of the local people, Count Roger tore his red-and-white quartered banner in two and gave half to the Maltese contingent, thus inventing Malta's national flag.

800–218 BC	218 BC–AD 395
Malta is colonised by the Phoenicians and then controlled by the Carthaginians	The Romans control Malta after their success in the Punic Wars

For the next 400 years Malta's history was closely linked to Sicily's, and its rulers were a succession of Normans, Angevins (French), Aragonese and Castilians (Spanish). Malta remained a minor pawn on the edge of the European chessboard, and its relatively small population of down-trodden islanders paid their taxes by trading, slaving and piracy, and were repaid in kind by marauding Turks and Barbary corsairs. During this period a Maltese aristocracy began to form, and a few of their elegant townhouses survive in Mdina and Victoria. Their distinctive architectural style is referred to as Siculo-Norman (Sicilian-Norman), but it is almost entirely Sicilian – there is little if any Norman influence.

The marriage of the Catholic monarchs Ferdinand II of Aragon and Isabella of Castile led to the unification of Spain in 1479, and under their grandson, the Holy Roman Emperor Charles V, Malta became part of the vast Spanish Empire. One of the greatest threats to Charles' realm was the expanding Ottoman Empire of Süleyman the Magnificent in the east. Süleyman had driven the Knights of St John from their island stronghold of Rhodes between 1522 and 1523 (for information on the history of the Knights of St John see the boxed text, p26). When the Knights begged Charles V to find them a new home, he offered them Malta along with the governorship of Tripoli, hoping that they might help to contain the Turkish naval forces in the eastern Mediterranean. The nominal rent was to be two falcons a year – one for the emperor and one for the viceroy of Sicily (see the boxed text, p43).

Knights of St John – www.orderofmalta.org The long, illustrious history of the Knights, as well as information about present-day knightly activities.

THE KNIGHTS ARRIVE

Grand Master Philippe Villiers de L'Isle Adam (1530–34) of the Knights of St John was not particularly impressed by the gift of the Maltese Islands, which seemed to him barren, waterless and poorly defended. Neither were the 12,000 or so local inhabitants, who were given no say in the matter. Nor were the aristocracy, who remained aloof in their palazzos in Mdina. However, determined to make the best of a bad job and hoping one day to return to Rhodes, in 1530 the Knights decided to settle in the fishing village of Birgu (now Vittoriosa) on the south side of Grand Harbour and set about fortifying the harbour. Visitors can wander around Vittoriosa (p77) and admire the early auberges of the Knights.

In Rhodes, the Knights had developed into a formidable marine fighting force and had been a constant thorn in the side of the Ottoman Turks. Their expulsion allowed Turkish corsairs to roam the central Mediterranean at will, raiding and pillaging and carrying off Christians to serve as slaves or to hold for ransom. Short of funds and lacking any real support from European powers, the Knights became pirates themselves, attacking Turkish trading ships and raiding along the Barbary Coast of North Africa.

Their greatest adversary was Dragut Reis, the Turkish admiral, who invaded Gozo in 1551 and carried off almost the entire population of 5000 into slavery. Then in 1559 the Knights lost half their galleys in a disastrous attack on Dragut's lair on the island of Djerba off the Tunisian coast. With the power of the Knights at a low ebb, Süleyman the Magnificent saw an opportunity to polish off this troublesome crew once and

AD 60	395–870
St Paul is shipwrecked on Malta and brings Christianity to the population	Malta falls under Byzantine rule

for all, while at the same time capturing Malta as a base for the invasion of Europe from the south.

THE GREAT SIEGE OF 1565

Jean Parisot de la Valette (see the boxed text, p60) was Grand Master between 1557 and 1568. He was a stern disciplinarian and an experienced soldier who foresaw the threat of a Turkish siege and prepared for it well. Following the disaster of 1559, la Valette ordered the building of ditches and defensive walls around the peninsulas of Birgu and Isla. Fort St Angelo on the tip of Birgu was rebuilt and strengthened, and Fort St Michael was built on Isla. A new fortress, Fort St Elmo, was constructed on the tip of the uninhabited Sceberras peninsula.

The Knights' galley fleet was taken into the creek below Birgu, and a great chain was stretched across the harbour entrance between Fort St Angelo and Fort St Michael to keep out enemy vessels. Food, water and arms were stockpiled, and la Valette sent urgent requests for aid to the emperor, the pope and the viceroy of Sicily. But no help came. In May 1565, when an enormous Ottoman fleet carrying more than 30,000 men arrived to lay siege to the island, la Valette was 70 years old, and commanded a force of only 700 Knights and around 8000 Maltese irregulars and mercenary troops.

The Turkish force, led jointly by Admiral Piali and Mustafa Pasha, dropped anchor in the bay of Marsaxlokk, and its soldiers set up camp on the plain of Marsa. The entire population of Malta took refuge within the walls of Birgu, Isla and Mdina, taking their livestock with them and poisoning the wells and cisterns they left behind. The Turks took their time, digging out gun emplacements and setting up batteries, before beginning their campaign with an attack on Fort St Elmo, which guarded the entrance to both Grand and Marsamxett Harbours. The fort was small and held a garrison of only 60 Knights and a few hundred men. Mustafa Pasha was confident that it would fall in less than a week.

Dragut Reis, the wily old corsair who had always been the scourge of the Mediterranean sea lanes, was now, like la Valette, an old man. The 80-year-old ex-pirate was in the employ of Sultan Süleyman and arrived in Malta a few weeks into the siege to advise Mustafa and Piali. He was unhappy with their decision to concentrate first on the taking of St Elmo, but preparations were too far advanced to change plans. Dragut tirelessly went around the Turkish positions, inspiring his men and helping to set up batteries on Dragut Point and Ricasoli Point to increase the pressure on the tiny garrison. It was while setting up one such battery on Mt Sceberras that he was struck in the head by a splinter of rock thrown up by an enemy cannonball and retired, mortally wounded, to his tent.

Dragut's fears over the wisdom of besieging St Elmo were proved right. Despite continuous bombardment and repeated mass assaults on its walls, Fort St Elmo held out for over four weeks, and cost the lives of no fewer than 8000 Turkish soldiers before it was finally taken; not one of the Christian defenders survived. On receiving the news that the fort had been captured, old Dragut smiled, and died. Looking across at the looming bulk of Fort St Angelo from the smoke and rubble of St Elmo,

Malta: A Guide to the Fortifications
Quentin Hughes, a British architect, has written the classic guide to the defences of Valletta, Floriana and the Three Cities, as well as the forts that dot the coastline.

870–1090	1090–1530
Malta is occupied by Arab rulers	Count Roger captures Malta and places the country under Norman control

Mustafa Pasha is said to have muttered, 'Allah! If so small a son has cost us so dear, what price shall we have to pay for so large a father?'

Hoping to intimidate the already demoralised defenders of Fort St Angelo, Mustafa Pasha ordered that several of the leading Knights should be beheaded and their heads fixed on stakes looking across towards Birgu. The Turks then nailed the decapitated bodies to makeshift wooden crucifixes and sent them floating across the harbour towards St Angelo. La Valette's response was immediate and equally cruel. All Turkish prisoners were executed and decapitated. The Knights then used their heads as cannonballs and fired them back across the harbour to St Elmo.

Then began the final Turkish assault on the strongholds of Birgu and Isla. Piali's fleet moved from Marsaxlokk to Marsamxett Harbour to unload heavy artillery, and several ships were dragged across the neck of the Sceberras peninsula – the entrance to Grand Harbour was still commanded by the guns of Fort St Angelo – to aid the ground forces with fire from the sea. Through the heat of summer, the Turks launched at least 10 massed assaults on the walls of Birgu and Isla, but each time they were beaten back. On 18 August, when a large section of wall was brought down and it looked as though the Turkish troops were on the verge of fighting their way into the town, Grand Master la Valette himself joined his Knights in the breach. The day was saved.

Turkish morale was drained by the long, hot summer, their increasing casualties, and the impending possibility of having to spend the entire winter on Malta (the Mediterranean sailing season traditionally ended with the storms of late September). The ferocity of their attacks decreased. Then on 7 September the long-promised relief force from Sicily finally arrived. Twenty-eight ships carrying some 8000 men landed at Mellieha Bay and took command of the high ground around Naxxar as the Turks scrambled to embark their troops and guns at Marsamxett.

Seeing the unexpectedly small size of the relief force, Mustafa Pasha ordered some of his troops to land again at St Paul's Bay, while the rest marched towards Naxxar from Marsamxett. But the tired and demoralised Turkish soldiers were in no mood to fight these fresh and ferocious Knights and men-at-arms, and they turned and ran for the galleys now anchored in St Paul's Bay. Thousands were hacked to pieces in the shallow waters of the bay as they tried to escape. That night the banner of the Order of St John flew once again over the battered ruins of St Elmo, and in their churches the Knights and the people of Malta gave thanks for the end of the siege.

The part played in the Great Siege by the ordinary people of Malta is often overlooked, but their courage and resilience was a deciding factor in the Turkish defeat. The defence force was made up of some 5000 or 6000 Maltese soldiers. Local women and children contributed by repairing walls, bringing food and ammunition to the soldiers and tending the wounded. Although their names do not appear in the official accounts, local heroes like Toni Bajada – who has streets named after him in Valletta, St Paul's Bay and Naxxar – live on in Maltese legend. The date of the end of the siege, 8 September, is still celebrated in Malta as the Victory Day public holiday.

The Great Siege
Marauding Muslims vs crusading Christians – a clichéd plotline, you have to admit. This is a page-turning account of the epic 1565 battle between the Ottoman Turks and the Knights of St John, by Ernle Bradford.

1530	1565
The Knights of St John arrive after being given Malta by Emperor Charles V	The Knights are victorious over the Turks in the Great Siege of Malta

KNIGHTS OF ST JOHN

Origins

The Sovereign and Military Order of the Knights Hospitaller of St John of Jerusalem – also known variously as the Knights of St John, the Knights of Rhodes, the Knights of Malta, and the Knights Hospitallers – had its origins in the Christian Crusades of the 11th and 12th centuries.

A hospital and guesthouse for poor pilgrims in Jerusalem was founded by some Italian merchants from Amalfi in 1070. The hospital, operated by monks who followed the Augustinian rule, won the protection of the papacy in 1113 and was raised to the status of an independent religious order known as the Hospitallers. The Order set up more hospitals along the pilgrimage route from Italy to the Holy Land, and Knights who had been healed of their wounds showed their gratitude by granting funds and property to the growing Order.

Other Knights offered their services as soldiers to provide protection for pilgrims, and thus the Order's dual role of healing the sick and waging war on the enemies of Christ began to evolve. Knights of the Order kept the road to Jerusalem free of bandits. To kill an infidel was to win glory for Christ, and to die in battle in defence of the faith was to become a martyr in heaven.

When the armies of Islam recaptured the Holy Land in 1291, the Order sought refuge first in the Kingdom of Cyprus. In 1309 they acquired the island of Rhodes, planning to stay close to the Middle East in the hope of reconquering Jerusalem. But here they remained for over 200 years, building fortresses, auberges and a hospital, and evolving from a land-based army into the most formidable naval fighting force the medieval world had ever seen.

Organisation

The Knights of St John were European noblemen who lived the lives of monks and soldiers. The objective of the Order was 'the service of the poor, and the defence of the Catholic faith'. The Order was financed by the revenue of properties and estates spread throughout Europe, which were either owned by members of the Order, or had been gifted to it.

There were three basic divisions within the Order. The Military Knights were the elite of the Order, and formed the core of its military fighting force. They were drawn from the younger male members of Europe's aristocratic families – in other words, those who were not the principal heirs – and had to prove noble descent. After a year as a Novice, a Knight then spent three years in the galleys and two years in service in the Convent (the name given to the Knights' headquarters) before becoming eligible for higher ranks.

The Chaplains did not need to prove noble descent, and were more monk than soldier, though they were still expected to serve in the galleys and to fight in times of need. Their main duties were in the hospital and in the Order's churches and chapels. Sergeants-at-Arms were likewise not restricted by birth, and served mainly as soldiers and nurses. The Order was ruled over by the Supreme Council, headed by the Grand Master, who was elected by his peers from among the highest ranks of the Knights of Justice.

The Knights' traditional attire was a hooded monk's habit, made of black camel hair with a white Maltese cross emblazoned on the breast. The distinctive eight-pointed cross is thought to have evolved from the symbol of the Italian city of Amalfi. It did not assume its present form until the 16th century, when the eight points were said to represent the eight virtues which the Knights strove to uphold: to live in truth; to have faith; to repent of sins; to give proof of humility; to love justice; to be merciful; to be sincere and whole-hearted; and to endure persecution.

The Order comprised eight nationalities or langues (literally 'tongues' or languages) – Italy, France, Provence, Auvergne, Castile, Aragon, Germany and England. (The English langue was dissolved by King Henry VIII in 1540 following his breach with the Roman Catholic Church.)

1566	1798–1800
Valletta is founded by the Knights' Grand Master Jean Parisot de la Valette	The French occupy Malta after Napoleon's conquest in 1798

Each langue was led by a *pilier* (literally 'pillar'), and its members lived and dined together in an auberge (hostel), which operated a bit like an Oxford college or an American fraternity house. Each langue was assigned to a particular task or part of the city walls during battle (hence the Poste de France, the Poste d'Aragon etc on the walls of Vittoriosa), and each *pilier* had a specific duty – for example, the *pilier* of the Italian langue was always the admiral of the galley fleet.

The Order's properties and estates in Europe were managed by a network of commanderies and priories, often headed by older Knights who had retired from active service in the Mediterranean. Although the Knights were bound by vows of individual poverty, the Order as a whole was immensely wealthy. A Knight was required to bequeath four-fifths of his personal wealth to the Order; the remaining fifth – known as the *quint* – could be disposed of as he chose.

Hospitals

The hospitals created by the Order – first in Jerusalem and the Holy Land, then in Rhodes and finally in Malta – were often at the leading edge of the development of medical and nursing science. Ironically, although the Knights had sworn to bring death and destruction to the 'infidel' Muslims, many of their medical skills and treatments were gleaned from the study of Arabic medicine.

The Sacra Infermeria in Valletta (built in the 1570s) had 600 beds – the Great Ward alone could hold 350 patients – and was famous throughout Europe. It was obliged to provide care for the sick of any race or creed, slaves included, though non-Catholics were put in a separate ward. Patients were nursed by the members of the Order – even the Grand Master tended the sick at least once a week – and treated by physicians, surgeons and pharmacists. The hospital's plate and cutlery was made of solid silver 'to increase the decorum of the Hospital and the cleanliness of the sick' and basic rules of hygiene were observed.

The hospital was overseen by the Grand Hospitaller, a post traditionally filled by the *pilier* of the French langue. The Order's surgeons performed many advanced operations including trepanation, bladder-stone removal and cataract removal as well as more commonplace amputations and wound treatments. From 1676 onwards the study of anatomy and human dissection was taken up. Anyone particularly interested in the medical services provided by the Knights should visit the Knights Hospitallers exhibition inside the Sacra Infermeria in Valletta (p68).

After Malta

Following the loss of their French estates and their expulsion from Malta by Napoleon in 1798, the Knights sought refuge first in Russia, where they were welcomed by Tsar Paul I, and later in Italy. After several years of uncertainty, they finally made their headquarters in the Palazzo di Malta (the former Embassy of the Hospitallers) in Rome.

In the late 19th and 20th centuries the Order rebuilt itself as a religious and charitable organisation. Now known as the Sovereign Military Order of Malta, it is an internationally recognised sovereign entity that mints its own coins and prints its own postage stamps. In effect, it's a state without a territory, although its properties in Rome enjoy extraterritorial status. It concerns itself largely with providing hospitals, medical supplies and humanitarian aid in regions stricken by poverty, war and natural disasters.

The Order now has diplomatic relations with 93 countries, has legations in several countries (including France, Germany, Belgium and Switzerland) and has been a permanent observer at the UN since 1994. The Order has an embassy in Malta (housed in the Cavalier of St John in Triq l-Ordinanza in Valletta), and since 1991 it has reoccupied its old home in the upper part of Fort St Angelo in Vittoriosa. Since 1988 the Grand Master has been Fra' Andrew Bertie, a Scot.

1814	1814–1964
Malta is formally recognised as a British colony after British forces help drive the French from Malta in 1800	The British rule Malta, allowing varying levels of Maltese self-government

AFTER THE SIEGE

The Knights of Malta, previously neglected, were now hailed as the sa-
viours of Europe. Money and honours were heaped on them by grateful
monarchs, and the construction of the new city of Valletta – named after
the hero of the siege – and its enormous fortifications began. Although
sporadic raids continued, Malta was never again seriously threatened
by the Turks. Süleyman the Magnificent died in 1566, and much of the
Turkish fleet was destroyed by a magazine explosion in the Istanbul
dockyards. What remained of Ottoman naval power was crushed at the
Battle of Lepanto in 1571, a victory in which the galleys of the Order of
St John played an important (and enthusiastic) part.

The period following the Great Siege was one of building – not only of
massive new fortifications and watchtowers, but of churches, palaces and
auberges. The military engineer Francesco Laparelli was sent to Malta
by the pope to design the new defences of Valletta and Italian artists
arrived to decorate its churches, chapels and palazzos. An influx of new
Knights, eager to join the now prestigious Order, swelled the coffers of
the treasury.

The pious Grand Master Jean de la Cassière (1572–81) oversaw the
construction of the Order's new hospital – the Sacra Infermeria (p68) –
and the magnificent new Cathedral of St John (p63). The cathedral
replaced the old Conventual Church of St Lawrence in Birgu (renamed
Vittoriosa, or Victorious, after the siege). La Cassière's successor, Hugues
Loubeux de Verdalle (1581–95), was more inclined to enjoy the privileges
rather than the responsibilities of power and built himself the grandiose
Verdala Palace near Rabat (p124).

Alof de Wignacourt (1601–22) initiated many worthy projects, including the construction of an aqueduct to bring water to Valletta from the
hills near Mdina. In contrast, the decadent Antoine de Paule (1623–36)
built the San Anton Palace (p126) as a summer retreat for hedonistic
parties, an unchivalrous tendency which was to increase in the ensuing
century. Grand Master Antonio Manoel de Vilhena (1722–36) adorned
Malta with many magnificent buildings, including the Manoel Theatre
(p67), Fort Manoel (p88) and the Palazzo de Vilhena (p119), but the long
reign of the haughty Emanuel Pinto de Fonseca (1741–73), who considered himself on a level with the crowned heads of Europe, epitomised
the change that had come over the Order. One glance at the portrait of
Pinto in the museum of St John's Co-Cathedral in Valletta (p63) will
reveal how far the Order had strayed from its vows of poverty, chastity
and obedience.

With the Turkish threat removed, the Knights occupied themselves
less with militarism and monasticism, and more with piracy, commerce,
drinking and duelling. Although the Order continued to embellish Valletta, the Knights sank into corrupt and ostentatious ways.

NAPOLEON IN MALTA

In the aftermath of the French Revolution, Grand Master Emmanuel de
Rohan (1775–97) provided money for Louis XVI's doomed attempt to
escape from Paris. By the late 18th century around three-quarters of the
Order's income came from the Knights of the French langue, so when

1853–56	1914–18
Malta is used as a base and supply station of the Royal Navy during the Crimean War	Malta serves as a military hospital during WWI

the revolutionary authorities confiscated all of the Order's properties and estates in France, the Order was left in dire financial straits.

In 1798 Napoleon Bonaparte arrived in Malta aboard his flagship *L'Orient* at the head of the French Navy, on his way to Egypt to counter the British influence in the Mediterranean. He demanded that he be allowed to water his ships, but the Knights refused. The French landed and captured the island with hardly a fight – many of the Knights were in league with the French, and the Maltese were in no mood for a battle. On 11 June 1798 the Order surrendered to Napoleon. Although the French Knights were allowed to remain, the German Grand Master Ferdinand von Hompesch (1797–98) and the rest of the Order were given three days to gather what belongings they could and leave.

Napoleon stayed in Malta for only six days (in the Palazzo de Parisio in Valletta), but when he left *L'Orient* was weighed down with silver, gold, paintings and tapestries looted from the Order's churches, auberges and infirmary. (Most of this treasure went to the bottom of the sea a few months later when the British Navy under Admiral Nelson destroyed the French fleet at the Battle of the Nile.) The French also abolished the Maltese aristocracy, defaced coats of arms, desecrated churches and closed down monasteries.

Napoleon left behind a garrison of 4000 men, but they were taken unawares by a spontaneous uprising of the Maltese people (see the boxed text, p121) and had to retreat within the walls of Valletta. A Maltese deputation sought help from the British, and a naval blockade was enforced under the command of Captain Alexander Ball, who was sympathetic to the islanders' aspirations. The French garrison finally capitulated in September 1800, but having taken Malta the British government was unsure what to do with it.

The Treaty of Amiens (March 1802) provided for the return of Malta to the Order of St John (then taking refuge in Russia and Naples), but the Maltese did not want them back and sent a delegation to London to petition the British to stay. Their pleas fell on deaf ears, and arrangements had been made for the return of the Order when war between Britain and France broke out again in May 1803. Faced with the blockade of European ports against British trade, the British government soon changed its mind regarding the potential usefulness of Malta. Even Admiral Nelson, who had previously dismissed the islands, wrote: 'I now declare that I consider Malta as a most important outwork...I hope we shall never give it up.'

While the latter stages of the Napoleonic Wars wore on, Malta rapidly became a prosperous entrepôt, and with the Treaty of Paris in 1814 it was formally recognised as a Crown Colony of the British Empire, with Lieutenant-General Sir Thomas Maitland as its first governor and commander-in-chief.

Britain & Malta: The Story of an Era Why does Malta have red phone boxes? Joseph Attard's interesting historical account of British involvement in Malta from 1800 until the 1970s gives a Maltese point of view.

CROWN COLONY

The end of the Napoleonic Wars brought an economic slump to Malta as trade fell off and little was done in the way of investment in the island. But its fortunes revived during the Crimean War (1853–56) when it was developed by the Royal Navy as a major naval base and supply station,

1919	1921
Riots against British rule demonstrate a growing desire for self-government	A new constitution grants a limited form of self-government

and with the opening of the Suez Canal in 1869 Malta became one of the chief coaling ports on the imperial steamship route between Britain and India.

The early 19th century also saw the beginnings of Maltese political development. In 1835 a Council of Government made up of prominent local citizens was appointed to advise the governor and a free press was established. The constitution of 1849 allowed for eight elected representatives to partake in the government of Malta, but it was not until 1887 that the elected members constituted a majority.

In the second half of the 19th century vast sums were spent on improving Malta's defences and dockyard facilities as the island became a linchpin in the imperial chain of command. The Victoria Lines (see the boxed text, p101) and several large dry docks were built during this period. Commercial facilities were also improved to cater for the busy trade route to India and the Far East. In 1883 a railway was built between Valletta and Mdina (it was closed down in 1931). Between 1800 and 1900 the population of Malta doubled to 200,000.

During WWI Malta served as a military hospital – it was known as the 'Nurse of the Mediterranean' – providing 25,000 beds for casualties from the disastrous Gallipoli campaign in Turkey. But prices and taxes rose during the war and the economy slumped. During protest riots in 1919 four Maltese citizens were shot dead by panicking British soldiers and several more were injured.

The British government replied to the unrest by giving the Maltese a greater say in the running of Malta. The 1921 constitution created a diarchic system of government, with a Maltese assembly presiding over local affairs and a British imperial government controlling foreign policy and defence. The 1921 elections saw Joseph Howard of the Unione Politica (which later merged to become the Nationalist Party) take his place as the first prime minister of Malta.

The interwar years were marked by economic depression and political turmoil (the constitution was revoked in 1930 and again in 1933) and by growing tensions with Italy. Emigration became an increasingly attractive option, and many Maltese moved to Britain, Canada, the USA and Australia. Emigration to Canada and Australia increased after WWII, and today Australia has one of the largest Maltese communities in the world.

In 1930s Malta, Italian was the language of law and of polite conversation among the upper classes. Malti was the everyday language of the common people, and an increasing number could also speak English. Mussolini made the ridiculous claim that Malti was merely a dialect of Italian and that the Maltese Islands rightly belonged within his new Roman Empire. In 1934 Britain decreed that Malti would be the language of the law courts, and that henceforth Malti and English would be Malta's official languages.

www.roots-malta.com If your ancestors were among the thousands of Maltese who emigrated and you want to know more about them and their homeland, start here.

FORTRESS MALTA

The outbreak of WWII found Britain undecided as to the strategic importance of Malta. The army and air force felt that the islands could not be adequately defended against bombing attacks from Sicily and should

1920s–1930s	1934
Economic depression and political turmoil result in large numbers emigrating	Britain decrees Malti and English as Malta's official languages

---

THE BRITISH LEGACY

For 150 years, from 1814 to 1964, Malta was part of the British Empire. The legacy of British rule takes many forms, most noticeably in the fact that almost everyone speaks English as well as Malti. But there are many others – the Maltese drive on the left, and many of the vehicles on the road are vintage British models from the 1950s, '60s and '70s; the local football teams have typically British names like United, Hotspurs, Wanderers, Rangers and Rovers; cafés serve sausage, egg and chips and pots of tea; and beer is sold in pints and half-pints. Traditional items of British street furniture – red telephone boxes, red pillar boxes, and blue lamps outside police stations – persist in Malta, though they have largely disappeared from British towns. And conversations in Malti are liberally sprinkled with the English expression 'Awright?'

---

be evacuated. However, Winston Churchill (then First Lord of the Admiralty) insisted that possession of Malta was vital to Britain's control of supply lines through the bottleneck of the central Mediterranean. As a result of this indecision Malta was unprepared when Mussolini entered the war on 10 June 1940. The very next day Italian bombers attacked Grand Harbour.

The only aircraft available on the islands on 11 June were three Gloster Gladiator biplanes – quickly nicknamed *Faith*, *Hope* and *Charity* – whose pilots fought with such skill and tenacity that Italian pilots estimated the strength of the Maltese squadron to be in the region of 25 aircraft! (What remains of *Faith* can be seen in Malta's National War Museum, p66) The Gladiators battled on alone for three weeks before squadrons of modern Hurricane fighters arrived to bolster the islands' air defences.

Malta effectively became a fortified aircraft carrier, a base for bombing attacks on enemy shipping and harbours in Sicily and North Africa. It also harboured submarines which preyed on Italian and German supply ships. These operations played a vital part in reducing the supplies of fuel and materiel to the Panzer divisions of Rommel's Afrika Korps, which were then sweeping eastwards through Libya towards British-held Egypt. Malta's importance was clear to Hitler too, and crack squadrons of Stuka divebombers were stationed in Sicily with the objective of pounding the island into submission.

Malta's greatest ordeal came in 1942, when the country came close to starvation and surrender. It suffered 154 days and nights of continuous bombing – in April alone some 6700 tonnes of bombs were dropped on Grand Harbour and the surrounding area. By comparison, at the height of London's Blitz there were 57 days of continuous bombing. On 15 April 1942 King George VI awarded the George Cross – Britain's highest award for civilian bravery – to the entire population of Malta. The citation from the king read: 'To honour her brave people I award the George Cross to the island fortress of Malta to bear witness to a heroism and devotion that will long be famous in history.' The award can be seen at the National War Museum in Valletta.

Just as Malta's importance to the Allies lay in disrupting enemy supply lines, so its major weakness was the difficulty of getting supplies to the island. At the height of the siege in the summer of 1942 the governor made an inventory of remaining food and fuel and informed London

Siege: Malta 1940–1943 Ernle Bradford writes well on his favourite topic: Malta under siege. This time the role of the bad guys is played by the bomb-dropping Italians and Germans. See also the sidebar reference on p25.

The Kappillan of Malta Nicholas Monsarrat's historical novel tells the story of a local priest's experiences during WWII, interspersed with lively accounts of Malta's history. Perfect holiday reading.

1940–43	1942
Malta experiences heavy bombing and great hardship during WWII	The people of Malta are awarded the George Cross for civilian bravery

The Malta Story (1953) Surprisingly the only movie made about the dramatic WWII events in Malta. Men in spiffy uniforms fight dangerous battles, perform heroic acts and win hearts (of course). Stars Alec Guinness and Jack Hawkins.

that if more supplies did not get through before the end of August then Malta would be forced to surrender. A massive relief convoy, known as Operation Pedestal, consisting of 14 supply ships escorted by three aircraft carriers, two battleships, seven cruisers and 24 destroyers, was despatched to run the gauntlet of enemy bombers and submarines. It suffered massive attacks, and only five supply ships made it into Grand Harbour – the crippled oil tanker *Ohio,* with its precious cargo of fuel, limped in lashed between two warships on 15 August. This date, the Feast of the Assumption of the Virgin Mary, led to the Maltese christening the relief ships 'The Santa Marija Convoy'.

In the words of Winston Churchill, 'Revictualled and replenished with ammunition and essential stores, the strength of Malta revived', and it was able to continue its vital task of disrupting enemy supply lines. The aircraft and submarines based in Malta succeeded in destroying or damaging German convoys to North Africa to the extent that Rommel's Afrika Korps was low on fuel and ammunition during the crucial Battle of El Alamein in October 1942, a situation that contributed to a famous Allied victory and the beginning of the end of the German presence in North Africa.

Malta Convoy More WWII drama. This book, by Peter Shankland & Anthony Hunter, describes the famous Operation Pedestal that succeeded in resupplying Malta at its lowest point in 1942.

In July 1943 Malta served as the operational headquarters and air support base for Operation Husky, the Allied invasion of Sicily. By co-incidence, the date on which the Italian Navy finally surrendered to the Allies – 8 September – was the same as that on which the Great Siege had ended 378 years previously. As the captured enemy warships gathered in Marsaxlokk Bay, Admiral Cunningham, Commander-in-Chief of Britain's Mediterranean Fleet, cabled the Admiralty in London: 'Be pleased to inform their Lordships that the Italian battle fleet now lies at anchor under the guns of the fortress of Malta.'

For a better understanding of this tumultuous period in Maltese history, travellers should visit the National War Museum (p66) and Lascaris War Rooms (p67), which housed the headquarters and operations rooms of the Royal Air Force and Royal Navy. Both sights are in Valletta.

INDEPENDENT REPUBLIC

After 1943 Malta's role in the war rapidly diminished. WWII left the islands with 35,000 homes destroyed and the population on the brink of starvation. In 1947 the war-torn island was given a measure of self-government, and a £30 million war-damage fund to help rebuilding and restoration. But the economic slump that followed Britain's reductions in defence spending and the loss of jobs in the naval dockyard led to calls either for closer integration with Britain, or for Malta to go it alone. On 21 September 1964, with Prime Minister Dr George Borg Olivier at the helm, Malta gained its independence. It remained within the British Commonwealth, with Queen Elizabeth II as the head of state represented in Malta by a governor general.

DID YOU KNOW?

When Malta gained independence in 1964 it was the first time since prehistory that the country had been ruled by the native Maltese and not by some outside power.

Borg Olivier's successor as prime minister in 1971 was the Labour Party's Dominic (Dom) Mintoff, whose name was rarely out of the news headlines in the 1970s. Mintoff was a fiery and controversial politician who was not afraid to speak his mind. During his prime ministership (1971–84) Malta became a republic (in 1974, replacing the queen as head

1947	1964
Self-government is restored	Malta becomes independent, with Queen Elizabeth II still the head of state

of state with a president appointed by parliament). In 1979 links with Britain were reduced further when Mintoff expelled the British armed services, declared Malta's neutrality and signed agreements with Libya, the Soviet Union and North Korea.

In 1987 the Nationalist Party assumed power under the prime ministership of Dr Eddie Fenech Adami, and won a second term with a landslide victory in 1992, when one of the party's main platforms was Malta's application to join the EC (European Community; now the EU). The 1996 general election saw the Labour Party, led by Dr Alfred Sant, narrowly regain power with a one-seat majority. One of its main policies was to suspend the country's application for full EU membership. However, in 1998, during a debate on development of the Cottonera waterfront into a marina for private yachts, Dom Mintoff, then 82 years old but still capable of causing controversy, crossed the floor of the house to vote with the Opposition. A snap general election in September 1998 was effectively a vote of confidence in the Labour government. Labour lost, Fenech Adami's Nationalist Party was returned to power, and under the Nationalist Party Malta's bid for EU membership was revived.

In 2002 Malta was formally invited to join the EU and in March 2003 the country voted in a referendum on the matter. Ninety-two percent of eligible voters cast their vote and, in a close result, just over 53% voted in favour of EU membership. This pro-EU result was confirmed when Fenech Adami's Nationalist Party won a general election one month later, in April 2003. Malta became a member of the EU on 1 May 2004. It is anticipated that the euro will eventually be adopted as the national currency (probably in 2007).

DID YOU KNOW?

An estimated crowd of 100,000 people attended the Mass celebrated by Pope John Paul II on his visit to Malta in May 2001, staged in St Publius Sq in Floriana.

Malta-EU Information Centre –
www.mic.org.mt
Lots of factsheets, FAQs and details of what it means for Malta to join the Big Boys of the EU in 2004.

1974	2004
Malta becomes a republic	Malta joins the EU

The Culture

THE NATIONAL PSYCHE

When Malta gained its independence in 1964 it was the first time since prehistory that the islands had been ruled by the native Maltese, and not by some outside power. Since early in the 1st millennium BC Malta had been occupied successively by Phoenicians, Carthaginians, Romans, Byzantines, Arabs, Normans, Sicilians, the Knights of St John, the French and the British. All of these temporary powers have influenced Maltese culture to varying degrees, yet through all this time the population has managed to preserve a distinctive identity and a strong sense of continuity with the past. Despite an easy blend of Mediterranean and British culture in the islands today, there's still a strong feeling of tradition. The people remain fairly conservative in outlook; the Catholic Church still exerts a strong influence, the church's buildings and parish activities remain at the core of village life and family values are held in high regard.

Malteasers for the Visitor Charles Flores' small, sweet and sometimes humorous volume is full of 'teasers' designed to give the visitor an insight into the Maltese way of life.

The Maltese are justifiably proud of their small country's historical importance and the local grit and determination (well demonstrated during WWII). Understandably, they have relished their independence since 1964 and the vast majority of the population takes great interest in political matters (one local spoke of a reverence for authority among many locals – perhaps a by-product of centuries of foreign rule, or of the strongly religious nature of the population). In elections, voter turnout is very high (around 90%) but, interestingly, margins are usually very close – the country seems fairly evenly split on major issues.

The Maltese are friendly, laid-back and generally welcoming of tourists. As in most southern European countries, things can move slowly here, but this is tempered by an efficiency that may be a result of British rule. People are a little more reserved than you might expect for a Mediterranean country (in comparison to, say, Italians and Greeks) – again, this may be a direct result of the British influence. Visitors will easily be able to observe the very Maltese quirks that have withstood globalisation and continue to make the country unique and fascinating – among them the language, the village festa, and the love of cars, sport, politics, fireworks and lotteries.

LIFESTYLE

Malta is a fairly conservative country, with traditions and attitudes similar to those of southern Italy. Although its influence is waning, the Roman Catholic Church still plays an important part in everyday life. A Sunday Mass census held in Malta in December 1995 showed an

---

A UNIQUE LANGUAGE

The native language of Malta is called Malti. Some linguists attribute its origins to the Phoenician occupation of Malta in the 1st millennium BC, but most link it to North African Arabic dialects. The language has an Arabic grammar and construction but is a melting pot of influences, laced with Sicilian, Italian, Spanish, French and English loan-words.

English is taught to schoolchildren from an early age, and almost everyone in Malta speaks it well. Many also speak Italian, helped by the fact that Malta receives Italian TV. French and German are also spoken, though less widely.

See also the Language chapter, p192.

attendance of around 67%, and a recent study has shown that an estimated 70% of the people in Malta, in contrast to the average 21% in Western Europe, find religion to be very important in their lives. Baptisms, weddings and funerals are still celebrated in church (weddings in the parish where the bride was born), and the most important event in the calendar is the annual parish festa. Divorce and abortion are illegal; however, the possibility of divorce being legalised is a widely discussed issue. Still, family values are very important, as is the love of socialising common to southern European countries – Sunday in particular is the day to gather with family and friends and enjoy good food and company.

Statistically, the Maltese enjoy a good standard of living, low inflation (around 2% to 3%) and low unemployment (around 5%). Schooling is compulsory between the ages of five and 16 and is provided free in state and church schools (church schools are subsidised by the government). A university education is also free to Maltese citizens and students receive an annual stipend. Statistics are only part of the equation – positive elements such as the warm climate, strong connection to the land, and healthy sense of tradition and community also play their part in creating what to many might seem an enviably relaxed lifestyle.

Folklore of an Island – Maltese Threshold Customs For aspiring anthropologists, Tarcisio Zarb's book covers Maltese traditions related to all of life's big occasions, including birth, puberty, marriage and death.

POPULATION

Malta's population is around 400,000, with most people living in the satellite towns around Valletta, Sliema and Grand Harbour. Of the total, approximately 30,000 live on Gozo, while Comino has a mere handful of farmers (six or seven) in winter, and a couple of hundred tourists in summer. Around 85% of the population lives in urban areas and only 15% in rural areas. More than 95% of the population is Maltese-born.

The foreign community in Malta is predominantly British. Most foreigners live in Sliema and its surrounding modern suburbs. There also is a growing North African Muslim community of over 2000, who are married to Maltese nationals. Unfortunately, some racism exists, with occasional reports of owners of some bars and clubs periodically discouraging or prohibiting darker-skinned persons, especially of African or Arab origin, from entering their establishments.

DID YOU KNOW? Malta is one of the most densely populated countries in the world, with 1266 persons per sq km (the comparable figure for the Netherlands is around 390).

SPORT
Football (Soccer)
The Maltese are great football fans, and follow the fortunes of local sides and international teams with equal fervour (many bars televise matches). The local football season runs from September till May, and there is a Maltese Premier League with 10 teams. League and international matches are held at the National Stadium at Ta'Qali, which is situated between Mosta and Rabat; results are reported in the local newspapers. More information can be obtained from the website of the **Malta Football Association** (www.mfa.com.mt), which details the leagues, teams and fixtures. Another website, www.maltafootball.com, is also a good resource for information.

DID YOU KNOW? It is estimated that there are as many Maltese living abroad as there are in Malta.

Water Polo
As the heat of summer increases, football gives way to water polo, with its season lasting from July till September. The fans who were shouting on the terraces now yell from the pool sides. Games are hard fought and physical, and it's worth trying to take in a match during your stay in Malta. The important clashes are held at the National Swimming Pool Complex on Triq Maria Teresa Spinelli in Gżira. Further information is available from the **Aquatic Sports Association** (☎ 21 322 884; www.asaofmalta.com).

Horse Racing

Horse racing is one of the Maltese Islands' most popular spectator sports, with race meetings held at the Marsa Racecourse, part of the Marsa Sports Complex outside Valletta (see p163), every Sunday from October to May. Races are mostly trotting – where the jockey rides a light two-wheeled gig drawn by the horse – and the betting is frantic.

DID YOU KNOW?

There are 359 Catholic churches in Malta, serving around 392,000 people – the 98% of Malta's population who are Catholic.

RELIGION

Under the constitution, Roman Catholic Christianity is the official state religion and must be taught in state schools, but the Maltese constitution guarantees freedom of worship.

ARTS
Crafts

Malta is noted for its fine crafts – particularly its handmade lace, hand-woven fabrics and silver filigree. Lace-making probably arrived with the Knights in the 16th century. It was traditionally the role of village women – particularly on the island of Gozo – and, although the craft has developed into a healthy industry, it is still possible to find women sitting on their doorsteps making lace tablecloths.

The art of producing silver filigree was probably introduced to the island in the 17th century via Sicily, which was then strongly influenced by Spain. Malta's silversmiths still produce beautiful filigree by traditional methods but in large quantities to meet tourist demand.

www.aboutmalta.com Click first on Arts & Entertainment, then Visual Arts, to reach a useful directory of links to numerous art-related topics, local galleries and the works of Maltese artists (including painters, sculptors, photographers and ceramists).

Other handicrafts include weaving, knitting and glass-blowing; the latter is an especially healthy small industry which produces glassware exported throughout the world. Head to Ta'Qali Crafts Village near Rabat (p123) or its smaller Gozitan equivalent, Ta'Dbieġi (p152) for the opportunity to see locals practising their craft and to buy souvenirs.

Literature

Pietro Caxaro's *Cantilena*, an epic poem composed in the mid-15th century, is the earliest known literary work in Malti but Italian remained the language of literature in Malta until the late 19th century. Important writers of this period include Ġan Anton Vassallo (1817–67) and Guże Muscat Azzopardi (1853–1927). *Inez Farruġ* by Anton Manwel Caruana (1838–1907), published in 1889, is considered to be the first literary novel written in Malti.

Probably the best-known and best-loved of Maltese writers is Carmelo Psaila (1871–1961). Under his pen name of Dun Karm he became Malta's national poet, movingly chronicling the island's sufferings in WWII. Anton Buttiġieġ (1912–83) was another important poet, who captured the essence of the Maltese landscape and man's relationship with nature in his lyric poetry and tightly written vignettes.

Among modern writers, the playwright and novelist Francis Ebejer (1925–93), who wrote in both Malti and English, stands out. His novels deal with the tensions between tradition and modernity. *For Rozina... A Husband* is a collection of short stories (in English) that attempt to capture the essence of Maltese village life. Oliver Friġġieri (b 1947), Professor of Maltese at the University of Malta, is Malta's best-known and most prolific living novelist.

Music

The Maltese are great music lovers and the *għana* (arna; song) is Maltese folk music at its most individual and traditional. A tribute to Malta's

EDWARD DE BONO

lateral thinking *n.* a way of solving problems by rejecting traditional methods and employing unorthodox and apparently illogical means

Collins English Dictionary

Type 'Edward de Bono' into an Internet search engine and you will retrieve a list of over 156,000 Web pages. Do the same with 'lateral thinking' and the number is around 300,000.

Dr Edward de Bono (b 1933) is a world authority on cognitive science and the study of thinking and creativity. A pioneer in the teaching of creative thinking, he was born in Malta and educated at St Edward's College, Malta, and the University of Malta, where he qualified in medicine at age 21. He later gained an honours degree in psychology and physiology at Oxford University and holds postgraduate degrees from Oxford, Cambridge and Malta universities.

Inventor of the widely used technique of 'lateral thinking', Dr de Bono's principal achievement has been to remove the mystique from creativity and to develop tools and methods for teaching, enhancing and using creative thinking. His book *The Mechanism of Mind*, published in 1969, took the novel viewpoint that the human brain was a self-organising information system and suggested that creativity was quite simply a necessary behaviour in any such system. The Nobel Prize–winning physicist Murray Gell-Mann praised the book as being 10 years ahead of its time in tackling the subject of nonlinear systems – a forerunner of chaos theory.

De Bono believes that the traditional emphasis on analysis, critical thinking and argument is important, but not sufficient. He seeks to put an equal emphasis on constructive and creative thinking, and to promulgate these techniques in educational and business settings around the world. To this end he has written over 60 books – notably *Lateral Thinking* (1967), *Po: Beyond Yes and No* (1972), *Six Thinking Hats* (1985) and *I Am Right, You Are Wrong* (1990) – which have been translated into around 35 languages, and produced three television series as well as speaking and lecturing around the world. There is a De Bono Institute (www.debono.org) in Melbourne which serves as a world centre for creative thinking, and a De Bono Foundation (www.edward debonofoundation.com) in Dublin.

Dr de Bono's methods are taught and used in a vast range of environments, from primary-school classrooms to the boardrooms of the world's biggest corporations. De Bono himself was invited to give the keynote address to Microsoft's first-ever marketing meeting in Seattle.

In 1995 he was awarded the National Order of Merit by the president of Malta, the country's highest civilian award. He has had a planet named after him (Edebono) by the International Astronomic Union and was named by a group of university professors in South Africa as one of the 250 people in all history who have contributed most to humanity.

Edward de Bono lives in Venice (he owns homes all over the world, including in Malta) and runs international seminars on thinking, creativity and education.

geographic location, *għana* verses are a mixture of a Sicilian ballad and the rhythmic wail of an Arabic tune, and were traditionally viewed as the music of the farmers, labourers and working classes. In its truest form, lyrics are created fresh each time and tell stories of village life and events in local history. The verses are always sung by men with guitar accompaniment. Some band clubs and bars, especially in the centre and south of Malta, organise *għana* nights or you might chance upon an impromptu *għana* in a rural bar. The St James' Cavalier Centre for Creativity in Valletta (p67) occasionally holds *għana* nights and you may also see performances at various heritage events.

Etnika is a traditional folk group reviving ethnic Maltese musical forms and instruments. Their music, using traditional bagpipes, horns and drums, was once part of Malta's daily life, and was used in a variety of social contexts – from weddings to funerals. Etnika reinterpret this musical heritage for a contemporary audience, and sometimes fuse it with *għana*, jazz

www.allmalta.com
Intrigued by *għana*? Read all about it (and listen to samples) on this website.

www.eurovisionmalta
.com
The highs! The lows!
The bright outfits and
big hair! Read all about
Malta's performance at
Eurovision over the years.

and flamenco for a unique sound – you should be able to pick up a CD of their music at music stores throughout Malta. See also www.etnika.com.mt for information.

Band music is one of the most popular traditions on the islands. Every town and village has at least one band club (sometimes two, and they are often engaged in strong rivalry). Bands play a vital role in the village festa and other open-air events.

There is also a modern music scene and live music is featured in many pubs and clubs. The Eurovision Song Contest is taken very seriously in Malta – don't upset a local by mentioning Malta's worst-ever result at the 2003 competition (second-last) after the country came a close second in 2002.

Architecture

Malta's architectural heritage is dominated by two influences – the Knights of St John and the Roman Catholic Church. Together they created a distinctive variation of the baroque style of architecture that swept across Europe between the end of the 16th century and the 18th century.

MALTA'S CHURCHES

The Maltese claim to be one of the oldest Christian peoples in the world, having been converted by St Paul after his shipwreck on Malta in AD 60.

There are 64 Catholic parishes and 313 Catholic churches on Malta, and 15 Catholic parishes and 46 Catholic churches on Gozo. These range from full cathedrals down to tiny wayside chapels and were built between the 15th and 20th centuries. The main period of church-building in Malta took place after the arrival of the Knights of St John, in the 16th, 17th and 18th centuries. The oldest surviving church in Malta is the tiny medieval Chapel of the Annunciation at Ħal Millieri near Żurrieq (p135), which dates from the mid-15th century, and is in Maltese vernacular style.

The 16th century saw the Renaissance style imported from Italy by the Knights, followed by the more elaborate forms of Maltese baroque which evolved throughout the 17th century and culminated in the design of St Paul's Cathedral in Mdina. The 19th and 20th centuries saw the addition of several large churches in the neogothic style, including St Paul's Anglican Cathedral in Valletta (1839–41) and the Church of Our Lady of Lourdes in Mġarr, Gozo (1924–75). Two huge rotundas were also built by public subscription: the Church of St Mary at Mosta (1833–60) and the Church of St John the Baptist (1951–71) at Xewkija on Gozo.

The following list includes some of Malta's most impressive examples of church architecture.

St John's Co-Cathedral, Valletta (p63)

(1573–77; Gerolamo Cassar, interior by Mattia Preti) The austere Renaissance façade of St John's – the Conventual Church of the Order of St John from 1577 to 1798 – conceals a richly ornamental interior. The tombs of Grand Masters Nicolas Cotoner and Ramon Perellos in the Chapel of Aragon are floridly baroque.

Church of St Paul's Shipwreck, Valletta (p70)

(c 1580; Gerolamo Cassar, remodelled by Lorenzo Gafa in 1680) Don't be fooled by the largely 19th-century façade on Triq San Pawl – this is one of Valletta's oldest churches. The wooden statue of St Paul was carved in 1657 by Melchiorre Gafa, Lorenzo's brother, and is paraded through the streets on the festa day (10 February).

Church of St Lawrence, Vittoriosa (p80)

(1681–97; Lorenzo Gafa) St Lawrence's occupies the site of a small church built by Count Roger in 1090. It was enlarged and taken over by the Knights as their original conventual church in

The greatest Maltese architect of the 16th century was Gerolamo Cassar (1520–86). He was born in the fishing village of Birgu 10 years before the Knights of St John arrived from Rhodes and worked as an assistant to Francesco Laparelli, the military engineer who designed the fortifications of Valletta. He studied architecture in Rome and was responsible for the design of many of Malta's finest buildings, including the Grand Master's Palace, the façade of St John's Co-Cathedral, and many of the Knights' auberges.

The prolific architect Tommaso Dingli (1591–1666) created many of Malta's parish churches. His masterpiece is the Church of St Mary in Attard, which was designed when he was only 22 years of age. Lorenzo Gafa (1630–1704) designed many of the Maltese Islands' finest examples of Maltese baroque, among them the cathedrals of Mdina and Gozo.

Other important architects who also worked in the Maltese baroque style were Giovanni Barbara (Palazzo de Vilhena, Mdina, 1730), Giuseppe Bonnici (the Old Customs House, Valletta, 1747) and Domenico Cachia (the Auberge de Castile, Valletta, 1744).

5000 Years of Architecture in Malta Author Leonard Mahoney provides comprehensive coverage of the topic, from Neolithic temples to the auberges of the Knights and beyond.

Malta in 1530 and houses relics brought from Rhodes, a silver processional cross, and a fine altarpiece by Mattia Preti showing the martyrdom of St Lawrence. The dome was rebuilt after being damaged by a bomb in 1942.

Church of St Mary, Attard (p126)

(1613–16; Tommaso Dingli) This is one of the finest examples of Renaissance-style architecture in Malta, built on a Latin cross plan with an elegant and restrained façade adorned with statues of the saints.

St Paul's Cathedral, Mdina (p117)

(1697–1702; Lorenzo Gafa) Designed by Gafa at the height of his career, this is probably the finest example of the Maltese baroque style (rather more restrained and less florid than the baroque of Italy). The cathedral occupies the site of a Norman church built in the 1090s, and there may have been a church here since the 4th century.

Cathedral of the Assumption, Victoria, Gozo (p142)

(1697–1711; Lorenzo Gafa) Gozo's cathedral is another fine example of Maltese baroque designed by Gafa. Lack of funds meant the dome was never built, but an 18th-century trompe l'oeil painting looks convincingly like one on the inside. The cathedral occupies the site of an older Norman church, and possibly of a Roman temple.

Church of Sts Peter & Paul, Nadur, Gozo (p157)

(1760–80; Giuseppe Bonnici) The extravagance of Bonnici's original design has been tempered by a more sober 19th-century façade, but the beautiful and ornate marble interior is pure baroque. The twin statues of its patron saints have given it the nickname *iż-Żewġ* (the pair, or the twins), and its festa (29 June) is one of the liveliest on the islands.

Church of St John the Baptist, Xewkija, Gozo (p149)

(1951–71; Joseph D'Amato) This huge rotunda was built with money and labour donated by the parishioners of Xewkija. It is the biggest church in the Maltese Islands, and can seat up to 4000 people.

IL CAVALIER CALABRESE

Mattia Preti (1613–99) was a painter from Calabria, Italy who lived and worked in Malta for 30 years. In 1661 he was commissioned by Grand Master Rafael Cotoner to decorate the vault of St John's Co-Cathedral in Valletta (see p63). The 18 vivid scenes depicting events in the life of St John the Baptist – from Zachary in the Temple to the beheading of St John – took five years to complete. Preti also designed the ornately carved decoration on the walls and pillars of the cathedral – a rich confection of gilded leaves, scrolls, flowers, Maltese crosses and coats of arms – and painted several of the altarpieces in the side chapels. Some of his best work can be seen in Valletta's National Museum of Fine Arts (p66). Preti was eventually accepted into the Order of St John, and came to be known as *Il Cavalier Calabrese* – the Calabrian Knight.

Painting

As in architecture, Maltese art was much influenced by neighbouring Italy. Many Italian artists worked in Malta (most famously Caravaggio; see the boxed text below) and most Maltese artists went to study in Italy.

The greatest Maltese painter of the 17th century was Mattia Preti (1613–99; see the boxed text above), who painted the vault frescoes in St John's Co-Cathedral as well as many altarpieces for parish churches and for the cathedral at Mdina.

Giuseppe Cali (1846–1930) was a portraitist and religious artist who painted altarpieces for parish churches and also created the murals in the Mosta Dome (p125).

Exhibitions by contemporary Maltese artists are regularly held in the Museum of Fine Arts in Valletta, and a great spot to check out what is happening on the local scene is the St James' Cavalier Centre for Creativity (p67).

www.angelfire.com/ma /architecture
This website has loads of information on the various eras of architecture in Malta, with good accompanying photographs and useful links.

Sculpture

Antonio Sciortino (1879–1947) was the leading Maltese sculptor of the 20th century. Born in Żebbuġ, he spent 25 years in Rome before returning

---

CARAVAGGIO IN MALTA

Michelangelo Merisi (1571–1610), better known by the name of his home town, Caravaggio, was a revolutionary Italian painter whose naturalistic representation of religious subjects replaced the traditional symbolism of 16th-century art. In particular, he introduced the bold use of shadow and selective lighting to dramatise his subjects.

He made his name in Rome with a series of controversial paintings, but also earned a reputation as a wild man, and numerous brawls and encounters with the law culminated in Caravaggio murdering a man during an argument over a tennis game. He fled Rome and went into hiding in Naples for several months. Then, towards the end of 1607, he moved to Malta.

In Malta, Caravaggio was welcomed as a famous artist and was commissioned to produce several works for the Knights of St John, including the famous *Beheading of St John the Baptist*, now on display in the oratory of the cathedral in Valletta (p64). In July 1608 he was admitted into the Order as a Knight of Justice, but only two months later he was arrested for an unspecified crime – it may be that news arrived of the murder he had committed – and he was promptly imprisoned in Fort St Angelo.

He escaped to Sicily, but was expelled from the Order and spent the next two years on the run. He created some of his finest paintings during this period, before dying of exhaustion and fever before the age of 38.

to Malta, creating lively and thrusting compositions like the *Arab Horses* displayed in the National Museum of Fine Arts in Valletta (p66). You can see other examples of his work outdoors in Valletta's public spaces.

Vincent Apap (1938–2003) also created many of the sculptures that adorn public spaces in Malta, notably the Triton fountain in the centre of the City Gate bus terminus between Valletta and Floriana.

At the Cathedral Museum in Mdina (p118) you can view a permanent display of the clever, contemporary olive-wood sculptures created by Anton Agius (b 1933).

Environment

THE LAND

The Maltese Islands cover a total area of only 316 sq km – less than the Isle of Wight in the UK or Martha's Vineyard in the USA. There are three inhabited islands – Malta, Gozo and Comino – and two uninhabited islets, Cominotto and Filfla. They lie in the central Mediterranean Sea, 93km south of Sicily, 290km east of Tunisia and 290km north of Libya.

There are no mountains on the islands. The highest point is Ta'Żuta (253m) on the southwest coast of Malta. This high plateau is bounded on the southwest by sea cliffs, and drops away gradually towards rolling plains in the south and east. Northwest Malta is characterised by a series of flat-topped ridges running generally northeast to southwest – the Victoria Lines escarpment, the Wardija Ridge, the Bajda Ridge, the Mellieħa Ridge and the Marfa Ridge – separated by broad valleys. The landscape of Gozo is greener than Malta and consists of flat-topped hills and terraced hillsides, with high cliffs in the south and west. The highest point is Ta'Dbieġi (190m) to the south of Għarb.

The soil is generally thin and rocky, although some valleys are terraced and farmed intensively. There are few trees and, for most of the year, little greenery to soften the stony, sun-bleached landscape. The only notable exception is Buskett Gardens (p124), a lush valley of pine trees and orange groves protected by the imposing Dingli sea cliffs of the south coast.

There is virtually no surface water and there are no permanent creeks or rivers. The water table is the main source of fresh water, but it is supplemented by several large desalination plants – a good 60% of all tap water is desalinated seawater, produced by means of a reverse osmosis operated on electricity. So please use water carefully while here (and you may prefer to drink bottled water).

Geology

Geologically speaking, the Maltese Islands are lumps of the Mediterranean sea bed that have been warped upward until they are poking above sea level. The warping was caused by the collision between the African tectonic plate to the south and the European plate to the north. This collision is ongoing and is also responsible for the volcanoes of Etna and Vesuvius, and for the earthquakes which occasionally strike southern Italy and Malta (see p142).

The rocks that make up Malta are between seven million and 30 million years old, and are layered one on top of the other. From the bottom up, there are four main layers – the Lower Coralline Limestone, the Globigerina Limestone, the Blue Clay and the Upper Coralline Limestone. The limestones are rich in fossils, especially at the junction between the Lower Coralline and Globigerina Limestones, where there is a huge concentration of fossil scallop shells and sand dollars (flat, disc-shaped relatives of sea urchins).

The Upper and Lower Coralline Limestones are hard and resistant to weathering, and form the great sea cliffs of southwest Malta and Ta'Ċenċ, and the crags that ring the flat tops of Gozo's hills. The golden-coloured Globigerina Limestone is softer, and underlies much of central and eastern Malta. The sticky Blue Clay is rich in nutrients, and is responsible for the more fertile soils of Gozo – you can see it in the cliffs west of Ramla Bay.

Local quarrymen refer to the easily worked Globigerina Limestone as *franka;* the harder-wearing Coralline Limestones are called *zonqor.* Both were widely used in the building of the islands' massive fortifications.

WILDLIFE
Animals
The sparse vegetation supports little in the way of land-based wildlife – just a handful of rats, mice, hedgehogs, weasels and shrews. Rabbits have been hunted almost to extinction (the rabbit you'll see on menus has been bred). Geckoes and other lizards are fairly common – the dark green and red lizard *Lacerta filfolensis* is found only on the islet of Filfla – and there are three species of snake, none of them poisonous.

There are barely a dozen resident bird species, including sparrows, rock doves, linnets, corn buntings, herring gulls and the blue rock thrush – Malta's national bird, which appears on the 25c coin – but more than 150 species have been recorded as migrants and winter visitors; these are favourite targets for Maltese hunters, sadly.

The seas around Malta and Gozo are clean and clear, and support a rich and diverse marine fauna that attracts scuba divers from all over Europe. For more information, see p51.

Plants
Malta has little in the way of natural vegetation. Much of the island is cultivated, and where it is not the land is often bare and rocky. The only extensive area of woodland is at Buskett Gardens (see p124), which is dominated by Aleppo pines. The rough limestone slopes of the hilltops and sea cliffs support a typical Mediterranean flora of stunted olive, oleander and tamarisk trees, with growths of thyme, euphorbia, rosemary and brambles. Samphire, sea campion, spurge and saltwort can be found on the rocks beside the sea, and the rare parasitic plant *Cynomorium coccineus* is found at Dwejra on Gozo (see p153).

NATIONAL PARKS
Malta has no national parks – hardly surprising, given its diminutive size.

DID YOU KNOW?

With 49 cars per 100 inhabitants, Malta has the highest number of cars in the EU on a per-capita basis – and the least amount of land on which to drive them.

Malta Environment & Planning Authority – www.mepa.org.mt The best part of this website is the EcoExplore section, with lots of detail on local flora and fauna – click first on Environment, then EcoExplore.

THE MALTESE FALCON

Falconry was the great passion of the Holy Roman Emperor Frederick II (1194–1250) – he wrote a famous treatise on the subject, *De arte venandi cum avibus,* and chose as his emblem a peregrine falcon, the king of birds. He grew up in Sicily, and learned from his own experience that the finest peregrines came from Malta (the Maltese falcon is a subspecies of peregrine, *Falco peregrinus brookei*).

When Malta was gifted to the Knights of St John in 1530, the only condition attached was an annual rent of two Maltese falcons – one for the Spanish emperor and one for the viceroy of Sicily. Unfortunately, by the 1970s trapping and shooting had reduced these magnificent raptors to just one or two breeding pairs. There are occasional reports of peregrines – known as *bies* in Malti – being seen on the remote southwestern cliffs of Malta and Gozo, but there have been no confirmed sightings since the mid-1980s.

All this, of course, has nothing to do with Dashiell Hammett's famous detective story, *The Maltese Falcon.* If you've read the book you'll know that the eponymous black bird is actually a red herring.

ENVIRONMENTAL ISSUES

The combined pressures of population, land use and development, as well as pollution and the lack of protection of natural areas, have had a significant environmental impact on the islands. There is also a severe shortage of fresh water – the only natural supply comes from ground water, which is increasingly contaminated with nitrate run off from farmland. This has been eased slightly by the construction of several large desalination plants.

Air pollution is caused by the high concentration of cars, lorries and buses – many of them old – in the congested roads around Grand Harbour, and by discharges from coal-fired power stations and factories. With such a small land area, disposal of rubbish in landfill sites is also increasingly problematic.

During our time in Malta an interesting survey was published and received a good deal of media attention. The survey dealt with the impact of the environment on Malta's tourism, and the results may eventually see some action from tourism authorities and the government in the main areas of concern. The survey's results showed that the state of the roads, increasing urbanisation, traffic congestion and low levels of cleanliness in urban areas were the environmental issues generating the highest levels of dissatisfaction in visitors to Malta (on the up side, the cleanliness of the seas, accessibility of beaches and the cultural heritage generated positive feedback).

Bird Hunting

One of the favourite Maltese sports is shooting or trapping anything that flies. Bird shooting is still a very popular pastime in Malta, and one of the more unpleasant aspects of the islands for many foreign visitors. The shooters will take a pot shot at almost anything that flies – from a sparrow to a swift – though the main prey are turtledoves and quail. Shooters hides can be seen in the quieter corners of the countryside and the crack of shotguns is a common accompaniment to an evening walk.

Bird netting is also very popular – the rickety little towers of stones and metal poles you see in the Maltese countryside are for supporting the drop-nets and for holding cages containing decoy birds. Greenfinches are a popular prey, and you can often see them being bought and sold at the markets in Valletta. Conservative estimates are that around half a million birds are shot or trapped in Malta each year – but we also came across reports that put this number at six million. The truth probably lies in the middle of these extremes, at around three million – a phenomenal amount for such a small country. Most birds are shot or trapped while migrating between Africa and Europe in the spring and autumn.

Laws were introduced in 1980 designating a close season for shooting and trapping, protecting many bird species (especially migrants), and making shooting and trapping illegal in certain protected areas. They include Il-Għadira Nature Reserve at Mellieħa Bay, Filfla island, Buskett Gardens, the Ta'Qali area and Gozo's Ta'Ċenċ cliffs. However, these laws are regularly flouted and poorly policed (in January 2004, for example, hunters broke into Il-Għadira and killed two spoonbills – a protected species).

The close season for shooting is 22 May to 31 August (one of the shortest in Europe) – but these dates are routinely ignored by hunters. BirdLife Malta, a large organisation of bird-lovers, is seeking a ban on spring hunting and trapping as well as a stop to hunting at sea, but it faces an uphill battle – the hunters are a large and powerful lobby group

DID YOU KNOW?

It is believed bird hunters were responsible for vandalising the 5000-year-old Mnajdra temple in 1996 and 2001, when authorities tried to close off the surrounding area to hunting.

(estimated at around 20,000) that have actively opposed government measures to curb their activities by resorting to violence and extreme vandalism. In a country where electoral victories usually involve very small margins, political parties want to keep hunters on side, even going in to bat for them against EU authorities.

EU laws prohibit bird hunting and bird trapping in spring. Hunters had been led to believe that these pastimes might not be allowed if Malta joined the EU. But the Maltese government made it clear from the very start of EU negotiations that since hunting and trapping were traditional hobbies in Malta, they should be allowed to continue. During negotiations, Malta argued that hunting in Malta is mostly practised in spring because it depends on migratory birds. The EU acknowledged these arguments and Malta will retain hunting in spring and autumn after membership, and retain the right to trap birds.

Fatal Flight: Maltese Obsession with Killing Birds
A thought-provoking account by Natalino Fenech of the massacre of millions of migrating birds that takes place each year in Malta.

Diving & Snorkelling

The Maltese Islands – and Gozo in particular – offer some of the best scuba diving in Europe and have many advantages for divers, especially beginners, including a pleasant climate; warm, clear water; a wide range of interesting dive sites (caves, reefs, wartime wrecks), many of them accessible from the shore; and a large number of dive schools with qualified, professional instructors. There are also sites perfect for experienced open-water and cave divers.

Most schools in Malta offer courses that lead to qualifications issued by one or more of the internationally recognised diving bodies. The websites of these organisations offer general information about diving and dive qualifications, plus details of accredited diving schools in Malta:

Dive Sites of Malta, Gozo & Comino Lawson & Leslie Wood's comprehensive guide with details on marine life, plus a very helpful star-rating system grading the diving and snorkelling at each of the 80-odd sites reviewed.

British Sub-Aqua Club (BSAC; www.bsac.co.uk)
Confédération Mondiale des Activités Subaquatiques (CMAS; www.cmas.org)
Professional Association of Diving Instructors (PADI; www.padi.com)

DIVING
Requirements
If you want to learn to dive in Malta, there are a few things required of you, not the least of which is the ability to swim. The minimum age is 14 years and those under 18 must have written parental consent.

You will have to pass a simple medical examination to make sure you are fit to dive – this will be organised by the dive school and may be included in the cost of a course (or cost Lm3 to Lm5). Asthma, diabetes and epilepsy are some of the disqualifying factors for diving in Malta. You should also heed medical warnings and not fly within 24 hours of your last dive. Your last day in Malta should be spent reacclimatising to sea-level pressures.

Qualified divers wishing to lead their own groups will need to obtain a local diving instructor's permit known as Card C. To obtain this you will need a medical certificate, two passport-sized photos and a diving logbook. Your dive school will help arrange this for you.

www.visitmalta.com /en/diving Loads of stuff here including safety regulations, marine life, dive operators and an excellent interactive map with the country's best dive sites.

Courses & Qualifications
Most schools offer a 'taster course' or 'beginner's dive', which begins with one or two hours of shore-based instruction on the workings of scuba equipment and safety procedures. You will then be introduced to breathing underwater in a pool or shallow bay, and will end up doing a 30-minute dive in the sea. A beginner's course should cost around Lm15 including the compulsory medical examination.

A so-called 'resort course' gives you shore-based instruction plus four to six open-water dives accompanied by an instructor, and costs Lm40 to Lm70. These courses do *not* result in an official qualification.

A course that will give you an entry-level diving qualification (CMAS One-Star Diver, PADI Open Water Diver, BSAC Ocean Diver) should take four or five days and cost around Lm130.

Safety
Speedboat and ferry traffic can be quite heavy, especially in peak summer months and in the Gozo Channel area. For their own protection, divers are required to fly the code-A flag or use a surface marker buoy.

Divers should ensure that their travel insurance policy covers them for diving. Some policies specifically exclude 'dangerous activities', which can include scuba diving.

Malta's public general hospital is **St Luke's Hospital** (Map p86; www.slh.gov.mt; Triq San Luqa, Gwardamanġa), near Pietà (southwest of Valletta), and there is a decompression chamber here. Staff at the hospital can be contacted for any diving incidents requiring medical attention on ☎ 21 234 765 or ☎ 21 234 766, or by dialling the emergency telephone number ☎ 196. Divers on Gozo can be transferred by helicopter to Malta in the case of an emergency.

Dive Schools

There are over 30 dive school operators in Malta. The majority are members of the **Professional Diving Schools Association** (PDSA; www.digigate.net/divers; 1 Msida Ct, 61 ix-Xatt Ta'Msida, Msida), an organisation dedicated to promoting high standards of safety and professionalism.

The following dive schools all offer PADI-, BSAC- or CMAS-approved courses and most rent out equipment to experienced divers. Some are located at large resorts (especially those in northwest Malta).

Note that Zero Gravity on Gozo (p48) is able to cater to disabled divers and is a member of the **International Association for Handicapped Divers** (www.iahd.org).

SLIEMA & ST JULIAN'S AREA

Aquarrigo Scuba Diving Centre (☎ 21 330 882; www.planetsea.net; Preluna Beach Club, Triq it-Torri, Sliema)

AquaWorld (☎ 21 318 893; www.maltadiving.net; Sliema Aquatic Sports Club, Triq it-Torri, Sliema)

Cresta Diving Centre (☎ 21 310 743; www.crestadivingcentre.com; Cresta Quay Beach Club, St George's Bay, St Julian's)

Dive Systems (☎ 21 319 123; www.divesystemsmalta.com; Taht it-Torri, Triq it-Torri, Sliema)

Divecare (☎ 21 369 994; www.digigate.net/divecare; St Julian's Aqua Sports Club, Triq Ġorġ Borg Olivier, St Julian's)

Diveshack Scuba School (☎ 21 320 594; www.divemalta.com; ix-Xatt Ta'Qui-si-sana, Qui-si-sana, Sliema)

Divewise (☎ 21 356 441; www.digigate.net/divewise; Westin Dragonara Complex, St Julian's)

Northeast Diving Services Ltd (☎ 21 340 511; www.digigate.net/nds; 9 Triq Belvedere, Gzira)

Starfish Diving School (☎ 21 373 822; www.starfishdiving.com; Corinthia Beach Club Hotel, St George's Bay, St Julian's)

NORTHWEST MALTA

Aquatica Diving & Fishing Centre (☎ 21 579 753; www.aquaticamalta.com; Triq Toni Bajjada, Buġibba)

AquaVenture (☎ 21 522 141; www.aquaventuremalta.com; Mellieħa Bay Hotel, Mellieħa Bay)

Buddies Dive Cove (☎ 21 576 266; www.buddiesmalta.com; 24/2 Triq il-Korp Tal-Pijunieri, Buġibba)

Dive Deep Blue (☎ 21 583 946; www.divedeepblue.com; 100 Triq Ananija, Buġibba)

Luna Diving Centre (☎ 21 521 645; www.lunadiving.com; Luna Holiday Complex, Triq Marfa, Mellieħa Bay)

Maltaqua (☎ 21 571 873; www.maltaqua.com; Triq Mosta, Buġibba)

Meldives Dive School (☎ 21 522 595; www.digigate.net/meldives; Tunny Net Lido Complex, Triq Marfa, Mellieħa Bay)

Octopus Garden (☎ 21 584 318; www.octopus-garden.com; Sol Suncrest Hotel, Dawret il-Qawra, Qawra)

Paradise Diving (☎ 21 574 116; www.paradisediving.com; Paradise Bay Hotel, Ċirkewwa)

Scubatech Diving Centre (☎ 21 580 617; www.digigate.net/scubatech; Triq I-Alka, St Paul's Bay)

Maltese Islands Diving Guide
By Ned Middleton, this guide is good but considerably more expensive than its main competitor (by Lawson & Leslie Wood; see the sidebar on p46). Excellent photography and lots of dive-site details and practical information.

DID YOU KNOW?

The average sea temperature in Malta is above 20°C from June to October. The average temperature in June is 21.1°C, in August it is 25.6°C, and in October it's 22.2°C.

Strand Diving Services (☎ 21 574 502; www.scubamalta.com; 15 Triq Ramon Perellos, St Paul's Bay)
Subway Scuba Diving School (☎ 21 570 354; www.subwayscuba.com; Triq il-Korp Tal-Pijunieri, Buġibba)

Sea Fishes & Invertebrates of the Mediterranean No more wondering 'what on earth is that?' while diving or snorkelling in the Med. Lawson Wood provides full descriptions of nearly 300 species, plus good photos.

SOUTHEAST MALTA

Aquabubbles Scuba Diving School (☎ 21 639 292; www.aquabubbles.co.uk; Corinthia Jerma Palace Hotel, Dawret it-Torri, Marsaskala)
Dive Med (☎ 21 639 981; www.divemed.com; Iż-Żonqor, Marsaskala)

GOZO

Atlantis Diving Centre (☎ 21 561 826; www.atlantisgozo.com; Triq il-Qolla; Marsalforn)
Blue Waters Dive Cove (☎ 21 565 626; www.divebluewaters.com; Triq il-Kuncizzjoni, Qala)
Calypso Diving Centre (☎ 21 561 757; www.calypsodivers.com; Seafront, Marsalforn)
Frankie's Gozo Diving Centre (☎ 21 551 315; www.digigate.net/frankie; Triq Mġarr, Xewkija)
Gozo Aqua Sports (☎ 21 563 037; www.gozoaquasports.com; Green Valley, Triq Rabat, Marsalforn)
Moby Dives (☎ 21 551 616; www.gozo.com/mobydives; Triq il-Gostra, Xlendi Bay)
Nautic Team Diving Centre (☎ 21 558 507; www.nauticteam.com; cnr Triq il-Mungbell & Triq ir-Rabat, Marsalforn)
Scubatech Gozo (☎ 21 561 221; www.divemalta-gozo.com; Marsalforn waterfront)
St Andrews Divers Cove (☎ 21 551 301; www.gozodive.com; Triq San Ximun, Xlendi)
Zero Gravity (☎ 21 566 703; www.0-grav.com; off Xwenji Rd, Qbaijar)

RESPONSIBLE DIVING

The popularity of diving is placing immense pressure on many sites – over 40,000 divers a year visit the Maltese Islands. Please consider the following tips when diving and help preserve the ecology and beauty of Malta's underwater world:

▪ Avoid touching living marine organisms with your body or dragging equipment across the rocks.

▪ Be conscious of your fins. Even without contact the surge from heavy fin strokes can damage delicate organisms.

▪ Practise and maintain proper buoyancy control. Make sure you are correctly weighted and that your weight belt is positioned so that you stay horizontal. If you have not dived for a while, have a practice dive in a pool before taking to the sea. Be aware that buoyancy can change over the period of an extended trip: initially you may breathe harder and need more weight; a few days later you may breathe more easily and need less weight.

▪ Take great care in underwater caves. Spend as little time within them as possible as your air bubbles may be caught within the roof, leaving previously submerged organisms high and dry. Taking turns to inspect the interior of a small cave will lessen the chances of damaging contact.

▪ Resist the temptation to collect or buy shells or other remains of marine organisms. Aside from the ecological damage, taking home marine souvenirs depletes the beauty of a site and spoils the enjoyment of others. The same goes for marine archaeological sites (mainly shipwrecks). Respect their integrity; some sites are protected from looting by law.

▪ Ensure that you take home all your rubbish and any litter you may find as well. Plastics in particular are a serious threat to marine life.

▪ Resist the temptation to feed fish. You may disturb their normal eating habits, encourage aggressive behaviour or feed them food that is detrimental to their health.

▪ Minimise your disturbance of marine animals. *Never* ride on the backs of turtles.

COMINO

Comino Dive Centre (☎ 21 572 997; www.cominodivecentre.com; Comino Hotel, Comino)

Top Diving Spots

NORTHWEST MALTA

Aħrax Point (average depth 7m, maximum depth 18m) Caverns and a tunnel opening up to a small inland grotto with good coral growth. Suitable for all levels of experience. Shore dive. Can be viewed by snorkelling.

Anchor Bay (average depth 6m, maximum depth 12m) Not much to see in the bay itself, but around the corner are good caves. Suitable for all levels of experience. Shore dive.

Ċirkewwa Arch (average depth 15m, maximum depth 36m) Underwater walls and a magnificent arch, where you can encounter a variety of fish and possibly a seahorse. Suitable for all levels of experience.

Marfa Point (average depth 12m, maximum depth 18m) Large site with caves, reefs, promontories and tunnels. Can be accessed from the shore. Decent snorkelling opportunities.

St Paul's Islands (multiple sites, average depths 6m to 12m, maximum depth 25m) Popular dive sites with a wreck between the shore and inner island, a reef on the eastern side of the northernmost

www.ifyoudive.com
Not a Malta-specific
website, but has loads of
information on world-
wide diving holidays,
courses, gear and sites.

TOP DIVING SPOTS ON MALTA

DIVING/SNORKELLING (pp49–50)	
Anchor Bay	1 A2
Aħrax Point	2 A1
Blenheim Bomber	3 D4
Carolita Barge	4 C3
Ċirkewwa Arch	5 A1
Delimara Point	6 D4
Ghar Lapsi	7 B4
HMS Maori	8 C3
Marfa Point	9 A1
St Paul's Islands	10 B2
Tugboat Rozi	11 A1
Wied iż-Żurrieq	12 C4

island, and a valley between the two islands. Suitable for all levels of experience. The wreck can be accessed from the shore.

Tugboat Rozi (average depth 30m, maximum depth 36m) A boat deliberately sunk in 1991 as an underwater attraction and now colonised by thousands of fish.

VALLETTA AREA

Carolita Barge (average depth 12m, maximum depth 22m) Possibly mistaken for a submarine, this barge was hit by a torpedo in 1942 and sank immediately. Well preserved and home to grouper and octopus. Popular training site for divers and therefore busy. Suitable for all levels of experience. Shore dive.

HMS Maori (average depth 13m, maximum depth 18m) Below Fort St Elmo is the wreck of the HMS *Maori*, sunk in 1942. Silted up, but home to fish and octopuses. Suitable for all levels of experience. Shore dive.

SOUTHEAST MALTA

Blenheim Bomber (average depth 42m, maximum depth 42m) Exciting dive to explore the well-preserved wreck of a WWII bomber, with engine and wings intact. For experienced divers only.

Delimara Point (average depth 12m, maximum depth 25m) Usually excellent visibility, with vertical cliffs and many caverns. Varied and colourful flora and fauna. Suitable for all levels of experience. Shore dive.

Għar Lapsi (average depth 6m, maximum depth 15m) Popular training site for divers. Safe, shallow cave that winds through the headland. Shore dive, reasonable snorkelling and suitable for all levels of experience.

Wied iż-Żurrieq (average depth 9m, maximum depth 30m) Close to the Blue Grotto. Underwater valley and labyrinth of caves. Shore dive, reasonable snorkelling and suitable for all levels of experience.

GOZO

Billinghurst Cave (average depth 20m, maximum depth 35m) Long tunnel leading to a cave deep inside the rock, with a multitude of coloured sea sponges. There's very little natural light (torch required). For experienced divers only.

Blue Hole & Chimney (average depth 20m, maximum depth 45m) The Blue Hole is a natural rock formation and includes a large cave plus a fissure in the near-vertical wall. Popular, busy site. Shore dive, excellent snorkelling and suitable for all levels of experience.

Coral Cave (average depth 25m, maximum depth 30m) Huge semicircular opening with a sandy bottom. Varied and colourful flora and fauna. Shore dive.

Crocodile Rock (average depth 35m, maximum depth 45m) Rocky reef between the shore and crocodile-shaped rock off the west coast. Natural amphitheatre and deep fissures. Shore dive, decent snorkelling and suitable for all levels of experience.

Double Arch Reef (average depth 30m, maximum depth 45m) Site characterised by a strange formation, with an arch dividing two large openings in the rock. Prolific marine life. For experienced divers.

Fessej Rock (average depth 30m, maximum depth 50m) A prominent column of rock. Vertical wall dive descending to 50m amid large schools of fish. A very popular deep-water dive.

Fungus Rock (average depth 30m, maximum depth beyond 60m) Dramatic underwater scenery with vertical walls, fissures, caverns and gullies. Good site for underwater photography and suitable for all levels of diving experience.

Għasri Valley (average depth in cave 12m, maximum depth 30m) A deep winding cut in the headland makes for a long, gentle dive. May view seahorses in the shallows. Cave with a huge domed vault and walls covered in corals. Can be done as a shore dive. Very good snorkelling and suitable for all levels of experience.

Reqqa Point (average depth 25m, maximum depth beyond 70m) Near-vertical wall cut by fissures, caves and crevices. Large numbers of small fish, plus groups of amberfish and grouper if conditions are favourable. Shore dive and good snorkelling.

San Dimitri Point (average depth 25m, maximum depth beyond 60m) Lots of marine life and exceptional visibility (sometimes exceeding 50m). Good snorkelling and suitable for all levels of experience.

DID YOU KNOW?

Malta is popular with underwater photographers due to the clarity of its waters. Natural colours can be captured on film without the use of a flash even at a depth of 10m to 12m.

www.gozo.com/core /divesites
Details of some of the best dive sites on Gozo, as well as links to local dive operators.

TOP DIVING SPOTS ON GOZO & COMINO

Ta'Ċenċ (average depth 25m, maximum depth 35m) Sheltered bay – access is by 103 steps from car park of nearby hotel. Canyon with large boulders, plus cave. Good marine life, but visibility can occasionally be poor. Good spot for night dives. Shore dive and suitable for all levels of experience.

Xatt L'Aħmar (average depth 9m, maximum depth 30m) Small bay, excellent for observing a large variety of fish including mullet, grouper, sea bream, octopus and cuttlefish. Shore dive, OK snorkelling and suitable for all levels of experience.

Xlendi Cave & Reef (average depth 6m, maximum depth 25m) Easy cave dive in shallow water and popular with beginners. Brightly coloured cave walls. Rocky headland dips steeply to the sea. An abundance of flora and fauna. Shore dive, OK snorkelling.

COMINO

Blue Lagoon (average depth 6m, maximum depth 12m) Easy site to the north of the sheltered lagoon, very popular with divers and snorkellers, plenty of boat traffic. Shore dive. Suitable for all levels of experience.

Lantern Point (average depth 30m, maximum depth 45m) Very popular site. Dramatic dive down a vertical wall. Rich fauna and an abundance of colour. OK snorkelling.

Santa Marija Cave (average depth 7m, maximum depth 10m) Large cave and cavern system, and one of the most popular sites for cave dives. An abundance of fish in the area. Very good snorkelling and suitable for all levels of experience.

SNORKELLING

If you don't fancy scuba diving, you can still sample the delights of the underwater world by donning mask, snorkel and fins and exploring the rocks and bays around Malta's coastline. The only qualification necessary is the ability to swim. You can usually rent or buy the necessary equipment from hotels, lidos and water sport centres in all the tourist areas.

Top snorkelling spots are off Comino and Gozo and include the **Blue Lagoon** and the crags and caves east of **Santa Marija Bay** on Comino; the cave-riddled coastline at **Dwejra**; the long, narrow inlet at **Wied il-Għasri**; and along the salt pan rocks west of **Xwieni Bay** near Marsalforn on Gozo.

MALTA'S MARINE LIFE

Malta's location in the narrows between Sicily and North Africa, far away from the pollution of major cities and silt-bearing rivers, means that its marine life is richer than in many other parts of the Med.

Invertebrates such as brightly coloured bryozoans, cup corals, sea anemones, sponges, starfish and sea urchins encrust the underwater cliffs and caves around the shores of Malta and Gozo. The countless nooks and crannies in the limestone provide shelter for crabs, lobsters, common octopus *(Octopus vulgaris)* and white-spotted octopus *(O. macropus)*. By night, cuttlefish *(Sepia officinalis)* graze the algal beds below the cliffs.

Most divers who visit Malta hope to catch sight of a seahorse. The maned seahorse *(Hippocampus ramulosus)* is fairly common around the Maltese coast, preferring shallow, brackish water. They grow up to 15cm in length and feed on plankton and tiny shrimps. They mate for life and display an unusual inversion of common male and female reproductive roles. Using her tube-like ovipositor, the female deposits her eggs in a brood pouch in the male's abdomen where they are fertilised. Here the eggs develop and finally hatch before the male 'gives birth' by releasing the live brood into open water.

Guide to Shore Diving the Maltese Islands Well-researched guide to 36 dive sites, with aerial photographs, good underwater plans and detailed text (but no details of boat dives). By Peter G Lemon.

Migratory shoals of sardine, sprat, bluefin tuna, bonito, mackerel and dolphin fish *(Coryphaena hippurus)* – known in Malti as *lampuka*, and a local delicacy – pass through the offshore waters in late summer and autumn. Swordfish *(Xiphias gladias)* are fairly common all year round. Sea bream, sea bass, grouper, red mullet, wrasse, dogfish and stingray frequent the shallower waters closer to shore, where moray and conger eels hide among the rocks and venture out at night to feed on octopus and fish.

The seas around Malta are known among shark-watchers as one of the 'sharkiest' spots in the Med. In April 1987 a great white shark *(Carcharodon carcharias)* caught by local fisherman Alfredo Cutajar off Filfla was claimed to be a world record at 7.13m in overall length. However, later investigations brought the accuracy of the original measurements into doubt. Photographs of the shark – including some of Alfredo with his head in the (dead!) shark's mouth – can be bought in souvenir shops at Wied iż-Żurrieq (p135).

www.locationmalta.com /theme/diving Click on 'Diving sites of the Maltese Islands' and browse through extensive notes on 34 dive locations on Malta, Comino and Gozo.

Other shark species known to haunt Maltese waters include the blue, thresher and mako. However, bathers and divers should not be unduly alarmed. Shark sightings in inshore waters are extremely rare. Indeed, the great white is considered to be an endangered species, and the decrease in its numbers is thought to have resulted from dwindling stocks of tuna, its main food source.

The loggerhead turtle *(Caretta caretta)* is another endangered species that is occasionally sighted in Maltese waters, but the lack of secluded, sandy beaches means that they do not nest on the Maltese Islands. The common dolphin *(Delphinus delfis)* – known as *denfil* in Malti – and the bottlenose dolphin *(Tursiops truncatus)* are fairly common in Maltese waters and are occasionally seen from cruise boats and dive boats.

The marine life of the Maltese Islands is under increasing pressure from divers, fishermen and pollution, but as yet there are no marine conservation areas. The **Gaia Foundation** (www.projectgaia.org), an organisation founded in 1994 to protect Malta's environment and promote sustainable living, states that authorities are working on giving conservation status to the sea around Ramla Bay on Gozo and Għajn Tuffieħa Bay on Malta (the land here is classified as specially protected coastal zones). Marine conservation would involve the protection of marine flora and fauna, and the enforcement of regulations against pollution and dumping.

Food & Drink

Like the Maltese language, Maltese cuisine demonstrates the different influences of the many foreign cultures that have ruled the country in its long and often turbulent history. The food is quite rustic, and meals are generally based on seasonal produce and the fisherman's catch.

Malta is not known as a destination for gourmets, but the food is generally good and cheap. The most obvious influence is Sicilian, and most of the cheaper restaurants serve pasta and pizza; there are also some upscale places serving more creative Italian specialities. English standards (eg grilled chops, sausages and mash, and roast with three veg) are also commonly available, particularly in the tourist areas. If you tire of the ubiquitous meat-fish-pasta-pizza menu, you'll also find Chinese restaurants, a few Indian eateries and some highly regarded new places offering Japanese and Thai cuisine.

Definitive(ly) Good Guide to Restaurants in Malta & Gozo edited by Lisa Grech. A must for travellers looking for great dining experiences. It's updated annually and includes reviews of 150 of Malta's best restaurants. Available from most major bookshops (Lm4).

STAPLES & SPECIALITIES

SNACKS

Ġbejniet You will either love or hate this small, hard, white cheese traditionally made from unpasteurised sheep's or goat's milk. They are dried in baskets and often steeped in olive oil flavoured with salt and crushed black peppercorns.

Ħobż Freshly baked Maltese bread is delightful. It is made in a similar manner to sourdough bread, using a scrap of yesterday's dough to leaven today's loaves.

FINE FOOD VENUES IN MALTA

We enjoyed some fabulous meals in Malta (and quite a few uninspiring ones). Here are our picks for top nosh.

Restaurants

Rubino (Valletta, p72) Earns rave reviews in the capital for reinventing traditional Maltese cuisine while staying true to its roots.

Zest (St Julian's, p93) Brand new and winning over trendsetters with its funky décor, great service and inspiring menu of treats from East and West.

Grabiel (Marsaskala, p132) Follow the suited business folk who know they're onto a good thing – fine service and exceptional seafood in Malta's south.

Bobbyland Restaurant (Dingli, p124) The best place to join the locals tucking into their Sunday lunch-time feasts of rabbit and/or lamb – then walk it off with a stroll along the cliff top.

Giuseppe's Restaurant & Wine Bar (Mellieħa, p112) The perfect package of casual atmosphere, fresh and imaginative dishes and a diverse clientele.

Cafés

Café Juliani (St Julian's, p95) Smooth and stylish – the ideal venue for high tea, coffee and cake or an evening cocktail.

Ta'Ricardo (Victoria, p145) Tucked away in Gozo's beautiful citadel and serving up platters of delicious Gozitan treats.

Café Jubilee (Valletta, p73, and Victoria, p145) Cosy and inviting eateries with old-world charm, plus the ability to transform from daytime cafés to cool night-time bars.

Café Deux Baronnes (Valletta, p73) Who cares about the food when the view is this good? Take in a panorama that'll make you understand what makes Grand Harbour grand.

Fontanella Tea Gardens (Mdina, p121) It's a good thing the cakes are so tasty here and the views so spectacular – if we were judging on service alone, we might never return!

Ħobż biż-żejt This is another traditional snack – slices of bread rubbed with ripe tomatoes and olive oil until they are pink and delicious, then topped with a mix of tuna, onion, capers, olives, garlic, black pepper and salt.

Ftira This is bread baked in a flat disc and stuffed with a mixture of tomatoes, olives, capers and anchovies.

Pastizza (plural *pastizzi*) The traditional Maltese snack is the *pastizza*, a small parcel of flaky pastry filled with either ricotta cheese or mushy peas. A couple of *pastizzi* make for a tasty – if somewhat high-fat – breakfast or afternoon filler. You'll probably pay around Lm0.10 for one, so they're also great for budget travellers. They're available in most bars or from special takeaway *pastizzerija* (usually hole-in-the-wall places in villages – follow your nose).

SOUPS

Aljotta A delicious fish broth made with tomato, rice and lots of garlic.

Kusksu Soup made from broad beans and small pasta shapes, often served with a soft fresh *ġbejniet* floating in the middle.

Minestra A thick soup of tomatoes, beans, pasta and vegetables, similar to Italian minestrone.

Soppa tal-armla The so-called 'widow's soup' (possibly named because of its inexpensive ingredients) is traditionally made only with components that are either green or white. Basically a vegetable soup, it contains cauliflower, spinach, endive and peas, poured over a poached egg, a *ġbejniet* and a lump of ricotta cheese.

MAIN DISHES

Braġioli These are prepared by wrapping a thin slice of beef around a stuffing of breadcrumbs, chopped bacon, hard-boiled egg and parsley, then braising these 'beef olives' in a red wine sauce.

Fenek *Fenek* (rabbit) is *the* favourite Maltese dish, whether fried in olive oil, roasted, stewed, served with spaghetti or baked in a pie (*fenek bit-tewm u l-inbid* is rabbit cooked in garlic and wine, *fenek moqli* is fried rabbit, *stuffat tal-fenek* is stewed rabbit).

Kapunata A Maltese version of ratatouille made from tomatoes, capers, eggplant and green peppers – it goes well with grilled fish.

Qarabali Baby marrows – particularly good baked, stuffed with minced beef and parsley, or made into a creamy soup.

Ravjuletti Maltese variety of ravioli (pasta pouches filled with ricotta, parmesan and parsley).

Timpana A rich pie filled with macaroni, cheese, egg, minced beef, tomato, garlic and onion, *timpana* is a Sicilian dish not dissimilar to Greek *pastitsio*.

Torta tal-lampuki The local fish speciality is *torta tal-lampuki*, or *lampuki* pie. Lampuka (*Coryphaena hippurus*) – plural lampuki – is known in English as dolphin fish, dorado or *mahi-mahi*. It is delicious simply fried in olive oil, but the traditional way to prepare it is to bake it in a pie with tomatoes, onions, black olives, spinach, sultanas and walnuts. *Lampuki biz-zalza pikkanti* is *lampuki* in piquant sauce.

SWEETS

Kannoli Believed to have originated in Sicily, *kannoli* is a tube of crispy, fried pastry filled with ricotta, and sometimes sweetened with chocolate chips or candied fruit.

Mqaret One of Malta's favourite sweetmeats is *mqaret,* diamond-shaped pastries stuffed with chopped, spiced dates and deep-fried.

Qubbajt Maltese nougat, flavoured with almonds or hazelnuts and traditionally sold on festa (feast) days.

Qagħaq tal-għasel Honey or treacle rings made from a light pastry, served in small pieces as an after-dinner accompaniment to coffee.

DRINKS
Nonalcoholic Drinks

Good Italian coffee – espresso and cappuccino – is widely available in cafés and bars, and in the main tourist areas you will also find a cup of good strong British tea, heavy on the milk and sugar.

Cold soft drinks are available everywhere. Kinnie – you will see its advertising signs all over the place in Malta – is the brand name of a local soft drink flavoured with bitter oranges and aromatic herbs. It makes a change from cola and lemonade, and slips down nicely when mixed with rum or vodka.

Alcoholic Drinks

Maltese bars serve up every kind of drink you could ask for, from pints of British beer to shots of Galliano liqueur. The good locally made beers, Cisk Lager and Hopleaf Ale, are about half the price of imported brews.

The main local wine producers are **Marsovin** (www.marsovin.com.mt) and **Delicata** (www.delicata.com), which both make wine from local grapes and also produce more expensive 'special reserve' wines – merlot, cabernet sauvignon, chardonnay and sauvignon blanc – using imported grapes from Italy and France. The resulting products can be surprisingly good, and the quality is improving all the time. Head along to somewhere like the Castille Wine Vaults (p72) in Valletta for the chance to learn more about winemaking in Malta and sample some local drops.

www.aboutmalta.com /FOOD_and_DRINK A website with links to loads of topics in the Food & Drink category, from a site purely about Kinnie soft drink to recipes for octopus.

CELEBRATIONS

A *fenkata* is a big, communal meal of rabbit, usually eaten in the countryside. It supposedly originated as a gesture of rebellion against the occupying Knights (p23), who hunted rabbits and denied them to the local population. The most important *fenkata* is associated with the L-Imnarja harvest festival at the end of June, when hundreds of people gather at Buskett Gardens to eat rabbit, drink wine, sing folk songs and dance the night away (see the boxed text, p124). *Fenkata* is also eaten on special occasions, when a group of family and friends will take over a country restaurant for an afternoon and evening of food, drink and celebration. A number of village bars and small restaurants specialise in preparing a *fenkata* for large parties of merrymakers – these places are mainly concentrated in the off-the-tourist-track areas in the northern part of Malta. Your hotel or a friendly local should be able to recommend a favourite to you; see also the reviews for Bobbyland Restaurant (p124), Ta'Gagin (p124) and Il-Barri (p110).

WHERE TO EAT & DRINK

Many travellers to Malta opt for travel packages that include breakfast and dinner at their hotel (and sometimes even lunch too). This is a pity, as it means they don't get the chance to experience some of the great dining establishments in Malta, don't sample the local specialities or enjoy the views from scenically situated eateries, and never get the chance to chow down on rabbit among the locals. We recommend you opt only for a bed and breakfast arrangement and get out and travel your tastebuds in Malta. That said, many of Malta's finest restaurants are actually inside the four- and five-star hotels – and these are all open to the public.

Restaurants usually open for lunch between noon and 3pm, and for dinner between 7pm and 11pm. Many fine-dining restaurants are open only in the evening; conversely, some of Valletta's best eateries open for lunch only. Many restaurants open only six days a week, but days of closure vary (Sunday and Monday are popular – it can be worth calling ahead to find out if a place is open before setting off).

Cafés are usually open all day. Some popular cafés, such as Cara's Café (p94) in Sliema , Café Jubilee in both Valletta (p73) and Victoria (p145) and Café Juliani (boxed text, p95) in St Julian's transform from daytime café to night-time café-bar, staying open until midnight or later, serving cocktails, wine and snacks.

Quick Eats

Look out for small hole-in-the-wall *pastizzerijas* selling authentic *pastizzi* and other pastries – check out our favourite, Agius Pastizzerija (p73) in Valletta. You can also buy decent snacks from one of the many kiosks at the City Gate bus terminus.

VEGETARIANS & VEGANS

www.gozocooking
holidays.com
Your chance to get up
close and personal with
Maltese and Gozitan
cuisine.

Vegetarians are reasonably well catered for, vegans less so. Some restaurants offer meat-free dishes as main courses, and most offer vegetarian pizza and pasta options (these usually include egg and/or dairy ingredients). Vegetarians who eat seafood will have their options increased; alternatively, vegetarians and vegans might want to make a beeline for the local Chinese restaurant for a greater selection of suitable dishes. It is probably best to steer clear of the types of off-the-beaten-track village restaurant that specialise in rabbit – the menu will most likely also feature lamb, beef and quite possibly horse, and you'll go away hungry and disheartened.

WHINING & DINING

Like most Mediterranean cultures, the Maltese love children. (See p164 for more information on visiting Malta with children.) Generally speaking, babies and children are made welcome almost everywhere – in the world of eating out, the exception to this may be upmarket, fine-dining

DID YOU KNOW?

Many of the village
restaurants specialising in
rabbit also feature horse
meat on their menus.

establishments such as the Carriage (p72) in Valletta, Christopher's (p93) in Ta'Xbiex, Grabiel (p132) in Marsaskala and Mange Tout (p106) outside Buġibba. But then you'll encounter somewhere like the ritzy Restaurant Ta'Frenċ (p154) outside Marsalforn on Gozo that welcomes babies and children, and even offers a children's menu. Many restaurants offer highchairs and perhaps a kids' menu, or at least dishes that will appeal to kids, such as pasta and pizza. If in doubt, it pays to call ahead.

According to the locals, the most child-friendly restaurants in Malta include the Avenue (p94) in Paceville, Piccolo Padre (p92) in Sliema and Tal-Familja (p132) in Marsaskala – well it should be family-friendly, given its name!

Valletta

CONTENTS

When Valletta was built by the Knights of the Order of St John in the 16th and 17th centuries, its founder decreed that it should be 'a city built by gentlemen for gentlemen', and indeed it retains much of its aristocratic elegance to this day. The town is the seat of Malta's government, and is home to many of the country's most important museums and monuments – so much so that Unesco has named Valletta a World Heritage site, describing it as 'one of the most concentrated historic areas in the world'.

It's a compact place to explore, and in its streets, squares and alleys you're bound to stumble across scenes that will have you reaching for your camera – a commanding view over Grand Harbour and the Three Cities, a colourful row of overhanging 1st-floor balconies, a collection of bright yellow and orange buses, or a shopfront that looks like a relic of 1930s Britain.

The areas surrounding Valletta are also rich in history. On the southeastern side of the Grand Harbour lie the fortified peninsulas of Vittoriosa and Senglea – they are older and in some ways more interesting than Valletta itself, as this area was where the Knights of St John first settled when they arrived in Malta in 1530. If you want to go further back in history, a star attraction is the nearby Hypogeum, an underground necropolis dating from around 3500 BC.

And when you tire of all the history in and around Valletta, there are the treats you'd expect of most European capitals – albeit on a tiny scale (this capital has a population of only 7000!). Good restaurants, bars and theatre can be enjoyed here, but don't expect Valletta to be buzzing all night – it's far too small for that sort of action, but that's a large part of its charm.

HIGHLIGHTS

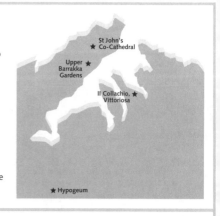

- Exploring the **streets of Valletta** (p68), admiring the monuments and soaking up the history
- Taking in the awesome views of Grand Harbour from the **Upper Barrakka Gardens** (p69)
- Marvelling at the magnificent baroque interior of **St John's Co-Cathedral** (p63)
- Stepping back in time at the remarkable **Hypogeum** (p82)
- Wandering through **Il Collachio** (p79), the historic alleys of Vittoriosa

■ POPULATION: 7030

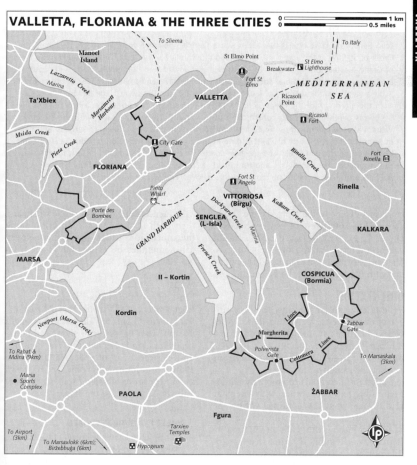

VALLETTA, FLORIANA & THE THREE CITIES

HISTORY

Before the Great Siege of 1565, the Sceberras peninsula was uninhabited and unfortified except for Fort St Elmo at its furthest point. Fearing another attack on Malta by the Turks, Grand Master la Valette began the task of financing and building new fortifications and a new city on what was then just a barren limestone ridge.

The foundation stone of Valletta was laid on 28 March 1566. Around 8000 slaves and artisans toiled on the slopes of Sceberras, levelling the summit, cutting a drainage system into the bedrock, and laying out a regular grid of streets – Valletta was to be the first planned city in Europe (see the boxed text, p64). A great ditch – 18m deep, 20m wide and nearly 1km long – was cut across the peninsula to protect the landward approach, and massive curtain walls and bastions were raised around the perimeter of the city.

Spurred on by the fear of a Turkish assault, the Knights completed the fortifications in a mere five years. With the defences in place, the new city was bestowed with churches, palaces, residential streets and, of course, a hospital. Valletta was considered a masterpiece of architecture and town planning, and today it remains one of Europe's finest and most distinctive cityscapes.

The threat of a Turkish attack in 1634 prompted Grand Master Antoine de Paule to begin the construction of a second line of

THE FOUNDER OF VALLETTA

Jean Parisot de la Valette (1494–1568) was a French nobleman from Provence. He joined the Order of St John at the age of 20, and served it faithfully for the rest of his life, holding the title of Grand Master from 1557 until his death. He was a hardened fighter who had been captured by Barbary pirates in 1541 and spent a year as a galley slave, and a natural leader whose greatest achievement was the defence of Malta against the Turks in the Great Siege of 1565.

In the aftermath of the Great Siege, la Valette immediately set about the fortification of the Sceberras peninsula and the construction of a new city. Three years later, with the streets of Valletta already laid out, he suffered a stroke after a day's hawking at Buskett Gardens, and died in August 1568 at the age of 73. His tomb in the crypt of St John's Co-Cathedral bears a Latin inscription which translates as: 'Here lies Valette, worthy of eternal honour. He who was once the scourge of Africa and Asia, and the shield of Europe, whence he expelled the barbarians by his holy arms, is the first to be buried in this beloved city, whose founder he was.'

landward defences, the Notre Dame Ditch, about 1km southwest of Valletta's Great Ditch. These were designed by the Italian engineer Pietro Paolo Floriani, who gave his name to the town (Floriana) that grew up within these walls in the 18th century.

ORIENTATION

Valletta and Floriana occupy the long finger of the Sceberras peninsula that divides Grand Harbour to the south from Marsamxett Harbour to the north. City Gate bus terminus (Malta's main bus station) lies between the two towns.

Valletta is a compact town barely a kilometre long and 600m wide, with a regular grid of narrow streets confined within the massive medieval fortifications at the tip of the peninsula. The main street, Triq ir-Repubblika (Republic St), runs in a straight line northeast from City Gate (adjacent to City Gate bus terminus) to Fort St Elmo, passing through Misraħ l-Assedju l-Kbir (Great Siege Sq), Misraħ ir-Repubblika (Republic Sq) and Pjazza San Ġorġ (St George's Sq).

Two other major streets run parallel to Repubblika – Triq il-Merkanti (Merchants' St) two blocks to the southeast, and Triq l-Ifran (Old Bakery St) two blocks to the northwest. Triq ir-Repubblika and Triq il-Merkanti roughly follow the spine of the peninsula, and side streets fall steeply downhill on either side. The main sights, St John's Co-Cathedral and the Grand Master's Palace, are on Triq ir-Repubblika within 500m of City Gate.

Street signs in Valletta are in both Malti and English. Note that houses are numbered in sequence along one side of the street, and then back in the opposite direction along the other side, which means that No 20 can sometimes be across the street from No 200!

Maps

Most maps of the Maltese Islands include an inset street plan of Valletta. Half a dozen different tourist maps of Valletta can be bought cheaply from the souvenir shops and bookshops on Triq ir-Repubblika. You can pick up free street maps of Valletta and Floriana at the tourist information office (p63), as well as free brochures detailing walking tours of Valletta, Floriana and the Three Cities.

VALLETTA STREET NAMES

It's helpful to know the names of Valletta's main streets in both Malti and English, as many maps feature only one language or the other, and many businesses advertise in English and use the English street name.

Triq ir-Repubblika	Republic St
Triq il-Merkanti	Merchants' St
Triq San Pawl	St Paul's St
Triq Sant'Orsla	St Ursula's St
Triq San Zakkarija	St Zachary's St
Triq id-Dejqa	Strait St
Triq l-Ifran	Old Bakery St
Triq iz-Zekka	Old Mint St
Triq Nofs in-Nhar	South St
Triq Melita	Melita St
Triq San Ġwann	St John's St
Triq Santa Luċija	St Lucija's St
Triq it-Teatru l-Antik	Old Theatre St
Triq l'Arċisqof	Archbishop St

VALLETTA IN...

Two Days

Start your day with coffee at **Caffè Cordina** (p73), then take in the **Malta Experience** (p68) for some historical background. Spend a few hours wandering Valletta's streets, stopping to admire the beautiful architecture and the magnificent views, especially those over Grand Harbour and the Three Cities from the **Upper Barrakka Gardens** (p69). Follow the walking tour outlined on p68 for more direction. Spend the afternoon visiting **St John's Co-Cathedral** (p63), the **Grand Master's Palace** (p65) and Valletta's **National Museum of Archaeology** (p66), before enjoying dinner at one of Valletta's fine restaurants. Afterwards, take in a show at the **Manoel Theatre** (p67) or sample some local wine at the atmospheric **Castille Wine Vaults** (p72). On the second day, take a tour of the **Hypogeum** (p82) – be sure to prebook – then spend the rest of the day exploring the nooks and crannies of the intriguing **Three Cities** (p77) area.

Four Days

Follow the two-day itinerary, then on the third day see the **Wartime Experience** (p68) and visit the **National War Museum** (p66) to learn of WWII heroism and hardships in Malta. Then, for a change of scenery, stroll around **Floriana** (p75). In the evening, visit **St James' Cavalier Centre for Creativity** (p67) and take in an exhibition or performance. On the fourth day, take the bus to stunning **Mdina** (p117) or the ferry across to bustling **Sliema** (p84).

One Week

If you're based in the capital for a week or longer, you're well placed to explore Malta by public bus. Follow the four-day itinerary and then spend the remaining time exploring other Maltese attractions. Consider day trips to Mdina, Sliema, Marsaxlokk, the northern beaches, and the temples at Ħaġar Qim and Mnajdra.

INFORMATION
Airline Offices

Most airline offices are found at the airport (p174). Some airlines also have offices in Valletta, while others are located in Sliema, Msida or Gzira.

Air Malta (☎ 21 240 686; Misraħ il-Ħelsien; ☟ 8.30am-5pm Mon-Fri) Near the tourist office.

British Airways (☎ 21 242 233; 20/2 Triq ir-Repubblika) Above the Travelex office.

Bookshops

There are several good bookshops in Valletta, and most major attractions also have a shop selling a wide range of Malta books, and souvenirs.

Agenda (☎ 21 252 117; Embassy Complex, Triq Santa Luċija)

Aquilina (☎ 21 233 774; www.maltabook.com; 58 Triq ir-Repubblika) A very good selection of history books, travel guides, reference and fiction; most are available online.

Hertie Library (☎ 21 237 298; 35c Triq San Zakkarija) A small, old-world bookshop dedicated almost exclusively to books about Malta.

Newsstand (Triq il-Merkanti) A wide range of British, German and Italian newspapers and magazines is available from this hole-in-the-wall place near the Auberge d'Italie.

Sapienzas (☎ 21 233 621; www.sapienzas.com; 26 Triq ir-Repubblika) Another excellent selection of history books, travel guides, reference and fiction; also available online.

Cultural Centres

Valletta and the surrounding area have a number of cultural centres, which offer a variety of exhibitions, lectures, language courses and cultural events.

Alliance Française de Malte (Map p59; ☎ 21 220 701 or 21 238 456; http://site.voila.fr/alliancefr.mt; 108 Triq San Tumas, Floriana)

British Council (Map p86; ☎ 23 232 301; www.british council.org/malta; British Embassy, Whitehall Mansions, Xatt Ta'Xbiex, Ta'Xbiex)

German-Maltese Circle (☎ 21 246 967; www.german maltesecircle.org; Messina Palace; 141 Triq San Kristofru, Valletta)

Italian Cultural Institute (☎ 21 221 462; www.iicmalta .org; Pjazza San Ġorġ, Valletta)

Russian Centre for Science & Culture (☎ 21 222 030; 36 Triq il-Merkanti, Valletta)

Emergency

Malta Police Headquarters (Map p59; ☎ 21 224 001; Pjazza Vicenzo Buġeja, Floriana)

Police Station (☎ 21 225 495; Triq Nofs in-Nhar, Valletta) Opposite the site of the old Opera House.

VALLETTA

Internet Access

MelitaNet (☎ 21 222 380; 28 Triq Melita; per hr Lm1)
YMCA Internet Café (☎ 21 240 680; 178 Triq il-Merkanti; 30 min Lm0.60) Drinks and snacks available.
Ziffa (☎ 21 224 307; 194 Triq id-Dejqa; 2hr Lm1.80; ♥ 9am-11pm Mon-Sat, 10am-5pm Sun) Fast Internet access, lots of computers, and good rates for overseas phone calls.

Medical Services

Royal Pharmacy (☎ 21 234 321; 271 Triq ir-Repubblika) Central pharmacy open during shopping hours.
St Luke's Hospital (Map p86; ☎ 21 241 251; Gwardamanġa Hill, Gwardamanġa) Malta's public general hospital, near Pietà (about 3km southwest of Valletta); take bus No 75.

Money

There are plenty of places to change money and cash travellers cheques on and near Triq ir-Repubblika in Valletta.

Bank of Valletta (cnr Triq ir-Repubblika & Triq San Ġwann; ♥ 8.30am-2pm Mon-Thu, 8.30am-3.30pm Fri, 8.30am-12.15pm Sat) Foreign exchange machine and ATMs.
HSBC (233 Triq ir-Repubblika & 15 Triq il-Merkanti) Foreign exchange machine and ATMs.
Travelex (☎ 21 235 948; 20 Triq ir-Repubblika; ♥ 8.30am-1pm & 2-5.30pm Mon-Fri, 9am-1pm Sat) Currency exchange bureau.

Post

Main Post Office (Pjazza Kastilja; ♥ 8.15am-4.30pm Mon-Fri, 8.15am-12.30pm Sat) Found under the St James' Cavalier, opposite the Auberge de Castile.

VALLETTA

Tourist Information

Tourist Information Branch (☎ 23 696 073/4; Malta International Airport; ◷ 10am-10pm)

Tourist Information Office (☎ 21 237 747 or 21 255 844; Misraħ il-Ħelsien; ◷ 9am-5.30pm Mon-Sat, 9am-12.30pm Sun, closed public holidays) In the City Arcade immediately on the right as you enter the town through City Gate.

Travel Agencies

National Student Travel Service (NSTS; ☎ 21 244 983; www.nsts.org; 220 Triq San Pawl) Specialises in student and youth travel; can arrange budget holiday packages, water-sports facilities and English-language courses (for more information see p160).

SMS Travel & Tourism (☎ 21 232 211; www.smstravel .net; 311 Triq ir-Repubblika) A good general agency, offering excursions, guided tours, currency exchange and plane and ferry tickets.

Universities

University of Malta (Map p86; ☎ 21 333 903; www .um.edu.mt) Founded as a Jesuit college in 1592, the university became a state institution in the 18th century. It now has more than 9000 students and boasts a prestigious medical school. The modern campus is at Tal-Qroqq near Msida, about 3km west of Valletta.

SIGHTS
St John's Co-Cathedral

Malta's most impressive church, **St John's Co-Cathedral** (☎ 21 225 639; entrance on Triq ir-Repubblika; adult/child Lm1/free; ◷ 9.30am-12.30pm & 1.30-4.15pm Mon-Fri, 9.30am-12.30pm Sat, last admission 30 min before closing, closed Sun, public holidays & during services) was designed by the architect Gerolamo Cassar and built between 1573 and 1578 as the conventual church of the Knights of St John. It took over from the Church of St Lawrence in Vittoriosa as the place where the Knights would gather for communal worship. It was raised to a status equal to that of St Paul's Cathedral in Mdina – the official seat of the Archbishop of Malta – by a papal decree of 1816, hence the term 'co-cathedral'.

The façade is rather plain, and framed by twin bell-towers – a feature that has been copied by almost every church in Malta – but the interior is a colourful treasure house of Maltese baroque. The nave is long and low and every wall, pillar and rib is encrusted with rich ornamentation, giving the effect of a dusty gold brocade – the Maltese Cross and the arms of the Order (a white cross on a scarlet background) can be seen everywhere. The floor is a vast

---

MEDIEVAL TOWN PLANNING

The Knights who oversaw the construction of Valletta grabbed the opportunity to try out their ideas for urban improvement. In league with Francisco Laparelli, who designed the city, and Gerolamo Cassar, who designed many of its buildings, they laid out certain rules governing the construction of their city.

The buildings were made tall enough to shade the streets from the hot sun, and the regular grid of straight streets allowed cooling sea breezes to circulate. Drainage ditches were cut beneath street level to carry away household waste, and were flushed with sea water twice a day. Every house had to have a well to catch rainwater, and waste had to be disposed of in the underground ditches; façades had to be built to certain specifications to maintain uniformity of appearance; any porches or projections that narrowed the street were prohibited; and every building had to have a sculpture on each corner. Most of these features remain to this day.

---

patchwork quilt of colourful marble tomb slabs in black, white, blue, red, pink and yellow, and the vault is covered in paintings by Mattia Preti (see the boxed text, p40) illustrating events from the life of St John the Baptist. The altar is dominated by a huge marble sculpture of the baptism of Christ, with a painting, *St John in Heaven*, by Preti above it.

There are six bays on either side of the nave, eight of which contain chapels allocated to the various langues (or divisions, based on nationality) of the Order of St John, and dedicated to the patron saint of the particular langue. The first bay you'll encounter upon entering and walking to your right is the **Chapel of Germany**.

Opposite is the **Chapel of Castile**, with monuments to Grand Masters Antonio Manoel de Vilhena and Manuel Pinto de Fonseca. This is followed by the **Chapel of Aragon**, the most splendid in the cathedral. The tombs of the brothers – and consecutive Grand Masters – Rafael and Nicolas Cotoner compete for the title of most extravagant sculpture.

The last bay in this aisle, past the **Chapel of Auvergne**, contains the **Chapel of the Blessed Sacrament** (also known as the Chapel dedicated to the Madonna of Carafa), closed off by a pair of solid silver gates. It contains a 15th-century crucifix from Rhodes and keys of captured Turkish fortresses.

Opposite is the dark and moody **Chapel of Provence**, containing the tombs of Grand Masters Antoine de Paule and Jean Lascaris Castellar. The steps at the back lead down to the cathedral **crypt** (usually closed to the public), where the first 12 Grand Masters of Malta – from 1523 to 1623 – are interred.

The reclining effigies include Jean Parisot de la Valette, hero of the Great Siege and the founder of Valletta, and his English secretary Sir Oliver Starkey, the only man below the rank of Grand Master to be honoured with a tomb in the crypt. Darker still is the **Chapel of the Holy Relics** (also known as the Chapel of the Anglo-Bavarian Langue), which contains a wooden figure of St John that is said to have come from the galley in which the Knights departed from Rhodes in 1523.

The austere **Chapel of France**, with a Preti altarpiece of St Paul, was stripped of its baroque decoration in the 1840s. Preti's painting *The Mystic Marriage of St Catherine* hangs in the **Chapel of Italy**, looking down on a bust of Grand Master Gregorio Carafa.

CATHEDRAL MUSEUM

The first bay in the south aisle of St John's gives access to the **Cathedral Museum** (☎ 21 220 536; admission included in cathedral ticket price; ❧ same hours as cathedral). The first room is the Oratory, built in 1603 as a place of worship and for the instruction of novices. It is dominated by the altarpiece the *Beheading of St John the Baptist* (c 1608) by Caravaggio, one of the artist's most famous and accomplished paintings. The executioner – reaching for a knife to finish off the job that his sword began – and the horrified Salome with her platter are depicted with chilling realism. On the east wall hangs *St Jerome*, another of Caravaggio's masterpieces.

The rest of the museum houses collections of vestments, choral books, and a collection of Flemish tapestries depicting Bible scenes and religious allegories. The tapestries were based on drawings by Rubens,

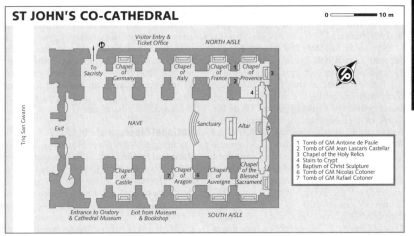

ST JOHN'S CO-CATHEDRAL

0 ————— 10 m

Visitor Entry & Ticket Office

NORTH AISLE

To Sacristy

Chapel of Germany

Chapel of Italy

Chapel of France

Chapel of Provence

1

2

3

4

NAVE

Sanctuary

Altar

5

Exit

Triq San Gwann

Chapel of Castile

Chapel of Aragon

Chapel of Auvergne

Chapel of the Blessed Sacrament

7

6

Entrance to Oratory & Cathedral Museum

Exit from Museum & Bookshop

SOUTH AISLE

1 Tomb of GM Antoine de Paule
2 Tomb of GM Jean Lascaris Castellar
3 Chapel of the Holy Relics
4 Stairs to Crypt
5 Baptism of Christ Sculpture
6 Tomb of GM Nicolas Cotoner
7 Tomb of GM Rafael Cotoner

and were commissioned by Grand Master Ramon de Perellos, whose escutcheon appears on each panel.

Grand Master's Palace

The 16th-century **Grand Master's Palace** (Pjazza San Ġorġ, visitor entrance on Triq il-Merkanti), once the residence of the Grand Masters of the Knights of St John, is today the seat of Malta's parliament and the official residence of the Maltese president.

There are two VIP entrances on Pjazza San Ġorġ, but these are not for general public admission. The right-hand arch leads to **Prince Alfred's Courtyard**, where two stone lions guard a doorway leading to the Great Hall (now occupied by Malta's parliamentary House of Representatives), and a clock tower built in 1745 marks the hours with bronze figures of Moorish slaves striking gongs. The left-hand arch leads into **Neptune's Courtyard**, named for the 17th-century bronze statue of the sea-god that stands there.

From the public entrance on Triq il-Merkanti, it is possible to visit the **Armoury** (☎ 21 249 349; adult/child Lm1/free; ⏰ 7.45am-2pm daily mid-Jun–Sep, 8.15am-5pm Mon-Sat & 8.15am-4pm Sun Oct–mid-Jun, closed public holidays) and the **State Apartments** (☎ 21 221 221; adult/child Lm1/free; ⏰ same hours as Armoury), although the State Apartments are closed from time to time when official state visits are taking place.

The **Armoury** is now housed in what was once the Grand Master's stables. The armour

and weapons belonging to the Knights were once stored at the Palace Armoury (now the Great Hall used by the parliament), and when a Knight died they became the property of the Order. The current collection of over 5000 suits of 16th- to 18th-century armour is all that remains of an original 25,000 suits – Napoleon's light-fingered activities, over-enthusiastic housekeeping by the British and general neglect put paid to the rest.

Some of the most interesting pieces are the breastplate worn by la Valette, the beautifully damascened (steel inlaid with gold) suit made for Alof de Wignacourt, and the captured Turkish sipahi armour. A second room contains displays of weapons, including crossbows, muskets, swords and pistols but the labelling of the exhibits is disappointingly sparse.

A staircase by the Armoury entrance provides access to the **State Apartments**. Only a few rooms are open to the public, depending on what is currently being used. The long **Armoury Corridor**, decorated with trompe l'oeil painting, scenes of naval battles, and the escutcheons of various Grand Masters, leads to the **Council Chamber** on the left. It is hung with 17th-century Gobelins tapestries gifted to the Order in 1710 by Grand Master Ramon Perellos. They feature exotic scenes of Africa, India, the Caribbean and Brazil, including an elephant beneath a cashew-nut tree; an ostrich, cassowary and flamingo; a rhino and a zebra being attacked by a leopard; and a tableau with palm trees, a tapir, a jaguar and an iguana.

Beyond lie the **State Dining Room** and the **Supreme Council Hall**, where the Supreme Council of Order met. It is decorated with a frieze depicting events from the Great Siege of 1565, while the minstrels' gallery bears paintings showing scenes from the Book of Genesis. At the far end of the hall a door gives access to the **Hall of the Ambassadors**, or Red State Room, where the Grand Master would receive important visitors, and where the Maltese president still receives foreign envoys. It contains portraits of the French kings Louis XIV, Louis XV and Louis XVI, the Russian Empress Catherine the Great, and several Grand Masters. The neighbouring **Pages' Room**, or Yellow State Room, was used by the Grand Master's 16 attendants, and now serves as a conference room.

National Museum of Archaeology

Housed in the Auberge de Provence, the **National Museum of Archaeology** (☎ 21 221 623; Triq ir-Repubblika; adult/child Lm1/free; ☼ 7.45am-2pm daily mid-Jun–Sep, 8.15am-5pm Mon-Sat & 8.15am-4pm Sun Oct–mid-Jun, closed public holidays) is well worth a visit, despite the fact that it is still undergoing renovation and expansion. At the time of research only the galleries on the ground floor (detailing the early Neolithic and Temple periods, c 5200 to 2500 BC) were open, but new exhibitions should be opening upstairs sometime in 2004, and these will explore the Bronze Age, Phoenician and Roman culture and the medieval period up to the modern period (c 2500 BC to AD 1800s).

In the downstairs galleries you can see the beautiful and often mysterious objects that have been found at Malta's prehistoric sites, along with displays showing the technology used to build Malta's prehistoric temples, and the evolution of temple design from simple stone huts to the elaborate layout of Ġgantija. There is also a very good model of the Hypogeum on display.

The exhibits include female figurines found at Ħaġar Qim, the so-called 'fat ladies' – perhaps representing a fertility goddess – with massive rounded thighs and arms, but tiny, doll-like hands and feet, wearing a pleated skirt and sitting with

legs tucked neatly to one side. The so-called *Venus de Malta*, also from Ħaġar Qim, is about 10cm tall and displays more realistic modelling. Best of all is the *Sleeping Lady*, found at the Hypogeum and dating from around 3000 BC – here the well-endowed Venus is seen lying on her side with her head propped on one arm, apparently in the depths of blissful sleep.

National Museum of Fine Arts

Occupying Admiralty House is Malta's **Museum of Fine Arts** (☎ 21 225 769; Triq Nofs in-Nhar; adult/child Lm1/free; ☼ 7.45am-2pm daily mid-Jun–Sep, 8.15am-5pm Mon-Sat & 8.15am-4pm Sun Oct–mid-Jun, closed public holidays). Admiralty House is a baroque palazzo that was used as the official residence of the Admiral Commander-in-Chief of the British Mediterranean Fleet from the 1820s until 1961. Lord Louis Mountbatten also had his headquarters here in the early 1950s.

The museum's collection of paintings – mostly Italian and Maltese – ranges from the 15th to the 20th century, and there are some fine examples of 17th- and 18th-century Maltese furniture. Highlights include Rooms 12 and 13 (at the top of the stairs on the first floor), which display works by Mattia Preti (see the boxed text, p40). Look out for the dramatic *Martyrdom of St Catherine*, Doubting Thomas poking a finger into Christ's wound in *The Incredulity of St Thomas*, and St John the Baptist dressed in the habit of the Knights of St John.

Downstairs, Room 14 contains portraits of several Grand Masters by the 18th-century French artist Antoine de Favray, including one of the imperious Manoel Pinto de Fonseca. Room 18 has scenes of Malta by 19th-century British artists, including poet Edward Lear and a wonderful watercolour depicting a Grand Harbour scene, painted by Turner – the museum's pride and joy. Room 19 has many 19th-century scenes of Valletta.

National War Museum

Opened in 1975 to commemorate the island's ordeal during WWII, Malta's **National War Museum** (☎ 21 222 430; entrance on Triq il-Fontana; adult/child Lm1/free; ☼ 7.45am-2pm daily mid-Jun–Sep, 8.15am-5pm Mon-Sat & 8.15am-4pm Sun Oct–mid-Jun, closed public holidays) is housed in the northwest corner of Fort St Elmo.

The collection of relics, photographs and equipment includes the Gloster Gladiator biplane called *Faith* (minus wings), the Jeep *Husky* used by General Eisenhower, and the wreckage of a Spitfire and a Messerschmitt Me-109 fighter aircraft recovered from the sea bed. The pictures of bomb damage in Valletta give some idea of the amount of rebuilding that was needed after the war. Pride of place goes to the George Cross medal that was awarded to the entire population of Malta in 1942.

St James' Cavalier

The St James' Cavalier has undergone a remarkable transformation from a 16th-century fortification into a bright and modern arts centre. Inside the **St James' Cavalier Centre for Creativity** (☎ 21 223 200; www.sjcav.org; entrance on Triq Nofs in-Nhar; admission free; ⏰ 10am-9.30pm) are a couple of exhibition spaces (with a bias towards the contemporary art scene), a theatre-in-the-round where live music and theatre performances are held, and a cinema showing art-house films. It's worth stopping in to check out the interesting interior and to grab a programme of what's on.

Manoel Theatre

The 600-seat **Manoel Theatre** (☎ 21 246 389; www.teatrumanoel.com; 115 Triq it-Teatru l-Antik), Malta's national theatre, was built in 1731 and is one of the oldest theatres in Europe. Take an interesting guided tour (conducted in English, French, Italian and German) to see the restored baroque auditorium with its gilt boxes and huge chandelier. Tours begin at 10.30am, 11.30pm and 5.15pm Monday to Friday, and 11.30am and 12.30pm Saturday. Tickets cost Lm1.65 and include admission to the theatre's small museum. See p74 for information on the theatre's programme of performances.

Fort St Elmo

At the furthest point of Valletta and guarding the entrance to both Marsamxett and Grand Harbours is **Fort St Elmo**, named after the patron saint of mariners. Although now much altered and extended, this was the fort that bore the brunt of Turkish arms during the Great Siege of 1565. It was built by the Knights in 1552 to guard the entrances to the harbours on either side of the Sceberras peninsula. The courtyard outside the

entrance to the fort is studded with the lids of underground granaries.

Today Fort St Elmo is home to the Malta police academy and is open to the public only for historical re-enactments, held on most Sunday mornings except during the peak summer months of July and August. **In Guardia** (☎ 21 237 747; adult/child Lm1.50/0.50; ⏰ 11am 1st & 3rd Sun of month Sep-Jun) is a colourful and photogenic military pageant in 16th-century costume, which includes a cannon-firing demonstration that will clear the wax from your ears. **Alarme!** (☎ 21 237 747; adult/child Lm1.50/0.50; ⏰ 11am 2nd Sun of month Feb-Jun & Sep-Nov) is a re-enactment of a military encounter between French and Maltese troops. Inquire about dates for these shows at the tourist office.

Lascaris War Rooms

WWII history boffins should be sure to visit the **Lascaris War Rooms** (☎ 21 234 936; adult/child Lm1.75/0.85; ⏰ 9.30am-4pm Mon-Fri, 9.30am-12.30pm Sat & Sun). These chambers, hewn out of the solid rock far beneath Lascaris Bastion, housed the headquarters of the Allied air and naval forces during WWII, and were used as the control centre for Operation Husky, the Allied invasion of Sicily in 1943.

The rooms are a little tricky to find. One option is to walk south from Pjazza Kastilja along Triq Girolamo Cassar and look for the path on the right (signposted) that leads down into the Great Ditch beneath St James' Bastion and doubles back under the road to the entry. An alternative route is to walk from City Gate along the Great Ditch outside the town walls, and enter through the Kalkara Gardens. Once inside, you take a self-guided audio tour through the operations rooms. You will need to use your imagination to fill these deserted control rooms and corridors with the clatter of typewriters, the crackle of radio transmissions, and the hushed urgency that must have permeated the air during major operations.

Casa Rocca Piccola

The 16th-century palazzo **Casa Rocca Piccola** (☎ 21 231 796; 74 Triq ir-Repubblika; adult/child Lm2.50/1; ⏰ tours on the hour 10am-4pm Mon-Sat) is the family home of the Marquis de Piro. The marquis has opened part of the palazzo to the public and guided tours give an insight into the privileged lifestyle of the aristocracy.

Toy Museum

Opposite Casa Rocca Piccola is the small **Toy Museum** (☎ 21 251 652; 222 Triq ir-Repubblika; adult/child Lm1/free; ⏰ 10.30am-3.30pm Mon-Fri, 10.30am-1.30pm Sat & Sun), housing an impressive private collection of model planes and boats from the 1950s, as well as Matchbox cars, farmyard animals, train sets and dolls. The collection is generally in glass display cabinets, so this place is better suited to nostalgic adults than hyperactive ankle-biters.

Audiovisual Shows & Exhibitions

The **Wartime Experience** (☎ 21 222 225; Triq Santa Luċija; adult/child Lm2/1.50) is a worthwhile 45-minute show made up of archive film from WWII, which movingly records the ordeal suffered by the Maltese people during the siege of 1940 to 1943. It's shown at the Embassy Cinemas (p74) inside the Embassy Complex daily at 10am, 11am, noon and 1pm. The Embassy Cinemas is a temporary home for this film – there are plans to resume showing it at the old Hostel de Verdelin on Triq l-Arċisqof (on the northeast side of Pjazza San Ġorġ), which is undergoing restoration. No-one knows when the restoration will finish, so don't hold your breath – and try the Embassy Cinemas first!

The **Malta Experience** (☎ 21 243 776 or 21 251 284; www.themaltaexperience.com; Triq il-Mediterran; adult/child Lm3/1.75) is a (somewhat pricey) 45-minute audiovisual presentation that provides a good introduction to Malta, especially for first-time visitors. The film is available in 12 languages; it showcases the country's long history and highlights many of its scenic attractions. Screenings begin on the hour from 11am to 4pm Monday to Friday, and from 11am to 1pm on weekends and public holidays (with an extra 2pm show from mid-October till June).

The Malta Experience is screened in the basement of the Mediterranean Conference Centre, which is housed in the **Sacra Infermeria**, the 16th-century hospital of the Order of St John. Here surgeons performed advanced operations as well as the more routine amputations and treatment of war wounds. See Hospitals in the boxed text, p27, for more details. A somewhat lacklustre **Knights Hospitallers exhibition** (☎ 21 224 135; entrance on Triq it-Tramuntana; adult/child Lm1.50/0.75; ⏰ 9.30am-4.30pm Mon-Fri, 9.30am-4pm Sat & Sun), with an entrance across the street from the Malta Experience, records the achievements of these medieval medics.

One heavily promoted exhibition is the **Great Siege of Malta & the Knights of St John** (☎ 21 247 300; Misraħ ir-Repubblika; adult/child Lm3.50/2.75; ⏰ 9am-last admission 4pm), beside the entry to the Bibliotheca. It rather grandly proclaims to be 'Europe's most exciting walk-through adventure' but doesn't live up to the hype. For the rather pricey admission fee you get a 45-minute, sometimes-tedious self-guided tour (audio provided) through re-creations of battle scenes from the 1565 siege.

WALKING TOUR

> Distance: approx 4.5km
> Duration: 3 hours

The first part of the walk outlined here follows the outer fortifications of Valletta, and offers some great views of Grand Harbour, the Three Cities, Marsamxett Harbour and Sliema. This is followed by some exploration of Valletta's narrow streets. Climbing the town's steep stairs is a good way of working up a thirst before retiring to the cool shade of a café for a well-earned drink. The route described can be completed in about 2½ to three hours. If you choose to visit all the sights detailed here, it could easily take an entire day.

Begin at **City Gate (1)** and go up the (pretty dingy and smelly) stairs on the left immediately inside the gate. These lead up to the bridge above City Gate, with a good view along Triq ir-Repubblika in one direction, and across the bus station to Floriana in the other.

Head northwest along Triq il-Papa Piju V, past **St John's Cavalier (2)**, which houses the Embassy of the Order of St John. Continue along Triq il-Mithna to **St Michael's Bastion (3)**. Nip into **Hastings Gardens (4)** here for a superb view over Marsamxett Harbour to Sliema and Manoel Island.

Descend steeply via Triq San Andrija and a flight of steps to Triq San Marku and continue straight on to Triq Marsamxett, the main road that runs along the top of the city walls. Head past the water polo pool on the shore below, and look out for the steep

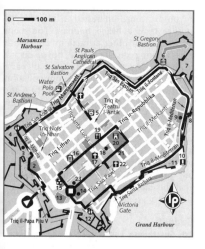

staircase of Triq it-Teatru l-Antik on the right, beneath the prominent spire of St Paul's Anglican Cathedral. A stiff climb leads up to **Manoel Theatre (5**; p74), built in 1731 and one of the oldest theatres in Europe.

Continue along Triq Marsamxett and around the walls of the Poste D'Angleterre and Poste de France. Drop in to the **National War Museum (6**; p66), then continue past **Fort St Elmo (7**; p67), which bore the brunt of Turkish attacks during the Great Siege of 1565.

A little further along Triq il-Mediterran lies the entrance to the **Malta Experience (8**; p68), an audiovisual presentation that provides a potted history of Malta. The show screens in the 16th-century hospital of the Order of St John, the **Sacra Infermeria (9**; p68). There is an exhibition here on the history of the medical care given by the Knights.

About 200m past the Sacra Infermeria the road forks, and on the left is a small park and a tall pillared cupola. This is the **Siege Bell Memorial (10)**, which commemorates those who lost their lives in the convoys of 1940 to 1943. Take the right hand fork in the road (still Triq il-Mediterran) past the entrance to **Lower Barrakka Gardens (11)**, which contains a little Doric temple commemorating Sir Alexander Ball, the naval captain who took Malta from the French in 1800.

Continue along Triq Santa Barbara, a charming tree-lined street with good views over the harbour to the Three Cities. Cross the bridge above Victoria Gate, and head through a sun-trap of a square, usually home to a handful of café tables, beside the Grand Harbour Hotel. Turn left and climb up steep Triq Sant'Orsla to reach the **Upper Barrakka Gardens (12)**. The balcony here provides a magnificent panorama of Grand Harbour and the creeks and dockyards of Vittoriosa and Senglea.

From the gardens continue to Pjazza Kastilja. On your left are the high walls of the **St James' Cavalier (13**; p67) which now houses exhibition spaces, a theatre and cinema. Pause to admire the façade of the **Auberge de Castile (14)**, on your right, designed by the architect Andrea Belli in 1741. It adorns a 16th-century building that was once the home of the Spanish and Portuguese langue of the Knights of St John, but now houses the offices of the Maltese prime minister (not open to the public).

Head straight along Triq Nofs in-Nhar towards Triq ir-Repubblika, passing the cracked steps and shattered column stumps of the ruined **Royal Opera House (15)** on your left. This once imperious building (you can check out an old photograph on the wall of Café Royale across the street) was built in the 1860s, but was destroyed during a German air raid in 1942. Its gutted shell has been left as a reminder of the war and is rather unceremoniously used as a car park while controversy rages as to what should be done with the site.

Turn right and walk east along Triq ir-Repubblika and you'll pass the 16th-century **Auberge de Provence (16)**, now home to the National Museum of Archaeology (p66) and the imposing **St John's Co-Cathedral (17**; p63). Stop in for a visit to one and/or both sights, then continue along the main street to Misrah ir-Repubblika, crammed with café tables and overlooked by the grand **Bibliotheca (18)** – Malta's national library and home to the archives of the Knights of St John – and a pigeon-spotted statue of Queen Victoria. Grab a coffee at the bar in **Caffè Cordina (19**; p73) on the left, then continue past the long façade of the **Grand Master's Palace (20**; p65), which dominates the southeast side of Pjazza San Ġorġ. You will need to walk around the block to Triq il-Merkanti to access the public entrance to the State Apartments and Armoury

VALLETTA

here. Continue southwest along Triq il-Merkanti – this street is home to a busy **market (21**; p74) that operates mornings from Monday to Saturday.

A short detour down the steep steps of Triq Santa Luċija leads to the side entrance of the **Church of St Paul's Shipwreck (22)** – the main door on Triq San Pawl is often closed – which dates from the 16th century. It has many treasures, including a dazzling gilded statue of St Paul, a golden reliquary containing some bones from the saint's forearm, and part of the column on which he is said to have been beheaded in Rome (see the boxed text, p38, for more information).

Continue back along Triq il-Merkanti, passing on your right the **Auberge d'Italie (23)**, built in 1574 and now home to the Ministry of Tourism. The ornate arms above the entrance are those of Grand Master Gregorio Carafa. You will emerge into Pjazza Kastilja; from here you can make your way back to City Gate, or pop into La Cave or the Castille Wine Vaults for refuelling.

VALLETTA FOR CHILDREN

Valletta is such a treasure trove of history and architecture – but, let's face it, there are not too many kids who get excited over such grown-up subjects. It's likely that your young offspring will enjoy walking along the city walls and taking in the great views, scenically situated gardens, café-filled squares and vaulted cellar restaurants of Valletta, but there are few attractions in the capital designed specifically for children. Older kids should enjoy the Malta Experience (p68) and younger kids will probably delight in some of the gory scenes depicted in exhibitions such as the Great Siege of Malta and Knights of St John (p68) or the Knights Hospitallers (p68) – but it's unlikely that much of the history lessons will sink in.

FESTIVALS & EVENTS

See p166 for details of some of the country's foremost festivals, most of which include a number of events staged in and around the capital.

SLEEPING

Although there are no more than 10 hotels in Valletta, it's a good place to base yourself if you are more interested in history and culture than a beach holiday. The main museums and other attractions are within easy walking distance, and buses depart from the City Gate terminus to all parts of the island. Most of the accommodation is within 10 minutes' walk of City Gate, and only the top-end option, Le Meridien Phoenicia Hotel, has car parking for guests. Many places offer discounts on stays of seven days or longer – it's worth asking. Many also offer half-board and full-board options: these are usually reasonable value, but you're better off with the freedom to visit the eateries of your choice – there are some very good ones in Valletta.

Budget

Asti Guesthouse (☎ 21 239 506; http://mol.net.mt /asti; 18 Triq Sant'Orsla; per person incl breakfast Lm5.50) Rooms in this classy old guesthouse are the best-value accommodation in Valletta. There is a charming hostess (Annie), spacious rooms (each with washbasin), and spotless shared bathrooms. Breakfast is served in a vaulted dining room complete with huge chandelier.

Coronation Guesthouse (☎ 21 237 652 or 99 406 080; 10E Triq M A Vassalli; per person incl breakfast Lm5.50 Jun-Aug, Lm5 Sep-May) There's a very warm welcome at this simple guesthouse, run by helpful Charlie and his family. Rooms (with washbasin; bathrooms are shared) are nothing flash but are airy and bright, and some have excellent views over Marsamxett Harbour. There's the added bonus of a kitchen for guest use. Charlie also has a self-contained apartment on offer (with its own entrance, kitchen, sitting room and room for three people, at around Lm5.50 per person).

Midland Guesthouse (☎ 21 236 024; http://mol .net.mt/midl&; 255 Triq Sant'Orsla; per person Lm6 May-Sep, Lm5.50 Oct-Apr) Down the hill from Asti Guesthouse, this is another elegant old townhouse offering similar facilities and prices to the Asti but not such a warm welcome. Rooms have older-style décor and are clean and comfortable.

Le Bonheur Guesthouse (☎ 21 238 433; 18 Triq l-Inġinieri; per person incl breakfast Lm5.50) At the top of the town in a quiet location, Le Bonheur offers six simple rooms (most with washbasin and shower; toilets are shared), plus an OK restaurant on the ground floor.

At the time of research, the **YMCA** (☎ 21 240 680; www.ymcavalletta.org; 178 Triq il-Merkanti; dm Lm3) was close to opening a hostel on Triq San Pawl, designed to cater to budget travellers as well as act as a temporary shelter for the homeless – so travellers with a social conscience can rest easy knowing that their accommodation costs are helping disadvantaged locals. There will be kitchen and laundry facilities, segregated dorms and common areas for mingling. Reception will be at the YMCA office, address above.

Mid-Range

Osborne Hotel (☎ 21 243 656/7; www.osbornehotel.com; 50 Triq Nofs in-Nhar; s/d Lm19/28; 🅿 🔊) The pick of the mid-range options, this former Knight's palace has an inviting ground-floor lobby, restaurant and lounge, but the smallish rooms don't quite live up to this high standard. Still, they're well equipped, with satellite TV (try for a room on the higher floors to ensure a view). On the 6th floor there's a roof terrace with great views and a small pool.

Castille Hotel (☎ 21 243 677/8; www.hotelcastillemalta.com; Pjazza Kastilja; s/d from Lm16/32; 🔊) Another good choice, this three-star place enjoys a grand position in an atmospheric old palazzo next door to the Auberge de Castile. Prices vary depending on the season; rooms are pleasant and have good amenities, including satellite TV. The bonus of staying here is the cellar restaurant, La Cave (p71), and the rooftop restaurant for breakfast or dinner with a great view.

British Hotel (☎ 21 224 730; www.britishhotel.com; 267 Triq Sant'Orsla, main entrance at 40 Triq il-Batterija; s/d Lm12/18, with sea view Lm16/22) You can enjoy excellent views over the Three Cities with your breakfast at this affordable, well-located hotel, and there are some good communal spaces here (the décor in the TV room and bar is so dated it's now retro-cool). But it's a bit of a rabbit warren, and the rooms, although clean, are basic and rather lacking in charm. It's worth paying extra for a balcony and view over Grand Harbour.

Grand Harbour Hotel (☎ 21 246 003; www.grandharbourhotel.com; 47 Triq il-Batterija; s/d Lm13/20 Jan-Mar & Nov-Dec, Lm15/29 Apr-Oct & Christmas-New Year period) Just downhill from the British, the Grand Harbour Hotel has similar facilities (and similarly tired rooms), plus great views

over the harbour, a small rooftop sundeck and an on-site restaurant.

EATING & DRINKING

Valletta is essentially a business district, and there are many restaurants and cafés that are open at lunch time but closed in the evenings. However, there are a few good places in which to enjoy dinner and a relaxed evening drink.

Restaurants

La Cave (☎ 21 243 677; Pjazza Kastilja; meals Lm1.80-3.75; 🕑 lunch Mon-Fri, dinner nightly) In an atmospheric 400-year-old cellar beneath Castille Hotel, this busy restaurant churns out crunchy pizzas big enough for two – the pizza Maltija is topped with goat's cheese, olives and Maltese sausage. There's also a good assortment of pasta dishes and a few salad options, and you can wash your food down with a selection of local wine – you might need more than one bottle though, as service can be slow.

La Sicilia (☎ 21 240 659; 1a Triq San Ġwann; snacks & meals Lm0.30-4.75; 🕑 8am-5pm Mon-Fri) You're sure to find something to fill a rumbling tum at this tiny, unpretentious eatery, which spills out onto a little sun-trap of a square at the foot of Triq San Ġwann. There are lots of hearty Italian pasta dishes (all under Lm3), grilled meats, steak and fish, plus burgers, sandwiches and salads. And – bonus – the prices are easy on the wallet.

Rubino (☎ 21 224 656; 53 Triq l-Ifran; mains approx Lm4-6; 🕑 lunch Mon-Fri, dinner Tue & Fri) Countless locals and return visitors agree that this restaurant, housed in an old confectionery, ranks among Malta's finest eateries. It serves up traditional Maltese cooking prepared to very high standards. There's no menu, just a selection of the day's dishes depending on seasonal produce and local tradition. Tuesday night is usually *fenkata* (a communal meal of rabbit) night. Bookings are advised.

Cocopazzo (☎ 21 235 706; Valletta Bldgs, Triq Nofs in-Nhar; mains Lm3.50-5; 🕑 lunch & dinner) With its cheery interior, friendly staff and well-prepared meals, this is an appealing option for lunch or dinner, and it's child-friendly too. There are good pasta and meat dishes, but the house speciality is seafood and the morning's catch is displayed on ice for diners to choose from.

Carriage (☎ 21 247 828; 22/5 Valletta Bldgs, Triq Nofs in-Nhar; mains lunch Lm2.50-6.60; 🕑 lunch Mon-Fri, dinner Fri & Sat) The entry to the Carriage is through a nondescript office building next door to Cocopazzo, and the restaurant is on the top floor. It's mainly a business-lunch spot, with crisp décor, efficient service and a set lunch menu for Lm7.50 (three courses plus a glass of wine). The food is imaginative: how about deep-fried camembert with avocado and parma ham, spicy crab cakes or roast quail with sage and eggplant stuffing?

Da Pippo Trattoria (☎ 21 248 029; 136 Triq Melita; mains Lm3-5; 🕑 lunch Mon-Sat) There's no menu at this cosy, cheerful place, with its tables covered in green-and-white checked tablecloths and usually crowded with locals. Check out the display cabinet filled with the day's offerings and take your pick from all the fresh seafood or meat, or one of the traditional dishes like rabbit, lamb or stuffed marrow.

Ristorante Giannini (☎ 21 237 121; 23 Triq il-Mithna; mains Lm7-8.50; 🕑 lunch & dinner Mon-Sat) Top-notch Italian at the top of town. Giannini, set in an elegant townhouse with a great view over Marsamxett Harbour, is one of Malta's top restaurants and is a good choice for a business lunch or romantic dinner. The menu is a mix of Italian and Maltese, eg monkfish tail fillets in chardonnay,

capers, sun-dried tomatoes and black olives, or gnocchi with clams and calamari on a bed of pesto.

Blue Room (☎ 21 238 014; 59 Triq ir-Repubblika; dishes Lm2-7; 🕑 lunch Tue-Sat, dinner nightly) Blue Room is a Chinese restaurant, but that's not too obvious on first inspection. The elegant blue décor and first-rate service create a lovely dining atmosphere, and the food is excellent. At the upper end of the price scale you'll find king prawns and other seafood creations, at the bottom end there are vegetable and rice/noodle dishes, and in between are all the standards, from sweet and sour pork to beef and black bean sauce. The aromatic crispy duck (with pancakes) is excellent.

Ambrosia (☎ 21 225 923; 137 Triq l-Arċisqof; mains Lm2.50-3; 🕑 lunch Mon-Fri) This new restaurant is the sister of the acclaimed Christopher's at Ta'Xbiex (p93), so you know the standards here will be high. Stop in for tasty lunch-time dishes like riso nero with calamari and pancetta, or fettucine with fresh prawns and orange sauce, then treat yourself to a dessert (Lm1.20) of lemon sorbet with grappa or honey panna cotta.

Castille Wine Vaults (☎ 21 237 707; Pjazza Kastilja; light meals Lm1.50-3) This fabulously situated café-bar is underneath the stock-exchange building, accessed by steps and a long passageway. In the dining area you can sate your hunger with light meals including panini and platters (of antipasto, cheese, seafood or dips), plus learn about and sample some very good local wine (Lm2 for four wines). After 10pm on Friday and Saturday this is a popular nightspot, playing ambient tunes by candlelight.

Labyrinth (☎ 21 248 002; 44 Triq id-Dejqa) This appealing antique shop, tucked away in an alley a block north of Triq ir-Repubblika, was undergoing renovations at the time of research, but by the time you read this it should be home to a piazza café for daytime tea, coffee and light meals, and a supper club/wine bar open every night and offering edibles and entertainment. There are plans for live music of an evening (including jazz) and a good selection of local wines to complement the menu.

Two inviting bars are luring cool locals and visitors to the southern end of town for evening drinks. **Maestro e Fresco** (☎ 21 233 801; Triq Nofs in-Nhar) and **Tra Buxu** (☎ 21 223 036; cnr

Triq Nofs in-Nhar & Triq id-Dejqa) lie across the road from each other, and both offer an array of platters and nibbles perfect for sharing among friends over a bottle of wine. Maestro has live music Wednesday to Saturday.

Cafés

Caffè Cordina (☎ 21 234 385; 244 Triq ir-Repubblika; snacks & light meals Lm0.70-3.60) The prime people-watching spot in Valletta is Misraħ ir-Repubblika, where several cafés command the ranks of tables around the statue of Queen Victoria. The oldest and best is Caffè Cordina, established in 1837 and now a local institution. You have the choice of waiter service at the tables in the square or inside, or joining the locals at the zinc counter inside – pay first at the till, and give the receipt to the guy behind the bar. And be sure to look up; the ceiling is exquisitely painted. Excellent for savoury pastries and decadent sweets.

Café Jubilee (☎ 21 252 332; 125 Triq Santa Luċija; snacks & meals Lm0.90-3; ⏰ 8am-1am) This is the kind of place you can drop in to anytime, for a breakfast of coffee and *pastizzi* (flaky pastry parcel filled with ricotta cheese or mushy peas), a lunch-time baguette, or a dinner of salad, pasta and risotto selections. It's a convivial continental-style bistro, with low lighting, cosy nooks and poster-plastered walls. It's also a great spot for a night-time drink, with good local wines on offer.

Café Deux Baronnes (☎ 21 226 718; Triq Sant'Orsla; light meals Lm0.60-2.70) At the foot of the Upper Barrakka Gardens, this is a great place to rest weary sightseeing bones and refuel. A sandwich, salad, pizza or plate of pasta tastes better with a view like this to savour.

Quick Eats

The major fast-food outlets are near the top of the town, but cheaper and tastier fare can be found at the kiosks beside City Gate bus terminus. **Millennium** (the first kiosk on your right after you exit City Gate) sells fresh hot *pastizzi* for a mere Lm0.08 each, and passable pizza for Lm0.30 a slice.

Agius Pastizzerija (☎ 21 237 965; 273 Triq San Pawl; pastries from Lm0.07) Search out this friendly hole-in-the-wall place for great traditional snacks – sweet and savoury – to take away, at bargain prices.

Self-Catering

Wembley Stores (☎ 21 225 147; 305 Triq ir-Repubblika; ⏰ 7.15am-7pm Mon-Sat) has a wide selection of groceries (tinned and dried food) and there is a **fresh produce market** (Triq il-Merkanti; ⏰ 7am-1pm Mon-Sat) behind the Grand Master's Palace, where you can buy fruit and vegetables, fish, meat, sausages and cheese.

ENTERTAINMENT

For years Valletta has seemed half-dead after 8pm, its streets hushed and empty after the business folk and day-trippers have left, and those seeking any form of nightlife automatically headed to the Paceville area (p96). But there seems to have been a revival of late, and Valletta is now home to a few café-bars where you can eat, drink and be merry among in-the-know locals. These places tend to draw an older crowd. There are no nightclubs in Valletta, so the overseas students and early-20-somethings still head to Paceville, and if that's more your scene you can take a night bus (Lm0.50). Bus No 62 runs from Valletta to Paceville every half-hour until around 1am on Friday and Saturday nights year-round, and until 2.30am every night from mid-June to mid-July.

Venues in Valletta worth seeking out of an evening include **Castille Wine Vaults**, **Labyrinth**, **Café Jubilee**, **Maestro e Fresco** and **Tra Buxu** (see Eating & Drinking on p71 for details on all these café-bars). There is often live music at Labyrinth and Maestro e Fresco. Another good venue for more formal musical performances is the **St James' Cavalier Centre for Creativity** (p67) – check the newspapers or pick up a programme at the centre.

See p77 for information about **Tom Bar**, a popular gay bar not far outside Valletta.

Theatre

The beautiful **Manoel Theatre** (☎ 21 246 389; www.teatrumanoel.com; 115 Triq it-Teatru l-Antik) is Malta's national theatre, and the islands' principal venue for drama, concerts, opera, ballet, and the hugely popular Christmas pantomime. The performance season runs from October to May, and during these months there are lunch-time concerts every Wednesday at 12.30pm. Check the website for details of the programme, or pick one up at the **booking office** (☎ 21 246 389; cnr Triq l-Ifran & Triq it-Teatru l-Antik; ☉ 10am-12.30pm & 5-7pm Mon-Fri, 10am-noon Sat).

Guided tours of the Manoel Theatre are also offered (see p67).

The **St James' Cavalier Centre for Creativity** (p67) also stages intimate performances in its theatre-in-the-round.

Cinemas

Embassy Cinemas (☎ 21 222 225; www.embassycomplex.com.mt; Triq Santa Luċija), inside the Embassy Complex, has six screens showing the latest from Hollywood. Tickets cost Lm2.25/1.40 adult/child (or Lm1.85/1.40 before 5pm).

The **St James' Cavalier Centre for Creativity** (p67) has a cinema screening alternative and art-house films nightly, with tickets costing Lm1.75.

Casino

Vegas meets Venice: travellers looking for a chance to make (or blow) some holiday dough should head to the ritzy **Casino di Venezia** (Map p78; ☎ 21 805 580; Vittoriosa waterfront; ☉ 2pm-4am Mon-Thu, 2pm-5am Fri-Sat, noon-4am Sun) in Vittoriosa, beside the new marina and part of the Cottonera waterfront redevelopment. Visitors must be aged at least 18 to enter (25 for Maltese citizens), be smartly dressed and carry a passport or ID card.

SHOPPING

There are small shopping centres and souvenir shops all along Triq ir-Repubblika, but little of interest to visitors after something uniquely Maltese. The **Malta Crafts Centre** (☎ 21 224 532; Misraħ San Ġwann) has a range of locally produced crafts, including glassware, ceramics and lace.

A **street market** (Triq il-Merkanti; ☉ around 7am-1pm Mon-Sat) set up between Triq San Ġwann and Triq it-Teatru l-Antik sells mainly clothes, shoes, watches and jewellery, pirated CDs and computer games. The **Monti** (St James' Ditch; ☉ Sun) is a much bigger market, just south of the City Gate bus terminus.

GETTING THERE & AWAY
Air

See the Transport chapter (p175) for information on flights into Malta International Airport at Luqa, 8km south of Valletta.

Bus

All bus routes lead to Valletta. The City Gate bus terminus is the source of services to all parts of the island. For information on routes, fares and timetables, inquire at the Public Transport Authority kiosk on the south side of the terminus, and also see p180 for more details.

Ferry

The **Marsamxetto ferry service** (☎ 21 338 981) provides a quick and easy way to travel between Valletta and Sliema. The crossing costs Lm0.35 each way and takes only about five minutes. There are departures every hour (every half-hour from 10am to 4pm) daily in both directions, beginning at around 8am and finishing at around 6pm. To reach the departure point in Valletta, follow Triq San Marku all the way north, then under the overpass and down to the water.

Ferries depart from Sliema on the hour and half-hour, and from Valletta at a quarter past and quarter to the hour.

GETTING AROUND
To/From the Airport

Bus No 8 runs between the airport and the City Gate terminus in Valletta, passing through Floriana on the way – the fare is Lm0.15, and the journey takes about 40 minutes. The airport bus stop is immediately outside the entrance to the departures hall.

Ignore any taxi drivers who tell you that the bus stop is a 20-minute walk away, or that the bus won't be along for another hour – they're just touting for business. You'll find a taxi information desk in the airport arrivals hall, and you can organise nd pay for your taxi there. The set fare or a taxi from the airport to Valletta or Floriana is Lm6.

o/From the Ferry Terminal

Ferry passengers seem sadly neglected by ourism authorities. There is no public ransport from the ferry terminal on Pinto Wharf in Floriana up to the city of Val-etta – you can either catch a taxi or make he steep 15-minute climb. If you decide o walk it's best to follow the waterfront northeast, under the Lascaris Bastion, hen veer left and climb the steps up at Victoria Gate. At the top of the stairs you'll be greeted by Grand Harbour Hotel (p71) nd La Sicilia restaurant (p71).

ar & Motorcycle

A car is more of a hindrance than a help in Valletta. The streets around City Gate are logged with cars, buses and taxis most of he day, and cars without a resident's per-mit are not allowed to park in Valletta – instead you must use the big underground ar park in Floriana, which is just southwest

of the bus station and charges Lm2 for 4½ hours or more.

Public Transport

Bus No 98 makes a circuit of Valletta from City Gate to Fort St Elmo along the outer road that follows the top of the city walls (Lm0.10), but walking is generally the fast-est and easiest way to get about.

AROUND VALLETTA

FLORIANA
pop 2300

The suburb of Floriana, immediately south-west of the capital, grew up in the 18th century within the landward defences of Valletta. The northern part is taken up with government buildings and offices, while the south side is mostly residential.

The broad avenue formed by Vjal ir-Re Edwardu VII (King Edward VII Ave) and Triq Sarria runs southwest from City Gate bus terminus for 500m, dividing the government buildings of Beltissebh to the

FLORIANA

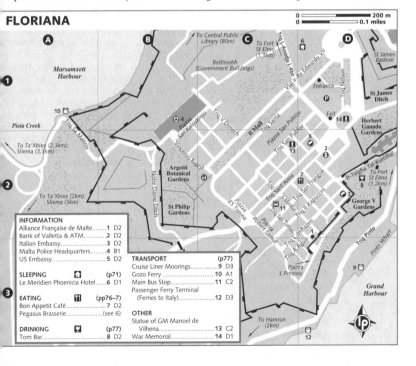

INFORMATION	
Alliance Française de Malte	1 D2
Bank of Valletta & ATM	2 D2
Italian Embassy	3 D2
Malta Police Headquarters	4 B1
US Embassy	5 D2

SLEEPING	(p71)
Le Meridien Phoenicia Hotel	6 D1

EATING	(pp76–7)
Bon Appetit Café	7 D2
Pegasus Brasserie	(see 6)

DRINKING	(p77)
Tom Bar	8 D2

TRANSPORT	(p77)
Cruise Liner Moorings	9 D3
Gozo Ferry	10 A1
Main Bus Stop	11 C2
Passenger Ferry Terminal (Ferries to Italy)	12 D3

OTHER	
Statue of GM Manoel de Vilhena	13 C2
War Memorial	14 D1

north from the long, open rectangle of Pjazza San Publiju (St Publius Sq) to the south. The main street of Floriana, Triq Sant'Anna (St Anne's St), lies two blocks south of the square. The main traffic route from Valletta to the rest of Malta exits from the southwest end of Triq Sant'Anna.

The terminal for passenger ferries from Sicily is on the southeast side of Floriana, beneath the fortifications. There is no public transport from here into town, unless you call a taxi. The shortest walking route to Floriana heads northeast along the quay, then doubles back up It-Telgha Tal-Kurċifiss (Crucifix Hill). It's a stiff climb, especially carrying a backpack – allow at least 15 minutes. A better route to get to the heart of Valletta is to follow the waterfront northeast, beneath the Lascaris Bastion, veer left and climb the steps up at Victoria Gate.

Street signs in Floriana are usually in Malti only.

Walking Tour

Distance: approx 1.5km
Duration: 45 minutes

Begin at the City Gate bus terminus and walk southwest along the central garden strip of Vjal ir-Re Edwardu VII and Triq Sarria. The **monument to Christ the King (1)**, opposite Le Meridien Phoenicia Hotel,

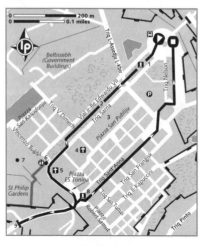

commemorates the International Eucharistic Congress held in Malta in 1913.

Cross Triq l-Assedju l-Kbir and continue along **Il-Mall (2)**. Now occupied by tree-lined gardens, the 400m-long Mall was laid out in the 17th century on the orders of Grand Master Lascaris, so that the younger Knights might play at pall-mall (an ancestor of croquet), in the forlorn hope that this might keep them from the temptations of wine, women and gambling.

The long open space on the south side of the Mall is Pjazza San Publiju. The circular slabs that stud its paved surface are the lids of underground **granaries (3)**. The square is dominated by the **Church of St Publius (4)**, dedicated to the patron saint of Floriana. Publius was the Roman governor of Malta in AD 60 when St Paul was shipwrecked on the island. He was converted to Christianity and became Malta's first bishop. The church was built in the 18th century, and badly damaged by WWII bombs.

Continue along Triq Sarria to the circular **Sarria Chapel (5)**, built in 1678 and designed and decorated by Mattia Preti. Across the street is the **Wignacourt Water Tower (6)**, part of an aqueduct system that brought water to Valletta from the central hills. Beside the tower is the entrance to the **Argotti Botanical Gardens (7)**.

Follow the street round to the left past the Sarria Chapel and downhill to the **Lion Fountain (8)**, and turn right on the main road out of town. A five-minute walk along this busy stretch of road leads to the **Porte des Bombes (9)**, an ornamental gateway dating from 1697 to 1720 that once formed part of the Floriana Lines fortifications. Pass through it to admire its decorations – reliefs of cannons and the coat of arms of Grand Master Perellos, under whose reign it was built.

Return to the Lion Fountain and then continue straight on along the grand, arcaded Triq Sant'Anna to return to Valletta.

Eating & Drinking

There aren't too many places to grab something to eat in Floriana. **Bon Appetit Café** (☎ 21 241 968; 19 Triq Sant'Anna; snacks & meals Lm1-4) will provide cheap and cheerful sustenance (burgers, salads, pizza, pasta etc), or at the end of your walk you could head to **Pegasus Brasserie** (☎ 22 911 084; The Mall; mains Lm4-6.50) a

Le Meridien Phoenicia Hotel (see the boxed text, p71) for upmarket café fare including locally influenced dishes like rabbit and pumpkin pie or pasta with Maltese sausage and mushrooms.

It's not the most likely location for one of Malta's prime gay nightspots, but the two-storey **Tom Bar** (☎ 21 250 780; www.geocities.com /tombarmalta; 1 It-Telgħa Tal-Kurċifiss; ☺ from 8.30pm year round, plus lunch 11.30am-2.30pm Oct-Mar) is very popular (especially among older gays, who prefer it to Paceville's offerings). Tom offers upstairs for chilling out, and downstairs for dance music.

Getting There & Away

Floriana is just a five-minute walk from Valletta. All buses to and from Valletta also pass through Floriana. The main bus stop on Triq Sant'Anna has an information board displaying the various route numbers and destinations.

There are two ferry terminals in Floriana. The daily car ferry to Gozo (used primarily by trucks) departs the Sa Maison wharf at Pieta Creek in Marsamxett Harbour (p184), while passenger ferries to/from Sicily dock at the ferry terminal on Pinto Wharf (p178). Pinto Wharf is also where cruise liners moor when in town.

THE THREE CITIES

When the Knights of St John first arrived in Malta in 1530, they made their home in the fishing village of Birgu, on a finger of land on the south side of Grand Harbour, overlooking the inlet (now known as Dockyard Creek) that was called the Port of the Arab Galleys. Here they built their auberges and repaired and extended the ancient defences. By the 1550s, Birgu (Fort St Angelo) and the neighbouring point of L-Isla (Fort St Michael) had been fortified, and Fort St Elmo had been built on the tip of the Sceberras peninsula. Bormla, at the head of Dockyard Creek, was not fortified until the 17th century.

From this base, the Knights withstood the Turkish onslaught during the Great Siege of 1565 (see p24 for more on this epic battle), but in the years that followed they moved to their new city of Valletta across the harbour. During WWII, the Three Cities and their surrounding docks were bombed almost daily throughout 1941 and 1942, and suffered terrible damage and bloodshed. Today, the towns of Vittoriosa, Senglea and Cospicua, as they are now known, are close-knit working communities largely dependent on their dockyards for employment. They are refreshingly untouristy and offer a welcome escape from the commercial hustle of Valletta and Sliema – although for how much longer this description will remain accurate is a matter for debate. The controversial Cottonera waterfront 'regeneration project' (www.cot tonerawaterfront.com) has seen the recent opening of a chi-chi casino at Vittoriosa, as well as a marina for so-called 'superyachts', with upmarket residential apartments under construction at the time of research and plans for a new five-star hotel, business centre and health spa in the pipeline. While projects such as these will hopefully bring employment and prosperity to a formerly neglected area, there is a danger of diluting the character and charm of the area in the rush to embrace development and attract wealthy locals and tourists.

At the time of research there were no tourist information offices, hotels or guesthouses in the Three Cities, and not a wide selection of cafés or restaurants – but this is likely to change in the not-too-distant future.

Vittoriosa

pop 3000

Vittoriosa is only 800m long and 400m at its widest, so it's hard to get lost. However, street signs are in Malti, while most tourist

---

WHAT'S IN A NAME?

The Three Cities were originally named Birgu, L-Isla and Bormla, but their names were changed after the Great Siege of 1565. Birgu became Vittoriosa (Victorious), L-Isla became Senglea (after Grand Master Claude de la Sengle), and Bormla became Cospicua (as in conspicuous courage). Local people and some road signs still use the old names, and all three together are sometimes referred to as 'The Cottonera', a reference to the Cottonera Lines – the landward fortifications surrounding the Three Cities that were built in the 1670s at the instigation of Grand Master Nicolas Cotoner.

VALLETTA

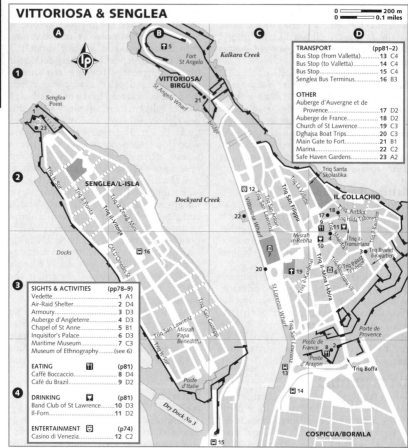

VITTORIOSA & SENGLEA

0 —— 200 m
0 —— 0.1 miles

Fort
St Angelo   *Kalkara Creek*

TRANSPORT   (pp81–2)
Bus Stop (from Valletta)...........**13** C4
Bus Stop (to Valletta)..............**14** C4
Bus Stop...................................**15** C4
Senglea Bus Terminus..............**16** B3

VITTORIOSA/
BIRGU

Senglea
Point

OTHER
Auberge d'Auvergne et de
Provence............................**17** D2
Auberge de France.................**18** D2
Church of St Lawrence...........**19** C3
Dghajsa Boat Trips.................**20** C3
Main Gate to Fort..................**21** B1
Marina...................................**22** C2
Safe Haven Gardens..............**23** A2

Triq Santa
Skolastika

SENGLEA/L-ISLA   *Dockyard Creek*   IL COLLACHIO

Docks

SIGHTS & ACTIVITIES   (pp78–9)
Vedette.............................**1** A1
Air-Raid Shelter................**2** D4
Armoury............................**3** D3
Auberge d'Angleterre.........**4** D3
Chapel of St Anne..............**5** B1
Inquisitor's Palace.............**6** D3
Maritime Museum..............**7** C3
Museum of Ethnography........(see 6)

EATING   (p81)
Caffè Boccaccio.................**8** D4
Café du Brazil...................**9** D2

DRINKING   (p81)
Band Club of St Lawrence...**10** D3
Il-Forn.............................**11** D2

ENTERTAINMENT   (p74)
Casino di Venezia..............**12** C2

*Misrah
Papa
Benedittu*

*Misrah
ir-Rebha*

*Poste de
France*

*Poste
d'Aragon*

Triq Boffa

*Poste
d'Italie*

Dry Dock No 3

COSPICUA/BORMLA

---

maps are in English only, which can be confusing. From the Poste de France, Triq il-Mina l-Kbira (Main Gate St) leads to the town's main square Misraħ ir-Rebħa (Victory Sq). From the square, the marina and Maritime Museum are downhill to the left, while Triq San Filippu (St Philip's St) leads on towards Fort St Angelo at the tip of the peninsula.

There's good information on Vittoriosa at www.cittavittoriosa.com.

SIGHTS
Inquisitor's Palace
The **Inquisitor's Palace** (☎ 21 827 006; Triq il-Mina l-Kbira; adult/child Lm1/free; ⏰ 7.45am-2pm daily mid-Jun–Sep, 8.15am-5pm Mon-Sat & 8.15am-4pm Sun

Oct–mid-Jun, closed public holidays) was built in the 1530s and served as law courts until the 1570s, when it became the tribunal (and prison) of the Inquisition, whose task it was to find and suppress heresy.

The palace is now undergoing renovation in order to play host to the **Museum of Ethnography**, which focuses on the religious values in Maltese culture up to the present day. In addition to the display areas in the tribunal room and prison complex, there is a permanent exhibition on the impact of the Inquisition on Maltese society.

Maritime Museum
The old naval bakery, built in 1578, now houses Malta's **Maritime Museum** (☎ 21 660

052; Vittoriosa Wharf; adult/child Lm1/free; ⏲ 7.45am-2pm daily mid-Jun–Sep, 8.15am-5pm Mon-Sat & 8.15am-4pm Sun Oct–mid-Jun, closed public holidays). Well-displayed exhibits include Roman anchors, traditional Maltese fishing boats, models of the Knights' galleys and British naval vessels. There are also displays of old navigational instruments, log books and signal books.

Fort St Angelo

The tip of the Vittoriosa peninsula has been fortified since at least the 9th century, and before that it was the site of Roman and Phoenician temples. The Knights took over the medieval fort in 1530 and rebuilt and strengthened it – Fort St Angelo served as the residence of the Grand Master of the Order until 1571, and was the headquarters of la Valette during the Great Siege. Further defences were added in the late 17th century by the engineer Don Carlos Grunenberg, whose florid coat-of-arms still sits above the gate overlooking St Angelo Wharf.

The British took over the fort in the 19th century, and from 1912 until 1979 it served as the headquarters of the Mediterranean Fleet, first as HMS *Egmont* and from 1933 as HMS *St Angelo*. The upper part of the fort, including the Grand Master's Palace and the 15th-century Chapel of St Anne, is now occupied by the modern Order of St John. The remainder of the fort is officially closed to visitors due to its poor state of repair, but access through the gate above St Angelo Wharf is usually pretty straight-forward and you can wander around parts of the site, an unusual mixture of medieval fortress and abandoned 20th-century offic-ers' mess.

WALKING TOUR: VITTORIOSA   Map p80

Distance: approx 2km
Duration: 1½ hours

Begin at the bus stop at the corner of Triq San Lawrenz (St Lawrence St) and Triq 79. Cross the road towards the Poste d'Aragon and enter the bastion through the **Advanced Gate (1)**, inscribed with the date 'MDCCXXII' (1722) and a relief of crossed cannons. Here you'll find a good café, and next door is a large WWII **air-raid shelter** (2; adult/child Lm1/0.50) open to the

public, but there's not a lot to see inside. Cross the bridge over the moat, which has been planted with orange trees and is now the Coronation Gardens, and pass through the Couvre Porte into the Poste de France (there's a good view of Senglea from the battlement up the ramp to the left).

Go through Porte de Provence Triq il-Mina l-Kbira and head left along Triq il-Mina l-Kbira, past the **Church of the Annunciation (3)** on your left and the **Inquisitor's Palace (4**; p78), now the National Museum of Ethnography, on your right, until you reach **Misraħ ir-Rebħa (5**; Victory Sq) with its two monuments: the Victory Monument, erected in 1705 in memory of the Great Siege; and a statue of St Lawrence, patron saint of Vittoriosa, dating from 1880. You will definitely notice the magnificent building dating from 1888 that stands on the eastern side of the square and is home to the Band Club of St Lawrence. Note its striking wooden balcony.

From the square head east on Triq Hilda Tabone (Britannic St, by Café du Brazil), then take the first left (Triq Santa Skolastika, or St Scholastica St) towards the massive blank walls of the **Sacra Infermeria (6**), the first hospital to be built by the Knights on their arrival in Malta. It now serves as a convent. Go down a stepped alley (signposted Triq il-Miratur) and walk along the wall's perim-eter. The ramp descending into a trench in front of the Infermeria leads to the **Bighi Sally Port (7)**, where the wounded were brought by boat to the infirmary under the cover of darkness during the Great Siege.

After doing a circuit of the Sacra Infer-meria head back onto Triq Hilda Tabone. To your right lies a small maze of charming alleys, collectively known as **Il Collachio (8)**, with some of the oldest surviving buildings in the city. Wander up Triq it-Tramuntana (North St) to the so-called **Norman House (9)** at No 11 (on the left) and look up at the 1st floor. The twin-arched window, with its slender central pillar and zigzag decoration, dates from the 11th century, and is in a style described as Siculo-Norman (similar win-dows survive in Il-Kastell on Gozo). Also in this area are the first auberges built by the Knights in the 16th century – the **Auberge d'Angleterre (10**; Triq il-Majjistral), the auberge of the English Knights, now serves as the local library.

VALLETTA

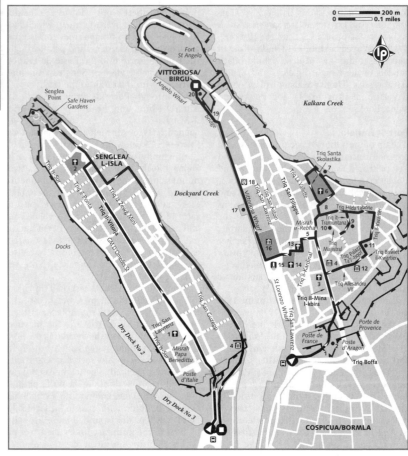

At the far end of Triq Hilda Tabone turn right along Triq il-Kwartier (Barrack St), and bear right at the corner of the imposing **Armoury (11)**. Turn left and then right along Triq Palazz Ta'l-Isqof (Bishop's Palace St) past the **Bishop's Palace (12)**. Return to Triq il-Mina l-Kbira and turn right to again reach Misraħ ir-Rebħa.

From the square, to explore the waterfront area turn left into the nearby chapel where the little **Oratory of St Joseph (13)** – now a fascinating museum – contains relics of Grand Master la Valette, and continue down past the **Church of St Lawrence (14)**. Built on the site of an 11th-century Norman church, St Lawrence's served as the conventual church of the Knights of

St John from 1530 until the move to St John's Co-Cathedral in Valletta (see the boxed text, p38, for more information on its history).

At the foot of the hill, pass to the left of the large building across the street. The palm and cactus garden on the left contains the **Freedom Monument (15)**, which commemorates the departure of the last British forces in Malta in 1979. Bronze figures show a bugler playing the 'Last Post' as his comrade lowers the flag, and a British sailor saying goodbye to a Maltese girl while, rather unromantically, shaking her hand.

Turn right along the waterfront and you will probably encounter a few boatmen offering cruises of Grand Harbour in a dgħajsa (traditional rowing boat or water taxi). Payment of about Lm2 per person is a reasonable price for a 40-minute trip. Continue along the waterfront past the interesting **Maritime Museum (16**; p78), housed in the old naval bakery, and you'll reach the new **marina (17)**, filled with flash boats, and **casino (18**; p74) in 17th-century buildings that were once the Knights' Treasury, the Captain-General's Palace, and a hostel for galley captains. At the far end of the quay you can cross the bridge over the moat and follow a path beyond St Angelo Wharf to the rocky point beneath the walls of **Fort St Angelo (19**; p79), where old cannons serve as bollards and the remains of WWII gun installations can be seen. The bridge was the original approach to the fort's **main gate (20)**, which can be seen above the wharf. This is the access point to the fort – it is usually open, although the fort is officially closed to visitors.

From the wharf, you can retrace your steps back along the waterfront and left up to the cafés of Misraħ ir-Rebħa, or continue walking south to make your way to Senglea (see below for a walking tour of the area).

EATING & DRINKING
There are a few options for eating in Vittoriosa. You'll encounter the first – and fanciest – option early, as you pass through the Advanced Gate. **Caffè Boccaccio** (☎ 21 675 757; Couvre Porte; mains Lm2-4) has outdoor seating and a menu of pizzas, pasta and grilled meat dishes. **Café du Brazil** and the **Band Club of St Lawrence** provide opportunities for a casual drink and offer limited lunch selections on Misraħ ir-Rebħa.

If you visit of an evening, call into **Il-Forn** (☎ 21 820 379; Triq it-Tramuntana; ☽ from 7.30pm Wed-Sun), an interesting art gallery and wine bar in Il Collachio (not far from the Norman House).

GETTING THERE & AWAY
Bus Nos 1, 4 and 6 from Valletta will take you to the bus stop on Triq 79 beneath the Poste d'Aragon; No 2 goes all the way to Misraħ ir-Rebħa. There's a bus every 15 to 20 minutes, and the fare is Lm0.15.

Bus No 627 runs from Buġibba via Sliema to the Three Cities (Lm0.40) hourly until 3pm.

Senglea
pop 3500

Senglea is even more difficult to get lost in than Vittoriosa, as the streets form a grid pattern. The town was pretty much razed to the ground during WWII, and little of historic interest remains, but there are great views of Valletta and Vittoriosa, and the little vedette (watchtower) at the tip of the peninsula is one of the classic sights of Malta.

WALKING TOUR: SENGLEA   Map p80

Distance: approx 2km
Duration: 1½ hours

From the bus stop in the square outside the fortifications, walk up the ramp and pass through the gate at the Poste d'Italie, and continue along Triq il-Vitorja (Victory St). At the first square is the **Church of Our Lady of Victory (1)**, which was completely rebuilt after WWII. Follow Triq il-Vitorja all the way to the **Church of St Philip (2)**, and follow the road right and then left (Triq iż-Żewġ Mini, or Two Gates St) to reach Safe Haven Gardens at the tip of the peninsula.

The **vedette (3)** here is decorated with carvings of eyes and ears symbolising watchfulness, and commands a view over the whole length of Grand Harbour and the southern flank of Valletta.

Bear left when you leave Safe Haven Gardens, and follow Triq iż-Żewġ Mini back past St Philip's Church. Turn left down Triq Sant'Anġlu and then right and descend to the quayside. Follow the waterfront, with its moored *dgħajsas* and impressive views of Vittoriosa, back to the starting point. There are a couple of reasonable restaurants along the quay.

Towards the end of the quay the road passes under the bastion, and a walkway goes around the outside beneath the socalled **Gantry House (4)**. This was where the galleys of the Knights of St John were moored while their masts were removed using machinery mounted on the wall above the walkway.

GETTING THERE & AWAY
Bus No 3 runs between Valletta and the central square in Senglea every half-hour or so. Alternatively, catch bus No 1 or 4 to

Vittoriosa and get off at Dry Dock No 1 (at the head of Dockyard Creek), walk back up the hill and turn right. It's only a 15-minute walk from the main gate at Vittoriosa around to the main gate at Senglea.

Cospicua
pop 6100

Cospicua was comprehensively flattened during WWII, and there is little to see in the town itself. However, if you are interested in **medieval fortifications**, you can spend half a day exploring the two concentric rings of 17th-century defences known as the Margherita Lines and the Cottonera Lines. A good map (*The mAZe Street Atlas* by Frans Attard) and a specialist book (*Fortresses of the Knights* by Stephen Spiteri) are recommended.

HYPOGEUM & TARXIEN TEMPLES

The suburb of Paola, about 2km southwest of Cospicua, conceals two of Malta's most important prehistoric sites. The **Hal Saflieni Hypogeum** (☎ 21 805 019 or 21 825 579; entry on Triq ić-Ċimiterju; adult/child Lm3/1; 🕑 5-7 tours conducted daily: 8.30am-12.30pm mid-Jun–Sep, 8.30am-3.30pm Mon-Sat & 8.30am-2.30pm Sun Oct–mid-Jun) is an incredible underground necropolis, discovered during building work in 1902. It consists of halls, chambers and passages hewn out of the living rock and covering some 500 sq metres; it is thought to date from around 3600 to 3000 BC, and an estimated 7000 bodies may have been interred here. Excellent 50-minute tours of the complex are available daily. Tours start with a brief introductory exhibition and multilingual film focusing on the temple-building people and the Hypogeum's relationship to Malta's overground temple sites. Touring the site is a fascinating experience, but leaves you with more questions than it does answers about the ancient civilisation responsible for the Hypogeum's construction – who were they, what exactly did they do here, and where did they go? (See p21 for more on Malta's temple builders.)

Carbon dioxide exhaled by visiting tourists was doing serious to damage the delicate limestone walls of the burial chambers of the Hypogeum, and it was recently closed to the public for several years. It has now been restored and reopened with Unesco funding and its microclimate is strictly controlled to ensure its conservation. For

HYPOGEUM AND TARXIEN TEMPLES

this reason, the maximum number of visitors to the site is 80 per day – tickets are understandably in demand, and you can't just turn up to the site and expect to join the next tour. Prebooking is essential (usually at least 10 days before you wish to visit); tickets are available in person from the Hypogeum and the Museum of Archaeology in Valletta (p66), or online (www.heritagemalta.org; info@heritagemalta.org).

The **Tarxien Temples** (☎ 21 695 578; Triq it-Templ Neolitiċi; adult/child Lm1/free; 🕑 7.45am-2pm daily mid-Jun–Sep, 8.15am-5pm Mon-Sat & 8.15am-4pm Sun Oct–mid-Jun, closed public holidays), pronounced tar-*sheen*, are hidden up a back street several blocks east of the Hypogeum – keep your eyes peeled, as the entrance is inconspicuous. These megalithic structures were excavated in 1914, and are thought to date from between 3600 and 2500 BC. There are four linked temples, built with massive stone blocks up to 3m by 1m by 1m in size, decorated with spiral patterns and pitting, and reliefs of animals including bulls, goats and pigs. The large statue of a broad-hipped female figure was found in the right-hand niche of the first temple.

Getting There & Away

More than a dozen buses pass through Paola, including Nos 1, 2, 3, 4 and 6. Get off at the main square, Pjazza Paola (look for landmarks such as the police station out the front of the prison at the northern end of the square, and the large Church of Christ

MOVIE-MAKING IN MALTA

From the road to Fort Rinella visitors have a good view of the huge water tanks of the **Mediterranean Film Studios** (not open to the public). There's not a lot to see, but these are the biggest film-production water facilities in Europe – the two main water tanks have a clear horizon behind them, allowing directors to create the illusion that on-screen characters are miles out to sea. Water scenes from such films as *The Spy Who Loved Me* (1977), *Raise the Titanic* (1980), *White Squall* (1996), *U-571* (2000) and *The League of Extraordinary Gentlemen* (2003) were shot here.

But it's not just the water tanks that are drawing film crews to Malta. The country's fortresses have long been popular with location scouts – the basement and casemates of Fort St Elmo were used for the Turkish prison scenes in the 1978 film *Midnight Express*, and Fort St Elmo has doubled as locations in Marseille and Beirut in more recent productions. Also out near Fort Rinella is Ricasoli Fort, controlled and managed by the Malta Film Commission (and also closed to the public). A large portion of the 2004 Trojan War epic *Troy* was filmed here on specially crafted sets. Many scenes of another sandals-and-swords blockbuster, *Gladiator* (2000), were also filmed here.

Comino's St Mary's Tower appears in *The Count of Monte Cristo* (2002), a film that features various locations in the Maltese Islands (including Mdina and Vittoriosa), while the Blue Lagoon provides a great backdrop to a dire film, *Swept Away* (2002), starring Madonna and produced by her husband, Guy Ritchie.

There are some good websites to check out if you're interested in learning more: see **Mediterranean Film Studios** (www.mfsstudios.com), the **Malta Film Commission** (http://mfc.com.mt), and especially the website of the **Malta Tourism Authority** (www.visitmalta.com), which has an excellent section dedicated to the subject – click on 'What to See', and then the 'Malta Movie Map' icon.

Be sure to keep your eyes peeled and ask around if you want to know what film sets (and stars) you might stumble across as you travel around the country.

the King). The Hypogeum is a five-minute walk from the square, the Tarxien Temples are 10 minutes.

FORT RINELLA

Built by the British in the late 19th century, **Fort Rinella** (Map p59; ☎ 21 809 713; Triq Santu Rokku, Kalkara; adult/child Lm1.50/0.50; ⓨ 10am-5pm Mon-Sat year-round, 10am-1pm Sun Jun-Sep, 1-5pm Sun Oct-May, closed public holidays), 1.5km northeast of Vittoriosa, was one of two coastal batteries designed to counter the threat of Italy's new ironclad battleships. The batteries (the second one was on Tigné Point in Sliema) were equipped with the latest Armstrong 100-ton guns – the biggest muzzle-loading guns ever made. Their 100-ton shells had a range of 6.4km and could penetrate 38cm of armour plating. The guns were never fired in anger, and were retired in 1906. Fort Rinella has been restored by a group of amateur enthusiasts from the Malta Heritage Trust (see www.wirtartna.org), and is now one of Malta's most interesting military museums. Guided tours are held at 11.30am and 2.30pm daily, but the best time to visit is Saturday afternoon; from 2.30pm to 4pm tours are given by volunteers dressed as late-19th-century soldiers, and historical re-enactments are staged (admission Lm2.50/1 per adult/child on Saturday afternoon).

Getting There & Away

To get to Fort Rinella, take bus No 4 from Valletta or the Three Cities. Ask the driver to let you off at Rinella; from here it's a 10-minute walk to the fort through quite a desolate area, and as you walk past what appears to be a junkyard you may well question if you're in the right place – you are, just head in the direction of the flying Union Jack.

Sliema & St Julian's

SLIEMA & ST JULIAN'S

The seaside suburb of Sliema was once the preserve of the Maltese upper classes, a cool retreat from the heat and bustle of Valletta. Although the waterfront streets have now been taken over by concrete hotels, restaurants, shops and bars, the back streets remain largely residential, and a Sliema address is still something of a status symbol in Maltese society.

Cosmopolitan St Julian's, north of Sliema, has been the focus of lots of recent tourist development, with new four- and five-star hotels and apartment complexes rising along the rocky shoreline (notably at Portomaso and St George's Bay). Paceville is in the heart of St Julian's and is the nightlife capital of Malta. This is also where many of Malta's English-language schools are located, so you'll hear a variety of languages and accents, and see lots of groups of students hitting the bars instead of the books! But the area is far from being a foreigners' ghetto – Sliema and St Julian's is also where the locals come to promenade, eat, drink, shop and play.

If you want to explore Valletta and the Three Cities, but are planning on taking a package holiday to save some money, then Sliema is the most convenient place to stay as there is a fast and regular ferry service to the capital. For more information, check out the website www.sliema-malta.com.

HIGHLIGHTS

- Dining at any of the great **Spinola Bay restaurants** (p93), preferably alfresco and with a great water view
- Ambling along Sliema's **waterfront promenade** (p87) and enjoying the local *passeggiata* (evening stroll)
- Letting loose on a big night out at a **Paceville nightclub** (p96)
- Landing a great low-season accommodation bargain, allowing you to live it up in a **five-star hotel** (p91)
- Escaping on a **cruise** (p89) to view the scenic Marsamxett and Grand Harbours

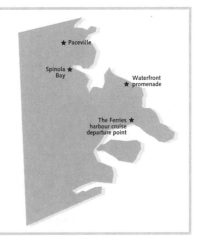

★ Paceville

Spinola ★
Bay

Waterfront
★ promenade

The Ferries ★
harbour cruise
departure point

SLIEMA & ST JULIAN'S

0 — 1 km
0 — 0.5 miles

ORIENTATION

Sliema occupies the peninsula to the north of Valletta, from which it is separated by Marsamxett Harbour. The main thoroughfare on the south side of the peninsula is Triq ix-Xatt (The Strand), which continues south along the Gżira waterfront and around the Ta'Xbiex peninsula to the marina at Msida. The focal point of Sliema, known as The Ferries, is located at the northeastern end of The Strand, where you will find the bus terminus and the ferry to Valletta. From here Triq it-Torri (Tower Rd) strikes north across the neck of the peninsula, then follows the coastline to the north and west to Balluta Bay and St Julian's.

St Julian's (San Ġiljan) lies between Balluta Bay and St George's Bay. The compact grid of streets packed with pubs and clubs to the north of Spinola Bay between Triq San Ġorġ and Triq id-Dragunara is known as Paceville (patchy-ville). North of St Julian's lies the rapidly developing district of St George's Bay.

INFORMATION
Airline Offices
Air Malta (Map p88; ☎ 21 330 275; 31 Triq it-Torri, Sliema)

Emergency
Police Station (Map p88; ☎ 21 330 502; cnr Triq Manwel Dimech & Triq Rudolfu, Sliema)

Police Station (Map p93; ☎ 21 332 196; Triq San Ġorġ, St Julian's) Close to McDonald's.

Internet Access

MelitaNet (Map p93; ☎ 21 337 557; Tropicana Hotel; Triq Ball, Paceville; per hr Lm1; ⏰ 24hr) Large Internet café also offering good-value rates for international calls.

CyberSurf (Map p88; Triq ix-Xatt, Sliema; per hr Lm1; ⏰ 10am-late) Close to the corner with Triq Manwel Dimech.

Magic Kiosk (Map p88; ☎ 21 335 653; cnr Triq ix-Xatt & Triq it-Torri, Sliema; per hr Lm1; ⏰ 9am-11pm) Also offers good rates for international calls.

Waves Internet Café & Cocktail Bar (Map p88; ☎ 21 342 242; 139 Triq it-Torri, Sliema; ⏰ noon-late)

Money

There are plenty of banks and ATMs throughout both Sliema and St Julian's.

American Express (Map p88; ☎ 21 334 051; Airways House, Triq il-Kbira, Sliema) Cashes travellers cheques and provides travel services.

Eurochange (Map p93; ☎ 21 356 272; cnr Triq id-Dragunara & Triq Ball, Paceville; ⏰ 8am-11pm)

Travelex (Sliema Map p88; ☎ 21 334 759; il-Piazzetta, Triq it-Torri; Paceville Map p93; ☎ 23 720 200; Bay St Complex, Triq Santu Wistin)

Post

Post Office (Map p88; Triq Manwel Dimech, Sliema; ⏰ 7.30am-12.45pm Mon-Sat)

Tourist Information

Tourist Information Office (Map p93; ☎ 21 381 392; Palazzo Spinola, enter from Triq Ross; ⏰ generally 8am-12.30pm & 1.30-5pm Mon-Fri) Complex opening hours that involve closing for an hour for lunch, and sometimes closing at 2pm in high season. And – strangest of all – it's closed Saturday, Sunday and public holidays (not terribly helpful for a tourist information office, really).

DANGERS & ANNOYANCES

The tidal wave of alcohol and testosterone that swills through the streets of Paceville at weekends occasionally overflows into outbreaks of violence. Some people also find that the noise levels in and around Paceville at night are high enough to be a nuisance. Unless you plan to party the night away, you will probably prefer to seek accommodation in a quieter part of town. If you decide to rent a car, bear in mind that finding a place to park in this area is a bit of a nightmare.

SIGHTS
Sliema

There's not a lot to see in Sliema itself, but there are good views of Valletta from Triq ix-Xatt (The Strand) and Tigné Point, especially at dusk as the floodlights are switched on. Triq ix-Xatt and Triq it-Torri (Tower Rd) make for a pleasant waterfront stroll, with plenty of bars and cafés to quench a thirst in. In the evenings these streets fill up with promenading families out for their daily *passeggiata* (evening stroll).

There are two towers on Triq it-Torri. **St Julian's Tower** is one of the network of coastal watchtowers built by Grand Master de Redin in the 17th century. **Il-Fortizza** was built by the British in the 19th century and has now been taken over by TGI Friday's (p95).

Sliema's **beaches** are mostly shelves of bare rock, and clambering in and out of the sea can be a bit awkward. In places along Triq it-Torri and at Qui-Si-Sana, square pools have been cut into the soft limestone – these were made for the convenience of upper-class Maltese ladies, but have since fallen into disuse. There are better facilities at the many private **lidos** along the coast,

---

TIGNÉ POINT DEVELOPMENT

Tigné Point, a promontory east of Sliema, was one of the sites where the Turkish commander Dragut Reis ranged his cannon to pound Fort St Elmo into submission during the Great Siege in 1565 (p24). The tip of the peninsula is still known as Dragut Point. This whole area is currently undergoing redevelopment, with construction of residential apartments set around large public areas. It's anticipated that there will be new restaurants, shops and sporting grounds as part of the development – the first stage is due for completion in 2005, with a later stage expected to open in 2006. The previously neglected Tigné Fort, built in 1792 by the Knights, will be restored and possibly used as a gallery or museum. When the Tigné Point revitalisation is complete, the developers will turn their attention to Manoel Island (see p88) – so expect big things there too (although possibly not until 2010!). If you're interested in all the goings-on here, check out www.tignepoint.com for more information.

SLIEMA & ST JULIAN'S

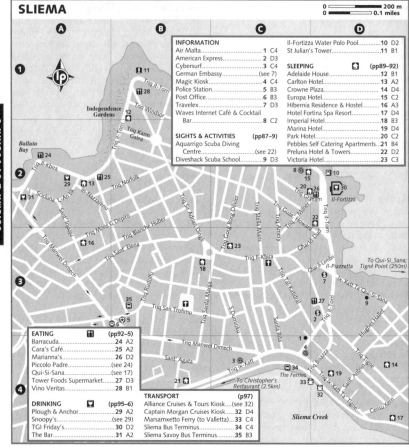

SLIEMA

INFORMATION	
Air Malta................................... 1 C4	
American Express.................... 2 D3	
Cybersurf................................3 C4	
German Embassy.................(see 7)	
Magic Kiosk...............................4 C4	
Police Station.........................5 B3	
Post Office..............................6 B3	
Travelex..................................7 D3	
Waves Internet Café & Cocktail	
Bar.......................................8 C2	
SIGHTS & ACTIVITIES (pp87–9)	
Aquarrigo Scuba Diving	
Centre.............................(see 22)	
Diveshack Scuba School.........9 D3	

Il-Fortiżża Water Polo Pool.............10 D2	
St Julian's Tower.............................11 B1	
SLEEPING (pp89–92)	
Adelaide House..............................12 B1	
Carlton Hotel.................................13 A2	
Crowne Plaza.................................14 D4	
Europa Hotel..................................15 C2	
Hibernia Residence & Hostel........16 A3	
Hotel Fortina Spa Resort..............17 D4	
Imperial Hotel................................18 B3	
Marina Hotel..................................19 D4	
Park Hotel.....................................20 C2	
Pebbles Self Catering Apartments...21 B4	
Preluna Hotel & Towers.................22 D2	
Victoria Hotel................................23 C3	

EATING (pp92–5)	
Barracuda.................................24 A2	
Cara's Café...............................25 A2	
Marianna's................................26 D2	
Piccolo Padre........................(see 24)	
Qui-Si-Sana..........................(see 17)	
Tower Foods Supermarket........27 D3	
Vino Veritas..............................28 B1	
DRINKING (pp95–6)	
Plough & Anchor.......................29 A2	
Snoopy's..............................(see 29)	
TGI Friday's..............................30 D2	
The Bar....................................31 A2	

TRANSPORT (p97)	
Alliance Cruises & Tours Kiosk.....(see 32)	
Captain Morgan Cruises Kiosk.....32 D4	
Marsamxetto Ferry (to Valletta)...33 C4	
Sliema Bus Terminus.....................34 C4	
Sliema Savoy Bus Terminus..........35 B3	

including swimming pools, sun lounges, bars and water sports – admission costs around Lm2 to Lm3 per day.

In summer, you can watch the local **water polo** teams in action at the Balluta Bay and Il-Fortiżża pools.

Around Sliema

Sliema merges southward into the suburb of Gżira. A short bridge gives access to **Manoel Island**, most of which is taken up by boat-building yards and the dilapidated ruins of Fort Manoel. The island was used as a quarantine zone by the Knights of St John, and their 17th-century plague hospital, the **Lazzaretto di San Rocco**, can still be seen on the south side – it served as an isolation hospital

during WWI and was last used during an epidemic in 1936. **Fort Manoel** was built in the early 18th century under Grand Master Manoel de Vilhena. It suffered extensive bomb damage during WWII, when nearby Lazzaretto Creek was used as a submarine base. The overgrown island is scheduled for long-overdue development, but not for a few years yet (see the boxed text, p87).

Ta'Xbiex (pronounced tashb-yesh), to the south of Manoel Island, is an upmarket area of gracious villas, mansions and embassies, with yacht marinas on either side.

St Julian's

Amid the heaving bars and packed restaurants of central St Julian's lies the elegant

Palazzo Spinola, built for the Italian knight Rafael Spinola in the late 17th century. Surrounded by a walled garden (the entrance is on Triq il-Knisja), it now houses an elegant (and expensive) restaurant. Another aristocratic residence that has found a new lease of life is the **Villa Dragonara**, set on the southern headland of St George's Bay. Built in the late 19th century for the Marquis Scicluna, a wealthy banker, it is now occupied by the Dragonara Casino (see p96).

Paceville is the in-your-face (and off-your-head) cluster of pubs, clubs and restaurants that forms the focal point for the wilder side of Malta's nightlife. This is party-all-night and sleep-all-day territory, and anyone over the age of 25 will probably feel old beyond their years. There is new development all around – notably the ultra-posh **Portomaso apartment & marina complex** on the site of the old Fort Spinola (featuring a five-star hotel, small marina and upmarket apartments), and the new Intercontinental Hotel – as the tourist authorities try to push Malta's image upmarket, but Paceville is likely to retain its raucous, rough-and-ready atmosphere for some time to come.

Most of the **beaches** around St Julian's are of the bare rock or private lido variety, but there is a genuine, if crowded, sandy beach at the head of St George's Bay.

ACTIVITIES
Water Sports
Traditional touristy stuff like banana rides, paragliding and paddle-boat hire are available at most of the private lidos along the shore. Many also offer waterborne activities, including windsurfing, water-skiing, dinghy sailing, motor-boating, snorkelling and scuba diving.

Boat Trips   Map p88
Captain Morgan Cruises (☎ 23 463 333; www.captain morgan.com.mt), at The Ferries in Sliema, has a boat trip for every traveller's taste and pocket. See p186 for details. Trips depart from The Ferries area and you can arrange a free transfer from your accommodation to the departure point.

Alliance Cruises & Tours (☎ 21 332 165; www .alliancecruises.com) offers a similar programme of boat tours out of Sliema (also from The Ferries area). See p186 also for more information.

Jeep Safaris & Bus Tours   Map p88
As well as its extensive programme of boat trips, **Captain Morgan Cruises** (☎ 23 463 333; www .captainmorgan.com.mt) also runs popular Jeep safaris exploring the more remote parts of Malta (Lm19.95/16.45 per adult/child) and Gozo (Lm21.95/18.65). These are full-day trips where you drive your own 4WD Jeep and follow the tour leader, who is in radio contact.

Alliance Cruises & Tours (☎ 21 332 165; www .alliancecruises.com) also offers land tours, including bus tours and a Jeep safari. See p186 for details.

Yachting   Map p88
That Captain Morgan is a busy man! **Captain Morgan Yacht Charter** (☎ 23 463 333; www .yachtcharter.com.mt) offers the chance for visitors to charter a yacht and join the throng of white sails on the harbour. Half-day, full-day or two-day (overnight) yacht charters (with skipper provided) start from Lm95, Lm160 and Lm320 respectively. Bareboat charter is also available to experienced sailors, from Lm1100 a week in low season (Lm1350 in July and August).

Diving
There are several dive operators in the area that can help you explore Malta's excellent dive sites (see p47). These include:
Aquarrigo Scuba Diving Centre (Map p88; ☎ 21 330 882; www.planetsea.net; Preluna Hotel & Towers; Triq it-Torri, Sliema)
Diveshack Scuba School (Map p88; ☎ 21 320 594; www.divemalta.com; ix-Xatt Ta'Qui-si-sana, Qui-si-sana, Sliema)
Divewise (Map p93; ☎ 21 356 441; www.digigate.net /divewise; Westin Dragonara Complex, St Julian's)

SLEEPING
Most of the accommodation in Sliema and St Julian's is aimed squarely at the package holiday and luxury hotel market, but you'll find that there are some bargains to be had during the low season. Very few hotels offer parking for guests (except for the more upmarket places on large grounds). You may find street parking hard to come by.

Budget
SLIEMA   Map p88
Hibernia Residence & Hostel (☎ 21 333 859; hib ernia@nsts.org; Triq Mons G Depiro; dm Lm2.15/3.45

low/high season, s/d/tr Lm8.85/8.40/10.35 low season, Lm15/17.80/20.55 high season; 🖥) Cheap hostel accommodation can be found at the well-run Hibernia, which offers private self-catering studios in a residence (popular with English-language students) as well as dorm beds in a hostel area. It has very good facilities, including helpful staff, a rooftop sun terrace, kitchens, a laundry and a cafeteria (breakfast is an additional Lm1). To get here from Valletta, take bus No 62 or 67 to Balluta Bay and walk up Triq Manwel Dimech for 300m – Triq Mons G Depiro is on the left.

Europa Hotel (☎ 21 334 070; www.europahotel -malta.com; 138 Triq it-Torri; s/d/tr Lm7/12/18 low season, Lm12/18/27 high season; 🖥) A friendly, well-located and well-priced option run by two brothers and their sister. There's an excellent restaurant serving good-value meals of pasta, pizza, noodles, salads and burgers downstairs. Upstairs, the rooms are nothing special but are spacious and well equipped for the price (en suite, ceiling fan, TV, phone). A sea view costs a little extra.

Adelaide House (☎ 21 330 361; adelaidehotel@cheer ful.com; 230 Triq it-Torri; d/tw incl continental breakfast per person Lm7-7.80; 🕙 May-Oct) This is a small, family-run guesthouse overlooking Balluta Bay, with a quiet garden at the back and public gardens and beach directly across the road. It's a lovely old townhouse but the décor is a little tired. The single supplement is Lm3.50. Some rooms have en suite bath or shower, but most have a shared toilet.

Pebbles Self Catering Apartments (☎ 21 311 889; www.maltaselfcatering.com; 89 Triq ix-Xatt; studio Lm14/16 low/high season; 🕃 🖥) Very handy to the bus terminus and Valletta ferry is this complex of good-value (but smallish) studio apartments. The studios all have a bathroom, a kitchenette, a phone and cable TV (sea views cost an additional Lm4). At the ground level is a café-bar with Internet; on the roof is a sun terrace. Air-con is via a user-pays system (Lm1 for seven hours).

ST JULIAN'S   **Map p86**
Pinto Guesthouse (☎ 21 313 897; www.pintohotel .com; Triq il-Qalb Imqaddsa; s/d/tr Lm5.50/8/10.50 low season, Lm8.50/13.50/15 high season) A steep walk up from Balluta Bay, but worth the hike for the warm welcome, bargain prices, clean, spacious rooms and excellent view (better than walking is to take bus No 42

from Valletta, which passes nearby). About half the rooms have an en suite, five have a sun terrace, and there's a TV lounge and small communal kitchen. The minimum stay is three nights.

PACEVILLE   **Map p93**
Tropicana Hotel (☎ 21 337 557; Triq Ball; s/d/tr Lm6/ 8/12; 🕃 🖥) Dirt-cheap and in the heart of Paceville, this hotel has small, somewhat dingy rooms (with good facilities like private bathroom, cable TV and air-con), but also tired décor and stained carpets; however, who can argue with the price, if all you're after is a bed to crash in? Prices get even cheaper if you stay for longer periods (single/double/triple for three nights costs Lm15/18/27).

Mid-Range
SLIEMA   **Map p88**
Marina Hotel (☎ 21 336 461; www.themarinahotel sliema.com; Triq ix-Xatt Ta'Tigné; s/d from Lm12/22 low season, Lm13.50/32 high season; 🕃) On the Tigné waterfront in Sliema (close to buses and ferries) and with great views across the harbour to Valletta, this nicely refurbished hotel is a good mid-range choice. All rooms have air-con and satellite TV, and there's a rooftop restaurant and ground-floor café. You'll pay more for a sea view (but it's worth it).

Imperial Hotel (☎ 21 344 093; www.imperial hotelmalta.com; Triq Rudolfu; s/d from Lm11/16 low season, Lm18/30 high season; 🕃 🔊) Things move slowly at the Imperial, in keeping with the old-world interior (it dates from 1865). It's tucked away in the heart of Sliema, and once inside you'll be impressed with the grand décor in the lobby (including chandelier and sweeping staircase). The rooms don't quite live up to the high standards set downstairs, but they're clean, comfortable and well equipped (you'll pay more for a garden/pool view and a balcony). Facilities include a courtyard garden and restaurant. There's good disabled access.

Carlton Hotel (☎ 21 315 764; Triq it-Torri; s/d from Lm10/15 low season, Lm18.50/26 high season; 🕃 🖥 🔊) At the western edge of Sliema, not far from the restaurants of Balluta Bay, the Carlton has good-value rooms, small but neat and well equipped. There's also a roof terrace with bar and small pool.

Park Hotel (☎ 21 343 780; www.parkhotel.com.mt; Triq Graham; s/d from Lm18/24 low season, Lm29/39 high season; ⚇ ▢ ⚞) This large, bright and modern complex has comfortable rooms with balcony and TV. There is also a 24-hour café, an indoor pool, an outdoor rooftop pool, a gym, sauna and massage centre, and a games room.

Preluna Hotel & Towers (☎ 21 334 001; www .preluna-hotel.com; 124 Triq it-Torri; s/d from Lm30/40 low season, Lm30/44 high season; ⚇ ▢ ⚞) Housed in one of Malta's tallest buildings, this hotel commands spectacular views along the coast. The hotel has recently been refurbished and presents a fresh, modern interior and good amenities, including a health spa, private beachfront lido, dive school and choice of bars and restaurants. Prices are quite reasonable given the five-star facilities. You'll pay about Lm6 per person extra to score a sea view.

AROUND SLIEMA　　　　　**Map p86**

Hotel Kappara (☎ 21 334 367; www.kappara.freeola .com; Triq Wield Ghollieqa; s/d Lm13/21 low season, Lm16/28 high season; ⚇ ▢ ⚞) The town of Kappara is about 10 minutes' walk west of Sliema and here, not far from the university, you'll find this 20-room hotel catering exclusively to gay men. The hotel has great décor and excellent amenities (including a roof terrace and a restaurant).

PACEVILLE　　　　　**Map p93**

Hotel Valentina (☎ 21 312 232; www.hotelvalentina .com; Triq Dobbie; s/d Lm10/12 low season, Lm20/31 high season; ⚇) Valentina is a pretty, boutique-style hotel, well positioned in a quieter street of Paceville. Rooms are small but attractive, spotless and well equipped. Low-season rates here are a bargain.

Hotel Bernard (☎ 21 373 900; www.hotelsmalta .com; Triq Santu Wistin; s/d Lm18/24 low season, Lm28/38 high season; ⚇ ⚞) If you want a short stumble home from Paceville's clubland, this could be for you (but others might find the noise of the area a sleep-deterrent). All rooms have TV and air-con and most have a balcony or terrace; there is also a rooftop swimming pool, restaurant, café and Irish pub downstairs.

Ir-Rokna Hotel (☎ 21 384 060; www.roknahotel .com; Triq il-Knisja; s/d Lm11/16 low season, Lm16/24 high season; ⚞) Well positioned opposite the Portomaso complex and within walking distance of all the restaurants and bars of Paceville (but far enough away to not suffer with noise), Ir-Rokna is a good-value option. Rooms and décor are uninspiring but the service is friendly, and it's home to a popular pizzeria that's stood the test of time.

Top End

There are lots of four- and five-star properties in this part of Malta (especially around Paceville). Competition to fill rooms can be tough, so there are often special offers and Internet deals to bring down the rack rates quoted here (especially outside July and August). It pays to shop around and ask what special rates are available. Deals can usually be done for longer stays and low-season holidays.

SLIEMA　　　　　**Map p88**

Hotel Fortina Spa Resort (☎ 23 460 000; www .hotelfortina.com; Triq ix-Xatt Ta'Tigné; full board per person from Lm32/45 low/high season; ⚇ ▢ ⚞) This huge complex overlooks Sliema Creek, with great views across to Valletta. There are oodles of distractions for guests, including seven swimming pools (yes, seven), a fitness centre, Pilates classes, a health spa, a beachfront lido, six restaurants and three bars. If your holiday is all about unwinding and you've got cash to splurge, how about a therapeutic-spa suite? You can enjoy spa services within the privacy of your own luxury room (from Lm80/109 per person low/high season, all inclusive). Prices listed here include all meals, drinks and snacks. Avoid the rooms at the rear of the hotel, which will be overlooking construction of a new hotel wing until about 2006.

Victoria Hotel (☎ 21 334 711; www.victoriahotel .com; Triq Ġorġ Borg Olivier; s/d Lm35/45 low season, Lm50/60 high season; ⚇ ▢ ⚞) In a quiet location away from the seafront, this elegant four-star hotel has the feel of a gentlemen's club, full of dark wood and leather club sofas. Facilities include a business centre, a sun terrace, free parking and a highly rated fine-dining restaurant, Copperfield's.

Crowne Plaza (☎ 21 343 400; www.malta.crowne plaza.com; Triq Tigné; d from Lm83/100 low/high season; ⚇ ▢ ⚞) The Crowne Plaza has views of the Med on one side and Valletta on the other, although the brochures don't show the construction going on to the east (as part of the Tigné Point development). Still, it's an excellent place to stay, occupying the site of an 18th-century fortress and partly housed in the century-old Officers' Mess of the Royal Malta Artillery. Facilities include an outdoor pool, a heated indoor pool, a gym, tennis courts, a private beach club and three restaurants.

ST JULIAN'S   Map p93
Hotel Juliani (☎ 21 380 000; www.hoteljuliani.com; 12 Triq San Ġorġ; r from Lm55; ✘ 🖳 ⚡) Finishing touches were going on at this fab new hotel on Spinola Bay at the time of research, and it promises great things. It's a beautifully restored seafront townhouse with stylish décor and modern facilities, including broadband Internet access in all rooms (you will pay an extra Lm10 for a sea view). There is a rooftop sundeck and swimming pool, and downstairs you can visit their excellent café, Café Juliani, and two of the best restaurants in Malta, Zest and Mezè (p93). Recommended.

PACEVILLE   Map p93
Westin Dragonara Resort (☎ 21 381 000; www .westin.com/malta; Triq id-Dragunara; r Lm90/100 low/high season; ✘ 🖳 ⚡) This is a vast, 300-room complex on Dragonara Point with high-quality service. The extensive amenities include large, well-equipped rooms (all with balcony), two outdoor and one indoor pool, a gym, two Jacuzzis, tennis courts, a diving school, casino and numerous restaurants and bars. There are also rooms designed for wheelchair users. Rack rates are given here, but good deals are often available to reduce these.

Hilton Malta (☎ 21 383 383; www.hiltonmalta .com.mt; Portomaso; r from Lm103/125 low/high season; ✘ 🖳 ⚡) This place is seriously swish. In the middle of the new Portomaso marina and apartment complex, the large hotel has everything you would expect from a Hilton, and then some: almost 300 luxury rooms, three outdoor swimming pools, an indoor pool, a health and fitness centre, beauty salons, tennis courts, a private beach club, water sports etc etc. Plus a variety of restaurants. You might not want to leave the complex.

EATING
Restaurants
SLIEMA   Map p88
Vino Veritas (☎ 21 324 273; 59 Triq Sir Adrian Dingli; mains Lm2.50-3.50; ✐ lunch & dinner) Popular with

both locals and tourists, convivial Vino Veritas has well-priced and appetising salad, pasta and pizza options, as well as decent vegetarian selections. Try the house specialities (home-made pasta, including swordfish-filled ravioli in a lemon butter sauce) or an interesting salad combo such as the Del Contadino – lettuce, sun-dried tomato, bacon, feta cheese, tangerine and pine nuts.

Marianna's (☎ 21 318 943; 132 Triq it-Torri; mains Lm3-6.50; ✐ noon-11.30pm) Across the road from Il-Fortiżża, Marianna's is a loud and lively Tex-Mex restaurant, with loads of meaty offerings (steak cuts, lamb chops, ribs, burgers), fish and seafood, and chilli-soaked Mexican favourites, including fajitas, burritos and enchiladas.

Barracuda (☎ 21 331 817; 195 Triq il-Kbira; mains Lm4.50-9; ✐ dinner nightly) On the western fringes of Sliema, this is a supremely elegant restaurant set in the drawing room of an early-17th-century seaside villa. Enjoy the tasteful décor, water views, good service and a menu of carefully prepared Italian and Mediterranean dishes. The starters include a selection of carpaccio (thinly sliced meats) – choose from smoked swordfish or tuna, octopus, marinated raw fillet, venison or smoked duck breast.

Piccolo Padre (☎ 21 344 875; Triq il-Kbira; mains Lm2.50-3.20; ✐ lunch & dinner) Beneath the Barracuda, this is a lively, informal and family-friendly pizzeria that is almost always crowded. Sit on their veranda overlooking the sea and chow down on traditional crunchy pizzas – it's worth queuing for a table to enjoy the house pizza: tomato, mozzarella, Maltese sausage, Gozo cheese, salami and egg. Also on the menu are good risotto and pasta options.

Qui-Si-Sana (☎ 21 342 976; Hotel Fortina Spa Resort; Triq ix-Xatt Ta'Tigné; mains Lm5.50-9.50) Marketing itself with the slogan 'fine dining for healthy appetites', this restaurant is a godsend for vegetarians and those with food allergies and intolerances. The menu has been put together by a nutritionist, and dishes are classified as low calorie/ low sodium/low fat/gluten-free/dairy-free/ vegetarian or suitable for diabetics. And it may surprise you to learn that the meals are tasty – fancy a stilton soufflé with pear and walnut salad, or grilled king prawns with Cajun spices?

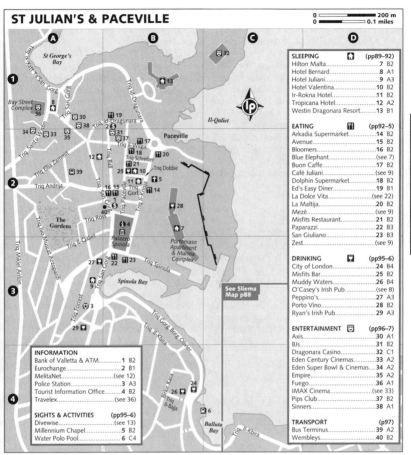

ST JULIAN'S & PACEVILLE

SLEEPING (pp89–92)
Hilton Malta...................................7 B2
Hotel Bernard................................8 A1
Hotel Juliani..................................9 A3
Hotel Valentina............................10 B2
Ir-Rokna Hotel.............................11 B2
Tropicana Hotel...........................12 A2
Westin Dragonara Resort............13 B1

EATING (pp92–5)
Arkadia Supermarket...................14 B2
Avenue...15 B2
Bloomers.....................................16 B2
Blue Elephant........................(see 7)
Buon Caffe..................................17 B2
Café Juliani............................(see 9)
Dolphin Supermarket..................18 B2
Ed's Easy Diner...........................19 B1
La Dolce Vita........................(see 22)
La Maltija...................................20 B2
Mezè......................................(see 9)
Misfits Restaurant......................21 B2
Paparazzi....................................22 B3
San Giuliano...............................23 B3
Zest.......................................(see 9)

DRINKING (pp95–6)
City of London............................24 B4
Misfits Bar..................................25 B4
Muddy Waters.............................26 B4
O'Casey's Irish Pub.................(see 8)
Peppino's....................................27 A3
Porto Vino..................................28 B2
Ryan's Irish Pub..........................29 A3

ENTERTAINMENT (pp96–7)
Axis...30 A1
BJs..31 B2
Dragonara Casino.......................32 C1
Eden Century Cinemas................33 A2
Eden Super Bowl & Cinemas.......34 A2
Empire...35 A2
Fuego..36 A1
IMAX Cinema.........................(see 33)
Pips Club.....................................37 B2
Sinners..38 B2

TRANSPORT (p97)
Bus Terminus..............................39 A2
Wembleys....................................40 B2

INFORMATION
Bank of Valletta & ATM..............1 B2
Eurochange...................................2 B1
MelitaNet...............................(see 12)
Police Station...............................3 A3
Tourist Information Office.............4 B2
Travelex..................................(see 36)

SIGHTS & ACTIVITIES (pp95–6)
Divewise................................(see 13)
Millennium Chapel.......................5 B2
Water Polo Pool...........................6 C4

AROUND SLIEMA   Map p86

Christopher's (☎ 21 337 101; Ix-Xatt Ta'Ta'Xbiex, Ta'Xbiex; mains Lm6-10; ☺ dinner Mon-Sat) A waterfront promenade of about 2.5km from The Ferries area of Sliema will take you along the marina south to the classy town of Ta'Xbiex and this well-known, upmarket restaurant, considered by many to be Malta's finest. Tastefully decorated and with a menu of tasty French dishes, this is a special-occasion place and it's worth booking ahead.

ST JULIAN'S   Map p93

Mezè (☎ 21 376 444; 12 Triq San Ġorġ; small dishes Lm1-3, mains Lm4-6.50; ☺ dinner Mon-Sat, lunch Sun) Part of the super-stylish trio of eateries below

Hotel Juliani, basement-level Mezè has low lighting, mosaics, pastel-coloured décor, an inviting bar area and a menu of treats designed to share. Come with a group and partake in cocktails and small plates of Mediterranean and Middle Eastern–inspired delectables such as dips, chorizo, mussels, calamari and prawns, and keftedes. Alternatively, order main dishes like souvlakia, tagine (stew) of roasted lamb shanks, prawns with tabbouleh or chicken with pumpkin and chickpeas. Yum! Bookings are advised.

Zest (☎ 21 387 600; 12 Triq San Ġorġ; mains Lm3-7.50; ☺ dinner Mon-Sat) More fabulousness upstairs from Mezè (accessible via the external staircase from ground level). Zest features monochrome décor with vibrant splashes of colour (red, hot pink), great service and possibly the most interesting menu in Malta. The theme here is 'East meets West', so you can choose from the West (Continental) section of the menu (seared salmon, pan-fried duck, lamb loin), or the East (Asian) section – and this is where things get interesting! Try king prawns in yellow curry and coconut sauce, Balinese grilled chicken, curry laksa soup or pad thai noodles. There's also a decent selection of sushi, and fabulous desserts (try the bento box combo of chocolate fondant and green tea sorbet). Bookings are advised.

Paparazzi (☎ 21 374 966; Triq San Ġorġ; mains Lm2.50-7) The terrace at Paparazzi is a prime people-watching spot, with a fine view of Spinola Bay. Fight your way through the huge portions on the kitsch, crowd-pleasing menu (with titles like Fork It Pasta, Cheeky Chick Burger and Octopussy Salad), then move on to dessert (fancy a Get Happy Banana Split?).

Spinola Bay could almost be described as Malta's gastronomic centre. There are more than half a dozen restaurants in the block next to Paparazzi, and most are very good. Other recommendations:

San Giuliano (☎ 21 332 000; Spinola Bay, entry from Triq San Ġorġ; mains Lm6-7; ☽ lunch Tue-Sat, dinner nightly) Upmarket Italian with a superb view over the bay.

La Dolce Vita (☎ 21 337 036; 159 Triq San Ġorġ; mains Lm4-7; ☽ lunch & dinner) Popular for great fresh fish and pasta dishes.

PACEVILLE   **Map p93**
Avenue (☎ 21 311 753; Triq Gort; mains Lm1-5; ☽ lunch Mon-Sat, dinner nightly) The Avenue is cheap and cheerful, always bustling and perfect for families. It's a long-standing favourite among tourists and locals, with simple, great-value meals of meat and fish (steak, lamb chops, beef kebabs, all under Lm5) plus huge portions of pizza, pasta, salads and burgers. The chicken salad comes highly recommended and the calzone's not bad either.

Bloomers (☎ 21 333 394; cnr Triq San Ġorġ & Triq Gort; mains Lm2.50-5; ☽ lunch & dinner) Cute Bloomers has the look and feel of an old French brasserie, with a décor of warm reds and blues and a simple but appealing menu. Choose from pasta, risotto, pizza and salad selections or go for the house

speciality – pot pies (with fillings such as steak, onion and ale or chicken, ham and mushroom).

La Maltija (☎ 21 339 602; 1 Triq il-Knisja; mains Lm3-5.50; ☽ dinner Mon-Sat) Close to all of Paceville's hotels is this restaurant, giving visitors the chance to sample authentic Maltese fare. But rest assured, it's not tacky and touristy! The menu is full of traditional dishes such as *soppa tal-Armla* (widow's soup, made with eggs, ricotta cheese, goat's cheese and vegetables), *aljotta* (fish soup), snails and quail. Mains include *timpana* (macaroni pie), *braġioli* (braised stuffed beef), rabbit, lampuki and stuffed eggplant. And don't be surprised to see locals eating here too.

Misfits (☎ 21 331 766; cnr Triq Paceville & Triq Schreiber; mains Lm5.50-9.50; ☽ dinner, closed Tue in winter, Sat in summer) A colourful place highly praised for its quality French cuisine and fine attention to detail. No doubt about it – the menu features all the well-known dishes, from *soupe de poissons* (fish soup) to foie gras and flambéed prawns, and you'll also find local produce (like rabbit and fish) given a Gallic going-over.

Blue Elephant (☎ 21 383 383; Hilton Malta, Portomaso complex; mains Lm5-8; ☽ dinner nightly) You'll know you're not in Thailand if you eat here and enjoy a view of the marina and luxury apartment complex (and the prices are another giveaway). What you will experience at this Thai restaurant are top service, wonderful fresh dishes and impressive Oriental décor – all extremely popular with locals and travellers. There are loads of spicy seafood creations, curries, stir-fries, noodles and more.

Cafés

Cara's Café (Map p88; ☎ 21 343 432; 249 Triq it-Torri, Sliema; snacks under Lm1; ☽ 9am-1am) Getting a table at Cara's might involve a short wait. This is a very popular café with good coffee and lots of sweet treats (cakes, pastries, sundaes) on offer, plus savoury snacks such as *pastizzi* (small pastries filled with ricotta cheese or mushy peas), sandwiches, *ftira* (flat bread filled with olives, tomatoes and anchovies). There's also a large outdoor area where you can have a late-night drink among the fairy lights.

Buon Caffè (Map p93; ☎ 21 388 545; Triq il-Wilga, Paceville; snacks & meals Lm0.75-3.25) This is a good (but smoke-filled) lunch-time pit stop. Pop in for a ham and mozzarella crepe, chicken caesar salad, club sandwich or lasagne, then finish with coffee and cake.

Quick Eats

You'll have no trouble finding the big multinational chains in St Julian's and Paceville. There are numerous fast-food eateries in the streets of Paceville, open late and serving snacks to quell the hunger and soak up the alcohol. A decent option for late-night munchies is **Ed's Easy Diner** (Map p93; Triq id-Dragunara), where you can get good burgers, hot dogs and kebabs for around the Lm1 mark.

Self-Catering

For self-caterers **Tower Foods Supermarket** (Map p88; 46 Triq il-Kbira, Sliema; ⏰ 8am-7.30pm Mon-Sat) sells a wide range of groceries, frozen foods and fresh fruit and veg. Other options include the **Dolphin Supermarket** (Map p93; Triq il-Wilga, Paceville; ⏰ 8am-7pm Mon-Sat) and **Arkadia Supermarket** (Map p93; Triq il-Knisja, Paceville; ⏰ 8am-7pm Mon-Sat).

DRINKING

This area has a bar for everyone, from the teenage clubber to the old-age pensioner. Paceville is the place for full-on partying, with wall-to-wall bars and clubs in the area around the northern end of Triq San Ġorġ in Paceville, while the St Julian's and Sliema waterfronts have everything from posh wine bars to traditional British pubs. Check out the nightclub venues listed on p96, as these are also popular drinking dens.

The American-themed **TGI Friday's** (Map p88; ☎ 21 346 898; Triq it-Torri, Sliema) is housed in Il-Fortiżża on the Sliema waterfront and is busy at lunch and dinner time – popular for its menu of fajitas, burgers and steak and ribs, as well as for the atmospheric vaults of the old watchtower. After dinner a youthful crowd enjoys margaritas and assorted cocktails at the bar.

Plough & Anchor (Map p88; ☎ 21 334 725; 263 Triq it-Torri, Sliema) offers good, cheap pub grub and a cosy bar downstairs crammed with maritime paraphernalia (there's a restaurant upstairs with a more extensive menu). Next door is **Snoopy's** (Map p88; ☎ 21 345 466; 265 Triq it-Torri, Sliema), a small pub popular with students. Either of these pubs is a decent option for a drink earlier in the night if

---

AUTHOR'S PICK

From the chic décor (soothing blues, greens and neutrals) to the comfy couches, cool artwork, water feature and smooth tunes being played, **Café Juliani** (Map p93; ☎ 21 377 888; 12 Triq San Ġorġ, St Julian's; snacks & meals Lm1.60-3.50; ⏰ until midnight Sun-Thu, until 2am Fri & Sat) oozes style – but it's not at all intimidating and is an ideal place to stop in for food and drink at any time of day or night. There's good service and a great modern menu of wraps, baguettes, salads and light meals. You can enjoy a huge selection of coffees and teas (or cocktails late into the night), a display cabinet full of sweet treats, and there's even a dainty high tea on offer of an afternoon (sandwiches, scones and pastries with tea or coffee).

---

you're en route from Sliema to Paceville, but if you're simply after a nightcap (or ice cream sundae as you head back to your hotel, consider **Cara's Café** (p94).

More good options are to be found on Balluta Bay. The **Bar** (Map p88; ☎ 21 337 349; 32 Balluta Bldgs, Triq il-Kbira, St Julian's) is housed in a beautiful building not far up from the church. It has a low-key profile on the bar scene and is frequented by in-the-know locals; it's a good choice for wining and reclining, and serves great snacks. Not far away are two more lively options: **Muddy Waters** (Map p93; ☎ 21 374 155; 56 Triq il-Kbira, St Julian's) has a great jukebox and regular live rock bands. It's favoured by the student crowd. **City of London** (Map p93; ☎ 21 331 706; 193 Triq il-Kbira, St Julian's) is packed at weekends and there's a great party atmosphere. It is popular on the gay scene (particularly with lesbians), but everyone is welcome, and there's a nicely mixed crowd of expats, locals and students.

Drinking options on Spinola Bay are equally varied. Pop into **Café Juliani** (see the boxed text, p95) for a chilled-out cocktail or vino, or opt for the fashionable wine bar on the first floor of **Peppino's** (Map p93; ☎ 21 373 200; 31 Triq San Ġorġ, St Julian's), a local institution.

If the pub scene is more your thing, head to **Ryan's Irish Pub** (Map p93; ☎ 21 350 680), high up overlooking the action on Spinola Bay, or **O'Casey's Irish Pub** (Map p93; ☎ 21 373 900; Triq

Santu Wistin), beneath Hotel Bernard in the heart of Paceville's clubland. Both Ryan's and O'Casey's are much as you'd expect of an Irish theme bar anywhere in the world – crowded, lively, friendly and well-stocked with cold Guinness. They also screen live football games.

An older crowd of stylish apartment-owners and their friends frequent **Porto Vino Wine Bar** (Map p93; ☎ 21 389 289), inside the slick Portomaso complex, while the hip, alternative crowd opts for the excellent bar-club **Misfits** (Map p93; ☎ 21 361 766; Triq Paceville), which hosts DJs on weekends (playing ambient, hip-hop or house music) but is a lot more laid-back during the week, holding jazz and art-house film nights.

ENTERTAINMENT
Nightclubs   Map p93

There are loads of clubs concentrated at the north end of Triq San Ġorġ in Paceville, but their names come and go with the seasons. Speaking of seasons, this area is pumping and jam-packed most nights of the week in the high season (June to September) but you won't experience the same level of action in the low season (although weekends year-round are definitely classified as party-time).

The best advice is to wander this area and check out the offerings, and see what takes your fancy (the right crowd, the right music, free entry or no need to queue, drinks promotions etc).

The only club that has managed to stand the test of time is **Axis** (☎ 21 318 078; Triq San Ġorġ), Malta's biggest and best venue, with three separate clubs (commercial house is usually served up) and seven bars providing space for 3500 people, plus loads of laser lighting. There is usually an entrance fee of around Lm2.50. Some sections of Axis are closed off in winter and the smaller version of the club is also known as Matrix.

Close to Axis are two more large clubs: **Sinners** (☎ 21 316 317; www.sinners.com.mt; Triq San Ġorġ) and **Empire** (☎ 21 351 120; Triq San Ġorġ), both cranking up the commercial music for crowds of students and holiday-makers.

For something a little less mainstream, get hot and sweaty dancing up a storm at the incredibly popular salsa bar, **Fuego** (☎ 21 373 211; www.fuego.com.mt; Triq Santu Wistin). Head first to its free salsa dancing classes (8.30pm

to 10.30pm Monday to Wednesday; Monday and Wednesday are for beginners, Tuesday is for the more advanced), then strut your stuff to the Latin grooves. The open terraces (covered and heated in winter) are full of people checking each other out – there's something of a meat-market atmosphere, but it's friendly, fun and not too sleazy!

BJ's (☎ 21 337 642; Triq Ball) is a recommended off-beat club offering live music (jazz, blues, rock) and drawing an older crowd than most of the neighbouring clubs. Weekends at **Misfits** (above) see this venue come alive with the cool crowd swinging to an eclectic mix of ambient, hip-hop or house music.

Pips Club (☎ 21 373 957; www.pips.com.mt; Triq il-Wilga) is a revamped, slightly campy gay bar and club (replacing the previous Lady Godiva bar). Entertainment includes resident DJs playing house music and regular live drag shows.

Casino   Map p93

Dragonara Casino (☎ 21 382 362; www.dragonara.com; entry from Triq Dragunara; admission free; ⏱ 10am-6am Mon-Thu, 24hr Fri-Sun) Out on the point beyond the Westin Dragonara Resort, this casino is housed in a 19th-century mansion that, appropriately enough, once belonged to a wealthy banker. The minimum age for tourists is 18 (it's 25 for Maltese citizens) and you'll need your passport or ID card to get in. The dress code is 'smart casual' (no

---

CHECKING OUT THE SCENE

Here are some useful websites for hooking into the local dance/music/party scene:

- www.starwebmalta.com/clubbing – lists clubs according to regions, with excellent links.

- www.manicmalta.com – a website promoting local bands, forthcoming events and hot venues.

- www.dansezee.com – online version of a local music magazine. Info on parties, clubs, gigs etc.

- www.strictlyhousemalta.com – info about regularly staged local events for house-music lovers.

shorts or jeans after 8pm). There is also a courtesy bus picking up and dropping off at many hotels in the area.

Cinemas   Map p93
Eden Century Cinemas (☎ 21 376 401; www.eden leisure.com/cinemas; Triq Santu Wistin) This large complex has 16 screens (on both sides of the road) showing first-run films. Tickets cost around Lm2. See the website or local newspapers for movie details and screening times.

At the same location is Malta's only **IMAX Cinema** (☎ 21 376 401; www.imax.com.mt), with a programme of big-screen spectacles. Tickets cost Lm9/3/2.45 for a family/adult/child.

Tenpin Bowling   Map p93
Good for a rainy day or to amuse the kids, the **Eden Super Bowl** (☎ 21 319 888; www.eden leisure.com/superbowl; Triq Santu Wistin; adult per game Lm1.50, shoe hire Lm0.45; ☺ 9am-around midnight), across the road from the ticket office of the cinemas, offers a 20-lane tenpin bowling alley.

GETTING THERE & AWAY
Bus
Bus Nos 62, 64 and 67 run regularly between Valletta and Sliema, St Julian's and Paceville. Nos 60 and 63 go to the Savoy terminus in Sliema (near the post office

on Triq Manwel Dimech). All journeys cost Lm0.15.

Bus No 645 goes from The Ferries in Sliema through St Julian's and on to St Paul's Bay, Mellieħa and the Gozo Ferry at Ċirkewwa (one way Lm0.40). Bus No 70 runs from The Ferries through Paceville and along the coast to the Buġibba terminus.

For other sightseeing, bus No 652 runs from The Ferries in Sliema via St Julian's and Buġibba to Għajn Tuffieħa and Golden Bay, while No 65 operates to Rabat.

Ferry
The **Marsamxetto ferry service** (☎ 21 338 981) crosses frequently between Sliema and Valletta. The crossing takes only about five minutes and there are frequent departures (see p185).

GETTING AROUND
Wembleys (Map p93; ☎ 21 374 141 or 21 374 242 for taxi; www.wembleys.net; 50 Triq San Ġorġ, St Julian's) provides a reliable 24-hour radio taxi service (similar to minicabs). Rates are cheaper than official taxi rates (to Valletta is Lm4, to the airport is Lm6, to the Gozo ferry is Lm9). Wembleys can also arrange car hire – the smallest car costs Lm14 for one day in the high season (Lm8 per day for rentals of six to 10 days), Lm10 for one day in the low season (reduced to Lm6 for six- to 10-day hire).

SLIEMA & ST JULIAN'S

Northwest Malta

CONTENTS

NORTHWEST MALTA

Most visitors will spend a good deal of time in Malta's northwest. Many of the country's large resorts – Buġibba, Qawra, St Paul's Bay (three neighbouring towns that have more-or-less blurred into one conglomeration of hotels) and Mellieħa Bay – are here, as well as a handful of excellent beaches, interesting activities (water sports, of course, but also horse riding and quad biking), good coastal walking in the region's remote corners and some of the country's best dive spots.

Beach bums should make a beeline for Mellieħa Bay if you like your facilities and water sports laid on thick, or either Għajn Tuffieħa Bay or Ġnejna Bay if you're after something more low-key and a chance to hang out with the locals. Golden Bay offers a choice midway between those two extremes. But there's little chance of finding solitude on any patch of sand or rock during the high season – locals and visitors will all be looking to cool off to escape the heat. In the low season, however, you may well get to experience those picture-perfect images the tourist brochures are so fond of.

Peace, solitude and natural beauty might best be found *under* the water – the rocky shores of the north boast some of the country's best diving outside Gozo.

If you do some travelling around Malta, you'll notice that the northwest is more rugged than the rest of the island. Geological faulting has produced a series of barren rocky ridges and fertile, flat-floored valleys. The Victoria Lines escarpment – a steep slope that follows the line of a geological rift known as the Great Fault – cuts across the island from the bay of Fomm ir-Riħ in the west to Baħar iċ Ċagħaq in the east, dividing northwest Malta from the more densely populated central region.

NORTHWEST MALTA

HIGHLIGHTS

- ▣ Taking a boat trip out of Buġibba on the schooner **Charlotte Louise** (p102)
- ▣ Enjoying the magnificent views from the wild headland of **Ras il-Qammieħ** (p113)
- ▣ Sunbathing on the sand of **Għajn Tuffieħa Bay** (p109) on a quiet spring day
- ▣ Taking a boat trip along the northwest coast with Charlie from **Golden Bay** (p108)
- ▣ Exploring the local marine life by scuba diving off the **Marfa Peninsula** (p113)

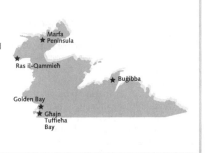

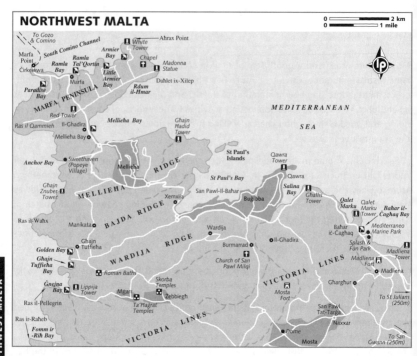

NORTHWEST MALTA

Map labels:
To Gozo & Comino
South Comino Channel
Ahrax Point
White Tower
Chapel
Madonna Statue
Marfa Point
Armier Bay
Ramla Tal'Qortin
Ramla Bay
Ċirkewwa
Marfa
Little Armier Bay
Dahlet ix-Xilep
Paradise Bay
MARFA PENINSULA
Rdum il-Ħmar
MEDITERRANEAN SEA
Red Tower
Ras il Qammieh
Il-Għadira
Mellieħa Bay
Għajn Madid Tower
Mellieħa Bay
St Paul's Islands
Qawra Tower
Anchor Bay
Sweethaven (Popeye Village)
Mellieħa
RIDGE
St Paul's Bay
Qawra
Għajn Żnuber Tower
MELLIEĦA
Xemxija
San Pawl-Il-Baħar
Buġibba
Salina Bay
Għallis Tower
Qalet Marku
Qalet Marku Tower
Baħar iċ-Ċagħaq Bay
Ras ik-Waħx
Manikata
BAJDA RIDGE
Wardija
Baħar iċ-Ċagħaq
Mediterraneo Marine Park
Golden Bay
Għajn Tuffieħa
WARDIJA RIDGE
Burmarrad
Il-Għadira
Splash & Fun Park
Madliena Tower
Għajn Tuffieħa Bay
Roman Baths
Church of San Pawl Milqi
VICTORIA LINES
Madliena Fort
Madliena
Għejna Bay
Lippija Tower
Mġarr
Skorba Temples
Żebbiegħ
Mosta Fort
Għargħur
Ras il-Pellegrin
Ta'Ħaġrat Temples
San Pawl Tat-Tarġa
To St Julians (250m)
Ras ir-Raħeb
Fomm ir-Riħ Bay
VICTORIA LINES
Dome
Naxxar
Mosta
To San Ġwann (250m)

0 — 2 km
0 — 1 mile

BAĦAR IĊ-ĊAGĦAQ

Baħar iċ-Ċagħaq (*ba*-har eetch *cha*-ag) – also known, less tongue-twistingly, as **White Rocks** – lies halfway between Sliema and Buġibba. It has a rather scruffy rock beach and a couple of family-friendly water-based attractions.

Splash & Fun Park (☎ 21 374 283; pool & slides adult/child Lm3/2, pool only adult/child Lm2/1.50; ☒ 9.30am-5pm April-Nov, until 6pm Jun-Sep) is a low-key water park with a large seawater swimming pool and a selection of fibreglass water slides and flumes. There is also a slightly shabby children's playground inhabited by bizarre-looking plastic dinosaurs in bright primary colours.

Next door, **Mediterraneo Marine Park** (☎ 21 372 218; mediterraneo@waldonet.net.mt; adult/child Lm4/2.50; ☒ 10am-12.30pm) is home to a group of performing Black Sea dolphins, rescued from an old Soviet marine park that went bust. The dolphins go through their routine at 11.30am daily, preceded by a sea-lion show at 10.45am. The cost of admission includes viewing of both shows. Also on offer through the marine park is the chance to

swim with dolphins, under the guidance of their carers. This costs Lm40 per person and bookings are recommended.

On Qrejten Point, west of Baħar iċ-Ċagħaq Bay, is **Qalet Marku Tower**, one of several 17th-century watchtowers along this coastline.

To get to Baħar iċ-Ċagħaq, take bus No 68 from Valletta, No 70 from Buġibba or No 645 from Sliema.

BUĠIBBA

pop 7800

St Paul's Bay is named for the saint who was shipwrecked here in AD 60 (see the boxed text, p102). The unattractive sprawl of Buġibba and Qawra, on the eastern side of the bay, is the biggest tourist development in Malta. Buġibba is the heartland of the island's cheap-and-cheerful package holiday trade, and is absolutely mobbed in summer. It is not the prettiest or most inspiring of places to end up on a holiday (and there are no sandy beaches), but at least it's cheap, especially in the low season when there are some real accommodation bargains and the swimming areas are not so crowded – just

THE VICTORIA LINES

The Victoria Lines are fortifications built by the British in the late 19th century. They were supposedly built to protect the main part of the island from potential invaders landing on the northern beaches, but they didn't see any military action and some historians think they were commissioned simply to give the British garrisons something to do. The lines were named for Queen Victoria's Diamond Jubilee in 1897.

The Victoria Lines run about 12km along a limestone escarpment that stretches from Fomm ir-Riħ in the west to Baħar iċ-Ċagħaq in the east and are excellent for country walking. There is talk of a heritage trail being developed along the lines in the future. Three forts – Madliena Fort, Mosta Fort and Binġemma Fort – are linked by a series of walls, entrenchments and gun batteries. The best-preserved section – the Dwejra Lines – is north of Mdina.

don't expect the same level of after-dark action during this quieter period.

Orientation

The tourist towns of Buġibba and Qawra (*aow*-ra) occupy the peninsula on the southeastern side of St Paul's Bay. Buġibba merges westward into the fishing village of St Paul's Bay (San Pawl il-Baħar in Malti). The smaller resort of Xemxija lies at the head of the bay on the northwest shore, about 3.5km from Buġibba. St Paul's Islands guard the northwestern point of the bay.

The main coast road from Valletta and Sliema to Mellieħa and the Gozo ferry bypasses Buġibba and St Paul's Bay village.

Information
BOOKSHOPS
Agenda (☎ 21 574 866; 91 Dawret il-Gżejjer) Sells foreign newspapers and magazines and a good range of English-language books.

EMERGENCY
Police Station (☎ 21 576 737; Triq it-Turisti)

INTERNET ACCESS
9-Ball Café (☎ 21 586 091; Triq it-Turisti; per hr Lm1; 🕑 9am-midnight) Large cybercafé as part of a café and snooker hall, opposite the bus station.

Browsers Internet Café (☎ 21 585 082; Triq Kavetta; per 40 min Lm1; 🕑 10am-1.30am) Fifty-three PCs, plus scanning and printing facilities, and a bar upstairs. Printing costs Lm0.15 per page, scanning is Lm0.25 per scan.
Mirabelle's Restaurant (☎ 21 572 163; Triq Bajja; per 40/100 min Lm1/2; 🕑 noon-11pm) There is an Internet café above the restaurant.

LAUNDRY
Lion Laundrette (☎ 21 580 578; Triq it-Turisti; 🕑 8.45am-4.30pm Mon-Fri, 8.45am-1.30pm Sat) A coin-operated, self-service laundrette, one of a dying breed in Malta. A load of washing costs Lm2.

MONEY
HSBC (Misraħ il-Bajja) Full bank services plus 24-hour foreign exchange machine and ATM.
Travelex (☎ 21 570 178; Triq Bajja; 🕑 9am-1.30pm & 2-5.30pm Mon-Fri, 9am-1pm Sat) Currency exchange bureau near Misraħ il-Bajja.
Travelex (☎ 21 577 691; Dawret il-Gżejjer; 🕑 9am-5pm Mon-Fri, 9am-1pm Sat) Near the entrance to the New Dolmen Hotel.

POST
Just Jase (Dawret il-Gżejjer) Sub–post office in a souvenir shop.

TRAVEL AGENCIES
You will be tripping over travel agencies in Buġibba, especially in the area around Misraħ il-Bajja (Bay Sq). All can help organise excursions, activities, car rental etc.

Sights & Activities
There's not much to see in Buġibba except acres of painted concrete and sunburnt flesh, and not much to do other than stroll along the promenade, lie around in the sun, go swimming or get towed around the bay on a variety of inflatable objects. There are a number of private lidos lining the waterfront (on both the east and west side of the peninsula), many offering sun lounges, water sports, swimming pools and café-bars (for a fee). Another option is to head for the harbour at the exotically named Plajja Tal'Bognor (Bognor Beach) and get away from it all on a **boat trip** (p102).

Salina Bay, to the east of Qawra Point, is a popular venue for local anglers. The narrow head of the bay is filled with **salt pans**, which have been in use since at least the 16th century. On the eastern edge of the bay, beside the steps leading from the

ST PAUL IN MALTA

The Bible (Acts 27–8) tells how St Paul was shipwrecked on Malta (most likely around AD 60) on his voyage from Caesarea to stand trial in Rome. The ship full of prisoners was caught in a storm and drifted for 14 days before breaking up on the shore of an unknown island. All aboard swam safely to shore, '…and when they were escaped, then they knew that the island was called Melita'.

The local people received the shipwrecked strangers with kindness and built a bonfire to warm them. Paul, while adding a bundle of sticks to the fire, was bitten by a venomous snake – a scene portrayed in several religious paintings on the island – but suffered no ill effects. The Melitans took this as a sign that he was no ordinary man.

Acts 28 goes on to say that Paul and his companions met with 'the chief man of the island, whose name was Publius; who received them, and lodged them three days courteously', during which time Paul healed Publius' sick father. The castaways remained on Melita for three months before continuing their journey to Rome, where Paul was imprisoned and sentenced to death.

According to Maltese tradition, Paul laid the foundations of a Christian community during his brief stay on the island. Publius, later canonised, was converted to Christianity and became the bishop of Malta and later of Athens. The site of the shipwreck is traditionally taken to be St Paul's Islands. The house where Publius received the shipwrecked party may have occupied the site of the 17th-century church of San Pawl Milqi (St Paul Welcomed) on the hillside above Burmarrad, 2km south of Buġibba, where excavations have revealed the remains of a large Roman villa and farm.

main coast road up to the Coastline Hotel, are the remains of a 16th-century redoubt and **fougasse** (Map p107; also see the boxed text, p104).

The old fishing village of St Paul's Bay, now merged with Buġibba, has retained something of its traditional Maltese character and has a few historical sights.

The 17th-century **Church of St Paul's Bonfire** (Map p103) stands on the waterfront to the south of Plajja Tal'Bognor, supposedly on the spot where the saint first scrambled ashore. A bonfire is lit outside the church during the festa of St Paul's Shipwreck (10 February).

The **Wignacourt Tower** (Map p107; ☎ 99 477 806; Triq it-Torri; adult/child Lm0.50/free; ☯ 9.30am-noon & 1-3pm Mon, 9.30am-12.30pm Tue, Wed, Fri, Sat), built in 1609, was the first of the towers built by Grand Master Wignacourt. It guards the point to the west of the church, and houses a tiny museum with exhibits on local fortress history, including a small selection of guns and armour.

West again, near the fishing-boat harbour at the head of the bay, is **Għajn Rasul** (Apostle's Fountain; Map p107), where St Paul is said to have baptised the first Maltese convert to Christianity. On the festa of Sts Peter and Paul (29 June), people gather at the fountain before taking fishing boats out to St Paul's Islands, where they hear mass beneath a large white **statue of St Paul** (Map p107) that was erected in 1845.

BOAT TRIPS & WATER SPORTS

Captain Morgan Cruises (☎ 23 463 333; www.captain morgan.com.mt) offers an hour-long 'underwater safari' in a glass-bottomed boat exploring the marine life around St Paul's Islands, and the wrecks of HMS *Kingston* (sunk during WWII) and the MV *Hanini* (once a private yacht). Underwater safaris set off at 10.30am, 12.30pm and 2.30pm Monday to Saturday from May to October (daily in July and August). In March, April and November there are departures at 10.30am, 12.30pm and 2pm Monday to Friday only. Safaris leave from il-Menqa, the quay just west of Gillieru Harbour Hotel and restaurant, in St Paul's Bay village. Tickets cost Lm4.95/3.95 per adult/child.

Captain Morgan also offers a full-day cruise out of Buġibba to Comino and Gozo on the graceful gaff-rigged schooner *Charlotte Louise*, with stops for swimming and snorkelling. The *Charlotte Louise* cruises depart at 10am and return at 6pm daily from July to September (Monday to Saturday from mid-May to late June, and in October). The price is Lm23.95/14.95 per adult/child, which includes a buffet lunch,

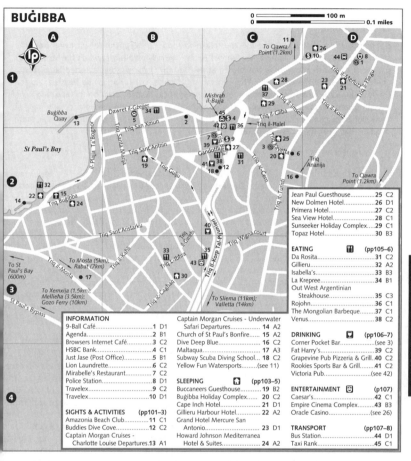

BUĠIBBA

INFORMATION	
9-Ball Café	1 D1
Agenda	2 B1
Browsers Internet Café	3 C2
HSBC Bank	4 C1
Just Jase (Post Office)	5 B1
Lion Laundrette	6 C2
Mirabelle's Restaurant	7 C2
Police Station	8 D1
Travelex	9 C2
Travelex	10 D1

SIGHTS & ACTIVITIES	(pp101-3)
Amazonia Beach Club	11 C1
Buddies Dive Cove	12 C2
Captain Morgan Cruises -	
Charlotte Louise Departures	13 A1
Captain Morgan Cruises - Underwater	
Safari Departures	14 A2
Church of St Paul's Bonfire	15 A2
Dive Deep Blue	16 C2
Maltaqua	17 A3
Subway Scuba Diving School	18 C2
Yellow Fun Watersports	(see 11)

SLEEPING	(pp103-5)
Buccaneers Guesthouse	19 B2
Buġibba Holiday Complex	20 C2
Cape Inch Hotel	21 C2
Gillieru Harbour Hotel	22 A2
Grand Hotel Mercure San	
Antonio	23 D1
Howard Johnson Mediterranea	
Hotel & Suites	24 A2

Jean Paul Guesthouse	25 C2
New Dolmen Hotel	26 D1
Primera Hotel	27 C2
Sea View Hotel	28 C1
Sunseeker Holiday Complex	29 C1
Topaz Hotel	30 B3

EATING	(pp105-6)
Da Rosita	31 C2
Gillieru	32 A2
Isabella's	33 B3
La Krepree	34 B1
Out West Argentinian	
Steakhouse	35 C3
Rojohn	36 C2
The Mongolian Barbeque	37 C1

DRINKING	(pp106-7)
Corner Pocket Bar	(see 3)
Fat Harry's	39 C2
Grapevine Pub Pizzeria & Grill	40 C2
Rookies Sports Bar & Grill	41 C2
Victoria Pub	(see 42)
Venus	38 C2

ENTERTAINMENT	(p107)
Caesar's	42 C1
Empire Cinema Complex	43 B3
Oracle Casino	(see 26)

TRANSPORT	(pp107-8)
Bus Station	44 D1
Taxi Rank	45 C1

NORTHWEST MALTA

---

free open bar and use of snorkelling equipment. Cruises on the *Charlotte Louise* depart from the main quay, off Dawret il-Gzejjer (one block west of Triq Santa Marija).

Yellow Fun Watersports (☎ 23 552 570; www
.yellowfunwatersports.com; Dawret il-Gżejjer) operates from the Amazonia Beach Club in front of the Oracle Casino and offers powerboat trips to the Blue Lagoon on Comino (p158). Trips leave at 10am, 11am, noon and 1pm, returning at 3pm, 4pm, 5pm and 6pm. The cost is Lm4 per person. Yellow Fun can also arrange boat charter, sea taxi service, fishing trips and lots of water sports like water-skiing, jet-skiing, canoeing, windsurfing and paragliding.

DIVING
There are several dive operators in Buġibba that can help you explore the excellent nearby dive sites (p49) or sites around the Maltese Islands. These include:
Buddies Dive Cove (☎ 21 576 266; www.buddies
malta.com; 24/2 Triq il-Korp Tal-Pijunieri)
Dive Deep Blue (☎ 21 583 946; www.divedeepblue
.com; 100 Triq Ananija)
Maltaqua (☎ 21 571 873; www.maltaqua.com; Triq
il-Mosta)
Subway Scuba Diving School (☎ 21 570 354; www
.subwayscuba.com; Triq il-Korp Tal-Pijunieri)

Sleeping
Most accommodation around St Paul's Bay is taken up by package holiday companies

---

THE FOUGASSE

A *fougasse* was a cheap and primitive mortarlike weapon – a deep, circular pit hewn from the solid rock, and angled at around 45 degrees to the vertical, pointing towards the sea. An explosive charge with a long fuse was placed at the bottom of the pit, and assorted large stones and other shrapnel piled on top. When enemy ships came within range, the fuse was lit and the resulting explosion would send a shower of heavy rocks raining down on the invading fleet. Several dozen *fougasses* were dug along the northern coast of Malta during the early days of the Knights' occupation, and a few can still be seen – notably the one preserved on the shore of Salina Bay near the Coastline Hotel.

---

from April to October, so book in advance if you want to stay in summer. In the low season you can get some good deals, especially for stays of a week or more (although many smaller establishments may close during this period). There is very little by way of small and intimate hotels, except in the budget category. Most hotels are large and have good facilities (pool, restaurant etc), but are somewhat impersonal. They usually offer a choice of hotel rooms or self-catering studios and apartments; the latter are usually good value as you'll get a larger room (to accommodate a kitchen/ kitchenette and dining area) and you can cut costs by preparing your own meals. Half- and full-board arrangements are available at most guesthouses and hotels. There are supplements for solo travellers, sea views and for stays of less than three days at many hotels.

BUDGET

Jean Paul Guesthouse (☎ 21 576 142; www.jean paulguesthouse.com; Triq Kavetta; per person incl breakfast Lm7.50; ☒ Feb-Nov) You'll be warmly welcomed at this friendly, family-run place just a few minutes' walk from the seafront. There are 12 simple, spotless double and family rooms available, all with en suite, plus a restaurant downstairs.

Buccaneers Guesthouse (☎ 21 571 671; www .buccaneers.com.mt; Triq Ġulju; per person incl breakfast Lm6; ☒ Apr-Oct; ☒) Another friendly, well-run guesthouse, large (30 rooms) and with good facilities (rooms have phone, air-con and private shower and washbasin – toilets are shared). The rooms are nothing flash but are clean, comfy and very well-priced, and there is a lively bar and restaurant downstairs (half-board is a bargain at Lm7.50 per person).

Sea View Hotel (☎ 21 573 105; seaview@waldo net.net.mt; cnr Dawret il-Gżejjer & Triq il-Imsell; per person incl breakfast Lm5/8.25 low/high season; ☒ year-round; ☒) This budget hotel, on the promenade north of Misraħ il-Bajja, has rather small and basic rooms, but all have balconies and bathroom, and there's a small pool here too. Prices are based on two people sharing a room; the single supplement is Lm2 per night. There is also a sea-view supplement of Lm1.25 per person in high season, and you'll pay a little extra if you're staying only one night.

MID-RANGE

Sunseeker Holiday Complex (☎ 21 575 619; www.sun seekerholidaycomplex.com; Trejqet il-Kulpara; 1-bedroom apt from Lm60/90 low/high season; ☒) This central complex has helpful staff, indoor and outdoor pools, gym, sauna, Jacuzzi and mini-market. On offer are one- to three-bedroom self-catering apartments for weekly lets (although shorter stays are welcome). Apartments sleep up to seven, and all have ceiling fans, kitchenette and lounge area. Low season prices (November to April) are particularly good value.

Buġibba Holiday Complex (☎ 21 580 861; www .islandhotels.com; Triq it-Turisti; hotel r per person incl breakfast Lm11/17 low/high season, 1-bedroom apt per person Lm8/15 low/high season; ☒ ☒ ☒) One of the veterans of the Buġibba tourist trade, having opened in 1982. There are more than 200 hotel rooms and over 100 self-catering apartments of varying sizes. One-bedroom apartments sleep up to four. Facilities include three swimming pools, games room, cocktail bar, restaurant and pizzeria, plus a very pleasant courtyard garden.

Topaz Hotel (☎ 21 572 416; www.tumas.com/topaz; Triq iċ-Ċagħaq; hotel r per person incl breakfast Lm8/18 low/high season, 2-person studio Lm9/22 low/high season;

☒ ▫ ☒) If you don't mind the slightly impersonal, big-hotel feel, this large complex of modern hotel rooms (nearly 260) and self-catering studios offers excellent facilities. There's a large, inviting lobby area, two swimming pools (indoor and outdoor), friendly staff, a pub, pizzeria, buffet restaurant and gym – so you might not need to leave the premises. Studios are very good value (note that studio prices given here are per room, not per person).

Howard Johnson Mediterranea Hotel & Suites
(☎ 21 578 758; Triq Buġibba; www.hojomed.com.mt; hotel r per person incl breakfast Lm8/18 low/high season, 1-bedroom apt Lm18/35 low/high season; ☒ ☒) More of the same in terms of hotel rooms and self-catering studios and apartments (one-bedroom sleeping up to four; two-bedroom, sleeping up to six), but the rustic décor of the HJ accommodation is a cut above the other places listed in this category. There is a rooftop pool and gym, a restaurant, and a good location high above the bay close to St Paul's Bay village.

Also recommended if you're travelling in summer and struggling to find accommodation in Buġibba:

Primera Hotel (☎ 21 573 880; primera@daystar.com.mt; cnr Triq Pijunieri & Triq il-Ħalel; per person incl breakfast from Lm9/12 low/high season; ☒ ☒) Bang in the centre of Buġibba.

Gillieru Harbour Hotel (☎ 21 572 716; gillieru@vol.net.mt; Triq il-Knisja; per person incl breakfast Lm9/14 low/high season; ☒ ☒) In front of the excellent Gillieru Seafood restaurant (p106).

Cape Inch Hotel (☎ 21 572 025; www.capeinchhotel.com; cnr Triq it-Turisti & Triq il-Merluzz; per person incl breakfast Lm8/14 low/high season; ☒) Small and pleasant old hotel opposite the bus station.

TOP END

New Dolmen Hotel (☎ 23 552 355 or 21 581 510; entrance at end of Triq il-Merluzz; d from Lm39/56 low/high season; ☒ ☒) On the waterfront about 200m northeast of Misraħ il-Bajja, this huge hotel (380 rooms) takes its name from the remains of a prehistoric temple which has been incorporated – none too sympathetically – into the hotel garden. It has all the comforts you would expect of a four-star hotel, and more – including four outdoor swimming pools, sports facilities, bars and restaurants, and a casino.

Grand Hotel Mercure San Antonio (☎ 21 583 434; www.accorhotels.com; Triq it-Turisti; d from Lm44/60

low/high season; ☒ ☒) The whitewashed entrance and colourful, stylish lobby create an excellent first impression for this hotel; the high standards carry through to the restaurants, pool areas and rooms, which are airy and well equipped.

Sol Suncrest (Map p107; ☎ 21 577 101; www.suncresthotel.com; Dawret il-Qawra; s/d from Lm25/35 low season, Lm35/50 high season; ☒ ☒) This vast, 458-room, four-star hotel is on the Qawra waterfront facing Salina Bay and is the biggest hotel in Buġibba. There are four restaurants, four bars and a nightclub, and guests have free use of a wide range of leisure facilities, including four swimming pools (three outdoor, one indoor), gymnasium, Jacuzzi, sauna, squash and tennis courts, beachside lidos and a summer water-sports centre. Rates quoted here are for the cheapest (inland) rooms – you'll pay extra for a sea view.

Eating

Buġibba is awash with cheap eating places, many offering 'full English breakfast' and 'typical English fish and chips', as well as pizzas, burgers and kebabs. But there's a reasonable selection of other cuisines and a few good Maltese places too.

The Buġibba promenade is lined with jewellery and souvenir stores and some fairly average eateries, but there is a decent array of ice-cream kiosks, and a good creperie, **La Krepree** (☎ 21 571 517; Dawret il-Gżejjer; crepes Lm0.70-1.30; ☺ until midnight), for an inexpensive late-night snack (sweet or savoury).

Da Rosita (☎ 21 571 158; Triq il-Ħalel; mains Lm3.25-6; ☺ dinner) It is hard not to like this bright and breezy, family-run Italian-Maltese restaurant, with its colourful décor, varied menu and friendly service. There should be something to please most diners, with pasta selections, traditional Maltese dishes such as *braġioli* (beef slices wrapped around a savoury filling and braised in red wine), fried rabbit and rabbit stew, fish, seafood, steaks, pizzas and vegetarian dishes.

Rojohn (☎ 21 574 454; Triq il-Ħalel; mains Lm2-3.50; ☺ dinner) Down the road from Da Rosita is this Indian restaurant, with wisecracking waiters and classic curries like lamb rogan josh, chicken tikka massala (Lm2) and prawn korma. Octopus balti adds a bit of Maltese colour to the menu.

Venus (☎ 21 571 604; cnr Triq Bajja & Gandoffli; mains Lm5-6.50; 🕑 dinner) Venus adds a touch of class to a neighbourhood of fast-food places and tourist restaurants. There's a bright and sophisticated interior and the modern menu adds an imaginative twist to traditional ingredients – try the spicy home-made fishcakes or char-grilled baby squid, followed by roast rabbit with garlic and star anise or marinated Moroccan chicken.

Mongolian Barbeque (☎ 21 574 072; Dawret il-Gżejjer; meals Lm5.25; 🕑 dinner) With its funky modern dining room, sea views and novel menu, this new restaurant should do well. For your money you get a choice of starters, then get to choose raw produce from a buffet (meat, fish, veggies and a sauce to accompany), and then have these cooked to order in front of you (rice and noodles also included). You can revisit the buffet as often as you like.

Out West Argentinian Steakhouse (☎ 21 580 666; Empire Cinema Complex, Triq il-Korp Tal-Pijunieri; mains from Lm5; 🕑 dinner) It calls itself Argentinian but serves Canadian beef and there's a touch of the cowboy in the décor. Still, the food is very good – and the choice of meats extensive (including fillet steak, ribeye, T-bone, lamb fillet, kangaroo, kebabs and burgers). Each meal includes soup, bruschetta, garlic bread, a choice of salads and potatoes. Needless to say, there's little joy for vegetarians here.

Isabella's (☎ 21 572 834; Triq I-Ibħra; mains Lm3.50-5; 🕑 dinner) Isabella's is a cheerful, laid-back Mexican-American eatery in the southern part of town where you can eat your fill of burgers, fried chicken, steak, nachos, tacos, burritos etc – the kind of food that goes perfectly with beer or margaritas.

Gillieru (☎ 21 573 269; 66 Triq il-Knisja; mains Lm4-8; 🕑 lunch & dinner) Gillieru enjoys a five-star location on a terrace overlooking the harbour. The building is designed to resemble the front of a ship – sit at a window and you'll feel you're on a cruise liner. The restaurant has been around for decades and is a local institution famed for its fresh seafood (prawns, lobster, grilled swordfish, calamari), but there are good choices for nonseafood-eaters too.

Mange Tout (Map p107; ☎ 21 572 121; 356 Triq San Pawl; mains Lm6.50-7.50; 🕑 dinner Mon-Sat) Tucked well away from the tourist areas in St Paul's Bay village (indeed it's closer to Xemxija than Buġibba) is this acclaimed French-Mediterranean restaurant. It's tiny seating only 30, so a booking is highly advised. Everything on the menu sounds amazing – try to choose between mains of slow-roasted fillet of beef with truffled mash and blue cheese, roasted barbary duck breast or pot-roasted pork cutlet with a white bean and apple puree. And that's only mains – starters and desserts are just as difficult to choose!

Drinking

Take your pick from the dozens of bars along Triq it-Turisti and the streets around Misraħ il-Bajja (particularly Triq Sant'Antnin) There are basically two species of bar in Buġibba. There's the 'typical British pub with a name like the Victoria or the Red Lion, drawing tourists looking for the comforts of home. In these places you can down pints of bitter, play darts and sing along with the karaoke machine. Then there are the bars for the younger party crowd where the mission for the evening is to get sloshed and maybe get lucky. The bars catering to the boozy crowd come alive in the high season and usually vary from year to year – but it shouldn't take too long to find them if that's your scene. Don't expect the same level of hedonism in the low season.

Fat Harry's (☎ 21 581 298; Triq Bajja) Fat Harry's belongs firmly to the first category. It is a central English-style pub doing traditional pub grub like fish and chips, and offering plenty of draught beer, outdoor tables for people-watching and, inside, live sports on the big screen.

Victoria Pub (☎ 21 571 355; Misraħ il-Bajja) On Buġibba's main square, with a sign out the front boldly claiming to be 'Malta's No I karaoke venue' – consider yourself warned

Corner Pocket Bar (☎ 21 581 073; Triq Kavetta A great after-dark spot with something for everyone – karaoke, DJs, big screens for sports coverage, pool tables and video games. It's above Browsers (p101), a large Internet café.

Rookies Sports Bar & Grill (☎ 21 574 550; Triq Sponoż) Fourteen TVs and two giant screens televise sports from around the world at this large and popular American-style sports bar. There are also regular live bands and a wide range of international beers (and meals) to get you going.

Grapevine Pub, Pizzeria & Grill (☎ 21 572 973; Triq il-Korp Tal-Pijunieri) The Grapevine is of Irish persuasion, as evidenced by the Guinness on tap, among other things. There are good pizzas and snacks, plus the ubiquitous TV screens broadcasting sports and regular live bands.

Entertainment
NIGHTCLUBS
Fuego (Map p107; ☎ 21 386 746; Dawret il-Qawra; admission free) Due to the enormous popularity of the first Fuego in Paceville, a sister salsa bar opened in Qawra. With its unique music policy (DJs playing pure and commercial Latin music), free salsa dancing classes (8.30pm to 10.30pm Tuesday and Wednesday in high season) and open terraces (covered and heated in winter), this place is sizzling!

Caesar's (Map p103; ☎ 21 571 034; Misraħ il-Bajja) Near the Victoria Pub, Caesar's is a mainstream nightclub playing summer anthems for the holiday-makers (open nightly in high season).

CASINO
Oracle Casino (Map p103; ☎ 21 570 057; www.oracle casino.com; entry on Dawret il-Gżejjer; admission free; ⌚ 10am-4am) Buġibba's casino is smaller and less formal than the other two casinos on the island (at St Julian's and Vittoriosa). It's part of the New Dolmen Hotel and is open daily until the wee small hours. The minimum age is 18 for visitors (25 for Maltese citizens). The dress code is 'smart casual' and you'll need your passport or ID card.

CINEMAS
Empire Cinema Complex (Map p103; ☎ 21 581 909; Triq il-Korp Tal-Pijunieri) Cinemas showing first-run movies. Tickets cost Lm2.40/1.40 per adult/child.

Getting There & Away
Buġibba bus station is on Triq it-Turisti near the New Dolmen Hotel. Bus Nos 49 and 58 run frequently between Valletta and Buġibba (one way Lm0.15).

Direct bus services to and from Buġibba (avoiding Valletta) include the following (all fares one way Lm0.40):

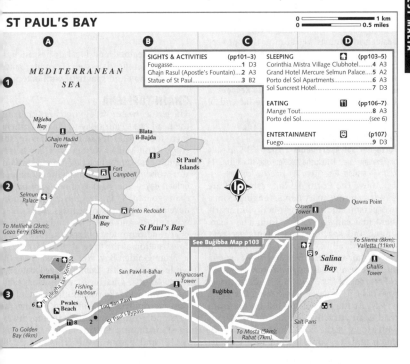

ST PAUL'S BAY

SIGHTS & ACTIVITIES	(pp101–3)
Fougasse	1 D3
Għajn Rasul (Apostle's Fountain)	2 A3
Statue of St Paul	3 B2

SLEEPING	(pp103–5)
Corinthia Mistra Village Clubhotel	4 A3
Grand Hotel Mercure Selmun Palace	5 A2
Porto del Sol Apartments	6 A3
Sol Suncrest Hotel	7 D3

EATING	(pp106–7)
Mange Tout	8 A3
Porto del Sol	(see 6)

ENTERTAINMENT	(p107)
Fuego	9 D3

No 48 – to Mellieħa town, Mellieħa Bay and Ċirkewwa
Nos 51 and 652 – to Għajn Tuffieħa and Golden Bay
No 70 – to Sliema
No 86 – to Mosta and Rabat
No 427 – to Mosta, Attard, Paola and Marsaxlokk
No 627 – to Sliema, the Three Cities and Marsaxlokk

There is a taxi rank on Misraħ il-Bajja in Buġibba, and a notice of the official (expensive) fares is posted on a sign near the HSBC Bank. From the rank to Xemxija is Lm4, to Mellieħa town Lm5, Mellieħa Bay Lm6, the Gozo ferry Lm7, Sliema Lm7 and Valletta Lm8.

XEMXIJA

The small, south-facing resort of Xemxija (shem-*shee*-ya), on the north side of St Paul's Bay, takes its name from *xemx*, meaning sun in Malti. There are a couple of private lidos along the waterfront, but Pwales Beach at the head of St Paul's Bay is just a narrow strip of gravelly sand. There are a few very good accommodation options if you prefer to be away from the hustle and bustle of Buġibba and Qawra.

About 300m west of the roundabout at the top of the hill in Xemxija a minor road leads to **Mistra Bay**, which has a tiny, gravelly beach and a tourist restaurant. It's not very pretty and the bay itself is filled with fish-farm pens, but there's good swimming and snorkelling off the rocks; and good hiking along the coast beyond the **Pinto Redoubt**, a 17th-century gun battery at the far end of the bay.

Sleeping & Eating

Porto del Sol Apartments (☎ 21 573 970; porto sol@maltanet.net; It Telegħa tax-Xemxija; studio Lm7/13 low/high season, 2-bedroom apt Lm12/18 low/high season) Above the Porto del Sol restaurant are 18 self-catering apartments, ranging from a two-person studio to a two-bedroom apartment that can sleep up to four. The clean, simple and spacious apartments are very well priced; all have private bathroom and fan (no air-con or TV), and most have a kitchenette and balcony with bay views.

Porto del Sol (☎ 21 573 970; It Telegħa tax-Xemxija; mains Lm4-6.50; ☽ lunch & dinner Mon-Sat, lunch Sun Oct-May) At the foot of the hill on the main road is an attractive family-run restaurant with views of the bay. The service is top-notch and it's popular with locals for its

One of the nicest accommodation options on the island, and a family-friendly place too, is the **Corinthia Mistra Village Club-hotel** (☎ 21 580 481; www.corinthiahotels.com; Xemxija Hill; 1-bedroom apt for up to 4 people Lm19/50/80 in Nov/Apr/Aug, 2-bedroom apt for up to 6 people Lm32/80/160; ⚌ ⛶ ⚑). It has over 200 one- and two-bedroom apartments set in lush landscaped gardens in a great location on top of the ridge above Xemxija. These spacious apartments are well equipped for a long stay (full kitchen, lounge, satellite TV, balcony) and well spread out over the property; some have spectacular views. The hotel's many high-quality facilities include swimming pools, sun terraces, a gym, sauna and massage parlour, tennis and squash courts, mini-market, laundrette and children's club. There are good restaurants and bars on the premises; breakfast is an additional Lm2/3 low/high season, and half- and full-board arrangements are also possible. The low-season rates (November to March) are a phenomenal bargain, then there's a steady climb in prices until August's peak.

excellent seafood and local dishes, including a delicious fish soup, rabbit, baked lamb, *braġioli* and spaghetti with octopus.

GĦAJN TUFFIEĦA

The fertile Pwales Valley stretches 4km from the head of St Paul's Bay to Għajn Tuffieħa (ayn too-*fee*-ha, meaning 'Spring of the Apples') on Malta's west coast. Here, two of Malta's best sandy beaches draw crowds of sun-worshippers. The misleadingly named **Golden Bay** – the sand is more grey-brown than golden – is the busier and more developed of the two beaches, with cafés, water sports and boat trips, and a couple of nearby accommodation options (one under construction at the time of research).

From Golden Bay, you can take a worthwhile cruise with **Charlie's Speedboat Trips** (☎ 99 486 949). Charlie is a knowledgeable guide who will take you south from Golden Bay, viewing rugged cliffs and visiting the bays and grottoes indenting the northwest coast, including Għajn Tuffieħa, Ġnejna (p110) and Fomm ir-Riħ (tricky to get to on land – see p123). Trips leave at noon and 2.30pm daily and cost Lm3.50/2 per adult/child. Look out for Charlie and his boat at the northern part of the beach, or ask at Munchies Bar-Pizzeria on the sand. Charlie also operates a trip every day at 4pm from April to October to Comino's Blue Lagoon – a great chance to visit this beautiful spot and take a swim after most of the crowds have left. This trip costs Lm4.50/3 per adult/child.

Landlubbers don't miss out though. Behind the beach (well signposted) is **Golden Bay Horse Riding** (☎ 21 573 360; ⏰ 8am-8pm Jun-Sep, 9am-5pm Oct-May), offering enjoyable one- and two-hour rides on fields overlooking the northwest beaches (but marred by the sight of so many bird hunters in the area). A one-hour ride costs Lm5, two hours is Lm8. All levels of experience are welcome, and free transport to the stables can be arranged for people staying in the north of the island.

Around the headland and to the south, guarded by a 17th-century watchtower, is **Għajn Tuffieħa Bay**. It is reached via a long, long flight of 186 steps from a car park beside the derelict Old Riviera Hotel, which is slowly sliding downhill towards the sea. The 250m strip of red-brown sand, backed by slopes covered in acacia and tamarisk trees, is more attractive than its neighbour.

There are good coastal walks south to Gnejna Bay and north to Anchor Bay.

Sleeping & Eating

The old Golden Sands Hotel above Golden Bay has been demolished and at the time of research the **Radisson SAS Golden Sands Resort & Spa** was being built in a prime site overlooking the beach. With an anticipated completion date of spring 2005, this five-star, 300-room resort is another example of the drive to push Malta's tourism industry upmarket and attract the more discerning traveller.

Ħal Ferħ Holiday Village (☎ 21 573 883; www hal-ferh.com; per person incl breakfast Lm10.50-17.75; ⏰ Apr-Oct; ☒) Tucked away behind Golden Bay is this holiday complex set in 9.6-hectare grounds. The walled-in compound was originally a British military barracks and has a slightly dilapidated air, but the rooms and apartments are bright and comfortable, and the facilities are family

friendly: pool, minigolf, water sports, tennis courts, children's entertainment programmes. There's also a restaurant and bar, and a minimarket.

Apple's Eye Restaurant (☎ 21 573 359; meals Lm2-4), on a terrace overlooking Golden Bay, peddles an uninspiring menu of tourist fare such as burgers and pizzas. It's better to come here just for a drink, as many of the locals do – especially on a sunny Sunday afternoon. Down on the beach are a number of cafés and kiosks selling snacks and drinks to parched and hungry sunbathers.

At Għajn Tuffieħa Bay there's just a kiosk selling drinks and ice creams at the top of the steps leading down to the beach.

Getting There & Away

By car, turn south at the roundabout at the west end of the St Paul's-Buġibba Bypass, or catch bus No 51 or 652 from Buġibba, No 652 from Sliema, or No 47 from Valletta.

MĠARR & AROUND

The village of Mġarr (mm-jarr), 2km to the southeast of Għajn Tuffieħa (and not to be confused with Mġarr on Gozo), would be unremarkable were it not for the conspicuous dome of the famous **Egg Church**. The Church of the Assumption was built in the 1930s with money raised by local parishioners, largely from the sale of locally produced eggs. Across the village square from the church is the **Mġarr Shelter** (☎ 21 573 235; entry through Il Barri restaurant; adult/child Lm1/0.50; ⏰ 9am-2pm Tue-Sat, 9-11.30am Sun), used by locals during the WWII bombings of Malta. It's one of the largest underground shelters in Malta, with a depth of 12m and a length of over 225m. You can only imagine the long uncomfortable hours spent down here in the humidity, but to show that life went on under such tough conditions, there are rooms on display that served as classrooms and hospitals.

The site of the **Ta'Ħaġrat Temple** (dating from around 3600 to 3300 BC and the earliest temple building in Malta) is concealed down a side street near the police station (on the road towards Żebbiegħ), but it's hardly worth seeking out. The site is fenced off and there is nothing to see except a few tumbled stones. The **Skorba Temples** (in the neighbouring village of Żebbiegħ are slightly more interesting, but probably only to archaeology enthusiasts. The excavation of the site was important in providing evidence of village habitation on Malta in the period between 4500 and 4100 BC (earlier than the temple-building period), now known as the Skorba Phase. Fragments of pottery and figurines found on the site are displayed in the National Museum of Archaeology in Valletta (p66). Both the Skorba and Ta'Ħaġrat temple sites are open to visitors by appointment only; call ☎ 21 222 966 if you'd like to arrange a viewing.

A minor road leads west from Mġarr past the ornate early-19th-century **Zammitello Palace** – originally a manor house, and now a wedding and function hall – to **Ġnejna Bay**. The red-sand beach is backed by terraced hillsides and enjoys a distant view of the Ta'Ċenċ cliffs on Gozo. There is good swimming off the rocks on either side of the bay. The **Lippija Tower** on the northern skyline makes a good target for a short walk.

On the road between Għajn Tuffieħa and Mġarr are the fenced remains of the **Roman Baths**. There are only scant remnants of floor mosaics, the fire-bricks beneath the caldarium (hot room), and the stone toilet seats from the latrine, but the site is closed to the public.

Il-Barri (☎ 21 573 235; mains Lm3.25-5.20), also known as Charlie's, is on the village square in Mġarr. It's a favourite local venue for a *fenkata* – whole fresh rabbit served in a casserole, either fried in garlic or in a thick brown gravy (Lm11.25 for a whole rabbit, which serves three, or Lm3.75 for a single portion). There are also grilled steaks, lamb chops, *braġioli*, and a 'Maltese special mix' (a selection of rabbit, horse and quail).

MELLIEĦA
pop 6300

The town of Mellieħa (mell-ee-ha) perches picturesquely atop the ridge between St Paul's Bay and Mellieħa Bay. Because of its distance from the beach, Mellieħa escaped the tidal wave of development that blighted Sliema and Buġibba in the early days of Malta's package-holiday boom. Although there are now several large hotels in town, Mellieħa today exudes a certain atmosphere of exclusivity, and is home to some very good restaurants. A 15-minute walk leads down the steep hill to **Mellieħa Bay**, the biggest and best sand beach in the

Maltese Islands. It's also, predictably, one of the most popular.

Although Mellieħa township was founded in the 15th century, the site was abandoned for several hundred years because of its vulnerability to attacks by corsairs landing in the bay below. The town was reoccupied in the 19th century.

Orientation & Information

Triq Ġorġ Borg Olivier – Mellieħa's main drag – runs north–south along a narrow gorge in the limestone plateau of the Mellieħa Ridge, and descends via a series of hairpin bends towards Mellieħa Bay. The older part of the town lies to the west of this street, with the Church of Our Lady of Victory at the northern end. Newer houses, luxury villas and apartments spread along the ridge to the east. The bus terminus is in Misraħ iż-Żjara Tal'Papa, beneath the church. The main road to Ċirkewwa and the Gozo ferry bypasses Mellieħa to the south and west.

The **Bank of Valletta** (Triq Ġorġ Borg Olivier) and **HSBC Bank** (Triq il-Kbira) both have central branches with ATMs. **Ta'Peter** (☎ 2 523 537; Triq Ġorġ Borg Olivier) is a bar and café with 1970s décor and a few computers for Internet access.

Sights
MELLIEĦA

The **Church of Our Lady of Victory** sits prominently on a rocky spur overlooking Mellieħa Bay. Stairs lead down on the eastern side of the church to a little pedestrian plaza beside the **Shrine of the Nativity of Our Lady of Mellieħa** (☼ 8am-noon & 4-6pm). It has been a place of pilgrimage since medieval times and it walls are covered with votive offerings. The fresco of the Madonna above the altar is said to have been painted by St Luke.

Across the main street from the shrine a gate in the wall and a flight of steps lead down to the **Grotto of the Madonna**, another shrine dedicated to the Virgin. It is set deep in a cave lit by flickering candles, beside a spring with waters that are said to heal sick children. Baby clothes hung on the wall are votive offerings given in thanks for successful cures.

MELLIEĦA BAY

The warm, shallow waters of Mellieħa Bay are great for swimming and safe for kids, so

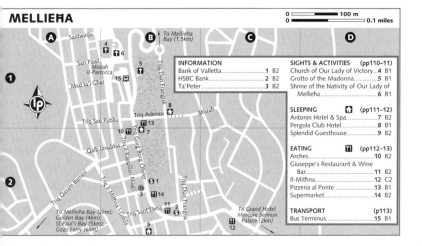

MELLIEĦA

INFORMATION		
Bank of Valletta	1	B2
HSBC Bank	2	B2
Ta'Peter	3	B2

SIGHTS & ACTIVITIES	(pp110–11)	
Church of Our Lady of Victory	4	B1
Grotto of the Madonna	5	B1
Shrine of the Nativity of Our Lady of Mellieħa	6	B1

SLEEPING	(pp111–12)	
Antonin Hotel & Spa	7	B2
Pergola Club Hotel	8	B1
Splendid Guesthouse	9	B2

EATING	(pp112–13)	
Arches	10	B2
Giuseppe's Restaurant & Wine Bar	11	B2
Il-Mithna	12	C2
Pizzeria al Ponte	13	B1
Supermarket	14	B2

TRANSPORT	(p113)	
Bus Terminus	15	B1

the sea gets almost as crowded as the sand. Add the water-skiers, rental canoes, banana rides, parascending boats and the fact that the reliable northeasterly breeze blowing into the bay in summer makes it ideal for windsurfing, and you begin to realise that Mellieħa Bay is not the place to get away from it all. Still, there are good summertime facilities, including sun beds and umbrellas for rent, windsurfing and kitesurfing gear for hire, and numerous kiosks serving drinks and snacks. At the southern edge of the bay is the **Tunny Net Complex**, with restaurants and a few shops, a lido, a watersports operator open from April to October (parascending, ringo rides, jet skis for hire, canoes and paddle boats etc), plus a diving operator: **Meldives Dive School** (☎ 21 522 595; www.digigate.net/meldives).

Ironically, on the other side of the road from Malta's busiest beach is **Il-Għadira** (www .birdlifemalta.org; admission free, donations welcome; ⊙ 10.30am-4.30pm Sat-Sun Oct-Nov & Feb-May, 9.30am-3.30pm Sat-Sun Dec-Jan, closed public holidays). This area of shallow, reedy ponds surrounded by scrub is an important resting area for migrating birds. The name, pronounced il-aa-dee-ra, means 'the marsh', and this was Malta's first national nature reserve, managed by passionate volunteers of BirdLife Malta on behalf of the government. Visitors are accompanied for a walk along a nature trail that eventually leads to a birdwatching hide, and it's wonderful to visit an area in Malta where birdlife is respected and admired in its natural habitat, rather than hunted and trapped.

Sleeping

MELLIEĦA

Splendid Guesthouse (☎ 21 523 602; www.splendid malta.com; Triq il-Kappillan Magri; per person incl breakfast from Lm5.50; ⊙ Apr-Oct) At the southern end of town is this pleasant, affordable guesthouse. All 14 rooms have a private shower and washbasin, a fan and a heater, and there's a sunbathing terrace on the rooftop.

Pergola Club Hotel (☎ 21 523 912; www.pergola hotel.com.mt; Triq Adenau; hotel r per person incl breakfast Lm6/15 low/high season, 2-person studio Lm10/28 low/ high season, apt Lm15/40 low/high season; ✷ ⬛ ⬤) Across the bridge from the main road is the Pergola, offering comfortable hotel rooms and self-catering apartments (entry is at the top of the steps). All rooms have satellite TV and a balcony overlooking the swimming pool. The views from the sun terraces towards the church are lovely. There is also a gym, an indoor pool and a children's play area, plus the obligatory choice of bars and restaurants. Studios and apartments are very good value (note that studio/apartment prices given here are per room, not per person; apartments sleep up to five).

Antonin Hotel & Spa (☎ 21 520 923; www.maritim .de; Triq Ġorġ Borg Olivier; s/d from Lm21/32 low season, Lm36/60 high season; ✷ ⬛ ⬤) The glossy new Antonin dominates the main street in the middle of Mellieħa. Here you'll find 108 high-quality rooms and suites, each with balcony, minibar, satellite TV and Internet connection. Hotel facilities are first-rate and include restaurants, a health spa, rooftop sun terrace, and lovely gardens with a large pool.

Grand Hotel Mercure Selmun Palace (Map p107; ☎ 21 521 040; www.accorhotels.com; half-board per person Lm11/20 low/high season; 🍴 🏊) This beautifully situated hotel lies 2km east of Mellieħa town centre, next to the grand, fortlike 18th-century Selmun Palace. There are 150 rooms in a modern block behind the palace, overlooking a garden courtyard, and six luxury suites in the palace itself. The hotel has outdoor and indoor pools, gym, sports facilities, tennis courts and a fine-dining restaurant in the palace (Le Chateau, open only two nights a week). Living it up in the palace suites will cost Lm23/27 per person with breakfast in the low/high season (Lm27/32 on a half-board basis).

MELLIEĦA BAY

Seabank Hotel (☎ 21 521 460; www.seabankhotel.com; Triq Marfa; s/d Lm12/13 low season, Lm26/40 high season; 🍴 🏊) Seabank is strategically situated on Mellieħa Bay, right next to Malta's biggest sandy beach. It has four-star facilities, including pool, sauna, Jacuzzi and fitness room, and opposite the hotel is the Tunny Net Complex, an area for swimming and water sports, with a couple of restaurants plus a diving school. The rooms are well equipped, but you'll pay more for a sea view. Low season rates are a bargain.

Mellieħa Holiday Centre (☎ 21 573 900; www.mell iehaholidaycentre.com; Triq Marfa; bungalows per person Lm11/17 low/high season; 💻 🏊) Set back off the street in expansive grounds, this family-friendly 'village' has excellent facilities including disabled facilities, a well-stocked supermarket, a choice of restaurants, sports grounds, an Internet café, a playground and a large pool and sun terrace. It's often totally booked out by Danish tour operators in the high season, but it's worth inquiring after vacancies. You can rent spacious self-catering bungalows that sleep up to six; each bungalow has a private, sheltered courtyard.

Eating & Drinking

MELLIEĦA

Giuseppe's Restaurant & Wine Bar (☎ 21 574 882; cnr Triq Ġorġ Borg Olivier & Triq Sant'Elena; mains Lm3-6; 🕑 Tue-Sat evenings) Run by Malta's favourite TV chef, Michael Diacono, this inviting place has a winning formula of stylishly rustic décor, a relaxed feel and a great menu of treats that changes regularly according to seasonal produce. Try the fresh fish (reliably good), beef carpaccio, barbary duck breast or risotto of basil, prosciutto and fresh mozzarella. Bookings are recommended.

Arches (☎ 21 523 460; 113 Triq Ġorġ Borg Olivier; dinner mains Lm5.50-10.50; 🕑 lunch & dinner, closed Sun in summer) Another main-street favourite is this acclaimed restaurant. It's large and elegant, with a menu and prices befitting the décor and formality. The food is delicious. Try roasted scallops and prawns on a leek and aubergine sauté, or monkfish with sun-dried tomatoes, basil and parma ham. Bookings advised.

Pizzeria al Ponte (☎ 21 520 923; cnr Triq Ġorġ Olivier & Triq Adenau; snacks & meals Lm1-3.50; 🕑 lunch & dinner) For a snack or light lunch in stylish surroundings, head to this friendly, relaxed place below the Antonin Hotel. There's a good menu of pizzas, pasta, sandwiches and burgers, plus a kids' menu and good desserts.

Il-Mitħna (☎ 21 520 404; 45 Triq il-Kbira; mains Lm4.50-7; 🕑 dinner Thu-Tue) This atmospheric eatery is housed in an early-17th-century windmill, the only survivor of three that used to sit atop Mellieħa Ridge. There are outdoor tables in a pretty courtyard, and a menu of local dishes with a twist, like braised rabbit in a bacon, tomato and sweet pepper sauce, slow-roasted cernia (fish) on citrus couscous, or seafood ravioli. There's a good-value set menu for early diners – Lm4.75 for three courses, from 6pm to 7.45pm.

For self-caterers, there's a **supermarket** (Triq Ġorġ Borg Olivier; 🕑 closed Sun) on the main street.

MELLIEĦA BAY

At the southern edge of the bay, near the roundabout where the bypass rejoins the coast, is the Tunny Net Complex, home to some good dining options. The casual **Café Latino Punta Rena** (☎ 21 523 254; mains Lm2-7.50; 🕑 lunch & dinner) has outdoor seating over the water and a Tex-Mex menu, with selections like paella, jerk chicken burger, fajitas and steaks any which way. There are also cakes and sundaes, a good kids' menu, and a wide choice of cocktails. Next door, the more formal **Trattoria de Buono** (☎ 21 521 332; main

Lm3-8; ☾ dinner) serves up high-quality Italian and local dishes, including a casserole of octopus and stuffed squid or king prawns on a bed of leek risotto.

Self-caterers should head to the **supermarket** (Triq Marfa; ☾ daily) inside the Mellieħa Holiday Centre (p112).

Getting There & Away

Bus Nos 43, 44 and 45 from Valletta pass through Mellieħa. No 43 terminates here, No 44 continues to Mellieħa Bay and No 45 goes on to Ċirkewwa. To/from Sliema, catch bus No 645; to/from Buġibba, you need bus No 48 or 645. Both these routes run to Mellieħa town and Mellieħa Bay.

There are a number of car-rental places lining the main street in town – shop around and you should find a good price, especially given the competition along here.

AROUND MELLIEĦA

The crest of Mellieħa Ridge offers some good walking to the east and west of the town. To the east, the fortresslike **Selmun Palace** (Map p107) dominates the skyline above St Paul's Bay. It was built in the 18th century for a charitable order called the Monte di Redenzione degli Schiavi (Mountain of the Redemption of the Slaves), whose business was to ransom Christians who had been taken into slavery on the Barbary Coast. The palace, which now houses a hotel and restaurant (p112), mimics the style of the Verdala Palace south of Rabat (p124).

A right turn just before you get to Selmun Palace leads in just over 1km to derelict **Fort Campbell**, an abandoned coastal defence built by the British between WWI and WWII. The headland commands a fine view over St Paul's Islands, and you can hike down to the coastal salt pans of Blata il-Bajda and around to Mistra Bay, or westwards along the cliff top to the ruined **tower of Għajn Ħadid** above the little beach at Mġieba Bay.

A left turn at the foot of the hill leading down to Mellieħa Bay puts you on the road to Anchor Bay about 1.5km away on the west coast. This steep-sided, pretty little bay was named after the many Roman anchors that were found on the sea bed by divers, some of which can be seen in the National Maritime Museum at Vittoriosa (p78).

However, in 1979 Anchor Bay was transformed – less than convincingly, it must be said – into the fishing village of **Sweethaven** (☎ 21 572 430; www.popeyemalta.com; adult/child Lm3.30/1.50; ☾ 9.30am-4.30pm Oct-Mar, 9.30am-5.30pm Apr-Sep) and was used as the set for the Hollywood musical *Popeye*, starring Robin Williams. The film was a turkey – as was the idea of retaining the set as a tourist attraction. The place is as interesting as, well, an abandoned film set, and the marketing is aimed squarely at kids, with audiovisual shows, puppets and a small fun park (where you pay extra for rides). You can get a good view of the village for free from the southern side of the bay (drive on past the car park entrance).

From the car park of Sweethaven (or Popeye Village, as it is also called) travellers have a unique chance to go off-road and explore some of the rugged terrain in the area. **Ride 4 Fun** (☎ 79 065 746; ☾ 10am-5pm) offers one-hour self-drive trips (guided and tailored to experience) on all-terrain quad bikes – great fun and easy to drive. The cost is Lm10 per person (or Lm5 for passengers) – beginners are welcome.

Bus No 441 runs hourly from Mellieħa Bay to Anchor Bay between 10am and 5pm Monday to Saturday (one way Lm0.40).

MARFA PENINSULA

The Marfa Peninsula is Malta's final flourish before dipping beneath the waters of the Comino Channel. Some of Malta's best diving spots are found along its northern coast (see Map p49). For information on requirements, dive schools and the best locations see the Diving & Snorkelling chapter, p46.

The peninsula is a barren ridge of limestone, steep on the south side and dipping more gently north and east from the high point of Ras il-Qammieħ (129m). A minor road leads west from the top of the hill up from Mellieħa Bay, passing the **Red Tower**, built in 1649 for Grand Master Lascaris as part of the chain of signal towers that linked Valletta and Gozo. The road continues west to the wild headland of **Ras il-Qammieħ**, which commands stunning views north to Gozo and south along the western sea cliffs of Malta.

Opposite the Red Tower road, another road leads east along the spine of the peninsula, with side roads giving access to various little coves and beaches. These places are very popular with local people and are best avoided at weekends, when the crowds can be enormous.

First up is **Ramla Bay**, with its small, sandy beach monopolised by the hotel of the same name. Immediately to its east is **Ramla Tal'Qortin**, which has no sand and is surrounded by an unsightly sprawl of Maltese holiday huts amid a forest of TV aerials and telephone cables.

The next two roads lead down to **Armier Bay** and **Little Armier Bay** and meet in the middle. The scrap of sand at Little Armier is probably the most pleasant beach around here.

The last road goes to **White Tower Bay**, which has another seaweed-stained patch of sand and a rash of holiday huts combining to form a small, unattractive shanty town. A track continues past the tower to the low cliffs of Aħrax Point, from which a pleasant coastal walk leads 1km south to a statue of the Madonna on Daħlet ix-Xilep. You can also reach the Madonna statue and a small chapel by following the main road east across the Marfa Peninsula.

The main road from Valletta ends at **Ċirkewwa**, which consists of little more than a desalination plant, a hotel and the Gozo ferry terminal. A left turn just before the Paradise Bay Hotel leads to **Paradise Bay**, a narrow patch of sand below cliffs with a private lido and a grand view of the ferry slip. It's a pleasant enough small beach if you manage to look beyond the ferry docks to Gozo in the distance!

Sleeping & Eating

Given the remote location of the three resorts in this area (not within easy walking distance of any restaurants – except for those at other hotels), half- and full-board options are available to guests at each hotel (normally at an additional cost of Lm7.50 to Lm10 for full board per person per night). Some of Malta's best diving is found in this area, so all the resorts have diving schools, plus good water-sports facilities and regular boat trips to nearby Comino.

Barceló Riviera Resort & Spa (☎ 21 525 900; www.riviera.com.mt; s/d incl breakfast Lm20/25 low season, Lm34/48 high season; ✶ ✿) Easily the nicest accommodation option in the far north is

this new hotel, just off the main road about 1.5km from the Ċirkewwa ferry terminal. There's a fresh, bright décor and modern facilities, including a health spa, three restaurants (a bistro, pizzeria and more formal restaurant), two bars and three pools.

Paradise Bay Hotel (☎ 21 521 166; www.paradise -bay.com; s/d incl breakfast from Lm14.50/21 low season, Lm23.50/39 high season; ✶ ✿ ✿) Squeezed onto the tip of Marfa Point, opposite the Gozo ferry terminal, is this large (215-room) hotel, with somewhat gloomy décor but good facilities. All rooms have a balcony with sea view, a fridge, satellite TV and a trouser press – the latter is no doubt connected to the 'no shorts' dress code at the hotel's restaurant at dinner. There are also three outdoor pools and one indoors, as well as a games room and two tennis courts.

Ramla Bay Garden (☎ 21 522 181; www.garden hotels.net; per person incl breakfast Lm10/23.50 low/high season; ✿ ✿) Another well-equipped, remote northern resort is Ramla Bay Garden, with 111 hotel rooms. Facilities include indoor and outdoor pool, private beach and floodlit tennis court. There's a complex schedule of rates, with low season prices from Lm10 (less if you stay a few nights, Lm1 more if you want a room with a sea view). In high season prices rise to Lm23.50 from mid-July to August, with a sea-view supplement of Lm6 during this period.

The Marfa Peninsula is a bit of a culinary wasteland, with few eating places outside the three hotels. **Ray's Pizzeria** at Little Armier Bay has OK meals and also offers water-sports facilities.

The **café** at the ferry terminal serves sandwiches, pies and soggy, microwaved pizzas. The food on the ferry is even worse.

Getting There & Away

Bus No 45 runs regularly between Valletta and Ċirkewwa, and takes about an hour (one way Lm0.20). By car, you can make the trip in about 40 to 45 minutes. Bus Nos 48 and 645 run between Ċirkewwa and Buġibba and Sliema respectively (one way Lm0.40). Bus No 50 runs from Valletta to Armier Bay daily in July and August only. A taxi from Malta International Airport to Ċirkewwa should cost Lm13.

For details of the ferry services to Gozo and Comino, see p184.

Central Malta

This small region (well, every region in Malta is small!) offers visitors some surprising diversity. You can drive through tiny villages that see few tourists on your way between sprawling urban regions full of traffic-clogged roads. You can choose to visit remarkable medieval frescoes in ancient underground catacombs and then marvel at one of Europe's largest church domes. Natural attractions include stark cliffs that are the perfect place to watch a sunset, a scenic bay ideal for swimming (if only you can find it) and the only patch of woodland on this rather barren island. There are sleeping and eating options here ranging from luxury five-star hotels that play host to dignitaries and movie stars, to university residences and rustic village restaurants where locals come for their regular weekend feasts of rabbit.

But the jewel in the crown of this area, and an absolute must-see, is Mdina, once the ancient walled capital of Malta. It's a stunning town perched loftily on a crag about 10km west of Valletta, and its quiet streets ooze history and refinement (after the tour buses leave!). In the early morning and of an evening, especially, this is the kind of place that has you talking in whispers so as not to disturb the peace.

HIGHLIGHTS

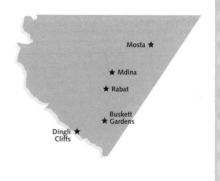

- Wandering the silent and beautiful streets of **Mdina** (p117)

- Taking a tour of **St Agatha's Catacombs** (p122) in Rabat and admiring the frescoes

- Strolling along the top of the **Dingli Cliffs** (p124), followed by lunch among the locals at Bobbyland Restaurant

- Joining in with the L-Imnarja festivities at **Buskett Gardens** (p124)

- Staring in awe at **Mosta Dome** (p125) and marvelling at the miracle of the unexploded bomb

CENTRAL MALTA

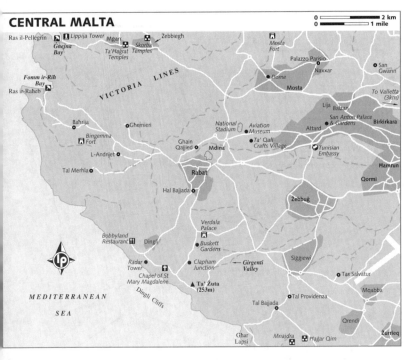

MDINA

pop 370

The citadel of Mdina was fortified from the earliest times. As long ago as 1000 BC the Phoenicians had built a protective wall here, and called their settlement Malet, meaning 'place of shelter'. The Romans built a large town here and called it Melita. It was given its present name when the Arabs arrived in the 9th century – *madina* is Arabic for 'walled city'. They built strong walls and dug a deep moat between Mdina and its suburbs (known as *rabat* in Arabic).

In medieval times Mdina was known as Città Notabile – the Noble City. It was the favoured residence of the Maltese aristocracy and the seat of the *università* or governing council. The Knights, who were largely a sea-based force, made Grand Harbour and Valletta their centre of activity, and Mdina sank into the background as a retreat of the Maltese nobility. Today, with its massive walls and peaceful, shady streets, it is often referred to as the Silent City.

Orientation & Information

Mdina is the walled city; Rabat is the town outside the walls. Mdina's main street, Triq Villegaignon, runs north from the Main Gate in the south to Pjazza tas-Sur (Bastion Sq), passing St Paul's Cathedral on the right. A second gate, the Greek's Gate, at the western corner of Mdina, is opposite the Museum of Roman Antiquities in Rabat.

The bus terminus is outside Mdina on Is-Saqqajja, 150m south of the Main Gate. Visitors' cars are not allowed into Mdina, but there is parking outside the Main Gate and on Triq il-Mużew.

You'll find banks and ATMs in Rabat, opposite the bus stop, but you can also change money at the **Maltese Falcon** (27 Triq Villegaignon), a souvenir shop near the cathedral. **Fontanella Tea Gardens** (p121) has a couple of computers for Internet access. There are public toilets outside the Main Gate.

Sights

ST PAUL'S CATHEDRAL

The **Cathedral** (Pjazza San Pawl; admission free, donations welcome; 9.30-11.45am & 2-5pm Mon-Sat, 3-4.30pm

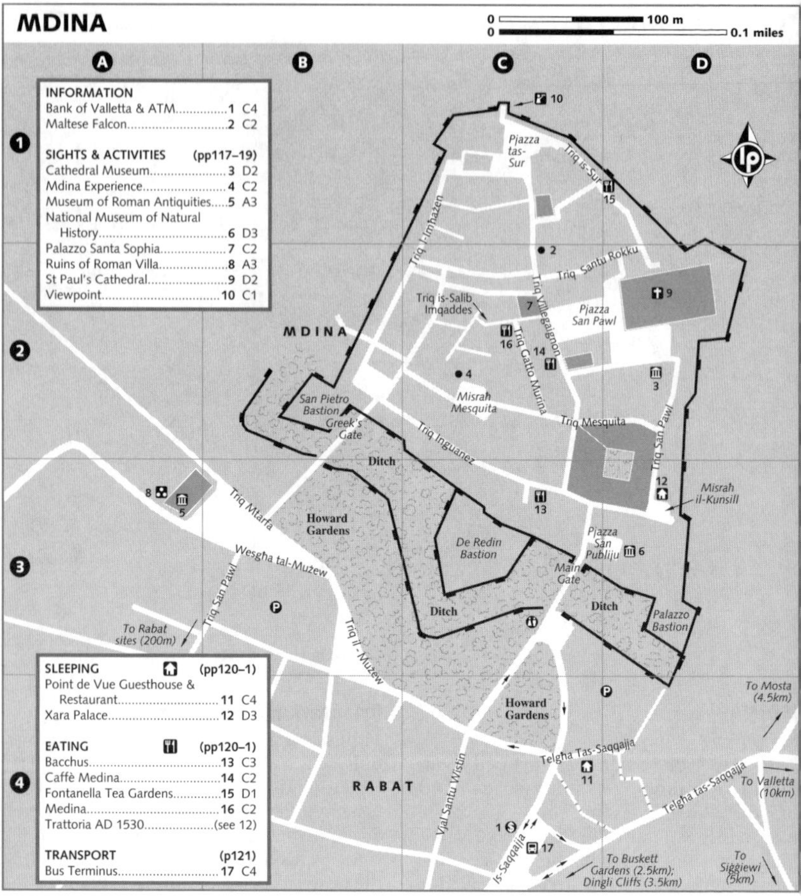

Sun) is said to be built on the site of the villa belonging to Publius, the Roman governor of Malta who welcomed St Paul in AD 60.

The original Norman church was destroyed by an earthquake, and the restrained baroque edifice that you see today was built between 1697 and 1702 by Lorenzo Gafa. Note the fire and serpent motifs atop the twin bell-towers, symbolising the saint's first miracle on Malta (see the boxed text, p102).

Echoing St John's Co-Cathedral in Valletta, the floor of St Paul's is covered in the polychrome marble tombstones of Maltese nobles and important clergymen, while the vault is painted with scenes from the life of St Paul. The altar painting *The Conversion of St Paul* by Mattia Preti survived the earthquake, as did the apse above it with the fresco *St Paul's Shipwreck* and the beautifully carved oak doors to the sacristy on the north side.

CATHEDRAL MUSEUM

Housed in a baroque 18th-century palace originally used as a seminary is the **Cathedral Museum** (☎ 21 454 697; Pjazza San Pawl; adult/child Lm1/free; ⏰ 10am-5.15pm Mon-Fri, 10am-3.15pm Sat). It contains important collections of coins, silver plate, vestments, manuscripts and religious paintings, as well as a series of woodcut and copperplate prints and lithographs by the German artist Albrecht Dürer. There is an interesting collection of weird and wonderful olive-wood carvings by Maltese artist Anton Agius.

NATIONAL MUSEUM OF NATURAL HISTORY

The displays of the **National Museum of Natural History** (☎ 21 455 951; Pjazza San Publiju; adult/child Lm1/free; ✆ 7.45am-2pm daily mid-Jun–Sep, 8.15am-5pm Mon-Sat & 8.15am-4pm Sun Oct–mid-Jun, closed public holidays), though housed in the elegant Palazzo de Vilhena, look a little tired and belong to another era, when museums were simply full of stuffed animals in dusty glass cabinets. The most interesting section is the geology exhibit, which explains the origins of Malta's landscape and displays the wide range of fossils that can be found in its rocks. The teeth belonging to the ancient shark *Carcharodon megalodon aggasiz* are food for thought – measuring 18cm on the edge, they belonged to a 25m monster that prowled the Miocene seas 30 million years ago. Also on display (in the Seashells Room) is the pickled body of a 16kg squid found at Xemxija in St Paul's Bay. The dusty and moth-eaten collection of stuffed mammals and birds can be safely ignored.

AUDIOVISUAL SHOWS & EXHIBITIONS

A worthwhile 25-minute audiovisual show, the **Mdina Experience** (☎ 21 454 322; Misraħ Mesquita; adult/child Lm1.60/0.80) does for Mdina's history what the Malta Experience in Valletta (p68) does for Malta's. The show begins roughly every half-hour from 10.30am to 4pm Monday to Friday, and 10.30am to 2pm Saturday.

Unfortunately, the Silent City appears to be succumbing to a rising tide of tawdry tourist traps, all hitching a ride on the back of the successful Mdina Experience show. You can soak up enough history from the streets and stones without paying to see endless gory tableaux of dying knights and tortured prisoners. Don't be forced into buying tickets to other 'visual attractions' by the pushy staff at the Mdina Experience.

Walking Tour

Distance: approx 750m
Duration: 30 minutes

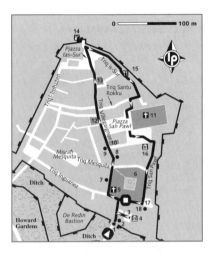

Enter Mdina by the **Main Gate (1)**, which was built in 1724 and bears the arms of Grand Master Manoel de Vilhena. The outline of the original gate can be seen in the wall to the right of the bridge. Immediately inside the gate on the right are the **Mdina Dungeons (2;** ☎ 21 450 267; Pjazza San Publiju; adult/child Lm1.50/0.75; ✆ 9.30am-5.30pm), which house a series of gruesome tableaux depicting torture and dismemberment, accompanied by a rather wearing soundtrack of screaming, groaning, chopping and choking noises. It's a last resort for a very wet day or with bored kids to entertain.

An imposing gateway on the right leads into the courtyard of **Palazzo de Vilhena (3)**, built as a summer residence for the Grand Master in the early 18th century. The palace served as a hospital from 1860 until 1956, and since the 1970s has housed the **National Museum of Natural History (4;** p119). Go left and then right onto Triq Villegaignon. On the right-hand corner of the street is **St Agatha's Chapel (5)**, which dates from the early 15th century. The entire block on the right here is occupied by the **Nunnery of St Benedict (6)**, whose members live in strict seclusion. No man is permitted to enter the convent and the sisters are not allowed to leave. Even after death they remain, buried in a cemetery within the walls of the nunnery.

On the left is the **Casa Inguanez (7)**, the ancient seat of Malta's oldest aristocratic family, who have lived here since the 14th century. Further along Triq Villegaignon

CENTRAL MALTA

THE TRAGEDY OF ST AGATHA

St Agatha was a 3rd-century Christian martyr from Sicily – Catania and Palermo both claim to be her birthplace – who fled to Malta to escape the amorous advances of a Sicilian governor. On returning to Sicily she was imprisoned and tortured, and her breasts were cut off with shears – a horrific punishment gruesomely depicted in many paintings and statues in Malta. She was then burnt at the stake. There is a chapel dedicated to St Agatha in Mdina (p119) and catacombs in Rabat (p122) that are said to have been her hiding place in Malta.

---

on the right, the **Casa Testaferrata (8)** is the residence of the Marquis of St Vincent Ferreri, another member of the Maltese nobility (the title was created by King Phillipe of Spain and donated to the family in 1716). Across the street on the left is the **House of Notary Bezzina (9)**. It was from Bezzina's balcony that the French commander Masson was lobbed to his death in 1798 (see the boxed text opposite).

Next up on the right is the beautiful baroque façade of the **Banca Giuratale (10)**, built in 1730, which once housed Mdina's city council and is now home to the National Archives. Beyond that, Pjazza San Pawl opens out on the right, dominated by the elegant baroque façade of **St Paul's Cathedral (11;** p117). Facing it is the **Palazzo Santa Sophia (12)**, which bears a stone tablet with the date 1233. Though this year is probably inaccurate, the building is still the oldest in Mdina.

Keep on along Triq Villegaignon past the Carmelite Church and monastery to the **Palazzo Falzon (13)**, also called (inaccurately) the Norman House. The building dates from 1495, and was used for a time by Grand Master de L'Isle Adam when the Knights first arrived in Malta in 1530. Look up to see the beautiful medieval windows. The ground floor houses a private museum with displays of 16th- and 17th-century weapons, furniture and cooking utensils. At the time of research the museum was closed for extensive restoration and modernisation; it plans to reopen in late 2004.

Triq Villegaignon ends at Pjazza tas-Sur. The **views (14)** from the city walls take in all of northern and central Malta, including St Paul's Bay, Mosta Dome and the Valletta bastions. On an exceptionally clear day, you might even see the peak of Mt Etna in Sicily, 225km away to the north-northeast (scan the horizon just to the left of Mosta Dome).

Follow the walls to the right along Triq is-Sur, pausing for a cuppa at the **Fontanella Tea Gardens (15)** if you wish, and bear right at Triq Santu Rokku into Pjazza San Pawl. The entrance to the cathedral is on the far side, and opposite the entry is the **Cathedral Museum (16)**, housed in the former seminary.

Go to the left of the Cathedral Museum along Triq San Pawl, which leads to the pretty little square of **Misraħ il-Kunsill (17)**. Facing the Xara Palace Hotel is the **Corte Capitanale (18)**, the former Court of Justice – note the figures on the balcony representing Justice and Mercy. Turn right to return to the Main Gate, or continue to the end of Triq Inguanez and exit through the Greek's Gate to visit the Museum of Roman Antiquities (p121).

Sleeping & Eating

There is very little accommodation in Mdina, but there are a number of good places to eat.

Point de Vue Guesthouse & Restaurant (☎ 21 454 117; http://mol.net.mt/point; 5 Is-Saqqajja; per person incl breakfast Lm7-8) Just outside Mdina's Main Gate is this a very affordable guesthouse, with simple but comfortable rooms (with private bathroom). Book ahead, as this is the only budget option in the area and its position can't be bettered. Downstairs from the guesthouse is a restaurant catering to the tourist crowds and offering Maltese specialities like fish, rabbit and lamb, and pizzas for around Lm2.

Xara Palace (☎ 21 450 560; www.xarapalace.com.mt; Misraħ il-Kunsill; ste from Lm85; 🔀) The only other accommodation option in the area is this exclusive five-star hotel in one of Mdina's 17th-century palazzos. The building served as an RAF officers' mess during WWII and now houses one of Malta's most elegant places to stay (in keeping with the refined atmosphere of Mdina). There are 17 luxury suites, each with cable TV, a stereo music centre and modem connection. There is also a gym and sauna, plus atrium bar, trattoria (see below) and rooftop fine-dining restaurant. Buffet breakfast is Lm8 extra per person.

THE MDINA UPRISING

After the French invasion of Malta in June 1798, Napoleon stayed on the island for only six days before continuing his journey to Egypt, where his fleet was defeated by the British Navy at Aboukir. He left behind a garrison of only 4000 troops under the command of General Vaubois.

With revolutionary fervour, the French tried to impose their ideas on Maltese society. They abolished the nobility, defaced their escutcheons, persecuted the clergy and looted the churches. But on 2 September 1798, when they attempted to auction off the treasures of Mdina's Carmelite Church – on a Sunday – the Maltese decided that enough was enough. In a spontaneous uprising, they massacred the French garrison at Mdina, throwing its commander, Capitaine Masson, off a balcony to his death.

The French retreated to the safety of Valletta, where the Maltese, under the command of Canon Caruana of St Paul's Cathedral, besieged them. Having learnt of Napoleon's misfortune in Egypt, the Maltese asked for help from the British, who imposed a naval blockade on Malta under the command of Captain Alexander Ball. The Maltese forces suffered two hard years of skirmishing and stand-off until the French finally capitulated on 5 September 1800.

Trattoria AD 1530 (☎ 21 450 560; Misraħ il-Kunsill; mains Lm3-7; ☯ lunch & dinner) Next door to the entrance to Xara Palace, this stylishly casual restaurant offers outdoor seating on the pretty square, and warm, yellow-washed walls inside. There's a kids' menu, and the grown-ups can choose from pizza and pasta choices, plus more substantial mains of fish and meat (such as roasted pork loin, grilled fillet of beef).

Medina (☎ 21 454 004; 7 Triq is-Salib Imqaddes; mains Lm3-8; ☯ dinner Mon-Sat) The Medina (not to be confused with Caffè Medina on the main street) is one of Malta's most romantic venues – a medieval townhouse with vaulted ceilings and fireplaces for cooler evenings, and an attractive garden-courtyard for alfresco dining in warmer months. The menu offers a mix of Maltese, Italian and French dishes, with good vegetarian selections.

Bacchus (☎ 21 454 981; Triq Inguanez; snacks & lunch Lm2-3.50, dinner mains Lm5-7; ☯ 10am-11pm) This excellent restaurant and reception venue is built into a vault beneath the De Redin Bastion that used to serve as a powder magazine; blocks of original Roman masonry can be seen in one of the walls. Snacks and lunch dishes are a good option – how about minestrone, roast chicken or a traditional Maltese platter of *ftira* (flat bread filled with tomatoes, anchovies and olives) and goat's cheese? At dinner time carefully presented, French-influenced meals include grilled shrimp in prosciutto or roasted duck breast.

Fontanella Tea Gardens (☎ 21 454 264; Triq is-Sur; snacks & meals Lm0.50-3; ☯ 10am-7pm winter, 10am-11pm summer) Enjoy coffee and a huge array of cakes and sweets at this wonderful setting on top of the city walls. Fontanella – a Maltese institution – serves delicious home-baked cakes (Lm0.70 per piece), good sandwiches and light meals and passable coffee, and you'll have ample time to admire the sweeping views from its terrace – service is very ordinary.

Caffè Medina (☎ 21 451 917; 19 Triq Villegaignon; snacks & meals Lm0.65-3) There are no impressive views from here, but the service is better and the café fare (baguettes, jacket potatoes, salads, pasta) is very good and a little more creative than at the Fontanella (eg salad with apple, blue cheese and walnuts). There's also a kids' menu, and a tempting selection of cakes and pastries on display.

Getting There & Away
See p123 for information on getting to Rabat. The bus terminus in Rabat is on Is-Saqqajja, 150m south of Mdina's Main Gate.

RABAT
pop 11,500

The town of Rabat sprawls to the south of Mdina and is home to a few sites of historical interest. Triq San Pawl is the street to follow – it begins opposite Mdina's Greek's Gate and runs south to St Paul's Church and the town square.

Sights
The **Museum of Roman Antiquities** (Map p118; ☎ 21 454 125; Wesgħa tal-Mużew; adult/child Lm1/free;

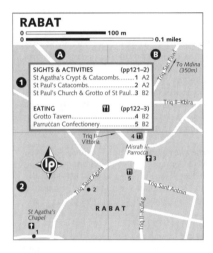

RABAT

SIGHTS & ACTIVITIES (pp121–2)
St Agatha's Crypt & Catacombs........1 A2
St Paul's Catacombs.........................2 A2
St Paul's Church & Grotto of St Paul..3 B2

EATING (pp122–3)
Grotto Tavern...............................4 B2
Parruċċan Confectionery.................5 B2

7.45am–2pm daily mid-Jun–Sep, 8.15am–5pm Mon-Sat & 8.15am–4pm Sun Oct–mid-Jun, closed public holidays), also called the Roman Domus, is yet another museum closed for restoration and renovations at the time of research; the scheduled reopening date is mid-2004. When it does reopen it will have the admission costs and opening hours outlined above.

The museum was built in the 1920s to incorporate the excavated remains of a large Roman townhouse dating from the 1st century BC. The centrepiece is the original peristyle court (formerly an open courtyard surrounded by columns). The mosaic floor has a geometric border around the image of two birds perched on a water bowl; a cistern in one corner was used for collecting rainwater.

Mosaic fragments mounted on the walls show nymphs punishing a satyr, grinning clowns and the famous (though surprisingly small) wide-mouthed woman surrounded by fruits and vegetables. There is also a collection of artefacts from the Roman period in Malta, including sculptures, amphorae, pottery fragments and oil lamps.

From the Museum of Roman Antiquities, walk south along Triq San Pawl for 400m to **St Paul's Church**, built in 1675. Beside the church, stairs lead down into the **Grotto of St Paul** (Misraħ il-Parroċċa; admission free, donations welcome; 10am-5pm Mon-Sat), a cave where the saint is said to have preached during his stay in Malta. The statue of St Paul was gifted by the Knights in 1748, while the silver ship to its left was added in 1960 to commemorate the 1900th anniversary of the saint's shipwreck.

From the church, numerous signposts point the way across the parish square and along Triq Sant'Agata towards two groups of early Christian underground tombs. First up, on the left, are **St Paul's Catacombs** (21 454 562; Triq Sant'Agata; adult/child Lm1/free; 7.45am-2pm daily mid-Jun–Sep, 8.15am-5pm Mon-Sat & 8.15am-4pm Sun Oct–mid-Jun, closed public holidays), which date from the 3rd century AD. They were rediscovered in 1894. The labyrinth of rock-cut tombs, narrow stairs and passages is poorly lit and there's not a lot to see, but it's fun to explore (note that there are a number of uneven surfaces, so mind your step). Unfortunately there are no explanatory boards detailing the history and purpose of the catacombs – you will learn more by taking a tour of the nearby St Agatha's Catacombs.

Another 100m down the street and on the right are **St Agatha's Crypt & Catacombs** (21 454 503; Triq Sant'Agata; adult/child Lm0.75/free; 9am-5pm Mon-Fri, 9am-1pm Sat Jul-Sep, 9am-noon & 1-4.30pm Mon-Fri, 9am-12.30pm Sat Oct-Jun, closed public holidays). These are more interesting than St Paul's as they contain a series of remarkable frescoes dating from the 12th to the 15th century. According to legend, these catacombs were the hiding place of St Agatha when she fled Sicily (see the boxed text, p120). Tours of the catacombs are conducted regularly, and explain the history of the site and point out features of the artwork. Back at ground level is an unusual little museum containing everything from fossils and minerals to coins, church vestments and Etruscan, Roman and Egyptian artefacts.

Sleeping & Eating

See p120 for details of hotels and restaurants in Mdina. If you're exploring Rabat, you might like to stop by **Parruċċan Confectionery** (Misraħ il-Parroċċa) to pick up a bag of sweet treats from the huge selection of cookies and cakes, including Maltese specialities like nougat and fig rolls.

Also on the parish square, opposite St Paul's Church, is **Grotto Tavern** (21 455 138; Misraħ il Parroċċa; lunch mains Lm2-5, dinner Lm4-6), owned by a friendly French-Maltese couple and offering subterranean wining and dining. The extensive lunch menu offers snacks, salads, chicken, rabbit and fish dishes, while the dinner menu has a heavy French accent, with dishes like poached salmon or rabbit Provençale, plus fondues and raclettes perfect for sharing (Lm6 to Lm7.50 per person). Finish with crepes, chocolate fondue or tarte aux pommes.

Getting There & Away

From Valletta, take bus No 80 or 81 (one way Lm0.15); from Sliema and St Julian's No 65 (Lm0.40); and from Buġibba and St Paul's Bay No 86 (Lm0.40).

By car, the road from Valletta is well signposted. From St Paul's Bay, begin by following signs to Mosta.

AROUND RABAT
Ta'Qali Crafts Village

The arts and crafts workshops at Ta'Qali are housed in the old Nissen huts on this WWII RAF airfield, which is badly in need of a makeover – the place looks like a building site. Although it's rather scruffy, the workshops are worth a look. You can watch glass-blowers at work, and shop for gold, silver and filigree jewellery, paintings by local artists, leather goods, Maltese lace, furniture, ceramics and ornamental glass.

The individual workshops are open varying hours, but most are open from 9am to 4pm Monday to Friday. Try to get here early (before 10am) if you want to avoid the coach-tour crowds.

Bus No 65 operates between Sliema and Rabat and calls in at Ta'Qali, as does the No 86 bus between Buġibba and Rabat.

Malta Aviation Museum

The **Malta Aviation Museum** (☎ 21 416 095; www .digigate.net/aviation; adult/child Lm1.50/0.50; ⊙ 9am-5pm) is tucked away in an unassuming shed between Ta'Qali Crafts Village and the National Stadium, 2km northeast of Mdina. It's a real enthusiast's museum, with bits of engines, airframes and instruments lying around, and numerous restoration projects under way – including a WWII Hawker Hurricane IIa, salvaged in 1995 after 54 years at the bottom of the sea off the southwest coast. You can watch locals working on the aircraft and other exhibits. Star of the show here is a WWII Spitfire Mk IX; other aircraft on display include a

vintage Flying Flea, a DeHavilland Vampire T11, a Fiat G91R and a battered old Douglas Dakota DC-3.

Fomm ir-Riħ

Fomm ir-Riħ (meaning 'mouth of the wind') is the most remote and undeveloped bay on Malta. During rough weather it can be a drab and miserable place, the grey clay slopes and limestone crags merging with the grey clouds and the wave-muddied waters. But on a calm summer's day it can be a beautiful spot, with good swimming and snorkelling in the clear blue waters off the southern cliffs, and few other people to disturb the peace.

It's a long hike to get here – and locals will marvel at any nonlocals who manage to find it! From central Rabat, follow Triq Gheriexem (passing to the left of the Museum of Roman Antiquities) to the roundabout on the edge of town (this can also be reached via the bypass from the roundabout on the Rabat–Mosta road). Follow signs for Baħrija (they're a bit hard to spot). After the roundabout, head left at the first fork and right at the next (Fiddien Bridge), passing Fiddien Reservoir on the right. Continue straight and after about 3km bear left towards Baħrija (signed). After passing through the centre of Baħrija village, fork right, then right again.

About 1.2km from Baħrija's town square the road drops into a valley; you need to turn right on a potholed road indicated by low brick gateposts (but no gate), labelled RTO – this track ends 600m downhill above the southern cliffs of Fomm ir-Riħ. This is best accessed by car – on foot it's an 8km hike (about 1¾ hours) from the bus terminus in Rabat.

But you're not there yet! To reach the head of the bay, you need to follow a precarious footpath across a stream-bed and along a ledge in the cliffs. Locals say that the former Maltese prime minister, Dom Mintoff, used to ride his horse along this path – today posts have been cemented in place to prevent horses and bicycles using it.

From here, you can hike north to the wild cape of Ras il-Pellegrin and down to Ġnejna Bay (p110), or west to Ras ir-Raħeb and south along the top of the coastal cliffs to the tiny village of Mtaħleb and back into Rabat.

FOMM IR-RIĦ BY BOAT

If the directions to Fomm ir-Riħ sound far too complicated, you can take the easy option and view the bay from the water, on a boat trip out of Golden Bay (see p108 for more details).

Ta'Gagin (☎ 21 450 825; mains Lm3.50-5; ☯ dinner nightly, lunch Sun), on the village square in Baħrija, is a good place to sample authentic local dishes, including horse-meat and rabbit – the latter comes with something called 'rabbit sauce', a rich gravy flavoured with juniper berries. This place is well off the tourist trail and allows you to participate in the true Maltese Sunday lunch ritual among the locals.

Dingli Cliffs

Named after the famous Maltese architect Tommaso Dingli (1591–1666) – or possibly his 16th-century English namesake Sir Thomas Dingley, who lived nearby – Dingli is an unremarkable little village. But only 500m to the southwest the land falls away at the spectacular 220m-high **Dingli Cliffs**. A potholed tarmac road runs along the top of the cliffs. There are also some great walks south, past the incongruous radar tower to the lonely little **Chapel of St Mary Magdalene**, built in the 17th century, and onwards to Ta'Żuta (253m) the highest point in the Maltese Islands. Here, you'll enjoy excellent views along the coast to the tiny island of Filfla.

Heading northwest along the cliffs, you'll find **Bobbyland Restaurant** (☎ 21 452 895; mains Lm4-7; ☯ closed lunch Sat, dinner Sun & all day Mon), a friendly place 500m from the Dingli junction. This is a hugely popular weekend venue for locals, and the indoor and outdoor tables are regularly crowded with diners munching contentedly on house specialities like rabbit pan-fried in garlic, onions and herbs, or roast fillet of lamb, wrapped in puff pastry and served with garlic and rosemary sauce. Vegetarians will struggle here.

Bus No 81 runs every half-hour or so from Valletta to Dingli (one way Lm0.18) via Rabat.

Buskett Gardens & Verdala Palace

The fertile valley about 2km south of Rabat (east of Dingli) harbours the only extensive area of woodland in Malta. Known as **Buskett Gardens** (from the Italian *boschetto*, meaning 'little wood'), the gardens were planted by the Knights as a hunting ground. Today they are a hugely popular outing for the Maltese, and the groves of Aleppo pine, oak, olive and orange trees provide shady picnic sites in summer and orange-scented walks in winter. Buskett Gardens is the main venue for the L-Imnarja festival, held on 28 and 29 June (see the boxed text below). The gardens are open at all times and entry is free. Bus No 81 from Valletta to Dingli via Rabat stops at the entrance. Buskett is well signposted from Rabat.

En route to Buskett you'll pass the rather grand **Verdala Palace**, built in 1586 as a summer residence for Grand Master Hugues Loubeux de Verdalle. It was designed by Gerolamo Cassar in the form of a square castle with projecting towers at each corner,

---

THE FESTIVAL OF L-IMNARJA

L-Imnarja (sometimes spelt Mnarja), held on 28 and 29 June (the feast day of Sts Peter and Paul), is Malta's biggest and most boisterous festival. Its origins lie in a harvest festival dedicated to St Paul – the name is a corruption of the Italian *luminaria*, meaning 'illuminations', after the traditional bonfires that once lit up Rabat during the festival.

The festivities begin on 28 June with a huge party in Buskett Gardens, complete with folk music, singing and dancing. Vast quantities of rabbit stew are consumed, washed down with plenty of local wine. The carousing continues well into the small hours and many people end up spending the entire night at Buskett Gardens.

The following day, a public holiday, continues with an agricultural show at Buskett Gardens, where farmers and gardeners exhibit their produce, accompanied by local band performances. In the afternoon, bareback horse and donkey races are held at Saqqajja Hill in Rabat, attended by crowds from all over the island. The winners are awarded with *palji* – colourful banners – which are taken home to adorn the victor's village.

THE RIDDLE OF THE RUTS

One of the biggest mysteries of Malta's prehistoric period is the abundance of so-called 'cart ruts' throughout the islands. In places where bare limestone is exposed, it is often scored with a series of deep parallel grooves, looking for all the world like ruts worn by cart-wheels. But the spacing of the ruts varies, and their depth – up to 60cm – means that wheeled carts would probably get jammed if they tried to use them.

A more likely explanation is that the grooves were created by a travois – a sort of sled formed from two parallel poles joined by a frame and dragged behind a beast of burden, similar to that used by the Plains Indians of North America. The occurrence of the ruts correlates quite closely to the distribution of Bronze Age villages in Malta.

This still leaves the question of what was being transported. Suggestions have included salt and building stone, but it has been argued that whatever the cargo was, it must have been abundant, heavy and well worth the effort involved in moving it. The best suggestion to date is that the mystery substance was topsoil – it was carted from low-lying areas to hillside terraces to increase the area of cultivable land, and so provide food for a growing population.

In some places the ruts are seen to disappear into the sea on one side of a bay, only to re-emerge on the far side. In other spots they seem to disappear off the edge of a cliff. These instances have given rise to all sorts of weird theories, but they are most convincingly explained as the results of long-term erosion and sea-level changes due to earthquakes – the central Mediterranean is a seismically active area and Malta is riddled with geological faults.

Good places to see the ruts include Clapham Junction near Buskett Gardens and the top of the Ta'Ċenċ cliffs on Gozo (see p150).

but this was only for show – it was intended to be a hunting retreat, not a defendable, fortified position. The British used Verdala Palace as the Governor of Malta's summer residence and today it's the summer residence of the Maltese president. It is not open to the public.

Clapham Junction

Just south of Buskett Gardens is a parking area. At its far end the road forks – head left, uphill, for 300m to where a rough track on the right is signposted 'Cart Tracks'. To the right (west) of this track is a large area of sloping limestone pavement, scored with several sets of intersecting prehistoric 'cart ruts' (see the boxed text above). The ruts are about 1.5m apart and up to 50cm deep. The name Clapham Junction – a notoriously complicated railway junction in London – was given to the site by British visitors.

MOSTA

pop 17,430

Mosta is a busy and prosperous town spread across a level plateau atop the Victoria Lines escarpment. It is famous for its Parish Church of Santa Maria, generally better known as the Rotunda or **Mosta Dome** (☎ 21 433 826; Pjazza Rotunda; admission free, donations welcome;

☉ 9-11.45am & 3-5pm), which was designed by the Maltese architect Giorgio Grognet de Vassé and built between 1833 and 1860 using funds raised by the local people. A visit is worthwhile to admire the stunning blue, gold and white interior, and also to check out the bomb that fell through it in 1942 (see the boxed text, p126). Its circular design with a six-columned portico was closely based on the Pantheon in Rome, and the great dome – a prominent landmark visible from most parts of Malta – is said to be one of the broadest unsupported domes in Europe. Its diameter of 39.6m is exceeded only by the Pantheon (43m) and St Peter's (42.1m) in Rome. But dome comparison is a tricky business open to dispute. The parishioners of Xewkija on Gozo claim that their church has a bigger dome than Mosta's – although the Gozitan Rotunda has a smaller diameter (25m), it is higher and has a larger volumetric capacity. So there!

Apart from the church, there's not much else to see in Mosta, but it does make a good starting point for exploring the Victoria Lines (see the boxed text, p101). To reach **Mosta Fort** from the Rotunda, head northwest on Triq il Kostituzzjoni (to the left of the church, facing the portico), cross the bridge over Wied il-Għasel, and turn right

CENTRAL MALTA

THE MIRACLE OF MOSTA

On 9 June 1942, during WWII, three enemy bombs struck the Mosta Dome while around 300 parishioners waited to hear Mass. Two bounced off and landed in the square without exploding. The third pierced the dome, smashed off a wall and rolled across the floor of the church. Miraculously, no one was hurt and the bomb failed to detonate. A replica of the bomb can be seen in the church sacristy.

along Triq il-Fortizza and walk through this quite industrial area. At the end of the street go straight on at the roundabout – the distance from the church to the fort is 2.5km.

At **Pjazza Café** (☎ 21 413 379; Pjazza Rotunda; snacks & meals Lm0.60-5.50) you can enjoy good views of the dome from a table by the window, while downing a light lunch or snack from a menu that includes pastries, salads, burgers, kebabs and pizza. The nearby **Tal-Koppla** (☎ 21 422 880; Pjazza Rotunda; snacks & meals Lm0.40-4.75) is a colourful lunch-time café with good selections, including sandwiches, pasta and a few local dishes such as rabbit stew, octopus stew and *braġioli* (beef slices wrapped around a savoury filling and braised in red wine).

A number of buses pass through Mosta. From Valletta take bus No 47, 49 or 58. From Sliema and St Julian's you can reach Mosta on bus No 65, and from Buġibba and St Paul's take No 86.

NAXXAR
pop 11,150

Naxxar, a couple of kilometres northeast of Mosta (and more-or-less joined by the urban sprawl), is another bustling town worthy of a visit for its few interesting attractions, the highlight of which is the lavish **Palazzo Parisio** (☎ 21 412 461; www.palazzoparisio.com; Pjazza Vittorja; adult/child Lm2.75/free; ☺ tours on the hour 9am-1pm). Originally built in 1733 by Grand Master Antonio Manoel de Vilhena, it was acquired by a Maltese noble family in the late 19th century. The new owners set about refurbishing and redecorating, and the end result was a stately home unique in Malta – the magnificent interior and baroque gardens have been described as a 'miniature Versailles'.

The entrance to the palazzo is directly opposite the **Parish Church of Our Lady**, one of the tallest baroque edifices on Malta. Construction was started in the early years of the 16th century according to the designs of Vittorio Cassar (son of the more famous Gerolamo Cassar, who designed Verdala Palace, p124).

To get to Naxxar, take bus No 55 or 56 from Valletta (one way Lm0.15).

THE THREE VILLAGES

The main road from Valletta to Mosta passes through the town of Birkirkara, one of the biggest population centres on the island (population 21,700), and part of the huge conurbation that encircles Valletta and the Three Cities. Birkirkara's **Church of St Helen** is probably the most ornate of Malta's churches, a late flowering of baroque exuberance built in the mid-18th century. On the strength of his performance here, the designer, Domenico Cachia, was given the job of designing the façade of the Auberge de Castile in Valletta.

Just west of Birkirkara is an upmarket suburban area known as the Three Villages, centred on the medieval settlements of **Attard**, **Balzan** and **Lija**. Although modern development has fused the three into a continuous urban sprawl, the old village centres still retain their parish churches and narrow streets, and there are some interesting historical sites to visit.

Triq il-Mdina, the main road which skirts the southern edge of Attard, follows the line of the **Wignacourt Aqueduct**, built between 1610 and 1614 to improve the water supply to Valletta. Substantial lengths of the ancient structure still stand beside the road. The **Church of St Mary** (Pjazza Tommaso Dingli) in Attard, designed by Tommaso Dingli and built around the same time as the aqueduct, is one of the finest Renaissance churches on the island (see the boxed text, p38). Lija's **Church of St Saviour** (Misrah it-Trasfigurazzjoni), designed in 1694, is the focus of one of Malta's liveliest festas, famed for its spectacular fireworks, on 6 August.

The main attraction in this area is **San Anton Palace & Gardens** (Palace closed to public; gardens entry on Triq Birkirkara; admission free; ☺ dawn-dusk) which lies between Attard and Lija. The palace was built in the early 17th century as the country mansion of Grand Master Antoine de Paule. It later served as the official residence of the British Governor of Malta, and is now the official residence of the Maltese president. The lovely walled gardens stretch between the palace and the main entrance on Triq Birkirkara, and contain groves of citrus and avocado, as well as a magnificent old fig tree. The Eagle Fountain, just inside the main gate, dates from the 1620s. The Mask Fountain is surrounded by unusual floss-silk trees with thick, thorn-studded trunks and beautiful pink flowers.

To get to San Anton Gardens, take bus No 40 from Valletta.

Sleeping & Eating

University Residence (☎ 21 436 168 or 21 430 360; www.university-residence.com.mt; Triq R M Bonnici, Lija; dm from Lm3.20/5.50 low/high season; 🖳 🖳) About 200m north of San Anton Gardens is the official student residence for the University of Malta. It's a well-equipped and well-run facility, and a good place to meet a mixture of travellers and local and international students. It can sleep a few hundred students and is in a fairly residential area. There are tennis courts, large grounds, a minimarket, café and laundrette. There's a three-night minimum on stays and a variety of very good accommodation available (including hotel-standard rooms – see the website). To get here, catch bus No 40 from Valletta.

Corinthia Palace Hotel (☎ 21 440 301; www.corinthiahotels.com; Vjal de Paule, Attard; s/d incl breakfast Lm75/100; 🔀 🖳 🖳) On the other side of San Anton Gardens, and at the other end of the accommodation spectrum to the uni residence, the five-star Corinthia Palace is sufficiently luxurious and elegant to entertain the entourages of foreign dignitaries visiting the president of Malta. Facilities include a health spa, landscaped gardens, indoor and outdoor pools, and a bistro, plus two fine restaurants (one serving Asian food). There are often good deals available on room rates – it pays to ask.

You can buy drinks and ice creams for your garden stroll from the kiosk beside the entrance to the San Anton Gardens. Also near the entrance is a casual restaurant-bar, **Il-Melita** (☎ 21 441 077; mains Lm2-5), serving up the usual suspects (pizza, pasta, chicken etc) nightly. A better option of an evening is to frock up a little and visit one of the restaurants at the Corinthia Palace Hotel.

Southeast Malta

CONTENTS

Much of Malta's industry is located in the southeast of the country, and the unattractive power station and port machinery located here have no doubt resulted in considerably less tourist development compared to the rest of the island. This also contributes to the feeling that, as with Italy (but on a much, much smaller scale), it is the south in Malta that is the working-class 'poor relation' of the more prosperous north.

Marsaskala is the only place in the southeast that could be described as a holiday resort, and it tends to be more popular with the Maltese than with foreign holiday-makers. But visitors to Malta would be unwise to dismiss the region and concentrate their sightseeing efforts elsewhere: several of Malta's most interesting historical sites are to be found in the south, including two impressive temples (Ħaġar Qim and Mnajdra) dating back over 5000 years, and the Għar Dalam cave, full of fossilised remains of prehistoric animals. There is some excellent coastal scenery with boat trips available to visit grottoes, plus enticing swimming spots well off the tourist track. Another highlight is the old fishing village of Marsaxlokk, with a harbour full of colourful boats and a waterfront lined with restaurants specialising in fresh fish. A day or so spent exploring the south brings a number of rewards; alternatively, most of the attractions in this chapter are accessible as day trips by bus from Valletta.

HIGHLIGHTS

- Watching the sunrise from mysterious **Mnajdra Temple** (p136)
- Eating a well-prepared fish meal by the colourful **Marsaxlokk harbour** (p134)
- Cruising the caves and grottoes on a boat from **Wied iż-Żurrieq** (p135)
- Hiking along the coast between **Wied iż-Żurrieq** and **Għar Lapsi** (p137)
- Enjoying lunch and a swim with the locals at **Għar Lapsi** (p138)

Marsaxlokk ★

Għar Lapsi ★ Mnajdra Temple ★ ★ Wied iż–Żurrieq

SOUTHEAST MALTA

SOUTHEAST MALTA

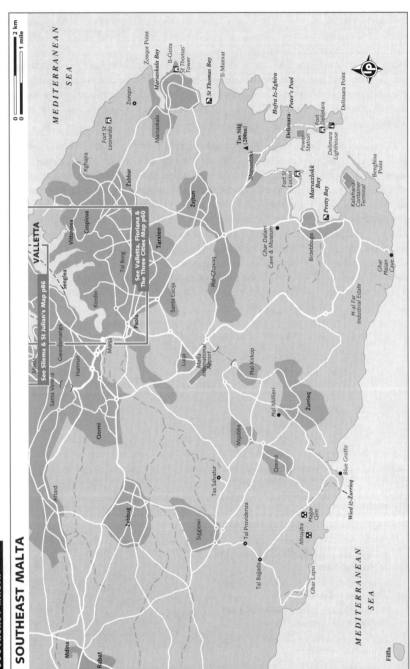

SOUTHEAST MALTA

MEDITERRANEAN SEA

Zonqor Point
Marsaskala Bay
Il-Gżira
St Thomas' Tower
St Thomas Bay
Il-Munxar
Zonqor
Marsaskala
Fort St Leonardo
Xgħajra
Żabbar
Tas Silġ (200m)
Marsaxlokk
Hofra tz-Żgħira
Peter's Pool
Delimara
Fort Delimara
Delimara Point
Power Station
Delimara Lighthouse
Benghisa Point
Żejtun
Fort St Lucjan
Marsaxlokk Bay
Pretty Bay
Kalafrana Container Terminal
Vittoriosa
Cospicua
VALLETTA
Tarxien
Senglea
Tal Borg
Kordin
Paola
See Sliema & St Julian's Map p86
See Valletta, Floriana & The Three Cities Map p60
Santa Luċija
Ħal-Ghaxaq
Ghar Dalam Cave & Museum
Birżebbuġa
Ghar Hasan Cave
Msida
Marsa
Gwardamanġa
Ħamrun
Santa Venera
Luqa
Malta International Airport
Ħal-Kirkop
Ħal Millieri
Żurrieq
Ħal Far Industrial Estate
Qormi
Mqabba
Qrendi
Blue Grotto
Attard
Tas Salvatur
Wied iż-Żurrieq
Żebbuġ
Siġġiewi
Mnajdra
Hagar Qim
Tal Providenza
Tal Bajjada
Ghar Lapsi
Mdina
Rabat
MEDITERRANEAN SEA
Filfla

0   2 km
0   1 mile

MARSASKALA

pop 5420

Marsaskala, gathered around the head of its long, narrow bay, was originally a Sicilian fishing community (the name means 'Sicilian Harbour'). Today it is an increasingly popular residential area and seaside resort, especially among the Maltese.

Orientation & Information

The Triq ix-Xatt promenade is the focus of the town and where most of the restaurants and cafés are to be found. The bus terminus is on Triq Sant'Antnin at the southern end of the promenade. On the north side of the bay, Triq iż-Żonqor goes past the Church of St Anne, with its distinctive Italianate campanile, to Żonqor Point, where a swimming pool and water polo stadium is located. Triq is-Salini, on the south side of the bay, leads to the headland of il-Gżira, where St Thomas' Tower and the Corinthia Jerma Palace Hotel are to be found.

Midas (Triq ix-Xatt) is a shop on the waterfront (a few doors from Sottovoce restaurant) that sells phonecards, souvenirs and acts as a post office. There's an **ATM** (cnr Triq il-Qaliet & Triq Tal-Gardiel) by the entry to Jakarta restaurant. **MelitaNet** (☎ 21 636 429; Pjazza Mifsud Bonnici; per hr Lm1; ☽ 11am-11pm) is a central Internet café that also offers cheap rates for overseas calls. It's a little tricky to find, hidden around the corner from Country Style.

Sights

Marsaskala is not big on sights or tourist attractions. The main activities are hanging out in cafés and bars along the waterfront, strolling along the promontory and fishing in the harbour. **St Thomas' Tower**, on the southern point of the bay, is a small fort that was built by the Knights of St John after a Turkish raiding party landed in Marsaskala Bay in 1614 and plundered the nearby village of Żejtun. The tower is closed to the public.

St Thomas Bay is a deeply indented – and deeply unattractive – bay to the south of Marsaskala, lined with concrete and breeze-block huts and a dirty, potholed road. There's a sandy beach of sorts, and the place is popular with local people and windsurfers. It's about a 10-minute walk from Marsaskala along Triq Tal-Gardiel (past the Sun City Cinema Complex). From St Thomas Bay you can continue walking along the coast to Marsaxlokk (about 4km).

Activities

There are a couple of dive operators in town that can help you explore the excellent nearby dive sites (p50), including **Aqua Bubbles Diving School** (☎ 21 639 292; www.aquabubbles.co.uk; Dawret it-Torri), based at the Corinthia Jerma Palace Hotel; and **Dive Med** (☎ 21 639 981; www.divemed.com; Iż-Żonqor), out near the water polo stadium at Żonqor Point.

Sleeping

The accommodation scene in Marsaskala is dominated by private self-catering apartments, but there are a couple of other options.

Summer Nights Guesthouse (☎ 21 637 956; m.cutajar@nextgen.net.mt; Triq ix-Xatt; s/d Lm8/10) Good-value rooms are on offer at this central, high-quality guesthouse in the heart of the town's action (there's a restaurant and pub downstairs). Rooms have private bathroom, fan, TV and fridge (some have kitchenette), and all have a balcony with sea view.

At the time of research the **Etvan Hotel** (Triq il-Bahhara) was about to close for extensive refurbishment and was not expected to reopen until possibly late 2005.

Charian Hotel (☎ 21 636 392; www.charianhotel.com; Triq is-Salini; d incl breakfast Lm12/16 low/high season) The Charian is an affordable, well-maintained two-star hotel about 600m from the centre. Rooms here are small but well equipped, with ceiling fan, TV and balcony (most with sea view), and there's a rooftop terrace with Jacuzzi, plus friendly management.

Corinthia Jerma Palace Hotel (☎ 21 633 222; www.corinthiahotels.com; Dawret it-Torri; s/d from Lm30/44 low season, Lm35/50 high season; ⊠ ▯ ▣) This huge, four-star hotel complex has 326 decent rooms and dominates the southern headland of Marsaskala Bay, about 1.5km from the centre of town. There are two restaurants, indoor and outdoor pools, a gym, an outdoor terrace filled with sun lounges, and the opportunity for loads of water sports, including diving. There are often special deals on the rack rates listed here.

Eating & Drinking

There are some very good dining options in Marsaskala.

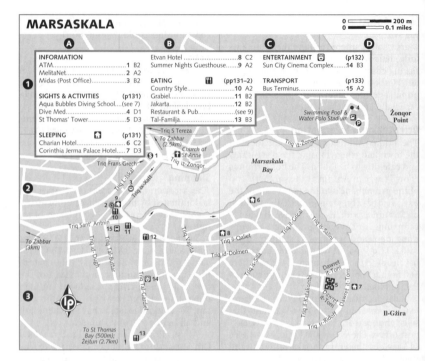

MARSASKALA

0   200 m
0   0.1 miles

INFORMATION
ATM..**1** B2
MelitaNet..............................**2** A2
Midas (Post Office)...............**3** B2

SIGHTS & ACTIVITIES (p131)
Aqua Bubbles Diving School....(see 7)
Dive Med................................**4** D1
St Thomas' Tower....................**5** D3

SLEEPING (p131)
Charian Hotel.........................**6** C2
Corinthia Jerma Palace Hotel...**7** D3

Etvan Hotel............................**8** C2
Summer Nights Guesthouse......**9** A2

EATING (pp131–2)
Country Style.........................**10** A2
Grabiel..................................**11** B2
Jakarta..................................**12** B2
Restaurant & Pub...................(see 9)
Tal-Familja............................**13** B3

ENTERTAINMENT (p132)
Sun City Cinema Complex........**14** B3

TRANSPORT (p133)
Bus Terminus.........................**15** A2

Grabiel (☎ 21 634 194; Pjazza Mifsud Bonnici; mains Lm5-6; ⏱ lunch & dinner Mon-Sat) Behind its unassuming façade (and in an unlikely location next to the bus stop) is one of Malta's most highly regarded restaurants. On offer are carefully crafted meat and seafood dishes. Choose from beef stroganoff, steak fillet, rabbit or prawns – or you can't go wrong choosing the fresh fish of the day. A favourite for business lunches and special-occasion dinners, bookings are advised if you want to see what all the fuss is about.

Jakarta (☎ 21 633 993; Triq Tal-Gardiel; mains Lm2.80-5.75; ⏱ dinner nightly, lunch Sun) Despite its name, Jakarta offers mostly Malaysian and Chinese cuisine from an extensive menu of meat and seafood dishes, as well as decent selections for vegetarians. Choose from the likes of crispy duck, Singapore noodles, wonton soup or green or red curry chicken. There are good-value set menus from Lm6.75 per person.

Tal-Familja (☎ 21 632 161; Triq Tal-Gardiel; mains Lm2-7; ⏱ lunch & dinner Tue-Sun) Another local favourite is Tal-Familja, away from the town centre (about 300m past the cinema) and offering

an attractive outdoor dining area. There are pasta and risotto dishes (spaghetti with rabbit, risotto pescatore) for around Lm2.50, plus lots of meat and seafood options (swordfish, octopus, calamari). Try the fresh fish à la Maltese – fish grilled and served in a green pepper, eggplant and tomato sauce.

For fast food, try **Country Style** at the southern end of the promenade. It has a simple selection of soups, sandwiches, doughnuts, cakes and coffee, and there's a playground outside where you can keep an eye on the kids.

There are a number of options on the promenade for sitting with a beer and just watching the world go by. There are several kebab and pasta places for a quick bite, and café-bars that liven up of an evening. **Summer Nights** (☎ 21 637 956; Triq ix-Xatt) has a bustling restaurant and English-style pub, plus a big screen for televising sports matches.

Entertainment
The five-screen **Sun City Cinema Complex** (☎ 21 632 857/8; Triq Tal-Gardiel) shows first-run films. Tickets are Lm2.50.

MALTESE BOATS

The brightly coloured fishing boats that crowd the harbours around the coast have become one of Malta's national symbols. Painted boldly in blue, red and yellow, with the watchful 'Eyes of Osiris' on the bows to ward off evil spirits, they are unmistakably Maltese. The harbour at Marsaxlokk is famous for its colourful vista of moored fishing boats.

There are different kinds of traditional Maltese vessel. The *luzzu* (*loots*-zoo) is a large double-ended fishing boat (for nonsailors, that means it's pointed at both ends). The *kajjik* (*ka*-yik) is similar in appearance, but has a square transom (it's pointed at the front end only). The *dgħajsa* (*dye*-sa) is a smaller and racier-looking boat, with very high stem and stern-posts – a bit like a Maltese gondola. These are not solid, seaworthy fishing boats, but sleek water taxis. A flotilla of *dgħajsas* was once used to carry passengers back and forth between Valletta and the Three Cities. They were powered by oars, but today's *dgħajsas* – used mainly for tourist trips – generally carry an outboard engine. Local enthusiasts maintain – and race – a small fleet of oar-driven vessels. The waterfront at Vittoriosa and Senglea is the best place to admire these classic boats.

Getting There & Away

Bus Nos 19 and 20 run regularly from Valletta to Marsaskala (one way Lm0.15).

MARSAXLOKK

pop 3000

Despite the encroachment of modern industry, the ancient fishing village of Marsaxlokk (marsa-shlock; from *marsa scirocco*, meaning 'southeasterly harbour') at the head of Marsaxlokk Bay remains resolutely a slice of real Maltese life, and attracts a number of camera-toting day-trippers. Old, low-rise houses ring the town's waterfront, and a fleet of brightly coloured *luzzu* (fishing boats; see the boxed text above) dance in the harbour. Men with weathered faces sit by the waterside mending nets and grumbling about the tax on diesel, while others scrape, paint and saw as they ready their boats for the sea.

The daily market on the waterfront sells mainly tourist tat aimed at the tour groups, who regularly sally forth from their buses for a lunch-time shopping break. Far more interesting is the **Sunday Fish Market**, where you can admire the riches of the Med before they're whisked off to Malta's top hotels and restaurants. It starts early in the morning and the best stuff is long gone by afternoon.

Marsaxlokk Bay is Malta's second natural harbour. It was here that the Turkish fleet was moored during the Great Siege of 1565 (p24), and Napoleon's army landed here during the French invasion of 1798 (p28). In the 1930s the calm waters of the bay were used as a staging post by the huge, four-engined Short C-Class flying boats of Britain's Imperial Airways as they pioneered long-distance air travel to the far-flung corners of the Empire. During WWII Marsaxlokk Bay was the base for the Fleet Air Arm, and in 1989 the famous summit meeting between Soviet and US presidents Mikhail Gorbachev and George Bush (senior) was held on board a warship anchored in Marsaxlokk Bay. Today the harbour is framed by the fuel tanks and chimney of a power station and the huge cranes of the Kalafrana Container Terminal – eyesores that will probably prevent any serious tourist development.

Delimara Point, southeast of Marsaxlokk, is blighted by a huge power station whose chimney can be seen for miles around, but there are a few good swimming places on the eastern side of the peninsula. **Peter's Pool** is the best, a natural lido in the rocks with large areas of flat slab for sunbathing between swims. Follow the narrow, potholed road out towards Delimara Lighthouse until you are practically under the power station chimney, and you will see a low building on the left with 'Peter's Pool' signposted on it. A sump-crunchingly rough track leads down to a parking area. Don't leave anything in your car – this is a favourite spot for thieves.

The road to Delimara passes **Tas Silġ**, where archaeologists have uncovered a Punic-Roman temple. This may be the famous Temple of Juno that was plundered by Verres, the Roman Governor of Sicily and Malta in 70 BC, as recorded in the writings of Cicero. Unfortunately the site is locked

SOUTHEAST MALTA

up and open only by appointment. To arrange a visit, phone ☎ 21 222 966 or contact info@heritagemalta.org.

South of Marsaxlokk, on the road to Birżebbuġa, is **Fort St Lucian**, built in 1610 to protect the bay. Today it houses a naval college and the offices of a government fish farm.

Sleeping & Eating

The only accommodation available in Marsaxlokk is at **Golden Sun Aparthotel** (☎ 21 651 762; www.goldensunhotelmalta.com; Triq il-Kajjik; r per person incl breakfast Lm6.50-8.50, apt per person Lm5-6.50; 🗩), two blocks back from the harbour in the northern part of town. You can choose from hotel rooms or self-catering apartments. Décor is very dated but the apartments are spotless and well equipped.

Good-quality restaurants line the harbour; most offer alfresco dining and, not surprisingly, fish features heavily on all menus. There are some casual places geared to tourists, plus more upmarket selections. Marsaxlokk is a favourite location for the Maltese to enjoy Sunday lunch among family and friends.

Ir-Rizzu (☎ 21 651 569; 89 Xatt is-Sajjieda; mains Lm2-6.50; ⏰ lunch & dinner) This is among the best upmarket eating options in town. Here you can select a variety of fresh fish (many priced according to weight) and have your choice cooked in the traditional Maltese way, steamed with tomatoes, onions, garlic and herbs. There's also lampuki, octopus or stuffed calamari, king prawns and lobster, and pasta and risotto with seafood and nonseafood sauces.

If you can't get in to Ir-Rizzu, never fear – two doors down is **La Campanna** (☎ 21 657 755; 80 Xatt is-Sajjieda; mains Lm2.50-6.50; ⏰ lunch & dinner), another great choice with similar fish and pasta selections. And in the middle of these two is **Ron's Restaurant** (☎ 21 650 382; Xatt is-Sajjieda; mains Lm2-6; ⏰ lunch & dinner), with outdoor tables for a casual drink or light snack, or a more formal upstairs dining area with funky blue walls, stylish décor, a great view over the boat-filled harbour and a menu of seafood favourites (try the tasty fish soup).

Getting There & Away

Bus No 27 runs every half-hour from Valletta to Marsaxlokk from around 6.30am to

---

ANY WAY THE WIND BLOWS

In Malti, the points of the compass are mostly named for the winds that blow from that direction. These are versions of the old Latin names used by Roman sailors.

North	Tramuntana
Northeast	Grigal
East	Lvant
Southeast	Xlokk
South	Nofs in-Nhar
Southwest	Lbiċ
West	Punent
Northwest	Majjistral

Xlokk is the Maltese equivalent of the Italian scirocco, both of which derive from the Arabic word *sharq,* meaning 'east.' The *xlokk* is a hot, humid and oppressive wind that blows from the southeast, usually in spring, bringing misty conditions to the island. It derives its heat from the Sahara Desert and picks up its humidity passing over the sea. The *tramuntana,* from the Italian for 'across the mountains', is the cold northerly wind from the direction of the Alps. The northeasterly *grigal* is the typical winter wind that batters the rocky coast of Malta, and makes for an uncomfortable ferry crossing to Gozo, while the northwesterly *majjistral* is the stiff sailing breeze of summer afternoons, the equivalent of the Turkish *meltem.*

9pm (services are more frequent on Sunday morning for the fish market). Tickets cost Lm0.15 one way. Bus No 627 runs hourly until 3pm from Buġibba via Sliema to Marsaxlokk (one way Lm0.40).

BIRŻEBBUĠA

pop 7650

Birżebbuġa (beer-zeb-*boo*-ja, meaning 'well of the olives') lies on the western shore of Marsaxlokk Bay. It began life as a fishing village, but today it's a dormitory town for workers from the nearby Malta Freeport. The misleadingly named **Pretty Bay** lies at the southern end of town. Although it has a pleasant sandy beach, it also has a wonderful view of the Kalafrana Container Terminal, only 500m away across the water.

There's little to see in town, but just 500m north on the main road from Valletta is the **Għar Dalam Cave & Museum** (☎ 21 657 419; adult/child Lm1/free; ☼ 7.45am-2pm daily mid-Jun–Sep, 8.15am-5pm Mon-Sat and 8.15am-4pm Sun Oct–mid-June, closed public holidays). Għar Dalam (aar-da-*lam*; the name means 'cave of darkness') is a 145m-long cave in the Lower Coralline Limestone (for more on this formation see p42). It has yielded a magnificent harvest of fossil bones and teeth belonging to dwarf elephants, hippopotamuses and deer – an estimated total of over 7000 animals – which lived between 180,000 and 18,000 years ago. The animals are all of European type, suggesting that Malta was once joined to Italy, but not to northern Africa.

The revamped museum at the entrance contains a new exhibition hall with displays on how the cave was formed, and how the remains of such animals came to be found here, plus how these animals adapted to new conditions. In the older part of the museum are display cases mounted with thousands and thousands of bones and teeth. It's not hugely interesting unless you're a palaeontologist, but impressive in terms of sheer numbers. Beyond the museum a path leads down through attractive gardens to the mouth of the cave, where a walkway leads 50m into the cavern. A pillar of sediment has been left in the middle of the excavated floor to show the stratigraphic sequence.

On the cliff-bound coastline south of Birżebbuġa lies another cave, **Għar Ħasan Cave** (admission free; ☼ always open). Follow the road towards Żurrieq, then turn left on a minor road that ends at an industrial estate (there are plenty of signposts). The cave entrance is down some steps in the cliff-face to the left; there is usually an enterprising local in the car parking area out the front with torches for hire (Lm0.30) to help you find your way inside the cave. The 'Cave of Ħasan' is supposed to have been used as a hide-out by a 12th-century Saracen rebel. With a torch you can follow a passage off to the right to a 'window' in the cliff-face.

To get to Għar Dalam and Birżebbuġa, take bus No 11 from Valletta. The cave museum is on the right-hand side of the road at a small, semicircular parking area 500m short of Birżebbuġa – look out for it as it's not well signposted. There is no public transport to Għar Ħasan – it's a 2.5km walk south of Birżebbuġa.

ŻURRIEQ
pop 9000

The village of Żurrieq sprawls across a hillside on the south coast, in a sort of no-man's-land to the south of the airport. This part of Malta feels cut off from the rest of the island, and although it's only 10km from Valletta as the crow flies, it seems much further. If you come by car, be prepared to get lost a couple of times.

The **parish church of St Catherine** was built in the 1630s and houses a fine altarpiece of St Catherine – painted by Mattia Preti in 1675, when the artist took refuge here during a plague epidemic – and there are several 17th- and 18th-century windmills dotted about the village. On a minor road between Żurrieq and Mqabba is the **Chapel of the Annunciation** in the deserted medieval settlement of Ħal Millieri. This tiny, plain church, set in a pretty garden, dates from the mid-15th century and contains important 15th-century frescoes. Both church and garden are normally locked, but are open to the public from 9.30am to noon on the first Sunday of each month. Telephone the chapel warden on ☎ 21 680 078 or ☎ 21 310 239 to confirm these times or to possibly arrange an alternative time for viewing.

About 2km west of Żurrieq lies the tiny harbour of **Wied iż-Żurrieq**, set in a narrow inlet in the cliffs and guarded by a watchtower. Here boats depart for enjoyable 30-minute cruises to the **Blue Grotto**, a huge natural arch in the sea cliffs 400m to the east. The boat trips take in about seven caves, including the Honeymoon Cave, Reflection Cave and Cat's Cave. The best time is before mid-morning, when the sun is shining into the grotto. **Boat trips** (☎ 21 640 058 or 21 649 925; adult/child Lm2.50/1.25) on small boats (up to eight passengers) depart from 9am to around 4pm daily, weather permitting (trips are less likely to run from December to February). If there is any doubt about the weather or sea conditions, call to check. You can see the Blue Grotto without a boat from a viewing platform beside the main road, just east of the turn-off to Wied iż-Żurrieq.

There are several souvenir shops and restaurants above the harbour in Wied iż-Żurrieq. The restaurants all offer similar menus of snacks, fish, rabbit, pasta, salads etc. **Congreve Channel Restaurant** (☎ 21 647 928; mains Lm2.50-6) is a down-to-earth place offering king prawns, shellfish and swordfish at the higher end of the price range, and jacket potatoes, simple pasta and salad meals at the lower end. If you like the décor in your eateries to be a little more elegant than vinyl chairs and wipe-clean tablecloths, head to nearby **Tax-Xiha** (☎ 21 680 684; mains Lm3-6), with seating on three levels (including a rooftop terrace with good water views).

Bus Nos 38 and 138 run from Valletta to Żurrieq and Wied iż-Żurrieq (on a circular route that also includes Ħaġar Qim and Mnajdra temples) every 30 minutes or so from 9.20am to 4.15pm. Tickets are Lm0.40 one way.

ĦAĠAR QIM & MNAJDRA
The megalithic temples of Ħaġar Qim (*adge*-ar eem – meaning 'standing stones') and Mnajdra (mm-*nigh*-dra) are perhaps the best preserved and most evocative of Malta's prehistoric sites, especially at dawn or sunset when the ancient stones are tinged pink and gold by the rising or setting sun. The temples are fenced off and the gates will be locked at these times but it's worth the effort, especially around the time of the winter solstice (21 December) when you can check out some of the supposed solar alignments.

It costs Lm1 to visit just one temple, Lm2 to visit both – but it's disappointing to find that there are no information boards provided by the authorities to explain a little about these temples and what makes them so remarkable. You might consider purchasing a booklet from the ticket office called *The Copper Age Temples of Ħaġar Qim and Mnajdra* by Professor Themistocles Zammit (Lm1) to help you get more from your visit and better understand these structures.

Ħaġar Qim (☎ 21 424 231; adult/child Lm1/free; ⏰ 7.45am-2pm daily mid-Jun–Sep, 8.15am-5pm Mon-Sat & 8.15am-4pm Sun Oct–mid-Jun, closed public holidays) is right next to the parking area. The façade, with its trilithon entrance, has been restored, rather too obviously, but gives an idea of what it may once have looked like. The temples were originally roofed over, but the wooden structures have long since rotted away.

Before going in, look round the corner to the right – the megalith here is the largest in the temple, and weighs more than 20 tonnes. The temple consists of a series of interconnected, oval chambers with no uniform arrangement, and differs from other Maltese temples in lacking a regular trefoil plan. In the first chamber on the left you will see a little altar post decorated with plant motifs, and in the second there are a couple of pedestal altars. The 'fat lady' statuettes and the so-called 'Venus of Malta' figurine that were found here are on display in the National Museum of Archaeology in Valletta (p66).

Mnajdra (☎ 21 424 231; adult/child Lm1/free; ⏰ 7.45am-2pm daily mid-June–Sep, 8.15am-5pm Mon-Sat

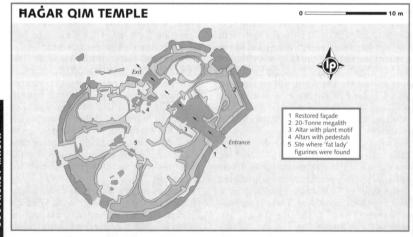

ĦAĠAR QIM TEMPLE

0 ⸺ 10 m

Exit

Entrance

1 Restored façade
2 20-Tonne megalith
3 Altar with plant motif
4 Altars with pedestals
5 Site where 'fat lady' figurines were found

MEGALITHIC TEMPLES

The megalithic temples of Malta, which date mainly from the period 3600 to 3000 BC, are the oldest freestanding stone structures in the world. They pre-date the pyramids of Egypt by more than 500 years.

The oldest surviving temples are thought to be those of Ta'Ħaġrat and Skorba (p109) near the village of Mġarr on Malta. Ġgantija (p156) on Gozo, and Ħagar Qim and Mnajdra (p136) on Malta are among the best preserved. Tarxien is the most developed, its last phase dating from 3000 to 2500 BC. The subterranean tombs of the Hypogeum date from the same period as the temples and mimic many of their architectural features.

The purpose of these mysterious structures is the subject of much debate. They all share certain features in common – a site on a southeasterly slope, near to caves, a spring and fertile farmland; a trefoil or cloverleaf plan with three or five rounded chambers (apses) opening off the central axis, which usually faces between south and east; megalithic construction, using blocks of stone weighing up to 20 tonnes; and holes and sockets drilled into the stones, perhaps to hold wooden doors or curtains. Most temple sites have also revealed spherical stones, about the size of cannonballs – it has been suggested that these were used like ball bearings to move the heavy megaliths more easily over the ground.

No burials have been found in any of the temples, but most have yielded statues and figurines of so-called 'fat ladies' – possibly fertility goddesses. Most have some form of decoration on the stone, ranging from simple pitting to the elaborate spirals and carved animals seen at Tarxien. There are also 'oracle holes' – small apertures in the chamber walls which may have been used by priests or priestesses to issue divinations. The temples' southeasterly orientation has suggested a relationship to the winter solstice sunrise, and one amateur investigator has put forward a convincing theory of solar alignment (see the website www.geocities.com/maltatemples/).

& 8.15am-4pm Sun Oct–mid-Jun, closed public holidays), a 500m walk downhill from Ħaġar Qim, is more interesting. There are three temples side by side, each with a trefoil plan and each with a different orientation. The oldest temple is the small one on the right, which is aligned towards the southwest and Filfla island. The central temple, pointing towards the southeast, is the youngest. All date from between 3600 and 3000 BC.

It has been claimed that the southern temple is full of significant solar alignments. At sunrise during the winter solstice, a beam of sunlight illuminates the altar to the right of the inner doorway. At sunrise during the summer solstice, a sunbeam penetrates the window in the back of the left-hand apse to the pedestal altar in the left rear chamber. In the right-hand apse there is a separate chamber entered through a small doorway, with a so-called 'oracle hole' to its left. The function of this is unknown.

On the cliff top to the southeast of Mnajdra is a 17th-century watchtower and a memorial to Sir Walter Congreve (Governor of Malta 1924–27) who was buried at sea off this point. You can hike east along the cliffs towards Wied iż-Żurrieq and the

Blue Grotto (p135), or west to Għar Lapsi (p137). The tiny uninhabited island **Filfla**, 8km offshore, is clearly visible. It suffered the ignominy of being used for target practice by the British armed forces until it was declared a nature reserve in 1970. It supports important breeding colonies of seabirds, including an estimated 10,000 pairs of storm-petrels, and a unique species of lizard. Landing on the island is forbidden.

Ħaġar Qim Restaurant (☎ 99 437 329; mains Lm2-5; 🕑 closed Mon), above the car park, serves the usual suspects (pizza, pasta, Maltese specialities). There's an outdoor terrace and an uninspiring view of the scruffy garden and the car park – you're better off heading to either the Blue Grotto or Għar Lapsi for more variety and better panoramas.

Bus Nos 38 and 138 run from Valletta to Ħaġar Qim and Mnajdra (on a circular route that also includes Wied iż-Żurrieq) every 30 minutes or so from 9.20am to 4.15pm. Tickets cost Lm0.40 one way.

GĦAR LAPSI

On the road west of the temples is a turn-off (signposted) to Għar Lapsi. The name means 'Cave of the Ascension', and there was once a fishermen's shrine here. The road winds steeply to the coast and ends at a car park beside a couple of restaurants and boathouses. The main attraction here is the swimming – a little cove in the low limestone cliffs has been converted into a natural lido, with stone steps and iron ladders giving access to the limpid blue water. It's a popular spot for bathing and picnicking among locals, and also well frequented by divers and fishermen.

To sate a swimmer's hunger, there are two contrasting restaurants above the cove. The 60-year-old **Lapsi View** (☎ 21 640 608; snacks & meals Lm0.50-6; ☹ daily) is housed in a somewhat crumbling blue building that looks a little worse for wear, but inside it's a taste of retro-Malta, with much of the original furniture still in place. There's a good menu catering to both tourists and locals, with omelettes,

burgers, sandwiches, salads and pizzas, plus rabbit, steak, lampuki and stewed octopus. If you're after a more modern dining experience, **Blue Creek** (☎ 21 462 786; snacks & meals Lm1-9; ☹ daily) is a slick new restaurant with an outdoor terrace directly above the water. It offers snacks and takeaway sandwiches, pasta and risotto dishes, and mains including fresh fish, king prawns, rabbit stew and even fillet of kangaroo or ostrich steak.

Getting to Għar Lapsi without a car is tricky. For hikers, there is a footpath along the 3km stretch of cliff top between Għar Lapsi, Ħaġar Qim and the Blue Grotto. For public transport users, the town of Siġġiewi is about 4km north of Għar Lapsi; and bus No 94 shuttles infrequently between the two points on Thursday and Sunday from July to September only. The alternative is to hike each way from Siġġiewi (bus No 89 runs from Valletta to Siġġiewi).

Gozo

CONTENTS

It would almost be a crime to visit Malta and not make it out to Gozo. A day trip won't allow enough time to sample this tiny island's treasures, however. It's well worth scheduling at least a few days here, or indeed making Gozo the primary focus of your trip to Malta, especially if you're after a relaxing getaway.

Gozo, called Għawdex (*aow*-desh) in Malti, provides soothing respite from the crowded resorts and manic drivers of Malta. Although it is more than one-third the size of its larger sister to the south, it has less than one-tenth of the population – only about 30,000 Gozitans live here (and they are Gozitans first, Maltese second).

Farming and fishing are the main activities. The land is more fertile, the scenery is greener (without the industry that blights some of Malta's landscapes), and the pace of life is much slower than in Malta. Despite all this (or perhaps because of it), for the holiday-maker Gozo has an air of exclusivity about it – and perhaps all the five-star hotels, luxuriously converted farmhouses and high-quality restaurants also have something to do with it.

The island offers good walking, superb coastal scenery and some of the best scuba diving in Europe, plus attractions like the megalithic temple of Ġgantija and Victoria's medieval citadel (a miniature version of Malta's Mdina). If you're looking for action-packed nightlife you'll be disappointed, but if you're interested in a chance to walk, swim, dive and snorkel, plus enjoy warm hospitality and see how the rest of Malta must have been before the advent of mass tourism, you're in luck.

In this chapter Gozo's main town, Victoria, is described first, then Mġarr, the main harbour. The rest of the island is covered in a clockwise direction from Mġarr.

There are some very good websites about Gozo. If you're looking for more information while planning your trip, try www.gozo.com or www.gozo.gov.mt (click on 'tourism'). And while you're in this part of Malta, consider slipping across to Comino for some swimming and snorkelling at the stunning Blue Lagoon (p158).

HIGHLIGHTS

- Exploring the ramparts of **Il-Kastell** (p142) and admiring the great views of the island
- Pondering the purpose of the **Ġgantija temples** (p156) in Xagħra
- Hiking the scenic coastline at **Dwejra** (p152) or **Ta'Ċenċ** (p149)
- Snorkelling at **Wied il-Għasri** (p153) and at Comino's **Blue Lagoon** (p158)
- Enjoying the stunning view from the terrace of Mġarr's **Xerri Il-Bukkett Restaurant** (p148)

GOZO & COMINO

0 ———— 2 km
0 ———— 1 mile

Labels on map:
San Dimitri Point
San Dimitri Church
Wied il-Għasri
Gordan Lighthouse
Salt Pans
Xwieni Bay
Salt Pans
Zebbuġ
Qbajjar
Marsalforn Bay
Marsalforn
Ta'Ghammar
Birbuba
Santa Pietru
Basilica of Ta' Pinu
Għarb
San Lawrenz
Ghasri
GOZO
Ramla Bay
Calypso's Cave
San Blas Bay
MEDITERRANEAN SEA
Dwejra Point
Ta'Dbieġi
Wilga
Aqueduct
Ramla Valley
Marsalforn Valley
Għasri Valley
Dahlet Qorrot
Dwejra Bay
Għajn Abdul
Santa Luċija
Kerċem
Xagħra
Ggantija Temples
Wardija
Wardija Point
Victoria (Rabat)
Xewkija
Nadur
Windmill
Qala
Qala Point
Xlendi Bay
Xlendi
Torri ta' Xlendi
Munxar
Rotunda
St Cecilia's Tower
Gozo Heliport
Għajnsielem
Mġarr
Redoubt
Hondoq ir-Rummien
San Niklaw Bay
Santa Marija Bay
Sannat
Ta'Ċenċ
Burial Mounds Cart Ruts and Dolmen
Torri ta' Mġarr ix-Xini
Fort Chambray
Mġarr Harbour
COMINO
Ta'Ċenċ Cliffs
Cart Ruts
Mġarr ix-Xini
Fessej Rock
Tafal Cliffs
NORTH COMINO CHANNEL
Blue Lagoon
Cominotto
MEDITERRANEAN SEA
SOUTH COMINO CHANNEL
To Cirkewwa

VICTORIA (RABAT)

pop 6640

Victoria, the chief town of Gozo, sits in the centre of the island, 6km from the ferry terminal at Mġarr and 3.5km from the resort town of Marsalforn. Victoria's main attraction is the compact and photogenic citadel, Il-Kastell, with its cathedral and museums.

Victoria is Gozo's main hub of shops and services. It was named for the Diamond Jubilee of Queen Victoria in 1897. Originally known as Rabat, it is still called that by many of the islanders (and by several road signs).

Orientation

Victoria is built on a hill crowned by the ramparts of Il-Kastell (the Citadel, also known by its Italian names, Gran Castello or the Cittadella). Telgħa Tal-Belt (Castle Hill) runs a short distance downhill from Il-Kastell to Pjazza Indipendenza. Triq ir-Repubblika, Victoria's main street, runs east (downhill) from Pjazza Indipendenza. The bus station and main car park are on Triq Putirjal, running south off Triq ir-Repubblika.

Victoria's narrow streets are locked into a labyrinthine one-way system – it may take several circuits of the town and one or two unintentional trips to the towns of Kerċem or Sannat before you find your way around.

Information

AIRLINE OFFICES

Air Malta (Map p143; ☎ 21 559 341; 13 Pjazza Indipendenza; 8.30am-5.30pm Mon-Fri)

BOOKSHOPS

Bookpoint (☎ 21 563 323; 49 Triq Putirjal) Opposite the bus station; sells books and newspapers, both local and British.

Bookworm (☎ 21 556 215; 105 Triq ir-Repubblika) Books and newspapers sold here, both local and British.

EMERGENCY

Police Station (☎ 21 562 040; Triq ir-Repubblika)

INTERNET ACCESS

Internet House (☎ 21 558 764; 44 Triq L'Assunta; 10am-7pm Mon-Sat) Printing and scanning facilities

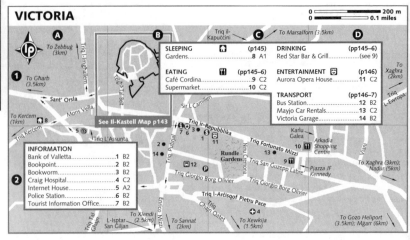

VICTORIA

0 — 200 m
0 — 0.1 miles

SLEEPING (p145)
Gardens...................................8 A1

EATING (pp145–6)
Café Cordina............................9 C2
Supermarket............................10 C2

DRINKING (pp145–6)
Red Star Bar & Grill................(see 9)

ENTERTAINMENT (p146)
Aurora Opera House.............11 C2

TRANSPORT (pp146–7)
Bus Station............................12 B2
Mayjo Car Rentals.................13 C2
Victoria Garage.....................14 B2

INFORMATION
Bank of Valletta......................1 B2
Bookpoint................................2 B2
Bookworm...............................3 B2
Craig Hospital.........................4 C2
Internet House.........................5 A2
Police Station..........................6 B2
Tourist Information Office.........7 B2

See Il-Kastell Map p143

---

available. Internet access Lm0.50/1/1.50 for up to 10/30/60 minutes.

Aurora Opera House (☎ 21 562 974; Triq ir-Repubblika) There are a few computers in the foyer of the opera house (see Entertainment, p146; buy your coupon for their use from the bar here.

MEDICAL SERVICES
Craig Hospital (☎ 21 561 600; Triq l-Arċisqof Pietru Pace)

MONEY
Bank of Valletta (Triq ir-Repubblika) With ATM.
Travelex (Map p143; cnr Triq ir-Repubblika & Telgħa Tal-Belt; ⏰ 9am-5pm Mon-Fri, 9.30am-2.30pm Sat) Cashes travellers cheques and changes money.

POST
Post Office (Map p143; Triq ir-Repubblika; ⏰ 8.15am-4.30pm Mon-Fri, 8.15am-12.30pm Sat)

TOURIST INFORMATION
Tourist Information Office (☎ 21 561 419; Tigrija Palazz; cnr Triq ir-Reppublika & Triq Putirjal; ⏰ 9am-12.30pm & 1-5pm Mon-Sat, 9am-12.30pm Sun & public holidays) On the ground floor of a shopping arcade, not far from the bus station.

Sights   Map p143
IL-KASTELL (CITTADELLA)
The **Cathedral of the Assumption** (Misraħ il-Katidral; Lm0.25; ⏰ 9am-4.30pm Mon-Sat) was built between 1697 and 1711 to replace the church that had been destroyed in the earthquake of 1693 (see the boxed text below). It was designed by Lorenzo Gafa, who was also

responsible for St Paul's Cathedral at Mdina (p117). The elegant façade is adorned with the escutcheons of Grand Master Ramon de Perellos and Bishop Palmieri. Due to lack of money the dome was never completed, but the impression of one was maintained inside by way of a clever trompe l'oeil painting.

The **Cathedral Museum** (☎ 21 556 087; Triq il-Fossos; ⏰ 9am-4.30pm Mon-Sat) is just northeast of the cathedral (the Lm0.25 ticket to the cathedral also covers admission to the museum). The downstairs vault contains church gold and silver, while the upstairs gallery is devoted to religious art and includes a disturbing 19th-century painting depicting the Martyrdom of St Agatha (see the boxed text, p120 for more on her grisly end). The ground floor houses various items including a 19th-century bishop's

---

THE 1693 EARTHQUAKE

On 11 January 1693 an earthquake of magnitude 6.8 on the Richter scale struck southern Italy. The epicentre was in the Val di Noto region of eastern Sicily, and several towns and villages were destroyed. Two-thirds of the population of Catania were killed, and the total death toll came to around 70,000. In Malta, the quake damaged many buildings including the cathedrals of Mdina and Victoria, both of which were built anew.

GOZO

carriage and an altar with a wax model of the Last Supper.

Besides the Cathedral Museum there are four other museums within the Citadel. If you plan to visit more than one, it's worth buying a **Citadel Day Ticket** (adult/child Lm1.50/free), which gives entry to all four sites and is available at each of them. The **Archaeology Museum** (☎ 21 556 144; Triq Bieb il-Mdina; adult/child Lm1/free; ⊙ 8.30am-4.30pm Mon-Sat, 8.30am-3pm Sun, closed public holidays) contains finds from the prehistoric temples at Ġgantija, though the model of the temple is more interesting than the array of pottery shards. Finds from the Punic and Roman periods are displayed upstairs, including inscriptions, terracotta cremation urns, lots of

amphorae and anchors, and some fascinating jewellery and amulets in the form of the Eye of Osiris – an ancient link to the symbols found on Maltese fishing boats of today.

The **Folklore Museum** (☎ 21 562 034; Triq Bernardo de Opuo; adult/child Lm1/free; ⊙ 8.30am-4.30pm Mon-Sat, 8.30am-3pm Sun, closed public holidays) is in a lovely old building that dates from around 1500, and shows Sicilian and Catalan influences; note the beautiful arched windows overlooking Triq Bernardo de Opuo. The museum is a maze of stairs, rooms and courtyards and the building is perhaps more interesting than the large collection of domestic, trade and farming implements that give an insight into rural life on Gozo.

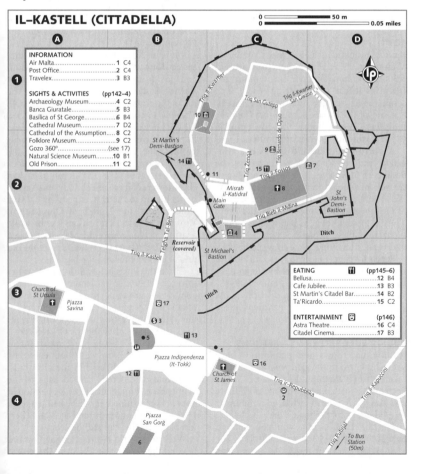

IL–KASTELL (CITTADELLA)

0   50 m
0   0.05 miles

INFORMATION	
Air Malta	1 C4
Post Office	2 C4
Travelex	3 B3

SIGHTS & ACTIVITIES	(pp142–4)
Archaeology Museum	4 C2
Banca Giuratale	5 B3
Basilica of St George	6 B4
Cathedral Museum	7 D2
Cathedral of the Assumption	8 C2
Folklore Museum	9 C2
Gozo 360°	(see 17)
Natural Science Museum	10 B1
Old Prison	11 C2

EATING	🍴 (pp145–6)
Bellusa	12 B4
Cafe Jubilee	13 B3
St Martin's Citadel Bar	14 B2
Ta'Ricardo	15 C2

ENTERTAINMENT	🎭 (p146)
Astra Theatre	16 C4
Citadel Cinema	17 B3

Triq l-Kwartier
Triq San Gużepp
Triq il-Kwartier San Gwann
Triq Bernardo de Opuo
St Martin's Demi-Bastion
Triq Zenqa
Triq il-Fossos
Misraħ il-Katidral
Main Gate
Triq Bieb il-Mdina
St John's Demi-Bastion
Ditch
Triq Ta'-Belt
Reservoir (covered)
St Michael's Bastion
Triq il-Kastell
Ditch
Church of St Ursula
Pjazza Savina
Pjazza Indipendenza (It-Tokk)
Church of St James
Triq ir-Repubblika
Triq il-Kapuċċini
Pjazza San Ġorġ
Triq Putirjal
To Bus Station (50m)

GOZO

The **Natural Science Museum** (☎ 21 556 153; Triq il-Kwartier; adult/child Lm1/free; 🕑 8.30am-4.30pm Mon-Sat, 8.30am-3pm Sun, closed public holidays), in another gracious old building, has low-key exhibits explaining the geology of the island and its water supply. On display upstairs is a rather sad collection of stuffed birds.

The **Old Prison** (☎ 21 565 988; Misraħ il-Katidral; adult/child Lm1/free; 🕑 8.30am-4.30pm Mon-Sat, 8.30am-3pm Sun, closed public holidays) served as a jail from the late 1500s to 1904. The cells here once held Jean Parisot de la Valette for the crime of 'aggressive behaviour' for a few months before he became Grand Master (for more about him see the boxed text, p60). The most interesting part of a visit to the prison is the extensive historic graffiti etched into the walls by the inmates, including crosses, ships, hands and the cross of the Knights.

TOWN

Pjazza Indipendenza, the main square of Victoria, hosts a daily market (from around 6.30am to 2pm) known throughout the island as **It-Tokk** (the meeting place). The semicircular baroque building at the western end of the square is the **Banca Giuratale**, built in 1733 to house the city council; today it contains government offices.

A narrow lane behind the Banca Giuratale leads to Pjazza San Ġorġ and the **Basilica of St George**, the original parish church of Rabat dating from 1678. The lavish interior contains a fine altarpiece of St George and the Dragon by Mattia Preti. The old town, known as Il-Borgo, is a maze of narrow alleys around Pjazza San Ġorġ and is an interesting place to wander.

Rundle Gardens (Map p142), south of Triq ir-Repubblika, were laid out by General Sir Leslie Rundle (Governor of Malta 1909–15) in around 1914. On the festa celebrating the Assumption (15 August) the gardens host a lively agricultural fair.

AUDIOVISUAL SHOWS & EXHIBITIONS

Audiovisual shows and exhibitions have yet to hit Gozo in the same manner they've taken off in Valletta and Mdina on Malta. Perhaps it's just a matter of time until there are dungeons and assorted gory tableaux around every corner inside the Citadel.

For the time being, you can take in **Gozo 360°** (☎ 21 559 955; entrance on Telgħa Tal-Belt; adult/child Lm1.75/0.85; 🕑 every half-hour 10am-3.30pm Mon-Sat, 10am-1pm Sun & public holidays), shown at the Citadel Cinema. It's a 30-minute audiovisual show on the history of Gozo, along the lines of the Malta Experience in Valletta (p68), with commentary available in eight languages.

Walking Tour: Il-Kastell

Distance: approx 600m
Duration: 20 minutes

From Pjazza Indipendenza, cross the main street and climb up Telgħa Tal-Belt to the Citadel's main gate. There are two gates into Il-Kastell – enter through the **Old Main Gate (1)** on the right (the larger new gate was opened in 1957), noting the Roman inscription on the left-hand inner wall from the 2nd century AD.

On your right after you enter is the **Archaeology Museum (2**; p143). Pass the museum and go up the stairs on the right into **St Michael's Bastion (3)** and continue along the top of the city wall to **St John's Demi-Bastion (4)**. There is a good panorama from here. Look for the huge dome of the Rotunda at Xewkija, with Comino and Malta in the background; the distant Gothic spire of the church above Mġarr harbour; the watchtower of Nadur, and the dome and twin clock-towers of its parish church; and Xagħra on its hilltop to the east, capped by Ta'Kola windmill and the Church of Our Lady of Victory. Off to the left you can see the white apartment blocks around Marsalforn Bay. The **Gozo Craft Centre (5**; 🕑 Mon-Sat) is in the old prison building behind the bastion.

Climb the stairs below St John's Cavalier to reach the upper battlements, with more good views to the north and west. The **fortifications (6)** were built at the beginning of the 17th century to guard against further Turkish attacks following the Great Siege of 1565. Until 1637, when the Turkish threat receded, all Gozitans were bound by law to spend each night within the city walls. After that date people drifted back to the countryside, and many of the abandoned houses were ruined in the earthquake of 1693 (see the boxed text, p142). Their tumbled remains can still be seen.

Walk down Triq il-Kwartier San Ġwann. Beyond the archway, at the little **Chapel of St**

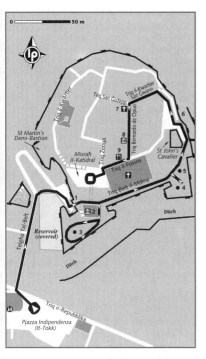

Joseph (7), turn left down Triq Bernardo de Opuo, past a beautifully restored medieval building that houses the **Folklore Museum (8;** p143), and then right on Triq il-Fossos. Stop in at **Ta'Ricardo (9**; see below) to sample some fine local produce, then continue along Triq il-Fossos to arrive in the little square in front of the cathedral.

Festivals & Events

See p166 for details of some of the country's foremost festivals, many with events held on Gozo.

Sleeping

Victoria is without a hotel, and the only accommodation option is at the **Gardens** (Map p142; ☎ 21 557 737 or 21 553 723; www.casalgo holidays.com; Triq Kerċem; per person incl breakfast Lm5), just west of the main square. Here the wonderfully hospitable owners rent out simple, comfortable rooms (shared bathrooms) for affordable prices. Facilities include guest kitchens and garden terraces. A very good budget option, in a good location (look out for the small sign on the front of the building – it's difficult to spot). The owners also have large self-catering apartments for rent – one in Victoria, and a few more scattered around Gozo – see the website for information.

Eating & Drinking
IL-KASTELL   Map p143

Ta'Ricardo (☎ 21 555 953; 4 Triq il-Fossos; platter for 2 Lm3; ⏱ 10am-6pm) An institution in Victoria, Ricardo's sells souvenirs and paintings as well as local produce such as honey, cheese and wine. Take a seat and order a cheap, delicious platter, which includes cheese, bread, locally grown fresh tomatoes, sun-dried tomatoes, capers and olives. Wash it all down with a glass or two of Gozitan wine.

St Martin's Citadel Bar (St Martin's Demi-Bastion; snacks & meals Lm0.40-2) Above the northeastern corner of the main square in Il-Kastell, St Martin's serves up lunches such as sandwiches, pasta, salads and omelettes, plus drinks, ice creams and various snacks, all with great views over Victoria.

TOWN
Café Jubilee (Map p143; ☎ 21 558 921; Pjazza Indipendenza; snacks & meals Lm0.40-2.25; ⏱ 8am-1am) This lovely old-fashioned bar (the sister establishment of Café Jubilee in Valletta, p73) has a classy interior featuring a marble counter, brass rails, lots of dark wood and waiters in black waistcoats and white aprons. As well as drinks and coffee, it serves soups, salads, pastries, pasta and sandwiches, which you can also enjoy at the outdoor tables on the main square. Of an evening it becomes a popular wine bar and serves good local drops.

Bellusa (Map p143; ☎ 21 556 243; Pjazza Indipendenza; snacks & meals Lm1.30-2.50; ⏱ 8am-10pm) Also well positioned for people-watching (just off the main square) is this casual café/snack bar. Stop by for a pizza, burger or salad and take your pick of dining alfresco or in the cosy interior.

Opposite the Arkadia shopping centre on Triq Fortunato Mizzi (the continuation of Triq ir-Repubblika), about 600m east of Pjazza Indipendenza, are a couple of good eateries. **Café Cordina** (Map p142; ☎ 21 559 859; Pjazza JF Kennedy) is a modern café with good coffee, cakes, sandwiches and pastries; next door **Red Star Bar & Grill** (Map p142; ☎ 21 556 026; Pjazza JF Kennedy; mains Lm2-5; ⏱ dinner nightly) is an

GOZO

GOZO FARMHOUSES

One of the best accommodation options for a stay on Gozo, especially if you're looking for a little local colour and rustic charm, is to rent a farmhouse. Dozens of these old, square-set farm buildings have been converted into accommodation, and many retain the beautiful stone arches, wooden beams and flagstone floors of their original construction (some are up to 400 years old). Most rental properties now have all the facilities you'll need for an easy holiday, including full kitchen, swimming pool, outdoor terrace and barbecue, laundry and cable TV. They can sleep anywhere from two to 16 people, so are perfect for families or groups of friends, and the costs are very reasonable – from around Lm350 per week for two people in high season (most high-season rentals are weekly), or from Lm28 per night for two people in low season. The farmhouses are usually inland in pretty, slow-paced villages like Xagħra and Għarb. Check the following websites for details of farmhouses for rent:

- www.aboutgozo.com
- www.gozo.com/gozodirectory /farmhouses.php
- www.gozofarmhouses.com
- www.gozorentals.com/farmhouses.htm
- www.gozogreatescapes.com

American-style restaurant with an interesting menu of burgers, salads and pizza. It also has decent platters that are good for sharing: the Deep Blue platter features calamari rings, scampi and fish croquettes. The bar here gets busy as the night wears on.

There are fruit and vegetable vendors around It-Tokk and at the car park beside the bus station, and a **supermarket** (Map p142; Triq Fortunato Mizzi) at basement level of the Arkadia shopping centre.

Entertainment

Despite its diminutive size, Victoria has two theatres to Valletta's one, a consequence of rivalry between two local band clubs. The **Aurora Opera House** (Map p142; ☎ 21 562 974) is the home of the Leone Philharmonic Society, and the **Astra Theatre** (Map p143; ☎ 21 556 256) is home to La Stella Philharmonic Society. Both are on Triq ir-Repubblika, and stage opera, ballet, comedies, drama, cabaret, pantomime and celebrity concerts. Check the local press for details of performances.

Victoria also has the two-screen **Citadel Cinema** (Map p143; ☎ 21 559 955; www.citadelcinema .com; Telgħa Tal-Belt; ticket adult/child Lm1.85/1.35) which shows mainstream films. Check the website or the *Times* newspaper to see what is showing.

Getting There & Away

A regular helicopter service operates between Malta International Airport and Gozo. For details see p180. The main ferry service between Malta and Gozo has frequent crossings during the day and also operates throughout the night during summer (see p184 for more information).

Getting Around

TO/FROM THE HELIPORT

Gozo's **heliport** (☎ 21 557 905) is just south of St Cecilia's Tower, about 3.5km southeast of Victoria on the main road to Mġarr. Most hotels will offer to pick you up from the heliport; otherwise, you could phone and arrange for a taxi to meet your flight. Alternatively, you can walk 200m up to the main road and catch bus No 25 into Victoria.

BUS

Victoria's **bus station** (Map p142; Triq Putirjal) is just south of Triq ir-Repubblika, about 10 minutes' walk from Il-Kastell. All the bus routes are circular, starting and finishing at Victoria. Except for bus No 25, which shuttles regularly between Victoria and Mġarr and connects with the ferries to Malta, the buses are slow and run according to the needs of the local schools and shoppers, so the schedule is not often convenient for sightseeing. There's a flat fare of Lm0.15.

CAR & BICYCLE

If you want to see as much of the island as possible, then it makes sense to rent a car. It's also very cheap – even cheaper than on Malta. You'll also find that the quieter roads and shorter distances make cycling a more attractive option on Gozo than on Malta.

GOZO

Victoria Garage (Map p142; ☎ 21 556 414 or 21 553 741; Triq Putirjal), opposite the bus station, rents out bicycles (Lm2 per day, or Lm1.50 per day for periods of a week or longer), motorbikes (Lm8 per day, or Lm5 per day for a week or longer) and cars (daily rate of Lm9, or Lm7 for longer periods).

Mayjo Car Rentals (Map p142; ☎ 21 556 678; www.intersoftgozo.com/mayjo; Triq Fortunato Mizzi) has a large range of vehicles and good rates (from Lm6/8 per day in low/high season for the smallest vehicle).

TAXI

Taxis hang around at the bus station and at Pjazza Indipendenza, or you can try phoning **Belmont Garage** (☎ 21 556 962) or **Mario's Taxis** (☎ 21 557 242).

WALKING

Gozo is so small that you could walk from Mġarr to Marsalforn in two hours. Away from the relatively busy road between Mġarr and Victoria the roads are pretty quiet and there are lots of attractive hikes around the coast.

MĠARR

Mġarr is Gozo's main harbour and the point of arrival for ferries from Malta. The row of buildings beside the harbour car park includes a **tourist information office** (☎ 21 553 343; ⏰ 9am-12.30pm & 1-5pm Mon-Sat, 9am-12.30pm Sun & public holidays). In the same block you'll also find a travel agent, public toilets and a bank (with ATM).

The 20th-century neogothic **Church of Our Lady of Lourdes** (Triq Lourdes) appears almost to hang over the village. Begun in 1924, lack of funds meant that its construction was not finally completed until the 1970s. The hilltop above it is capped by the ramparts of **Fort Chambray**, built by the Knights of St John in the early 18th century. It was originally intended to supplant the Citadel as Gozo's main fortified town, and the area within the walls was laid out with a grid of streets similar to Valletta. But with the decline of the Order in the late 18th century the plan came to naught. Instead, the fort served as a garrison and later as a mental hospital; developments to turn the fort into a hotel and residential complex seem to have stalled.

A right turn at the top of the harbour hill leads to a **belvedere** with a grand view over the harbour to Comino and northern Malta. Triq iż-Żewwiega (near the L-Imġarr Hotel) leads to an even better **viewpoint** just south of Qala (it's worth the effort to get here – it's 1.8km from the harbour to the viewpoint, and once here you can enjoy the magnificent panorama from Xerri Il-Bukkett Restaurant (p148).

Xlendi Pleasure Cruises (☎ 21 559 967; www.xlendicruises.com) offers half- and full-day boat trips around Gozo and/or Comino. A full-day trip (10.30am to 5.30pm) taking in Gozo and Comino costs Lm10/5 per adult/child and includes swimming stops and free use of snorkelling equipment. A half-day trip around Gozo is Lm7/3.50 per adult/child; around Comino and the Blue Lagoon is Lm6.50/3.50. Trips depart from Mġarr harbour, but there's free transport for participants from Xlendi and Marsalforn to the departure point. You can book trips through most travel agents in the resort towns on Gozo.

Sleeping

Both of Mġarr's accommodation options are decidedly upmarket.

L-Imġarr Hotel (☎ 21 560 455; www.l-imgarrhotel.com; Triq iż-Żewwiega; s/d from Lm30/40 low season, Lm42/60 high season; ❄ ⌁) Perched high above the marina and enjoying great views, this five-star hotel has all the facilities you'd expect, including two pools, a gym and a quality Italian restaurant. Prices quoted here are for a room with inland view; you'll pay Lm5-10 more per person for a sea view.

Grand Hotel (☎ 21 563 840; www.grandhotelmalta.com; Triq Sant'Antnin; s/d from Lm12.50/15 low season, Lm18.50/27 high season; ❄ ⌁) The four-star Grand Hotel also has a fine position overlooking the harbour, with bright, airy rooms and facilities including a sauna, gym, games room, restaurant and cocktail bar. Its least expensive rooms (prices listed here) have no view. From these it's a small step up to a 'country view' room, and sea view rooms cost around Lm8 more per person. There's an additional surcharge of Lm3 per person if you stay for only one night.

Eating & Drinking

Seaview Restaurant (☎ 21 565 541; 15 Triq ix-Xatt; mains Lm2-6.50) At the foot of the hill, close to the harbour, the Seaview has a large, pleasant

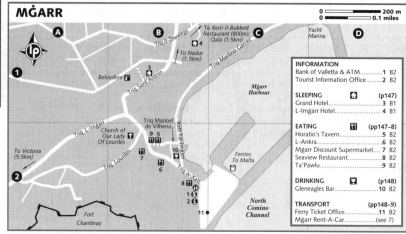

outdoor terrace, and a comprehensive menu of cheap pasta dishes (around Lm2), plus fresh fish, charcoal-grilled fillets of beef, lamb chops and a range of daily specials.

L-Ankra (☎ 21 555 656; Triq ix-Xatt; mains Lm2-5) A bit further up the hill from the Seaview, L-Ankra has a brightly coloured dining room and a menu full of the usual suspects (pasta, fresh fish, fried rabbit, king prawns) which it executes very well. Of an evening there are also pizza selections (Lm1.30 to Lm2.30), including the Gozitan: heavy with toppings of tomato sauce, anchovies, capers, black olives, potatoes, onions, basil, tuna and fresh tomato.

Horatio's Tavern (☎ 21 566 669; 9 Triq Manoel de Vilhena; snacks & meals Lm0.60-3) Triq Manoel de Vilhena is lined with restaurants. Horatio's, at the top of the hill, is a cosy, nautically themed tavern with outdoor seating and a menu of tempting sandwiches, salads and platters. Try a platter of local treats (including Gozitan cheeses and sausage), fish (marinated swordfish and salted tuna), Italian hams and salamis, or imported cheeses.

Ta'Pawlu (☎ 21 558 355; 4 Triq Manoel de Vilhena; mains Lm4.25-6; ⏱ dinner Wed-Mon) Next door to Horatio's, this restaurant raises the bar a little with a more elegant dining room and more upmarket selections. Mains might include sautéed calamari or king prawns, duck breast with honey and orange sauce, or veal with cognac sauce. Leave room for the crème caramel, home-made ice cream or crepes for dessert.

Xerri Il-Bukkett Restaurant (☎ 21 553 500; Triq iż-Żewwiega; snacks Lm1-2, mains Lm3-5.50) Who cares about the menu when the view is this good?! This restaurant is just south of Qala, about 1.8km from Mġarr harbour, and has a terrace with a stupendous view across the channel to Comino and northern Malta. It serves snacks like pizzas and burgers, or pasta, meat, fish and traditional dishes: fried rabbit, swordfish, *braġioli* (beef slices wrapped around a savoury filling and braised in red wine) and so on.

For picnics and self-caterers, the **Mġarr Discount Supermarket** (Triq ix-Xatt; ⏱ closed Sun) is just a few minutes' walk uphill from the harbour.

Gleneagles Bar (Triq ix-Xatt) is the place to head for a cold beer at the end of the day. It commands a view over the harbour, and is the social hub of the village, filling up in the early evening with a lively mix of locals, fishermen, yachties and tourists.

Getting There & Around

The car ferry from Ċirkewwa on Malta shuttles back and forth to Mġarr every 45 to 60 minutes from 6am to around 11pm (and every two hours throughout the night in the peak summer months from July to September). There is also a once-daily car ferry from Sa Maison in Floriana. The **Gozo Channel** (☎ 21 561 622; www.gozochannel.com) ticket office is in the harbour car park. For more information on ferry services see p184.

Bus No 25 runs from the harbour to Victoria, and taxi drivers tout for business among the crowds disembarking from the ferry. There are a couple of car hire agencies near the harbour. **Mġarr Rent-A-Car** (☎ 21 564 986; Triq ix-Xatt), above the supermarket a few minutes' walk uphill from the harbour, is good value.

GĦAJNSIELEM
pop 2400

Mġarr merges uphill into the town of Għajnsielem (ayn-*see*-lem, meaning 'spring of peace'). The huge, modern **Church of Our Lady of Loreto**, built in neogothic style, looms over the village square.

On the western edge of the village, on the main road from Mġarr to Victoria, is **Gozo Heritage** (☎ 21 561 280; Triq l-Imġarr; adult/child Lm1.75/0.90; ☽ 8.45am-4.45pm Mon-Sat), which advertises itself as a 'walk through 7000 years of living history'. It is a series of historical tableaux – the legend of Calypso, Ġgantija temple, the Romans, the Great Siege, WWII – accompanied by special light and sound effects.

Another 500m along the road to Victoria is **St Cecilia's Tower**. The level area around the tower served as a temporary airfield in 1943 during the invasion of Sicily. A left turn at the tower leads to Gozo heliport (see p180 for details on the Malta–Gozo helicopter service).

Casa di San Giuseppe or, as it is more commonly known, **St Joseph Home Hostel** (☎ 21 556 439; www.stjosephhomstel.com; Triq l-Imġarr; dm Lm3.75) is part of the NSTS network of hostels in Malta (p161), but this place should probably be considered only as a last resort – there's better budget accommodation in Victoria and Marsalforn. This hostel was once a home for poor and orphaned boys, and inside it feels as though not a lot has changed since that time. Its sleeping quarters are very much from a different era but there are a few redeeming features, including a pretty courtyard, large kitchen and good views. It's about 1.5km from the Mġarr harbour; bus No 25 between Mġarr and Victoria stops nearby.

MĠARR IX-XINI

The narrow, cliff-bound inlet of Mġarr ix-Xini (Port of the Galleys) was once used by the Knights of St John as their main harbour on Gozo – one of their watchtowers still guards the entrance. It was also used by the Turkish admiral Dragut Reis, who raided Gozo in 1551 and took most of the island's population into slavery.

There's a tiny shingle beach at the head of the inlet, and a paved area where tourists and locals stake out their sunbathing territories. The swimming and snorkelling along the rocks is very good, and the little cove near the western headland of the bay is a private lido that belongs to the Hotel Ta'Ċenċ.

The road from Sannat and Xewkija down to Mġarr ix-Xini is quite steep and narrow, and wouldn't be much fun on a day with lots of beach traffic. You can walk there from Victoria in just over an hour.

XEWKIJA
pop 3250

The village of Xewkija – and most of southern Gozo – is dominated by the vast dome of the Parish Church of St John the Baptist, better known as the **Rotunda** (☽ 5am-noon & 3-8pm). Work on the new church began in 1951 and it was finally completed in 1971. It was built mainly with the volunteer labour of the parishioners, and paid for by local donations. Its vast size – the dome is higher than St Paul's Cathedral in London, and the nave can seat 4000 people – is said to be due to rivalry with Mosta on Malta, whose rotunda was also funded by the local people.

The rotunda was built around the old 17th-century church, which was too small for the community's needs – the new one can seat around three times the village's population. The interior is plain, but impresses through sheer size. Paintings of scenes from the life of St John the Baptist adorn the six side-chapels. To the left of the altar is a **museum** where baroque sculptures and other relics salvaged from the old church are displayed. The wooden statue of St John was fashioned in 1845 by Maltese sculptor Paul Azzopardi.

TA'ĊENĊ

The quiet village of Sannat, once famed for its lace-making, lies 2km south of Victoria, and gives access to the Ta'Ċenċ plateau. Signs from the village square point the way to the Hotel Ta'Ċenċ, one of Gozo's best. The track to the left of the entrance to the walled hotel grounds leads to the high plateau of

Ta'Ċenċ – the **views** north to Victoria, Xewkija and Xagħra are good, especially towards sunset. Wander off to the left of the track, near the edge of the limestone crag, and you will find a prehistoric **dolmen** – a large slab propped up on three smaller stones like a table. The dolmen is not signposted and is a little tricky to spot, plus you may encounter some rifle-wielding hunters out this way, so take care!

The best walking is off to the right, along the top of the huge Ta'Ċenċ **sea cliffs**. These spectacular limestone crags, more than 130m high, were once the breeding ground of the Maltese peregrine falcon (see the boxed text, p43). Near the cliff top you can see traces of prehistoric 'cart ruts' (see the boxed text, p125).

The five-star **Hotel Ta'Ċenċ** (☎ 21 556 819 or 21 561 522; www.vjborg.com/tacenc; s/d from Lm33/56 low season, Lm55/80 high season; ✻ ☒) has a fine, remote setting on the cliff-top plateau just east of the village of Sannat. Its attractive, lowrise design and use of local stone, together with its large grounds and excellent facilities, have made it one of the most desirable hotels in the Maltese Islands. Get-away-from-it-all facilities include two swimming pools and a large terrace, a health spa, tennis courts, a private beach, bar and fine restaurant, **Il-Carrubo**, preparing excellent Italian and Maltese cuisine to enjoy alfresco.

XLENDI

Xlendi was once one of the most beautiful fishing villages on Gozo, but unregulated building on the south side of scenic Xlendi Bay has turned it into just another resort town. That said, it's a pleasant enough place to chill out by the sea, with good swimming, snorkelling and diving, and plenty of rocks for sunbathing.

Steps lead up the cliff above the little fishing boat harbour at the head of the bay to a tiny cove in the rocks where you can swim. Alternatively, you can keep walking up the hillside above and then hike over to Wardija Point and Dwejra Bay. On the south side of Xlendi Bay a footpath winds around to the 17th-century **watchtower** on Ras il-Bajda. From here you can hike east to the Sanap cliffs, and on towards Ta'Ċenċ.

There are a couple of dive operators in town that can help you explore the excellent nearby dive sites (p50):

Moby Dives (☎ 21 551 616; www.gozo.com/mobydives; Triq il-Gostra)

St Andrews Divers Cove (☎ 21 551 301; www.gozodive .com; Triq San Ximun)

By the bus stop and car park, a block back from the waterfront is an ATM and currency exchange machine. Nearby, **Herbees Diner** (p151) is a fast-food restaurant offering Internet access.

Sleeping & Eating

San Antonio Guesthouse (☎ 21 563 555; www.club gozo.com.mt; Triq it-Torri; s/d incl breakfast Lm9.50/13 low season, Lm15.80/25.60 high season; ✻ ☒) A fair climb up the hill on the south side of the bay is this affordable and very pleasant guesthouse, with 13 rooms and excellent facilities for the price: all rooms have TV, en suite and a balcony, and there are gardens to enjoy. The owners can also help with self-catering apartments and farmhouses – check the website for more information.

Serena Aparthotel (☎ 21 553 719; www.serena .com.mt; Triq Puniċi; per person incl breakfast from Lm8/12 low/high season; ✻ ☒) Serena is a large, well-equipped complex on the south side of the bay. The hotel has large rooms with kitchen and sitting area (if you want a sea view, you'll pay Lm4 per person more than the prices quoted here). Some of the communal areas have dated décor, but there's a new reception area, a gym, an indoor pool and restaurant, as well as a minimarket, an outdoor pool and a rooftop sun terrace.

St Patrick's Hotel (☎ 21 562 951; www.vjborg.com /stpatricks; Xatt ix-Xlendi; s/d from Lm11/18 low season, Lm21.50/30 high season; ☒) Bang in the middle of the Xlendi waterfront is the four-star St Patrick's, with attractive, well-appointed rooms set around an internal courtyard (you'll pay quite a bit more for a room with balcony and sea view). There's a rooftop terrace with small pool, and a ground-level waterside restaurant (half- and full-board arrangements are available).

Stone Crab (☎ 21 559 315; Xlendi Bay; mains Lm1.60–6.50; ⏰ lunch daily, dinner daily Apr-Oct, Sat & Sun Nov & Feb-Mar, closed Dec-Jan) This family-friendly restaurant attracts diners with a winning combination of tables right next to the water and a huge menu of well-priced pasta, pizza, seafood and meat favourites. Pasta dishes include spaghetti with octopus, clams or shellfish, or there are Maltese specialities like octopus cooked in garlic, king prawns in garlic and white wine, or stewed squid stuffed with mixed fish and rice.

Herbees Diner (☎ 21 556 323; meals from Lm1; ☽ 10am-1am daily Jul-Sep, 11.30am-3pm & 6-11pm daily Oct-Jun), a fast-food joint by the car park back from the waterfront, has a menu of fried chicken, kebabs, burgers and pizza. It also has Internet access.

It-Tmun (☎ 21 551 571; 3 Triq il-Madonna Tal-Karmnu; mains Lm4-7; ☽ lunch & dinner Wed-Mon) On a quiet, paved street well back from the waterfront is this highly regarded restaurant, a favourite with the locals for its innovative menu showing modern Mediterranean and Asian influences (fancy the baked Oriental vegetable parcels, or chicken in a spicy Thai sauce?). The desserts are worth leaving room for.

Iċ-Ċima Restaurant (☎ 21 558 407; Triq San Xmun; mains Lm2-6; ☽ lunch & dinner) High up over the village, this place has a great view over the bay from its wooden terrace. The menu is Italian and Maltese, with the emphasis on seafood, but there's also a good variety of inexpensive pizzas to choose from (the house speciality, the iċ-Ċima, is topped with mozzarella, local sausage and cheese, sun-dried tomatoes, eggplant and oregano).

Entertainment

La Grotta (☎ 21 551 149; www.lagrottaleisure.com; Triq ix-Xlendi; ☽ 10pm-dawn Fri & Sat May-Oct), on the road to Victoria about 1km east of Xlendi, is the best nightclub in the Maltese Islands. It's part open-air and part housed in a limestone cave in the cliffs above the valley, with two large dance areas. The admission price varies, depending upon the attraction that night (DJs, live music etc), but some nights are free. Above La Grotta and run by the same people, but on a smaller scale, is **Club Paradiso** (☎ 21 551 149; Triq ix-Xlendi; admission free; ☽ nightly May-Oct).

Getting There & Away

Bus No 87 runs between Xlendi and Victoria. By car, follow signs from the roundabout at the south end of Triq Putirjal in Victoria. Otherwise, it's a 40-minute walk from Victoria bus station.

GĦARB

pop 1040

The village of Għarb (pronounced aarb, meaning 'west') in the northwest of Gozo

has one of the most beautiful churches in the Maltese Islands. The baroque **Church of the Visitation** was built between 1699 and 1729, with an elegant curved façade and twin bell-towers. Three female figures adorn the front: Faith, above the door; Hope, with her anchor, to the right; and Charity. Inside, there is an altarpiece, *The Visitation of Our Lady to St Elizabeth*, which was gifted to the church by Grand Master de Vilhena.

The attractive **village square** was the location for the classic postcard, on sale throughout Malta and Gozo, showing a traditional British red telephone box beside a red letter box and a blue police station lamp (unfortunately the red letter box has been removed).

Next door to the police station is **Għarb Folklore Museum** (☎ 21 561 929; Triq il-Knisja; adult/child Lm1.50/free; ☽ 9am-4pm Mon-Sat, 9am-1pm Sun). This early-18th-century house has 28 rooms crammed with a fascinating private collection of folk artefacts. The exhibits, assembled by the owner over the past 20 years, include an early-18th-century printing press, a child's hearse, farming implements, fishing gear, jam-making equipment and much more.

A drive or pleasant walk of about 30 minutes (just over 2km) from Għarb leads to the tiny **Chapel of San Dimitri** (signposted on the road to the left of the church). This small, square church with its baroque cupola dates originally from the 15th century, though it was rebuilt in the 1730s. It stands in splendid isolation amid terraced fields. You can continue the walk down to the coast, and return via the hilltop of **Ġordan Lighthouse**, or the Basilica of Ta'Pinu.

The **Basilica of Ta'Pinu** (Triq ta'Pinu; ☽ 6.30am-12.30pm & 1.30-7pm) is Malta's national shrine to the Virgin Mary and an important centre of pilgrimage. It was built in the 1920s on the site of a chapel where a local woman, Carmela Grima, heard the Virgin speak to her in 1883. Thereafter, numerous miracles were attributed to the intercession of Our Lady of Pinu, and it was decided to replace the old church with a grand new one. Built in a Romanesque style, with an Italianate campanile, the interior of pale golden stone is calming and peaceful. Part of the original chapel, with Carmela Grima's tomb, is incorporated behind the altar. The basilica's name comes from the man, Filippino Gauci, who used to tend the old church – Pinu is the Malti diminutive for Filippino. The track leading to the top of the hill of Ta'Għammar opposite the church is punctuated by marble statues marking the Stations of the Cross. Visitors to the basilica should note that no shorts, miniskirts or sleeveless dresses are allowed.

Where the road to Għarb from Victoria forks (400m after the turning to Ta'Pinu) is **Jeffrey's Restaurant** (☎ 21 561 006; 10 Triq il-Għarb; mains Lm3-6; Ⓥ dinner Mon-Sat Apr-Oct). Set in a converted farmhouse with a pretty courtyard out the back, Jeffrey's offers meat, seafood and vegetarian dishes using fresh local produce. The signature dish of rabbit in wine and garlic is rated by many as among the best on Gozo. Bookings are advised.

Bus Nos 1, 2 and 91 go to Għarb; No 91 will take you to Ta'Pinu (Lm0.15).

SAN LAWRENZ

A left turn at Jeffrey's restaurant in Għarb (see above) leads to the village of San Lawrenz, where the novelist Nicholas Monsarrat (1910–79) lived and worked for four years in the early 1970s. His love for the Maltese Islands is reflected in his novel *The Kappillan of Malta*, which grew out of his experiences here.

En route from Għarb to San Lawrenz you'll pass the **Ta'Dbieġi Crafts Village** – a miniature clone of Malta's Ta'Qali (p123) – selling handicrafts, lace and pottery. The stalls have variable hours – it's best to go in the morning. A left turn just after the crafts village leads to the **Kempinski San Lawrenz Resort & Spa** (☎ 22 110 000; www.kempinski-gozo.com; Triq ir-Rokon; d Lm65/75 low/high season; ⛱ 🖥 🏊), a ritzy 'hideaway resort' set in lovely landscaped grounds. Facilities to help pass the time here include a health spa, tennis and squash courts, a gym, indoor and outdoor pools and pool bars. There's also a coffee shop, trattoria and fine-dining restaurant with strict dress code (no jeans, shorts, sandals or trainers).

DWEJRA

Geology and the sea have conspired to produce some of Gozo's most spectacular coastal scenery at Dwejra on the west coast. Two vast, underground caverns in the limestone

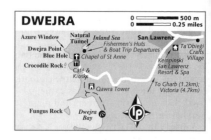

have collapsed to create two circular depressions now occupied by Dwejra Bay and the Inland Sea.

The **Inland Sea** is a cliff-bound lagoon connected to the open sea by a cave that runs for 100m through the headland of Dwejra Point. The cave is big enough for small boats to sail through in calm weather, and the Inland Sea has been used as a fishermen's haven for centuries. Today the fishermen supplement their income by taking tourists on **boat trips** (Lm3 for 2 people) through the cave.

A few minutes' walk from the Inland Sea is a huge natural arch in the sea cliffs, known as the **Azure Window**. In the rocks in front of it is another geological freak called the **Blue Hole** – a natural vertical chimney in the limestone, about 10m in diameter and 25m deep, that connects with the open sea through an underwater arch about 8m down. Understandably, it's a very popular dive site. The snorkelling here is excellent too. Between the Inland Sea and the Azure Window is the little **Chapel of St Anne**, built in 1963 on the site of a much older church.

The broad horizontal shelf of rock to the south of Dwejra Point has been eroded along the geological boundary between the Globigerina Limestone and the Lower Coralline Limestone – the boundary is marked by a layer of many thousands of fossil scallop shells and sand dollars (a kind of flattened, disc-shaped sea urchin). See p42 for more on these limestone layers. Just offshore is **Crocodile Rock** (seen from near Qawra Tower it looks like a crocodile's head).

Qawra Tower overlooks **Dwejra Bay**. This collapsed cavern has been completely invaded by the sea, and is guarded by the brooding bulk of **Fungus Rock** (see the boxed text opposite). A path below the tower leads to a flight of stairs cut into the rock which leads down to a little slipway on the edge of

FUNGUS ROCK

Known in Malti as Il-Ġebla tal-Ġeneral (The General's Rock), Fungus Rock takes both of its names from the fact that the Knights of St John used to collect a rare plant from the rock's summit. The plant *(Cynomorium coccineus)* is dark brown and club-shaped, and grows to about 18cm in height. It is parasitic and has no green leaves, which is why it was called a fungus or, in Malti, *gherq tal-Ġeneral* (the General's root). It is native to North Africa, and Fungus Rock is the only place in Europe that it is found.

Extracts from the plant had powerful pharmaceutical qualities, and were said to staunch bleeding and prevent infection when used to dress wounds. The plant cured dysentery and ulcers, and was used to treat apoplexy and venereal diseases. It was long known to the Arabs as 'the treasure among drugs', and when a general of the Knights of St John discovered it growing on a rock on Gozo, he knew he had struck gold. A rope was strung between the mainland and the rock, and harvesters were shuttled back and forth in a tiny, one-man cable car. Qawra Tower was built to guard the precious resource. The plant extract was much in demand in the Knights' hospitals; it was sold at a high price to the various courts of Europe.

---

the bay. There is good swimming and sunbathing here, away from the crowd of daytrippers who throng the rocks around the Azure Window. For even more peace you can hike right around to the cliff top on the far side of the bay, where the view back over Fungus Rock to Dwejra Point is spectacular.

You can get snacks and basic meals from a **café** by the car park at Dwejra, and there are a couple of **kiosks** here selling drinks and ice creams to the day-trippers.

To get to Dwejra, take bus No 2 or 91 to San Lawrenz, then walk down to the bay (15 to 20 minutes). Bus No 2 also sometimes goes down to the car park at Dwejra.

MARSALFORN

Marsalforn is Gozo's main holiday resort. The bay of this former fishing village (the name is possibly derived from the Arabic for 'bay of ships') is now lined with an ugly sprawl of hotels and apartment buildings, which is gradually spreading north along

the coast towards Qbaijar. Still, it's a lowkey resort compared to the fleshpots of Sliema and Buġibba on Malta, and offers some good out-of-season deals on accommodation.

Orientation & Information

Most of the restaurants, hotels and guesthouses are clustered around the waterfront. You can change money at the **Bank of Valletta** on the promenade, which has an ATM and a 24-hour moneychanging machine.

Sights & Activities

There is not much worth seeing in the town itself. At the head of the bay is a tiny scrap of sand but better swimming and sunbathing can be found on the rocks out to the west. You can hike eastward over the hill to Calypso's Cave and Ramla Bay in about 45 minutes.

Xwieni Bay, a 15-minute walk to the west, has a sandy beach beneath a headland with a small fort. Beyond Xwieni the rocky shore has been carved into a patchwork of **salt pans** which are still worked in summer.

Another 20-minute hike beyond the salt pans will bring you to the narrow, cliffbound inlet of **Wied il-Għasri**. Here a narrow staircase cut into the rock leads down to a tiny shingle beach at the head of the inlet. It's a gorgeously picturesque place and there is good swimming and snorkelling when the sea is calm. The beach is best avoided in rough weather when the waves come crashing up the narrow defile. You can also drive or walk to Wied il-Għasri from the village of Għasri, about 2km south, but it's a bit tricky to find – you'll need a decent map if you're coming from this direction.

There are a number of dive operators in town that can help you explore Gozo's great dive sites (p50), including:

Atlantis Diving Centre (☎ 21 561 826; www.atlantis gozo.com; Altantis Hotel; Triq il-Qolla)

Calypso Diving Centre (☎ 21 561 757; www.calypso divers.com; Triq il-Port) Near the Calypso Hotel.

Nautic Team Diving Centre (☎ 21 558 507; www .nauticteam.com; cnr Triq il-Munġbell & Triq ir-Rabat)

Sleeping

Lantern Guesthouse (☎ 21 562 365; romx@vol.net.mt; Triq il-Munġbell; per person incl breakfast Lm6.50/10 low/ high season) There's a lively bar and restaurant on the ground floor, and rooms upstairs

GOZO

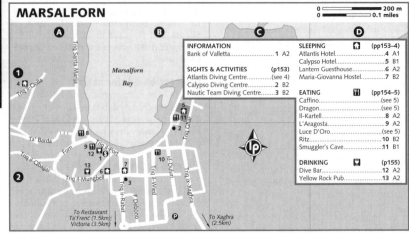

MARSALFORN

INFORMATION	
Bank of Valletta	**1** A2

SIGHTS & ACTIVITIES	(p153)
Atlantis Diving Centre	(see 4)
Calypso Diving Centre	**2** B2
Nautic Team Diving Centre	**3** B2

SLEEPING	(pp153–4)
Atlantis Hotel	**4** A1
Calypso Hotel	**5** B1
Lantern Guesthouse	**6** A2
Maria-Giovanna Hostel	**7** B2

EATING	(pp154–5)
Caffino	(see 5)
Dragon	(see 5)
Il-Kartell	**8** A2
L'Aragosta	**9** A2
Luce D'Oro	(see 5)
Ritz	**10** B2
Smuggler's Cave	**11** B1

DRINKING	(p155)
Dive Bar	**12** A2
Yellow Rock Pub	**13** A2

that are quite small but have decent facilities, including en suite, a fridge and TV.

Calypso Hotel (☎ 21 562 000; www.hotelcalypso gozo.com; Triq il-Port; s/d from Lm15/21 low season, Lm22.50/33 high season; ✖ ⍾) After closing for two years for renovation and refurbishment, the Calypso has recently reopened and is boasting fresh, stylish décor and excellent modernised facilities. Guests can take advantage of two excellent restaurants and a cool café, plus a lovely pool, bar and sun terrace on the roof. Sea-view rooms cost an additional Lm3 per person.

Atlantis Hotel (☎ 21 561 826; www.atlantisgozo.com; Triq il-Qolla; per person incl breakfast from Lm6/Lm14 low/

> ### AUTHOR'S PICK
> The pick of the budget accommodation on Gozo is **Maria-Giovanna Hostel** (☎ 21 553 630; www.gozohostels.com; cnr Triq il-Munġbell & Triq ir-Rabat; per person incl breakfast Lm4/7 low/ high season), a small hostel just back from the beach. It's a cut above most budget accommodation, and operates like a guesthouse in that rooms are rented out individually, so there are no dorm beds, and there is no need to share a room with a stranger. In a beautifully restored townhouse there are five rooms (two with en suite) with pretty, rustic décor, plus an inviting living room and guest kitchen. The friendly owners will gladly help with any inquiries. Highly recommended – but advance bookings are suggested, especially for the high season.

high season; ✖ ⍾) Above the west side of the bay is this large complex, which extends to both sides of the street and has loads of facilities, including indoor and outdoor pools, a fitness centre, a health spa and a diving school. The well-appointed rooms are very good value, particularly in the low season.

Eating & Drinking

Il-Kartell (☎ 21 556 918; Triq il-Port; mains Lm4-5.50; ✖ lunch & dinner Thu-Tue) Sit by the water or inside the atmospheric dining rooms at this laid-back place, housed in a couple of old boathouses in the southwestern corner of the bay. The menu includes pasta dishes around the Lm2 mark (penne Gozitana comes with local sausage, sun-dried tomatoes, garlic and herbs), along with fresh fish, traditional dishes and daily specials chalked up on the blackboard.

L'Aragosta (☎ 21 554 138; Triq ir-Port; mains Lm4-5.50; ✖ dinner Tue-Sun) This is a sweet little place serving up some fine nosh – choose from menu items that include quail in bacon and mustard, venison in an oriental sauce, fresh oysters or lobster, and fish of the day.

Restaurant Ta'Frenċ (☎ 21 553 888; Triq ir-Rabat; mains Lm5-8; ✖ lunch & dinner daily, closed Tue Nov-Mar) For a special occasion, head to this *très élégant* restaurant, about 1.5km south of Marsalforn on the road to Victoria. It's set in a lovingly restored 14th-century farmhouse and has an impressive menu of French, Italian and Maltese dishes. The

French influence is strongest; try starters of snails or lobster bisque, followed by grilled king prawns, duck breast with a walnut, apple and orange sauce, or pan-fried rabbit. There are a few vegetarian options, and even a children's menu, plus desserts like crepe suzette or soufflé.

Also at the Calypso Hotel is a very good Chinese restaurant, the **Dragon**, plus **Luce D'Oro** (mains Lm2.75-4), an elegant rooftop restaurant with a menu of innovative fusion dishes not often seen on Gozo – eg chicken caesar salad, tandoori chicken breast, or grilled teriyaki fish skewer on Asian noodles.

The **Ritz** (☎ 21 558 392; Triq il-Wied) is a cheap-and-cheerful café-bar selling snacks and sandwiches to settle a rumbling tum quickly (a ham omelette is Lm0.40, a cheeseburger is Lm0.70). **Smuggler's Cave** (☎ 21 551 005; snacks & meals Lm1.60-5), by the Calypso Hotel, has cheap pizzas and burgers (plus the usual pasta, meat and fish), but feels more like a British seaside restaurant than a Maltese one. Fashionable **Caffino**, at the ground level of the Calypso Hotel, is the best choice for a snack or drink, with lots of savoury pastries, toasted sandwiches and mouthwatering cakes (Lm0.60 to Lm0.95 each).

Dive Bar (☎ 21 559 931; Triq il-Port) is a good stop for after-beach drinks, in a bright, nautically themed interior reminiscent of a ship's galley. Internet access is also available. **Yellow Rock Pub** (☎ 21 550 983; Triq il-Munġbell), a block back from the waterfront, is another popular watering hole, with big screens televising sporting events.

Getting There & Away
Bus No 21 runs between Marsalforn and Victoria.

XAGHRA
pop 3750

The pretty village of Xaghra (shaa-ra) spreads across the flat summit of the hill east of Victoria, seemingly lost in a dream of times past. The early-19th-century Church of Our Lady of Victory looks down benignly on the tree-lined village square, Pjazza Vittorja, where old men sit and chat in the shade of the oleanders.

Orientation & Information
The main road from Mġarr and Victoria zigzags up the hill from the south and passes the site of the temples of Ġgantija before joining the village square in front of the church. A left turn here leads back towards Victoria on a rough, steep, minor road (affording brilliant views of Victoria and Il-Kastell). A right turn leads past the school and post office to the Marsalforn road. The **Bank of Valletta** (no ATM) is at the western end of the square.

Sights
A narrow lane beside the school leads to the restored **Ta'Kola Windmill** (☎ 21 561 071; Triq il-Bambina; adult/child Lm1/free; ☽ 8.30am-4.30pm Mon-Sat, 8.30am-3pm Sun, closed public holidays). Built in 1725, the windmill is now something of an attraction, housing a museum of country life with exhibits of woodworking tools, farm equipment and period bedroom and living quarters. Best of all is the climb up the narrow stairs to see the original milling gear complete with millstones.

Visitors can also purchase a **Xaghra Day Ticket** (adult/child Lm1.50/free), which includes entry to both the Ġgantija temples and Ta'Kola windmill on the same day. This ticket is available at both the temples and windmill.

In the back streets to the north of the village square lie **Xerri's Grotto** (☎ 21 556 863; l'Għar ta'Xerri; admission Lm1) and **Ninu's Cave** (Triq Jannar; admission Lm0.50). These underground caverns, complete with stalactites and stalagmites, are unusual in that they are both entered through private houses. Having discovered the caves beneath their homes, the owners decided to cash in on the tourist potential. Xerri's Grotto was discovered in 1923 when Antonio Xerri was digging a well. It's the bigger, deeper and more interesting of the two. Opening times are at the discretion of the owners, but are generally from 9am to 5pm in summer.

EDWARD LEAR ON GOZO

Edward Lear (1812–88), the English landscape painter and nonsense poet (Lear popularised the limerick as a form of comic verse), spent much of his life travelling around the Mediterranean. He visited Gozo in 1866, and described the scenery as 'pomskizillious and gromphiberous, being as no words can describe its magnificence'.

GOZO

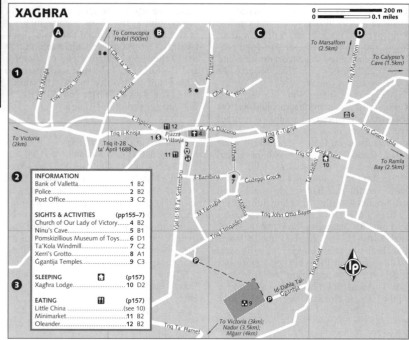

XAGĦRA

0 ——— 200 m
0 ——— 0.1 miles

To Cornucopia Hotel (500m)

To Marsalforn (2.5km)

To Calypso's Cave (1.5km)

To Victoria (2km)

To Ramla Bay (2.5km)

Triq il-Knisja

Triq it-28 ta' April 1688

il-Bambina

Gużeppi Grech

Triq John Otto Bayer

Id-Dahla Tal-Ġgantija

To Victoria (3km); Nadur (3.5km); Mgarr (4km)

Triq Ta' Hamet

INFORMATION	
Bank of Valletta	1 B2
Police	2 B2
Post Office	3 C2

SIGHTS & ACTIVITIES	(pp155–7)
Church of Our Lady of Victory	4 B2
Ninu's Cave	5 B1
Pomskizillious Museum of Toys	6 D1
Ta'Kola Windmill	7 C2
Xerri's Grotto	8 A1
Ġgantija Temples	9 C3

SLEEPING		(p157)
Xagħra Lodge	10	D2

EATING		(p157)
Little China	(see 10)	
Minimarket	11	B2
Oleander	12	B2

At the east end of town the road forks – left for Marsalforn, right for Ramla Bay. A few metres along the Ramla road on the left is the **Pomskizillious Museum of Toys** (☎ 21 562 489; Triq Ġnien Xibla; adult/child Lm0.90/0.40; ☒ 10am-noon & 3-6pm Mon-Sat May–mid-Oct, 10am-1pm Thu-Sat Apr, 10am-1pm Sat and public holidays mid-Oct–Mar), popular with kids for its impressive array of dolls houses, toy soldiers, dolls and various other old toys.

Signposts near the Pomskizillious Museum of Toys point the way through the maze of minor roads east of Xagħra down to **Calypso's Cave** overlooking the sandy beach of Ramla Bay – it's a 30-minute walk from the village square. The cave itself is hardly worth the hike – it's just a hollow under an overhang at the top of the cliff (a local near the entrance will try to get you to rent a candle from him, but you don't need it) – but the view over Ramla Bay is lovely. On a calm day visitors can usually see the remains of an artificial reef extending into the sea off the eastern headland of the bay. This was part of the defences built by the Knights of St John to prevent

attackers landing on the beach. In theory, the enemy ships would run aground on the reef, where they would be attacked using a couple of fougasses (primitive mortarlike weapons; for more information see the boxed text, p104).

ĠGANTIJA

Located on the crest of the hill to the south of Xagħra, the megalithic **temples of Ġgantija** (☎ 21 553 194; access from Triq l-Imqades; adult/child Lm1/free; ☒ 8.30am-4.30pm Mon-Sat, 8.30am-3pm Sun, closed public holidays) command a splendid view over most of southern Gozo and beyond to Comino and Malta. As the name implies (ġgantija – dje-*gant*-ee-ya – means 'giantess') these are the largest of the megalithic temples found in the Maltese Islands – the walls stand over 6m high, and the two temples together span over 40m.

Along with Ta'Ħaġrat and Skorba on Malta (p109), the Ġgantija temples are thought to be Malta's oldest, dating from the period 3600 to 3000 BC. Both temples face towards the southeast, and both have five semicircular niches within. The south

GOZO

CALYPSO'S ISLE

Gozo is one of the half-dozen or so contenders for the title of Calypso's Isle – the mythical island of Ogygia described in Homer's *Odyssey* where the nymph Calypso seduced the hero Odysseus and kept him captive for seven years. But she could not overcome his longing for his home in Ithaca, and Zeus eventually sent Hermes to command her to release him.

If the cave above Ramla Bay on Gozo was really Calypso's hideaway, then it is no wonder that Odysseus was keen to get home. Despite the pretty view and delightful island, it's a long, hot and scratchy climb up from the beach, and the cramped living quarters leave a lot to be desired.

temple (on the left) is the older, and is entered across a huge threshold slab with four holes at each side, thought to be for libations. The first niche on the right contains an altar with some spiral decoration – a pillar with a snake carved on it is now in the Archaeology Museum in Victoria (p143). The left-hand niche in the inner chamber has a well-preserved trilithon altar; on the right is a circular hearth stone and a bench altar.

There is little of interest in the north temple, but the outer wall of the temple complex is impressive in scale. The largest of the megaliths measures 6m by 4m and weighs around 57 tonnes, and the wall may originally have stood up to 16m tall.

As with other temples in Malta, it's disappointing that there's no information board explaining to visitors the history and significance of the site.

Sleeping & Eating

Xaghra Lodge (☎ 21 562 362; www.gozo.com/xaghra lodge; Triq Dun Ġorġ Preċa; s/d Lm15.75/21 low season, Lm18.75/25 high season; ❄ ❷) This is a cosy little guesthouse run by a friendly English couple. There are excellent facilities for the price, including en suite, a balcony and cable TV in all rooms, a terrace and an adjacent bar and Chinese restaurant. It's a five-minute walk east of the town square.

Cornucopia Hotel (☎ 21 556 486; www.vjborg.com /cornucopia; Triq Ġnien Imrik; s/d Lm11.25/22.50 low season, Lm26/39 high season; ❄ ❷) Cornucopia and its selection of accommodation options is set in and around a converted farmhouse about 1km north of the village square. Four-star accommodation is available in hotel rooms set around a courtyard, pool and pretty garden, or in self-catering villas, bungalows, apartments and farmhouses (all with an average price of Lm25/50 per unit low/high season).

Oleander (☎ 21 557 230; Pjazza Vittorja; mains Lm3.50-6; ❄ lunch & dinner Tue-Sun) On the pretty village square, the popular Oleander has a menu you've probably seen before (pastas, *braġioli*, rabbit, fresh fish, local lamb) but it's all well prepared and regulars rave over the rabbit dishes. It's a pleasant place to while away an evening, and there are a couple of other decent options on the square.

Little China (☎ 21 562 362; Triq Dun Ġorġ Preċa; mains Lm3-5.50; set menu per person from Lm5.90) If you need a break from pizza, pasta and rabbit, head to this place, adjacent to the Xaghra Lodge. On offer are a wide range of meat, poultry, vegetable and seafood dishes – favourites like sweet and sour pork, beef with black bean sauce, lemon chicken and crispy duck. There's lots of soups and starters, and vegetarian options.

For those who prefer to picnic or self-cater, there's a handy **minimarket** (Vjal it-18 Ta'Settembru) just south of the square.

Getting There & Away

Bus Nos 64 and 65 run between Victoria and Xaghra.

NADUR

pop 4000

Nadur is Gozo's 'second city', spreading along a high ridge to the east of Victoria. In Malti, Nadur means 'lookout', and a 17th-century watchtower overlooks the Comino sea lanes from the western end of the ridge.

Nadur's ornate **Church of Sts Peter & Paul** (Pjazza San Pietru u San Pawl) was built in the late 18th century – the entrance is framed between white statues of the two saints, giving the church its local nickname of iż-Żewġ (the pair). The interior is richly decorated with marble sculptures, and the vault is covered with 150 paintings. See the boxed text, p38 for more about the church.

A block south of the church (well signposted from the square) is the **Kelinu Grima Maritime Museum** (☎ 21 565 226; Triq il-Kappillan;

GOZO

COMINO

Comino (or *Kemmuna* in Malti), once reportedly the hide-out of pirates and smugglers, now regularly plays host to boatloads of bikini-clad invaders. Home to the Blue Lagoon, one of Malta's most hyped natural attractions, the island itself is a small and barren chunk of limestone wedged between Malta and Gozo. Almost the only inhabitants are the guests and staff of the island's single hotel, though they are joined in summer by hordes of day-trippers from Malta (and a few from Gozo). In winter, when the hotel is closed, only a handful of people remain.

Classified as a nature reserve and bird sanctuary, Comino is only 2.5km by 1.5km in size, and away from the hotel and the Blue Lagoon the island is peaceful and unspoiled. A walk along the rough tracks affords some great views of northern Malta or of Gozo. It's impossible to get lost here, given the island's tiny size and the fact that St Mary's Tower, the only landmark of note, is visible from almost everywhere on the island.

The main part of the Comino Hotel is on San Niklaw Bay, and the Comino Bungalows are on Santa Marija Bay, 500m to the west. A rough track lined with oleander trees, rather grandly named Triq Congreve, runs from Santa Marija Bay south to St Mary's Tower. Side tracks lead to the Blue Lagoon and San Niklaw Bay.

SIGHTS

The only man-made sights to see on Comino are the little **Chapel of Our Lady's Return from Egypt** at Santa Marija Bay and **St Mary's Tower**, built by the Knights in 1618. It was once part of the chain of signal towers between Gozo and Mdina but today it is just an observation post used by the Maltese military. Climb the steps and enjoy the views.

The island's biggest attraction is the **Blue Lagoon**, a sheltered cove between the western end of the island and the uninhabited islet of Cominotto (*Kemmunett* in Malti). This immensely photogenic cove has a white-sand sea bed and beautifully clear turquoise waters. It is an image repeated on countless souvenir postcards from Malta. In summer the bay is inundated with people each day between around 10am and 4pm, which detracts a little from the desert-island atmosphere (if you're staying at the hotel, of course, you can enjoy the lagoon in relative peace in the early morning and late afternoon). The southern end of the lagoon is roped off to keep boats out; there is excellent swimming and snorkelling here, plus you can swim over to Cominotto. Take care in the unrelenting summer heat – there is no shade here, and most sunbathing is done on

---

adult/child Lm1/0.50; 🕙 9am-4.45pm Mon-Sat, closed public holidays), a private collection of ship models, relics and maritime memorabilia.

To get to Nadur, take bus No 42 or 43 from Victoria.

AROUND NADUR

Narrow country roads radiate northward from Nadur to three beaches, all sign-posted. **Ramla Bay** (also called Ir-Ramla) is the biggest and best sandy beach on Gozo, and one of the prettiest in the islands – the strand of reddish-gold contrasts picturesquely with the blue of the sea and white statue of the Virgin Mary. As such, it is usually heaving with people in summer, when cafés, souvenir stalls and water-sports

facilities abound. It is much quieter and more pleasant in spring and autumn, and in winter you can have the place almost to your (goose-pimpled) self. The minimal remains of a **Roman villa** are hidden among the bamboo behind the beach, and Calypso's Cave (p156) looks down from the hilltop to the west. Ramla Bay is also easily accessed (on foot or by car) from Xaghra, and bus No 42 runs between the bay and Victoria.

The next beach to the east is **San Blas**, a tiny, rock-strewn bay with some patches of coarse rust-coloured sand backed by steep, terraced fields with prickly pear hedges. It's a lovely place to take a picnic lunch and a good book, and perhaps a mask and fins the exposed rocky ledges surrounding the cove, so wear a hat and heavy-duty sunscreen. There are public toilets and a few kiosks selling drinks, ice creams and snacks.

SLEEPING & EATING

Comino Hotel & Bungalows (☎ 21 529 821; www.cominohotels.com; half board per person Lm17-28; ❄️ 💻 🐾) is the only place to stay on the island, and it is open only from April to October. The four-star hotel has 95 rooms at San Niklaw Bay and 45 bungalows at Santa Marija Bay, but no self-catering options. Rooms are bright and simply furnished, but well equipped – each has a small balcony, TV, fridge and hairdryer. A garden-view room costs Lm17 per person per night for half board in low season (April, May and October), Lm23 in mid-season (June and from mid- to late September) and Lm28 in high season (July to mid-September). The supplement for a single room is Lm8, for a sea view is Lm3 per person. Full board costs an additional Lm6. The buffet meals are of a good standard.

The hotel has a café and bar, private beach (in San Niklaw Bay), swimming pools and tennis courts. Guests can also pay for bike rental, boat excursions, water-skiing and other water-sports facilities (including rental of windsurfing equipment, sailing and motor boats, and canoes) and instruction at the hotel's dive school, **Comino Dive Centre** (☎ 21 572 997; www.cominodivecentre.com).

Day-trippers can use the hotel facilities for a stiff fee of Lm12 a day (Lm14 at weekends), but this must be booked in advance through the hotel. The price includes lunch, a return boat ticket and use of the pool and private beach.

Apart from the public toilets above the Blue Lagoon, all facilities on the island – including telephones and currency exchange – belong to the hotel, and the management isn't too keen on nonresidents using them.

GETTING THERE & AWAY

The Comino Hotel runs its own ferry service, with around seven crossings a day from Ċirkewwa on Malta (between 7.30am and 11.30pm) and Mġarr on Gozo (between 6.15am and 10pm). Arriving and departing hotel guests are given priority on the boats and their return ticket price is Lm2/1 per adult/child. The ferry can also be used by nonresidents of the hotel (at a price of Lm3.50/1.75 return). The boats do not run from November to March when the hotel is closed.

You can also make a day trip to the Blue Lagoon from tourist areas like Sliema and Buġibba on Malta, and Xlendi on Gozo. **Charlie's Speedboat Trips** (☎ 99 486 949) runs an afternoon boat trip from Golden Bay (arriving as many of the crowds depart – see p108). Shuttle services (not operated by the hotel) also operate from Ċirkewwa and Mġarr harbours.

for snorkelling – the water is quite shallow and very clear. There are no facilities here, and parking space for only one or two cars on the very narrow track above the bay. You can walk there from Nadur in 20 to 30 minutes (take Triq San Blas off Triq it-Tiġrija, two blocks north of Nadur's church).

Attractive **Daħlet Qorrot**, the third bay, is popular with local weekenders. There's a small sandy beach, but most of the swimming is off the rocks beside the rows of little boathouses (carved out of the rock, and with brightly painted doors). There's usually plenty of space to park; you can buy drinks and snacks in summer only.

QALA

The village of Qala (a-la) has little to see except for a couple of 18th-century **windmills**. The road east of the village square (Triq il-Kunċizzjoni) leads down to the coast at **Ħondoq ir-Rummien**, a little cove with a scrap of sand, bathing ladders on the rocks, and benches with a view across the water to Comino.

Directory

CONTENTS

PRACTICALITIES

- Local English-language daily newspapers include the *Times* (online at www.timesofmalta.com) and the Malta *Independent* (www.independent.com.mt). The former has a good mix of local, European and world news, the latter has good coverage of domestic social issues. *Malta Today* (www.maltatoday .com.mt) is published weekly (on Sunday) and includes a useful supplement with listings of TV, cinema and events for the coming week.

- There are nearly 20 local radio stations broadcasting mostly in Malti but occasionally in English. There are two state-run TV stations and half-a-dozen small commercial channels broadcasting in Malti. Most of the main Italian TV stations can be received in Malta. Satellite and cable TV are widely available in hotels and bars, providing a wide range of stations from Europe and the US.

- Malta, like most of Europe and the UK, uses the PAL video system.

- Malta's electricity supply is 240V/50Hz and the plugs have three flat pins as in the UK. Continental European appliances (plugs with two round pins) will need an adaptor.

- Like the rest of Europe, Malta uses the metric system. However, the British legacy persists in the use of pint glasses in some pubs.

ACCOMMODATION

There is a wide range of accommodation available in the Maltese Islands, though much of it is in fairly uniform resort hotels and apartments. The government is attempting to drive Malta's tourist industry upmarket, and almost all the new hotels and developments are at the luxury end of the spectrum. However, there are still plenty of good budget options and loads of accommodation bargains in the low season (from November to March, excluding the Christmas and New Year period).

Camping

There are no official camp sites in Malta, and wild camping is not allowed. Travellers sometimes sleep out on the quieter beaches, particularly on Gozo, but strictly speaking this is illegal.

Guesthouses

Guesthouses in Malta are usually small (six to 10 rooms), simple, family-run places and are often good value at around Lm5 to Lm7 per person (and there is often no single supplement). Most rooms will have a washbasin, but showers and toilets are mostly shared. Breakfast is normally included in the price. Facilities will usually not include air-con or a swimming pool, but there are a few exceptions to this rule. Bear in mind that some guesthouses in resort areas close in the low season (however, all guesthouses in Valletta are open year-round).

Hostels

The **National Student Travel Service** (NSTS; Map pp62-3; ☎ 21 244 983; www.nsts.org; 220 Triq San Pawl, Valletta) is an associate member of Hostelling International (HI). It runs a few hostels in Malta and also has agreements with certain guesthouses to provide cheap accommodation to hostellers. An HI-membership card is required in order to stay at any of these hostels in Malta. Cards are available from the NSTS or from the main hostel, Hibernia Residence & Hostel, in Sliema. NSTS can arrange accommodation in the following hostels:

Hibernia Residence & Hostel (p89) Sliema
Pinto Guesthouse (p90) St Julian's
University Residence (p127) Lija
St Joseph Home Hostel (p149) Għajnsielem on Gozo

There is also a new hostel – Maria-Giovanna Hostel in Marsalforn, Gozo (see the boxed text, p154) – that is not affiliated with HI or the NSTS but is well worth investigating; it is an excellent choice for great-value accommodation.

Hotels

Hotels in Malta range from crumbling but characterful old townhouses in Valletta to modern, gilt and chrome palaces of five-star luxury overlooking a private marina. The majority (especially somewhere like Buġibba) are bland, faceless tourist hotels, block-booked by package tour companies in summer, and either closed or eerily quiet in winter. However, there are quite a few places that have real character, like the Castille Hotel in Valletta (p71), housed in an old mansion; the Xara Palace in Mdina (p120); and the Kempinski San Lawrenz Resort & Spa (p152) or Hotel Ta'Ċenċ (p150) on Gozo, but the latter three hotels are among the most expensive in the islands.

Most of the large four- and five-star places offer the kind of holiday where you may not need to leave the hotel's grounds – they're fully equipped with cafés, bars and restaurants (the majority of hotels include breakfast in their rates, and also offer half-board and full-board arrangements). At these places you'll usually find indoor and outdoor pools, a gym and/or sporting facilities, plus a programme of children's activities; and quite possibly a health spa, a dive company, and perhaps a beach-side lido offering pool and water sports (water-skiing, boat trips, canoe or boat hire, ringo rides etc).

Typical high-season hotel rates are Lm12 to Lm25 per person, but they rise to as high as Lm50 for the four- and five-star places. Prices may well halve in the low season. You should also be aware that many hotels and guesthouses quote their prices per person, not per room.

There are loads of Internet sites offering information on hotels and other accommodation options in Malta, including:

Holiday Malta (www.holiday-malta.com)
Malta Hotel (www.maltahotel.net)
Malta Hotels (www.malta-hotels.com)
Visit Malta (www.visitmalta.com/en/where_to_stay)

Rental Accommodation

There are hundreds of self-catering apartments with little to choose between them. Most have a private bathroom, a balcony and a kitchen area with fridge, sink and two-ring electric cooker. Though lacking a little in charm, they are often very good value at under Lm10 per person, even in high season. One of our favourites, and offering bargain prices in the low season, is the Corinthia Mistra Village Clubhotel (see the boxed text, p108).

If you're looking for something with a little local colour, then get in touch with a tour operator or agency that specialises in Gozo farmhouses (see the boxed text, p146).

High & Low Seasons

The cost of accommodation in Malta can vary considerably with the time of year, and low-season rates are often a bargain. Low season is almost always November to March. High season generally refers to the period April to October, but some accommodation providers have a 'shoulder' or 'mid' season covering April, May and October, with high-season prices restricted to June, July, August and September. Many hotels count the Christmas and New Year period as high season too. The high- and low-season prices quoted in this book are generally the maximum and minimum rates for each establishment.

Bear in mind that some places (small guesthouses and cheaper hotels) in some resort areas close in the low season – as does the Comino Hotel, making a stay on Comino impossible from November to March.

ACTIVITIES

One of the most popular activities for holiday-makers in Malta is diving – see the Diving & Snorkelling chapter (p46) for details.

The **Marsa Sports Complex** is used by various national sport associations. The complex, about 4km southwest of Valletta, includes a racecourse, the Marsa Sports & Country Club and the National Athletic Stadium. Facilities include five turf pitches, a rugby pitch, a baseball pitch, two netball courts, two basketball courts and one full-size football ground.

The **Marsa Sports & Country Club** (☎ 21 233 851; www.marsasportsclub.com) includes an 18-hole golf course (the only one in Malta – see Golf below), 30 tennis courts, five squash courts, minigolf, polo, a swimming pool, a cricket ground and a gymnasium. Visitors may use these facilities; a day membership costs Lm2, a week Lm10.

The website of the **Malta Tourism Authority** (www.visitmalta.com) has loads of information on the different types of activities possible in Malta, and organisations that can help you pursue them. Click onto the 'What to Do' pages.

Bird Watching

Although barely a dozen species of bird are permanent residents on Malta, the islands sustain important breeding colonies of sea-birds, including storm-petrels and Cory's shearwaters. Malta also lies on an important migration route between Africa and Europe, and in spring and autumn vast numbers of migrating birds can be seen (as can numerous bird hunters, unfortunately). See the Environment chapter (p44) for more information.

Wildlife of the Maltese Islands, a joint publication of BirdLife Malta and Nature Trust, edited by Joe Sultana and Victor Falzon, is a comprehensive book covering all types of animal found in Malta.

BirdLife Malta (☎ 21 347 646; www.birdlifemalta .org) is the best contact for birders visiting Malta. It manages the Il-Għadira nature reserve (p111) at Mellieħa Bay, monitors activity that threatens wild birds and has a website detailing recent sightings.

Golf

The **Royal Malta Golf Club** (☎ 21 239 302; www .maltagolf.org; 9/18 holes Lm10/15, clubs hire Lm5) is a private members' club established in 1888, located at the Marsa Sports & Country Club at Marsa, southwest of Valletta. Visitors are welcome to play the 18-hole, par-68 course, but reservations are essential (it's best to avoid Thursday and Saturday morning, as these days are reserved for members' competitions). Club facilities include a pro shop, bar, restaurant and driving range. There are plans drawn up for a second golf course, near Rabat in central Malta, but this is strongly opposed by environmental groups (bear in mind the size of this island and its lack of fresh water). See www.nogolfmalta.cjb.net for more information.

Horse Riding

Horses have long played an important part in Maltese life, and you can often see proud owners out exercising their favourite trotting horses. The quieter back roads offer enjoyable riding – hire of a horse and instruction can be organised through most major hotels.

Riding schools in Malta include:

Bidnija Horse Riding School (☎ 21 410 010; Triq il-Bdiewa, Mosta)

Golden Bay Horse Riding (☎ 21 573 360; Għajn Tuffieħa; ☼ 8am-8pm Jun-Sep, 9am-5pm Oct-May) See p109 for more details.

Pandy's Riding School (☎ 21 342 506; Triq Tobruk, Pembroke)

Wagon Wheel Horse Riding School (☎ 21 556 254; Triq Marsalforn, Victoria, Gozo)

Rock Climbing

There are more than 1200 established rock-climbing routes in the Maltese Islands (most on limestone), with some of the most popular sites for climbers below the Dingli Cliffs in the west, at Għar Lapsi, and near the Victoria Lines below Naxxar. **Malta Rock Climbing** (☎ 21 480 240; www.malta-rockclimbing.com) offers three-hour taster sessions (Lm15), guided climbing excursions (half day Lm20, full day Lm30), climbing courses and gear rental.

Running

Several major running events are held each year in Malta, including triathlons and half-marathons, culminating in the **Malta Marathon** (☎ 21 432 402; www.maltamarathon.com; PO Box 9, Hamrun) and half-marathon, held in late February. Application forms are available from the website; the entrance fee is €35.

Sailing

Malta is a major yachting centre, with a large marina at Msida, a smaller one at Gozo's Mġarr harbour, and two slick new marinas –

one at the Portomaso development in St Julian's, the other as part of the Cottonera waterfront redevelopment in Vittoriosa. Many yacht owners cruise the Med in summer and winter their vessels in Malta.

A full programme of races and regattas is held between April and November each year (great for participants and spectators). The popular **Rolex Middle Sea Race** (www.rolex middlesearace.com) is a highly rated offshore classic staged annually in October. The race is 607 nautical miles, from Malta, sailing anticlockwise around Sicily before returning to Malta. For details of events and opportunities for crewing, contact the **Royal Malta Yacht Club** (☎ 21 333 109; www.rmyc.org; Manoel Island) or check the website.

Qualified sailors are able to hire a yacht by the day or the week from one of several charter companies. If you don't have a RYA Coastal Skipper qualification you'll need to pay extra for a skipper. Try:

Captain Morgan Yacht Charter (☎ 23 463 333; www .yachtcharter.com.mt; per week from Lm1100/1350 low/ high season, including tax) Rates quoted are for an eight-berth Oceanis Clipper 411 sailing yacht. A professional skipper costs another Lm35 a day.

S & D Yachts (☎ 21 331 515; www.sdyachts.com)

If a yacht seems a little too much to handle, sailing dinghies can be rented by the hour at most tourist resorts for around Lm5 an hour.

Walking

There is some good walking to be enjoyed on the winding back roads and cliff-top paths of Malta and Gozo, although fences, dogs and bird-shooters can occasionally prove to be a nuisance. Distances are small and you can easily cover much of the islands on foot. A circuit of Gozo is a good objective for a multiday hike.

Windsurfing

Windsurfing is a popular sport enjoyed throughout the year in Malta. Equipment hire and instruction are available at all the main tourist resorts. Mellieħa Bay, St Paul's Bay and St Thomas Bay are popular venues. A good place for information is the website at www.holidays-malta.com/windsurf.

There are two major international competitions held in Maltese waters each year: the Sicily to Malta Windsurfing Race in May (the world's longest single-stretch race), and the International Open-Class Boardsailing Championships in September.

BUSINESS HOURS
Banks
Banking hours can vary from branch to branch, but they are all generally open from 8.30am to 12.30pm or 12.45pm Monday to Friday (some banks also open in the afternoon, from 2.30pm to 4pm) and 8.30am to noon on Saturday between October and mid-June. The summer hours (from mid-June to September) see branches opening at 8am and few banks are open in the afternoon.

There are 24-hour foreign exchange facilities at Malta International Airport all year round.

Museums
The standard opening hours for all government museums and historic sites on Malta (including the prehistoric temples of Tarxien, Ħaġar Qim, Mnajdra and Ġgantija) are: 8.15am to 5pm Monday to Saturday and 8.15am to 4.15pm Sunday from 1 October to 15 June; 7.45am to 2pm daily from 16 June to 30 September (closed public holidays).

The hours for government museums on Gozo are different from those on Malta. They are open from 8.30am to 4.30pm Monday to Saturday, 8.30am to 3pm Sunday (closed public holidays).

For inquiries about opening hours, contact **Heritage Malta** (☎ 22 954 000; www.heritage malta.org/visiting.html).

Pharmacies
Pharmacies are generally open from 9am to 1pm and 4pm to 7pm Monday to Saturday. Duty pharmacists that open late and on Sunday or public holidays are listed in local newspapers.

Restaurants & Cafés
See p55 in the Food & Drink chapter for an overview of opening hours for most eating establishments.

Shops
Shops are generally open between 9am and 1pm, and again between 4pm and 7pm. In tourist areas in summer they will usually be open all day. All shops are closed on Sunday and public holidays.

CHILDREN
Malta is a good destination for a family holiday. Children are made welcome everywhere and there are plenty of activities to keep them busy. Pharmacies are well stocked with baby products such as formula, bottles, pacifiers and nappies (diapers). Most hotels have cots available and safety seats can easily be arranged through most car-rental companies.

Kids might enjoy the Malta Experience and other audiovisual shows and exhibitions in Valletta (p68) and Mdina (p119). An option for older kids (who are not easily frightened) is a visit to the Mdina Dungeons (p119), which are fitted out with spooky sound effects and gory torture scenes.

The whole family can enjoy a boat trip out of Wied iż-Żurrieq (p135), Buġibba (p102), Golden Bay (p108) or Sliema (p89). More expensive distractions for older kids include Jeep safaris (p89), horse riding (p109) and quad biking (p113).

The Splash & Fun Park, with its waterslides and playground, is at Baħar iċ-Ċagħaq; and its neighbour, Mediterraneo Marine Park, puts on dolphin and sea-lion shows for the public. You can also swim with the dolphins here. See p100 for details. Popeye Village at Anchor Bay (also known as Sweethaven; p113) is always popular with younger children, even if they've never heard of Popeye.

In summer you can hire snorkelling gear, canoes, dinghies etc at most tourist resorts. A sandy beach with safe paddling and swimming for kids can be found at Mellieħa Bay.

Lonely Planet's *Travel with Children* by Cathy Lanigan is also packed with useful advice for travelling families.

CLIMATE CHART
The climate chart below is for Valletta, Malta's capital. For more detailed information

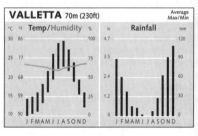

on climate and the best times for travel to Malta see p13.

COURSES

Malta is one of the few places where people wanting to learn or improve their English can combine a language course with a Mediterranean holiday. There are around 40 English-language schools in Malta, ranging from one-person operations to the Berlitz Language Centre, and together they cater to around 40,000 students a year from over 50 countries.

Sliema and St Julian's have the greatest concentration of schools, and most can organise accommodation for course participants in homestays, student residences, apartments or hotels.

For details of vacation and business courses contact:

Malta Tourism Authority (www.visitmalta.com) See also p172. The authority's website has loads of information in various languages and a full list of schools.

Federation of English Language Teaching Organisations Malta (FELTOM; fax 21 230 330; www.feltom .com; Foundation for International Studies, Old University Buildings, Triq San Pawl, Valletta)

CUSTOMS

Items for personal use are not subject to duty. The duty free allowance per person is: 1L of spirits, 1L of wine, 200 cigarettes or 100 cigarillos or 50 cigars or 250g of tobacco, 60ml of perfume and 250ml of eau de toilette. Duty will be charged on any gifts over Lm50 that are intended for local residents.

Meat and poultry (cooked or not), and plants and plant produce (including soil), must not be brought into the country, so forget about that Christmas turkey or the present of a pot plant. Speaking of pot plants, being caught trying to bring any kind of illegal drug into the country will land you in jail. Possession of even small amounts of cannabis for personal use is punishable by a prison sentence.

Customs regulations can be checked online at www.maltairport.com/customs.htm.

DANGERS & ANNOYANCES
Road Conditions & Driving

Much of the road network in Malta is badly in need of repair, which means that driving is often an uncomfortably bumpy experience.

Rules of the road are rarely observed, which adds to the stress of driving in unfamiliar territory, especially during rush hour conditions around Sliema and St Julian's.

There is something of a macho, devil-may-care culture among young male drivers and the accident rate is correspondingly high. This attitude extends to the buses too, and as a passenger there will be times when you might suspect that a kid has stolen his father's bus and is taking you on a joyride.

Taxi Drivers

Taxi drivers often try to rip off travellers – always agree on a fare before getting into a taxi. On arrival at the airport, ignore any taxi drivers who tell you that the bus stop is a 20-minute walk away, or that the bus won't be along for another hour – they're just touting for business.

Theft

Malta has a low rate of violent crime and crimes against visitors are a rarity. Incidents involving pickpockets and purse-snatchers are uncommon, but in past years there have been increasing reports of thieves breaking into cars parked in quiet areas like Marfa and Delimara Point. The only real defence is to lock the car and not leave anything of value in it.

Although Valletta is far safer than most European capitals, it's sensible to exercise a degree of caution, especially in the quieter side streets late at night.

Walking

If you go walking in the countryside, beware of the national obsession with shooting and trapping birds – the little stone shacks that pepper the cliff tops are shooters' hides. You will hear the popping of shotguns before you see the shooters – and they are not at all welcoming. The close season for shooting is 22 May to 31 August (one of the shortest in Europe), but even these dates are routinely ignored by hunters. See p44 for more information on this issue.

DISABLED TRAVELLERS

Maltese government policy is to improve access for people with disabilities, but many of Malta's historic places – notably the steep, stepped streets of Valletta – remain difficult, if not impossible, to negotiate in a wheelchair or for those with restricted mobility. Several sites are accessible, however, including the Malta Experience and the Museum of Archaeology in Valletta. A good number of the more expensive hotels have wheelchair access and some have rooms specially designed for disabled guests.

The **Malta Tourism Authority** (www.visitmalta .com) can provide information on hotels and sights that are equipped for wheelchair users; its website uses a wheelchair icon to indicate whether a venue has easy access or facilities for the disabled.

Other useful organisations:

National Commission for Persons with Disabilities (☎ 21 487 789; www.knpd.org; Triq il-Kbira San Ġużepp, Santa Venera) Can provide information on facilities and access for disabled travellers in Malta.

World Travel for Disabled Persons (WTDP; ☎ 21 570 326; www.wtdp.org; 9 New York Bldgs, Triq Qawra, Qawra) Specialises in holidays to Malta for disabled persons, their families and friends. Services include transfers, accommodation, activity programmes, therapy sessions and tours to other European destinations.

DISCOUNT CARDS
Senior Cards
In Malta, people over 60 are entitled to discounted admission to all government-owned museums.

Student & Youth Cards
A valid ISIC card is worth taking along. The **National Student Travel Service** (NSTS; p161) issues a booklet listing shops, restaurants, attractions and other establishments in Malta offering discounts of 15% to 40%. Admission to state-run museums is also discounted for students.

EMBASSIES & CONSULATES
Maltese Embassies & Consulates
Diplomatic representation abroad includes:

Australia (☎ 02-6290 1724; maltahc@bigpond.com; 38 Culgoa Circuit, O'Malley ACT 2606)
France (☎ 01 56 59 75 90; fax 01 45 62 00 36; 92 Avenue des Champs Elysées, 75008 Paris)
Germany (☎ 030-26 39 110; maltaembgrm@ndh.net; Tiergarten Dreieck, Block 4, Klingelhöferstrasse 7, 10785 Berlin)
Italy (☎ 06-687 99 90; maltaembassy.rome@gov.mt; 12 Lungotevere Marzio, 00186 Rome)
Netherlands (☎ 070-356 1252; malta.embassy@ planet.nl; 2 Scheveningensweg, 2517 KT, The Hague)

Tunisia (☎ 071-847 048; ambassade.malte@planet.tn; 5 Rue Achart, Nord Hilton, 1082 Tunis)
UK (☎ 020-7292 4800; maltahighcommission.london@ gov.mt; Malta House, 36-38 Piccadilly, London W1J 0LE)
USA (☎ 202-462 3611/2; malta_embassy@compuserve .com; 2017 Connecticut Ave NW, Washington DC 20008)

There's no representation in Canada, Ireland or New Zealand.

Embassies & Consulates in Malta
Countries with representation in Malta include:

Australia (Map p86; ☎ 21 338 201; Villa Fiorentina, Ir-Rampa Ta'Xbiex, Ta'Xbiex)
Canada (Map p62-3; ☎ 21 233 121; 103 Triq l-Arċisqof, Valletta)
France (Map p62-3; ☎ 21 233 430; 130 Triq Melita, Valletta)
Germany (Map p88; ☎ 21 336 531; Il-Piazzetta, Entrance B, 1st fl, Triq it-Torri, Sliema)
Italy (Map p75; ☎ 21 233 157/8/9; 1 Triq Vilhena, Floriana)
Netherlands (Map p62-3: ☎ 25 691 790; 19 Triq San Zakkarija, Valletta)
Tunisia (Map p117; ☎ 21 417 171; Valletta Rd, Attard)
UK (Map p86; ☎ 23 230 000; Whitehall Mansions, Ix-Xatt Ta'Ta'Xbiex, Ta'Xbiex)
USA (Map p75; ☎ 21 235 960; 3rd fl, Development House, Triq Sant'Anna, Floriana)

FESTIVALS & EVENTS
The festa is a hugely important event in Maltese family and village life. During the past 200 years festas have developed from simple village feast days into extravagant five-day spectacles, lasting from Wednesday to Sunday.

Every village has a festa, usually on a Sunday, to celebrate the feast day of its patron saint, and most villages try to outdo each other – the more spectacular (and costly) the show, the 'better' the parish and the stronger the saint. The church is decorated with coloured lights, its treasures and relics are cleaned and polished, and placed proudly on display.

Most festas are held from June to September. If a festa is held while you are visiting, do yourself a favour and go along. The timing of church services and events during a festa is usually as follows: on the eve of the feast day, vespers and Mass are at 6pm, followed by band club concerts and the main fireworks display at around 10pm; on the Sunday, pontifical High Mass is celebrated at 9am and 7pm, with the evening Mass followed by the procession. This is the climax of the festa, when the statue of the patron saint is paraded through the streets accompanied by brass bands, fireworks, petards and church bells. People then repair to the bars to drink, chat and sample savoury snacks or sweets such as *qubbajt* (nougat) sold from mobile kiosks that make the rounds of the festas.

The local tourist offices (p172) should be able to tell you when and where festas are being held during your stay. A good idea is to download an up-to-date list of festas before you travel – go to www.malta church.org.mt, then click on Feast Days.

But festas aren't the only excuse to throw a party in Malta, and the website of the Malta Tourism Authority has a comprehensive list of what's on, where and when – go to www.visitmalta.com/en/whats_on. Noteworthy annual events include the following:

FEBRUARY/MARCH
Carnival A week of colourful celebrations preceding Lent, with a traditional procession of floats, fancy dress and grotesque masks. It's celebrated throughout the islands but the main procession is in Valletta.
Malta Marathon A road race from Mdina to Sliema with a large international field (p163).

MARCH
Mediterranean Food Festival (www.mediterranean foodfestival.com) Four-day festival (usually held in the middle of the month) celebrating the food, music and dance of Malta and various ethnic cultures. Held at Eden Arena in St Julian's. See the website for information and schedules.

EASTER WEEK
Good Friday Pageants are held in several towns and villages. Life-size statues depicting scenes from the passion and death of Jesus Christ are carried shoulder high in procession along the main streets of the town, accompanied by men and women dressed as biblical characters.
Easter Sunday Early in the morning there are processions bearing the statue of the Risen Christ. Particularly interesting are those held at the three harbour towns of Vittoriosa, Senglea and Cospicua, where the statue bearers actually run with the statue. It is customary for children to have their *figolla* (an almond-based Easter cake), blessed by the Risen Christ during these processions.

MAY
Fireworks Festival A festival of fireworks, folk music, dance and entertainment, set against the awesome views of Grand Harbour's bastions.

JUNE
L-Imnarja Harvest festival with an agricultural show and traditional horse races; festivities are centred on and around Rabat (see the boxed text, p124).

JULY
Malta Jazz Festival (www.maltajazzfest.com) An increasingly popular event, with outdoor performances held beneath the bastions of Valletta. Held on the third weekend in July.
Farsons Great Beer Festival (www.farsons.com/beer festival/) Family fun (despite the name) with local artists performing, and a focus on local and international beer.

SEPTEMBER
Malta International Air Show (www.maltairshow.com) Held in late September at Luqa airfield. Exhibition of visiting aircraft and aerial displays.

CHRISTMAS IN MALTA

The festive season is celebrated with style in Malta. The strong Catholic tradition of the islands means that the religious aspect of Christmas is still very strong and the parish church, decorated with colourful lights, is the focus of the festivities. Candle-lit carol services are held in the days leading up to Christmas, and midnight Mass on Christmas Eve is the high point of the proceedings.

Every town and village has its crib (called *presepju* in Malti, and often signposted), showing the nativity scene. The tradition of the crib or nativity scene dates back to the 5th or 6th century, as shown by surviving sketches in the Catacombs of St Agatha in Rabat (p122). Villages compete to construct the most impressive nativity scenes, complete with motorised mechanical figures, elaborate lighting and even waterfalls. Some travel agents offer guided tours of the best cribs.

The commercial aspect of Christmas is fully celebrated too, with street lights and decorations, window displays, band club concerts and a frenzy of evening shopping in the streets of Valletta in the week or two before Christmas Day. It's a good time to visit. The weather in December is pleasantly mild and not too wet, the islands are quiet and at their greenest, and red poinsettia flowers – a traditional Christmas sight – brighten many a garden and windowsill.

OCTOBER
Historic Cities Festival Ten days of cultural activities including music, dance and pageantry in Malta's main historic cities – Valletta, the Three Cities, Mdina and Victoria on Gozo.
Rolex Middle Sea Race Offshore sailing classic (p163).

NOVEMBER
Mediterranea (www.mediterranea.com.mt) A week-long festival of culture on the island of Gozo, embracing the prehistoric temple culture, history of Gozo, art, crafts, opera, classical music, ethnic, choral and band music.

FOOD
See the Food & Drink chapter (p55) for details of *fenkata*, lampuki, Kinnie and other quirks of Maltese cuisine, also information on what to eat in Malta and where to eat it.

GAY & LESBIAN TRAVELLERS
Homosexual sex was legalised in Malta in 1973, and the age of consent for both males and females is 16. Attitudes towards homosexuality in Malta are much the same as in most of southern Europe. Younger people and women are likely to be more tolerant than older people and straight men – and bear in mind that this is a very Catholic country, and public displays of affection are generally frowned upon.

Still, although Malta is not a very 'out' destination, it is gay-friendly and there are a couple of openly gay and lesbian bars, and even a hotel exclusively for gay men. Check out **Hotel Kappara** (p91), **Tom Bar** (p77) and **Pips Club** (p96).

The best way to find out more on the local scene is to visit websites on the topic, including:
www.gaymalta.org
www.maltagayrights.com
www.gayroom.co.uk

HOLIDAYS
Malta observes 14 national public holidays:
New Year's Day 1 January
St Paul's Shipwreck 10 February
St Joseph's Day 19 March
Good Friday March/April
Freedom Day 31 March
Labour Day 1 May
Commemoration of 1919 independence riots 7 June
Feast of Sts Peter and Paul (L-Imnarja Festival) 29 June

Feast of the Assumption 15 August
Victory Day 8 September
Independence Day 21 September
Feast of the Immaculate Conception 8 December
Republic Day 13 December
Christmas Day 25 December

INSURANCE
A travel insurance policy to cover theft, loss and medical problems is a good idea. A wide variety of policies is available, so be sure to check the small print. Some policies specifically exclude 'dangerous activities', which can include scuba diving – a very popular attraction in Malta.

You may prefer a policy which pays doctors or hospitals directly rather than you having to pay on the spot and claim later. If you have to claim later make sure you keep all documentation. Some policies ask you to call back (reverse charges) to a centre in your home country where an immediate assessment of your problem is made.

Check that the policy covers ambulances or an emergency flight home.

INTERNET ACCESS
Malta is a well-wired destination, with most hotels and tourism-related organisations having a web page (or at least an email address). There are also numerous Internet cafés in Malta and more are springing up, while many hotels and cafés have at least one computer available for guest use. Rates vary, but typical charges for Internet access are around Lm1 to Lm1.50 an hour. Many computers belong to the **MelitaNet** (www.melita.net) or **Yellow Blue** (www.yellowblue.net) network of machines for public use – if you purchase a voucher for one network, you receive a password allowing the voucher to be used at any of their computers throughout the country. The websites for each network list computer locations; major MelitaNet cybercafés (in Paceville, Valletta, Sliema and Marsaskala) also offer good value rates for overseas telephone calls.

Most travellers make constant use of Internet cafés and free web-based email such as **Yahoo** (www.yahoo.com) or **Hotmail** (www.hotmail.com). If you need to access a specific account of your own, you'll need to carry three pieces of information with you: your incoming (POP or IMAP) mail server name, your account name and your password.

Your ISP or network supervisor will be able to give you these. With this information, you should be able to access your Internet mail account from any Net-connected machine in the world, provided it runs some kind of email software (remember that Netscape and Internet Explorer both have mail modules).

If you're travelling with a notebook or hand-held computer, be aware that your modem may not work outside your home country. The safest option is to buy a reputable 'global' modem before you leave home, or buy a local PC-card modem if you're spending an extended time in any one country. For more information on travelling with a portable computer, see www.teleadapt.com.

LEGAL MATTERS
All towns and most villages have their own police station, the smaller ones manned by a single officer and often marked by a traditional British-style blue lamp.

If you are arrested or detained by the police you have the right to be informed, in a language that you understand, of the reasons for your arrest or detention, and if the police do not release you they must bring you before a court within 48 hours. You also have the right to inform your consulate and to speak to a lawyer.

For an emergency requiring help from the police (*pulizija* in Malti), call ☎ 191. Useful addresses include:

Police headquarters (Map p75; ☎ 21 224 001; Pjazza Vicenzo Buġeja, Floriana)

Gozo's main police station (Map p142; ☎ 21 562 040; Triq ir-Repubblika, Victoria)

MAPS
There is a wide selection of maps of the Maltese Islands to choose from. A general one that is good value and hard-wearing is the *Malta FlexiMap* (Lm2) from Insight Maps. It shows Malta and Gozo at 1: 50,000 scale, and has street maps of Valletta, Sliema & St Julian's, Buġibba, Mdina and Victoria, with useful town and street indexes. The Berndtson *Malta & Gozo* map (Lm1) is another good option, at 1:45,000 with town plans covering Sliema, Mdina, Victoria, Valletta and Buġibba.

The *mAZe* by Frans A Attard is a comprehensive street atlas covering every town

---

ARE YOU OLD ENOUGH?

In Malta the legal drinking age is only 16; you can drive from age 18 and the age of consent (for both heterosexuals and homosexuals) is 16.

---

and village on Malta and Gozo; it costs around Lm5 from bookshops in Malta. Although the text is in English, street names are usually given in Malti only.

MONEY
The Maltese lira, plural liri (Lm) is divided into 100 cents (c). There are 1c, 2c, 5c, 10c, 25c, 50c and Lm1 coins, and Lm2, Lm5, Lm10 and Lm20 notes. The currency is often referred to as the pound, and a £ symbol is also sometimes used.

For new arrivals keen to get their hands on the local currency, there is a 24-hour exchange bureau at the airport and a number of ATMs. Travellers arriving by ferry should note that there are no exchange facilities at the ferry terminal.

ATMs
There are ATMs in all the main towns in Malta where you can withdraw Maltese cash using a credit or debit card and PIN. These transactions may incur a 'handling charge' of around 1.5% of the amount withdrawn – check with your bank before departing (and bear in mind that if you're withdrawing from a credit-card account, you'll be paying interest on the cash advance until you pay off your credit card bill).

Cash
Cash can be changed at hotels, banks, exchange bureaus and some tourist shops. There are also 24-hour exchange machines at banks in the main tourist towns, including Valletta, Sliema and Buġibba, where you can feed in foreign banknotes and get Maltese currency back automatically. The euro and US dollars are widely accepted.

Credit Cards
Visa, MasterCard and Amex credit and charge cards are widely accepted in hotels, restaurants, shops, travel agencies and car hire agencies.

DIRECTORY

International Transfers

You can have money wired to you in Malta via Western Union. Call ☎ 800 73 773 (free call) in Malta to find the nearest office.

Taxes & Refunds

VAT (value-added tax) was re-introduced to Malta in 1999, with two rates of tax: accommodation is charged at 5% (and is usually included in the rates quoted) and the rate for other items is 15%. Food, medicine, education, maritime services, air, sea and public transport are exempt from VAT.

Visitors to Malta can reclaim VAT provided they satisfy certain regulations. Repayment of VAT applies only to purchased goods valued at not less than Lm25 and bought from a single registered outlet, as shown on the receipt, and when the total value of the items is not under Lm100. If you wish to get a VAT refund, you should fill out an application form, available at the custom exit points at the airport or sea port. The next steps on how to obtain your refund are provided on the form and at the customs offices at the airport and sea port.

Tipping & Bargaining

Tipping etiquette generally follows normal practice in mainland Europe. In restaurants where no service charge is included in the bill, waiting staff expect a 10% tip. Baggage porters should get Lm0.50, car park attendants Lm0.20 to Lm0.50 and chamber maids in top-end hotels about Lm1 a week. Taxi drivers expect a tip of about 10% and you should make sure you agree on a fare before getting into the cab.

Bargaining for handicrafts at stalls or markets is essential, but most shops have fixed prices. Hotels and car-hire agencies will often be prepared to bargain in the off season between October and mid-June – stays/rentals of a week or more will often get a 10% discount.

Travellers Cheques

All the main brands of travellers cheques can be easily exchanged at hotels, banks and bureaux de change. You'll find that pounds sterling, euro and US dollars are the favoured denominations. Banks give better rates than hotels, but they often levy a charge of Lm0.20 to Lm0.25 per transaction.

Remember that you will need your passport when cashing travellers cheques.

PHOTOGRAPHY & VIDEO

Film, camcorder cassettes and camera equipment are easily obtained at dozens of photographic shops in all the main towns in Malta. Print film is also available from souvenir shops and hotels in the main tourist areas, but for B&W and slide film you'll usually need to go to a camera shop.

For the best results in your travel photos, shoot your pictures early and late in the day – before 10am and after 4pm. The blazing sun of a Maltese summer will give a flat and washed-out look to pics taken in the middle of the day. If you want to capture that 'tropical turquoise' look of the water in Comino's Blue Lagoon, you will need to use a polarising filter.

POST

Malta Post (☎ 25 961 303; www.maltapost.com) operates a reliable postal service. Post office branches are found in most towns and villages (in some towns the local newsagent/souvenir shop acts as a branch agent). Fax services are available at most branches.

Local postage costs Lm0.07; a 20g letter or postcard sent airmail to the UK or Europe costs Lm0.16, to the USA Lm0.22 and to Australia Lm0.27. Stamps are frequently available from hotels and souvenir shops as well as from post offices.

SHOPPING

Traditional handicrafts include lace, silver filigree, blown glass and pottery, and are available throughout the country. Hand-knitted clothing is produced in the villages and can be quite cheap, but remember to shop around before you make a purchase – the Malta Crafts Centre in Valletta (p74) or the Ta'Qali Crafts Village (p123) are good places to start. The best bargains (and often the most authentic pieces) are to be found on Gozo; inside Il-Kastell are a few options for purchasing handmade lace. Also check out the Ta'Dbieġi Crafts Village (p152) near Għarb.

SOLO TRAVELLERS

Solo travellers are not terribly common in Malta. Most people travel here on short-term summer package holidays with partner/family/friends, or make an annual pilgrimage from northern Europe for winter sun and meet up with people doing the same (at this time of year the average age of visitors to Malta increases significantly!).

Obviously many solo students head here to study English, but they invariably socialise with fellow students. If you are a solo traveller you may decide to stay at the University Residence (p127) in Lija or Hibernia Residence & Hostel (p89) in Sliema if you're looking for company.

Still, there is no real stigma attached to lone travellers. Many guesthouses rent rooms at a set rate per person and do not charge a single-room supplement. Others may charge a supplement of 50% of the per-person rate. Five-star hotels usually have a set rate per room and it doesn't matter whether there's one or two people staying in it – the rate remains the same. You may feel a little conspicuous dining solo in restaurants, surrounded by large groups of locals or travellers, but the service you receive shouldn't be affected.

Women travelling on their own should obviously exercise caution, but the chance of being the victim of crime in Malta is quite low and Maltese men are not nearly as troublesome as southern Italian men. Some solo women may feel uneasy at the levels of alcohol and testosterone in the streets of Paceville late at night (especially on weekends), which can result in aggressive behaviour.

TELEPHONE

Public telephones are widely available, and most are card-operated (there are also coin-operated phones, but these are not as common). There are over 1500 public cardphones installed in various localities – including public outdoor areas and indoor premises such as the airport, hospitals and restaurants. You can buy phonecards at many kiosks, post offices and souvenir shops. Telecards are available in denominations of Lm2, Lm3, Lm4 and Lm5. Easyline cards can be used from any line (even from hotels) and can be used in a wide range of overseas destinations. They are available in denominations of Lm2, Lm5, Lm6, Lm10 and Lm15.

Local calls cost Lm0.10. International calls are discounted by around 20% between 6pm and midnight Monday to Friday and all day Saturday and Sunday (off-peak rate), and by up to 36% between midnight and 8am (night rate) every day. A three-minute call to the UK or Italy costs Lm0.91 (standard rate), Lm0.72 (off-peak) and Lm0.59 (night), while a three-minute call to Australia or the US costs Lm1.62 (standard rate), Lm1.30 (off-peak) and Lm1.04 (night).

The international direct dialling code is ☎ 00. To call Malta from abroad, dial the international access code, ☎ 356 (the country code for Malta) and the number.

There are no area codes in Malta. In late 2001 Malta moved from six-digit local phone numbers to eight-digit numbers. You may see some old brochures using six-digit numbers – for most you should simply add a '21' prefix to the start of the old number.

Mobile Phones

Some 70% of Malta's population has a mobile phone and mobile phone numbers begin with either 79 or 99. Malta uses the GSM900 mobile phone network which is compatible with the rest of Europe, Australia and New Zealand, but not with the USA and Canada's GSM1900. If you have a GSM phone, check with your service provider about using it in Malta and beware of calls being routed internationally (very expensive for a 'local' call).

You may consider bringing your mobile phone from your home country and buying a Maltese SIM card, which gives you a Maltese mobile number. (Your mobile may be locked onto the local network in your home country, so ask your home network for advice before going abroad.) There are two mobile phone companies in Malta and at the time of research, **Vodafone** (www.vodafone.com.mt) and **Go Mobile** (www.go.com.mt) were offering local SIM cards for Lm5, plus prepaid vouchers for a minimum of Lm5 worth of calls. Prepaid vouchers for topping up credit are available at many stores and kiosks throughout Malta. Both Vodafone and Go Mobile have stores inside the Embassy Complex on Triq Santa Luċija in Valletta, and Go Mobile also has an outlet in the arrivals hall at the airport to help new arrivals get connected to the Maltese network.

You can rent a mobile phone from:
Telecom Electronics (☎ 21 376 050; www.telecom
.com.mt; Naxxar Rd, San Ġwann; rental 1 day/1 week/
2 weeks Lm5/23/38, plus a refundable deposit) Phone
delivery and pick-up can be arranged.

TIME

Malta is in the same time zone as most of
Western Europe (one hour ahead of the
UK). The country is two hours ahead of
GMT/UTC from the last Sunday in March
to the last Sunday in October (the daylight
saving period) and one hour ahead the rest
of the year. For more on international timing and to work out when's best to phone
home, see the map of world time zones on
p191.

TOILETS

Malta is well equipped with public toilets,
often at the entrance to a public garden or
near the village square. They are usually
clean and in good order, but it's a good idea
to have a small packet of tissues stashed in
your handbag or daypack as public toilets
are often short of loo paper. If there is an
attendant, it is good manners to leave a tip
of a few cents in a dish by the door.

TOURIST INFORMATION
Local Tourist Offices

The head office of the **Malta Tourism Authority**
(☎ 22 915 000; www.visitmalta.com; Auberge d'Italie, Triq
il-Merkanti, Valletta CMR02) is for postal and telephone inquiries only. Your best source of
information is the comprehensive website,
with directories, interactive maps and loads
of holiday and practical information.

There are local tourist information offices at Valletta and Malta International
Airport (for their contact details and
opening hours see p63), St Julian's (p87),
Victoria on Gozo (p142) and Mġarr Harbour, Gozo (p147).

Tourist Offices Abroad

The **Malta Tourism Authority** (www.visitmalta.com)
has many overseas offices, including the following (note that information on the official
website is available in seven languages):
France (☎ 01 48 00 03 79; info@visitmalte.com; Office
du Tourisme de Malte, 9 Cité Trévise, 75009 Paris)
Germany (☎ 069-285890; info@urlaubmalta.com;
Fremdenverkehrsamt Malta, Schillerstrasse 30-40, D-60313
Frankfurt-am-Main)

Italy (☎ 02-86 73 76; info@malta.it; Ente per il Turismo
di Malta, Via M Gonzaga 7, 20123 Milan)
Netherlands (☎ 020-6207 223; info@malta.nl; Verkeers-
bureau Malta, Singel 540, 4th fl, 1017 AZ Amsterdam)
UK (☎ 020-8877 6990; office.uk@visitmalta.com; Malta
Tourist Office, Unit C, Park House, 14 Northfields, London
SW18 1DD)
USA (☎ 212-430 3799; office.us@visitmalta.com; Malta
Tourist Office, 65 Broadway, Suite 823, New York NY
10006)

There are also representative offices in the
following countries:
Australia (☎ 02-9321 9154; office.au@visitmalta.com;
World Aviation Systems, 403 George St, Sydney NSW 2000)
Ireland (☎ 01-662 0332; office.uk@visitmalta.com;
Plunkett Communications, 46 St James's Pl, Dublin 2)

VISAS

Visas are not needed for visits of up to three
months by nationals of most Commonwealth countries (including UK, Australia,
New Zealand, Canada, but excluding South
Africa, India and Pakistan), most European
countries, the USA and Japan. The complete
list of countries whose nationals don't need
a visa is online at the website of the **Ministry
of Foreign Affairs of Malta** (www.foreign.gov.mt
/service/visa/). Other nationalities must apply
to the Maltese embassy, high commission
or consulate in their country, or directly to
the immigration police in Malta if there is
no official Maltese representation. Details
(and application forms) are also on the
website of Malta's Ministry of Foreign
Affairs.

If you wish to stay for more than three
months you should apply for an extension
at the immigration office in the police
headquarters in Floriana before your three
months are up. You will need four recent
passport photographs and proof that you
have enough money to support yourself
and not be a burden on the state. Exten-
sions are usually granted without a problem. Applications for temporary residence
should also be made at police HQ.

Visit Lonely Planet's website at www
.lonelyplanet.com/subwwway for links to
up-to-date visa information.

WOMEN TRAVELLERS

Malta remains a conservative society by
Western standards, and women are still
expected to be wives and mothers; however,

an increasing number of women are now joining the workforce. Young males have adopted the Mediterranean macho style, but they are not usually aggressive.

Malta presents no unusual dangers for women travelling alone. Normal caution should be observed, but problems are unlikely. If you are alone, Paceville – the nightclub zone at St Julian's – is hectic but not particularly unsafe.

WORK

When Malta joined the EU on 1 May 2004 the country opened to all EU nationals for study or residence purposes, but movement for work purposes might face restrictions for up to seven years. It's worth contacting the Maltese embassy or consulate in your home country for more information.

There is some work available to foreigners in Malta, including teaching English at one of the many language schools; in most cases you will need a TEFL (Teaching English as a Foreign Language) qualification. Some casual work is available in the hospitality industry, waiting tables, washing dishes and the like (perhaps even working as a diving instructor) – although these jobs can be tough to find, and the authorities take a hard line against illegal workers. See also www.labourmobility.com/guides/malta.pdf for tips on job hunting in Malta.

Transport

GETTING THERE & AWAY

ENTERING THE COUNTRY
Passport

Citizens of EU member states can travel to Malta with their national identity cards. People from countries that do not issue ID cards, such as the UK, must carry a valid passport. All non-EU nationals must have a full valid passport. If applying for a visa, check that the expiry date of your passport is at least six months off. See the Directory chapter, p172 for further information about visa requirements.

AIR

Malta is well connected to Europe, North Africa and the Middle East, with daily direct flights to/from Catania (Sicily), Frankfurt, London (Gatwick and Heathrow), Manchester, Rome and Tripoli (Libya); and at least two direct services weekly to/from Amsterdam, Athens, Berlin, Birmingham, Brussels, Cairo, Dubai, Dublin, Düsseldorf, Geneva, Istanbul, Larnaca, London (Stansted), Milan, Munich, Oslo, Paris, Sofia, Stockholm, Tunis, Vienna and Zürich.

There are no direct flights into Malta from places further afield. If you are flying from elsewhere in the world, your best bet is to travel to either Dubai (from Asia, Australia and New Zealand) or a major European city such as Rome, Frankfurt or London, then join a direct connecting flight to Malta.

Airports & Airlines

All flights arrive and depart from **Malta International Airport** (MLA; ☎ 21 249 600; www.maltairport.com) at Luqa, 8km south of Valletta. The airport has good facilities, including ATMs and currency exchange booths, a tourist office (open daily), left luggage, and a regular, inexpensive bus service to and from Valletta (see p74).

Gozo has a **heliport** (GZM; ☎ 21 557 905) with a helicopter link to Luqa (see p180).

The Maltese national airline is **Air Malta** (KM; ☎ 21 662 211; www.airmalta.com), with a very good safety record (no crashes or fatalities). Air Malta's overseas sales agents include:

Australia (☎ 02-9244 2011; fax 9290 3306; World Aviation Systems, 403 George St, Sydney, NSW 2000)

Canada (☎ 416-604 4112; transmed@interlog.com; Trans-Med Aviation Inc, General Sales Agents, 3323 Dundas St West, Toronto, Ontario M6P 2A6)

Egypt (☎ 02-578 2692; km_cairo@airmalta.com.mt; Air Malta Office, Nile Hilton Commercial Centre, Executive Suite, 34 Tahir Sq, Cairo)

France (☎ 01 58 18 64 10; info@airmalta.fr; Air Malta Office, 3 Rue Scribe, Paris 75009)

Germany (☎ 69-920 3521; office@airmalta.de; Air Malta Office, Rossmarkt 11, Frankfurt 60311)

Ireland (☎ 1800 397 400; Airline Business Ltd, Collins Town House, Level 1, Room 101-103, Dublin Airport)

Italy (☎ 06-482 3998; inforoma@airmalta.it; Air Malta Office, Via Barberini 29, Rome 00187)

Libya (☎ 21-335 0579; info.libya@airmalta.com.mt; Air Malta Office, Office 25, Ground Level, Al-Fatah Tower, Tripoli)

Netherlands (☎ 020-624 6096; info@airmalta.nl; Air Malta Office, Singel 540, 1017 AZ Amsterdam)

New Zealand (☎ 09-308 3354; fax 09-308 3388; World Aviation Systems, Level 12A, Toshiba Tower, 396 Queen St, Auckland)

Tunisia (☎ 071-703 229; airmaltatunisia@gnet.tn; Air Malta Office, Complexe Ariana Centre, Bureau A215, Ariana, Tunis 2080)

UK (☎ 020-8789 0480 or 0845 607 3710; telesales@airmalta.co.uk; Air Malta House, 314-316 Upper Richmond Rd, Putney, London SW15 6TU)

USA (☎ 800-756 2582; airmalta@worldaviationsystems
.com; World Aviation Systems, 300 N Continental Blvd,
Suite 610, El Segundo, Los Angeles, CA 90245)

AIRLINES FLYING TO AND FROM MALTA

Aeroflot (SU; ☎ 21 314 134; www.aeroflotmalta.com;
hub Moscow)

Alitalia (AZ; ☎ 21 237 115; www.alitalia.com; hub Rome)

British Airways (BA; ☎ 21 242 233; www.ba.com; hub
London)

Egyptair (MS; ☎ 21 322 256; www.egyptair.com.eg;
hub Cairo)

Emirates (EK; ☎ 23 696 455; www.emirates.com; hub
Dubai)

JAT Yugoslav Airlines (JU; ☎ 21 332 814; www.jat
.com; hub Belgrade)

KLM Royal Dutch Airlines (KL; ☎ 21 342 472; www
.klm.com; hub Amsterdam)

Libyan Arab Airlines (LN; ☎ 21 222 735; hub Tripoli)

Lufthansa (LH; ☎ 21 252 020; www.lufthansa.com;
hub Frankfurt)

Snowflake (SK; ☎ 45 77 66 10 05; www.flysnowflake
.com; hubs Stockholm & Copenhagen)

Swiss International Air Lines (LX; ☎ 21 802 777; www
.swiss.com; hub Geneva/Zürich)

Tuninter (UG; ☎ 21 320 732; hub Tunis)

Tickets

World aviation has never been so competitive and the Internet is fast becoming the easiest way of locating and booking reasonably priced seats. Full-time students and those under 26 years have access to discounted fares. You have to show a document proving your date of birth or a valid International Student Identity Card (ISIC) when buying your ticket. Other cheap deals are the discounted tickets released to travel agents and specialist discount agencies. One exception to this rule is the expanding number of 'no-frills' carriers, which sell direct to travellers. Many airlines also offer excellent fares to web surfers and there is an increasing number of online agents that operate only on the Internet, such as:

www.travelocity.co.uk
www.cheaptickets.com
www.travelcuts.com
www.expedia.com

High season in Malta is June to September and ticket prices are at their highest during this period. A month or two either side of this is the shoulder season (April, May, October), while low season is November to March. Holidays, such as Christmas and Easter, also see a jump in prices. Check the 'special fares' section of the Air Malta website to see if there are any good deals going for the period you are travelling.

From Asia

Bangkok, Singapore and Hong Kong are the best places to shop around for discount tickets. **STA Travel** (www.statravel.com) has offices in Hong Kong, Singapore, Taiwan and Thailand. Major Asian airlines (eg Thai Airways and Singapore Air) serve most of Western Europe, and also connect with Australia and New Zealand. Similarly, discounted fares can be picked up from Qantas, which usually transits in Kuala Lumpur, Bangkok or Singapore.

From Australia & New Zealand

For flights from Australia and New Zealand to Europe there are a number of competing airlines and a variety of air fares. It can sometimes work out cheaper to purchase a round-the-world ticket than do a U-turn on a return ticket.

Cheap flights from Australia/New Zealand to Europe generally go via Southeast Asian capitals, involving stopovers at Kuala Lumpur, Bangkok or Singapore. Some flights go via the Middle East, so another option might be to fly to Dubai and then direct to Malta with Emirates. Roughly speaking a return ticket to Europe will set you back A$1800/2200 from Australia in the low/high season.

Quite a few travel offices specialise in discount air tickets. Some travel agents, particularly smaller ones, advertise cheap air fares in the travel sections of weekend

TRANSPORT

newspapers, such as the *Age* in Melbourne and the *Sydney Morning Herald*. The *New Zealand Herald* has a travel section in which travel agents advertise fares.

Two well-known agents for cheap fares are STA Travel and Flight Centre, with branches throughout Australia and New Zealand. Contact details are:

STA Travel (Australia ☎ 1300 733 035; www.statravel .com.au; New Zealand ☎ 0508 782 872; www.statravel .co.nz)

Flight Centre (Australia ☎ 133 133; www.flightcentre .com.au; New Zealand ☎ 0800 243 544; www.flightcentre .co.nz)

For online bookings, try www.travel.com.au and www.travel.co.nz.

From Canada

Canadian discount air-ticket sellers are known as consolidators and their air fares tend to be about 10% higher than those sold in the USA. The *Globe & Mail*, the *Toronto Star*, the *Montreal Gazette* and the *Vancouver Sun* carry travel agents' ads and are a good place to look for cheap fares.

Travel Cuts (☎ 800-667-2887; www.travelcuts.com) is Canada's national student travel agency. For online bookings try www.expedia.ca and www.travelocity.ca.

Both Alitalia and Air Canada have direct flights from Toronto and Montreal to Rome, where you can connect with flights to Malta. Roughly speaking, expect to pay C$900/1800 for a return ticket to Rome from the Canadian east coast in the low/high season, and C$1200/2000 from the west coast.

From Continental Europe

Malta is well connected by air to many European cities. See p174 for those cities with regular direct flights to and from Malta.

FROM FRANCE

Direct Air Malta flights from Paris to Malta cost from €240 return. Recommended agencies in France include:

Anyway (☎ 0892 893 892; www.anyway.fr, in French)

Lastminute (☎ 0892 705 000; www.fr.lastminute.com, in French)

Nouvelles Frontières (☎ 0825 000 747; www.nouvelles -frontieres.fr, in French)

OTU Voyages (www.otu.fr, in French) This agency specialises in student and youth travellers.

Voyageurs du Monde (☎ 01 40 15 11 15; www.vdm .com, in French)

FROM GERMANY

A return ticket from Frankfurt to Malta costs from €230 with Air Malta; from Berlin it costs from €240 (prices can drop to €150 in the low season). Recommended travel agencies in Germany include:

Expedia (www.expedia.de, in German)

Just Travel (☎ 089 747 3330; www.justtravel.de)

Lastminute (☎ 01805 284 366; www.de.lastminute.com, in German)

STA Travel (☎ 01805 456 422; www.statravel.de, in German)

FROM ITALY

One recommended agent is **CTS Viaggi** (☎ 06 462 0431; www.cts.it, in Italian), specialising in student and youth travel. The nearest airport to Malta is at Catania in Sicily, which has daily flights to Malta for around €130 return (as low as €80 in the low season). From Rome the price of a ticket is around €300 (dropping to as low as €160 in the low season).

FROM THE NETHERLANDS

From Amsterdam to Malta costs from €240 with Air Malta. One recommended agency is **Airfair** (☎ 020 620 5121; www.airfair.nl, in Dutch).

FROM SCANDINAVIA

Kilroy Travel Group (www.kilroygroups.com, Scandinavian languages only) offers discounted travel to people aged 16 to 33, and has representative offices in Denmark, Sweden, Norway and Finland.

From summer 2004, the low-cost carrier of Scandinavian Airlines System (SAS), Snowflake, will fly twice a week between Stockholm and Malta (one way from around Skr1200), and once weekly between Copenhagen and Malta (one way from Dkr1000), with frequent special offers.

From the Middle East

Emirates has three direct flights a week between Dubai and Malta (from US$350), with connections to/from more distant destinations in Australia, India, Asia and other parts of the Middle East. Air Malta flies once or twice a week between Malta and Istanbul (from US$350).

Recommended agencies in the region include:

Al-Rais Travels (www.alrais.com) In Dubai.
Israel Student Travel Association (ISTA; ☎ 02-625 7257) In Jerusalem.
Orion-Tour (www.oriontour.com) In Istanbul.

From North Africa

There are frequent flights between Malta and various North African cities, including Cairo, Tripoli, Tunis and Casablanca. Flights cost from US$150 from Tunis or Cairo to Malta, US$250 from Casablanca and US$100 from Tripoli.

One recommended travel agency in the area is **Egypt Panorama Tours** (☎ 2-359 0200; www .eptours.com) in Cairo.

From the UK

Discount air travel is big business in London. Advertisements for many travel agencies appear in the travel pages of the weekend broadsheet newspapers, in *Time Out*, the *Evening Standard* and in the free magazine *TNT*.

Roughly speaking a return fare to Malta will cost you UK£150/300 in the low/high season from the UK, and there are some good winter prices (around UK£100) if you're prepared to shop around. Charter flights are usually much cheaper than scheduled flights, especially if you do not qualify for the under-26 and student discounts. You could also check out websites like www.bargainholidays.com (with scheduled and charter flights, plus package holiday offers) or www.lastminute.com.

Recommended travel agencies include the following:
Bridge the World (☎ 0870 444 7474; www.b-t-w .co.uk)
Flightbookers (☎ 0870 010 7000; www.ebookers.com)
Flight Centre (☎ 0870 890 8099; www.flightcentre .co.uk)
North-South Travel (☎ 01245 608 291; www.northsouth travel.co.uk) North-South Travel donate part of their profit to projects in the developing world.
Quest Travel (☎ 0870 442 3542; www.questtravel.com)
STA Travel (☎ 0870 160 0599; www.statravel.co.uk)
Trailfinders (www.trailfinders.co.uk)
Travel Bag (☎ 0870 890 1456; www.travelbag.co.uk)

From the USA

There are no direct scheduled flights from the USA to Malta. The best option is to fly into a European hub, such as London, Frankfurt or Rome, and connect with a flight from there to Malta. Flight options across the North Atlantic, the world's busiest long-haul air corridor, are bewildering and fares can vary wildly in price. A return fare to a major European city like Rome will cost you US$400/800 in the low/high season.

Discount travel agents in the USA are known as consolidators. San Francisco is the ticket consolidator capital of America, although some good deals can be found in Los Angeles, New York and other big cities.

The following agencies are recommended for online bookings:
www.cheaptickets.com
www.expedia.com
www.itn.net
www.lowestfare.com
www.orbitz.com
www.sta.com (for travellers under the age of 26)
www.travelocity.com

Discount and rock-bottom options from the USA include charter, stand-by and courier flights, although these will not take you to Malta, only to major European cities. Stand-by fares are often sold at 60% of the normal price for one-way tickets. Check out:
Courier Travel (☎ 303 570 7586; www.couriertravel .org) A comprehensive search engine for courier and stand-by flights.
Now Voyager (☎ 212 459 1616; www.nowvoyager travel.com)
International Association of Air Travel Couriers (IAATC; ☎ 308 632 3273; www.courier.org)

LAND

Bus

You can travel by bus from most parts of Europe to a port in Italy and catch a ferry from there to Malta. **Eurolines** (www.euro lines.com) is a consortium of coach companies that operates across Europe with offices in all major European cities. Bear in mind that a discounted air fare might work out cheaper than the long bus trip once you allow for food and drink to be bought en route.

As the saying goes, all roads lead to Rome; from there you will have to continue to Malta by bus or train to one of the ferry ports in southern Italy or Sicily (see p178).

You can contact Eurolines on the following:

TRANSPORT

TRANSPORT

Eurolines/National Express (☎ 0870 580 8080; www
.nationalexpress.com) In the UK.
Eurolines France (☎ 08 36 69 52 52; www.eurolines
.fr) in France
Eurolines/Touring (☎ 069-790350; www.deutsche
-touring.com) In Germany.
Eurolines Italia (☎ 055 357110; www.eurolines.it)
In Italy.
Eurolines Nederland (☎ 020-560 8788; www.euro
lines.nl) In the Netherlands.

Car & Motorcycle

With your own vehicle, you can drive to
southern Italy and take a car ferry from
Salerno, Reggio di Calabria, Pozzallo or
Catania (Sicily) to Malta (see below). From
northern Europe the fastest road route is
via the Simplon Pass to Milan, from which
Italy's main highway, the Autostrada del
Sole, stretches all the way to Reggio di
Calabria. From London the distance is
around 2200km.

Car drivers and motorbike riders will
need the vehicle's registration papers, a
Green Card, a nationality plate and their
domestic licence. Contact your local automobile association for details about necessary documentation.

Train

Rail travel from major European cities
to southern Italy and Sicily is convenient
and comfortable, but if Malta is your only
destination then you may want to rethink
your plans, as the train will prove considerably more expensive than a charter
flight. For the latest fare information on
journeys to Italy from the UK, contact
the **Rail Europe Travel Centre** (☎ 0870 848 848;
www.raileurope.co.uk). Another source of rail
information for all of Europe is **Rail Choice**
(www.railchoice.com).

If you're touring Europe on a Eurail or
Inter Rail Pass, then you can take the train
to Reggio di Calabria or Catania and catch
a ferry to Malta.

SEA
Departure Tax

All passengers leaving Malta by sea are required to pay a Lm6 departure tax, which
should be added by the travel agent when
you buy your ticket. Maltese nationals and
foreigners residing in Malta also pay a steep
'travel levy' of Lm10.

Ferry

Malta has regular sea links with Sicily (Pozzallo and Catania), southern Italy (Reggio
di Calabria and Salerno) and northern Italy
(Genoa). The ferry terminal is on Pinto
Wharf in Floriana, southwest of Valletta.

Virtu Ferries (www.virtuferries.com; Malta ☎ 21 318
854; Catania ☎ 095-535 711; Pozzallo ☎ 0932-954 062)
offers the shortest and fastest Malta–Italy
crossing with its fast catamaran service
(carrying cars and passengers) to/from
Pozzallo and Catania (in Sicily). The company also operates day excursions to Sicily
(see p186).

The Pozzallo–Malta crossing takes only
1½ hours and operates year-round (seven
times a week in June, up to 12 times a week
in August, dropping to three times a week
from November to April, weather permitting). Fares are as follows:

	From Pozzallo	From Malta
passenger	one way/return €70/86	one way/return Lm24/36
car	one way/return €104/140	one way/return Lm40/54
motorcycle	one way/return €52/68	one way/return Lm19/28
bicycle	one way/return €11/16	one way/return Lm5/7

The Catania–Malta crossing takes four
hours and operates from March to October (seven times a week in August, down to
once a week in March, April and October).
Fares are:

	From Catania	From Malta
passenger	one way/return €70/86	one way/return Lm24/36
car	one way/return €130/155	one way/return Lm45/65
motorcycle	one way/return €78/104	one way/return Lm25/35
bicycle	one way/return €16/21	one way/return Lm7/10

Departure taxes are not included in the
prices listed above (add Lm6 from Malta,
€8 from Sicily). Children under four travel
free of charge; children aged four to 11 pay
50% of the adult fares. If you are travelling
from Malta to Sicily, ask when booking

about transfers from your accommodation to the ferry terminal on Pinto Wharf – it's worth paying the extra charge (around Lm2.75 per person) as there is no public transport to the wharf, and taxis can prove expensive.

Ma.Re.Si Shipping (☎ 21 233 129; www.sms .com.mt/maresi.htm) has a ro-ro car ferry that makes one overnight return trip a week between Catania and Malta (12 hours) and one a week between Malta and Reggio di Calabria (15 hours). These services operate year-round; cabins are available (cabin supplement one way/return from Lm30/45). Prices (excluding taxes) are as follows:

	Malta–Catania	Malta–Reggio di Calabria
passenger	one way/return Lm20/35	one way/return Lm25/45
car	one way/return Lm35/55	one way/return Lm40/60
motorcycle	one way/return Lm12/24	one way/return Lm14/28
bicycle	one way/return Lm6/12	one way/return Lm10/20

Grimaldi Ferries (☎ 21 226 873; www.grimaldi-ferries .com) operates a weekly service year-round between Malta and Salerno, south of Naples. The journey takes about 19 hours and a cabin berth costs from €93. From Salerno, it is possible to sail on to Valencia in southern Spain. The same company also operates a weekly service from Salerno to Tunis then on to Malta (there is no direct service from Malta to Tunis; travellers must sail to Salerno, arriving on a Friday, and wait until the following Wednesday for the sailing to Tunis).

Grandi Navi Veloci (☎ 21 334 023; www.gnv.it /tunisia.asp), also part of the Grimaldi Group, has a twice-weekly car ferry service between Genoa and Tunis that calls in at Malta. Again, you can sail directly from Tunis to Malta, but there is no service from Malta to Tunis.

In past years TTT Lines has operated a car passenger service linking Malta with Catania and Naples, but at the time of research this service had ceased.

Ferry schedules tend to change from year to year, and it is best to confirm the information given here, either with the ferry company or with a travel agent. In Malta, **SMS Travel & Tourism** (☎ 21 232 211; www.smstravel.net; 311 Triq ir-Repubblika, Valletta) has information about all of the services on offer. In the UK, **Viamare Travel** (☎ 0870 410 6040; www.viamare.com; Graphic House, 2 Sumatra Rd, West Hampstead, London NW6 1PU) is an agent for Virtu Ferries.

Travellers should be aware that the Malta–Sicily catamarans do not have exchange facilities and there are none available (and no ATMs) at the ferry terminal in Floriana. Nor is there any public transport from the ferry terminal on Pinto Wharf up to the city of Valletta – you can either catch a taxi or make the steep 15-minute climb. If you decide to walk it's best to follow the waterfront northeast, under the Lascaris Bastion, then veer left and climb the steps up at Victoria Gate.

Yacht

Malta's excellent harbour and its strategic location at the hub of the Mediterranean has led to its development as a major yachting centre. There are berths for 700 yachts (up to 18m length overall) in Msida Marina near Valletta, and Mġarr Marina on Gozo has space for over 200 boats. There are also two upmarket new marinas – at the Portomaso complex in St Julian's (110 berths; www.portomasomarina.com), and the Cottonera waterfront in Vittoriosa (for the so-called 'superyachts'; www.cottonera waterfront.com). For more information on these marinas and details of the logistics and formalities of sailing to Malta, contact the **Malta Maritime Authority** (MMA; ☎ 21 332 800; www.mma.gov.mt; Yachting Centre Directorate, Ta' Xbiex Seafront, Ta' Xbiex).

Malta's popularity with the yachting fraternity means that it is possible to make your way there as unpaid crew. Yachts tend to leave Gibraltar, southern Spain and the Balearics in April and May to head towards the popular cruising grounds of the Greek Islands and the Turkish coast. It's possible to just turn up at a marina and ask if there are any yachts looking for crew, but there are also agencies that bring together yacht owners and prospective crew (for a fee). Check out one such agency, **Crewseekers** (☎ 01489-578 319; www.crewseekers.co.uk; Hawthorn House, Hawthorn Lane, Sarisbury Green, Southampton, Hampshire SO31 7BD, UK), which charges £50/75 for a six-/12-month membership.

Although complete novices are occasionally taken on, it's easier to get a berth if you have some experience to offer, or even better a paper qualification like the Royal Yachting Association's Competent Crew certificate (details on the RYA website at www.rya.org.uk).

TOURS

There are dozens of tour operators in the UK, Europe and North America that offer package holidays and organised tours to Malta. Package holidays, which include flights and accommodation, can offer some real bargains, particularly in winter – Malta is a year-round charter destination.

There are also many tour operators catering to a wide range of special interest groups, including walking, diving, history, archaeology, architecture and religion, and others offering holidays designed for senior travellers. The comprehensive website of the **Malta Tourism Authority** (www.visitmalta.com) allows you to search for tour operators based on country and speciality. Click on 'Getting Here', then 'Tour Operators'.

GETTING AROUND

AIR

Malta's only internal air service is the regular helicopter link between Malta International Airport and the heliport on Gozo. Operated by **Malta Aircharter** (MAC; ☎ 21 557 905; mac@airmalta.com.mt), a subsidiary of Air Malta, the service runs year-round with four flights a day in winter (November to March), and departures roughly every two to three hours throughout the day and night from April to October.

The aircraft used is the Russian-built 26-seat Mi-8, and the flight between Malta and Gozo takes only 10 to 15 minutes. The regular fare for foreign visitors one way/return is Lm18/27. Maltese residents pay one way/return Lm9/18. Children, students and senior citizens (aged 61 and over) receive discounts on these prices. There's a baggage allowance of 20kg plus one small piece of hand luggage.

Reservations should be made at least 24 hours in advance through Air Malta offices or any IATA travel agent. Check-in time is half an hour before departure, or an hour

if you are flying from Gozo to connect with an international flight at Malta.

BICYCLE

Cycling on Maltese roads can be a bit nerve-racking. The roads are often narrow and potholed, and drivers show little consideration for cyclists. Things are much better on Gozo – the roads are still rough, but there's far less traffic.

For spares and repairs, try the following bike shops:

Centrepoint Cycles (☎ 21 495 297; centrepoint@malta net.net; Triq I-20 Ta'Jannar, Qormi)

Magri Cycles & Spares (☎ 21 414 399; magricyc@ maltanet.net; 135 Triq il-Kungress Ewkaristiku, Mosta)

Shine Wheel Bicycle Centre (☎ 21 654 791; 60 Triq San Patriziju, Birżebbuġa)

Victoria Garage (☎ 21 556 414; Triq Putirjal, Victoria, Gozo)

You can rent bikes for Lm1.50 to Lm2 per day from Magri Cycles in Mosta and the Victoria Garage on Gozo.

BUS

There is an extensive network of buses in Malta (over 500 buses and around 85,000 passengers daily). Almost all bus routes on Malta originate from the City Gate bus terminus in Valletta and radiate to all parts of the island, which makes certain cross-country journeys (eg Marsaxlokk to Marsaskala) a little inconvenient, as you have to travel via Valletta. There are also a few direct services enabling tourists based in Sliema and Buġibba to do day trips to major sightseeing destinations (eg from Sliema and Buġibba to Marsaxlokk, Ċirkewwa, Mdina or the northern beaches of Golden Bay and Għajn Tuffieħa) that do not go through Valletta. In towns and villages the bus terminus is usually found on or near the parish church square.

Late-night buses (after 11pm) cost Lm0.50 and link the nightlife area of Paceville with Sliema, Valletta and Buġibba. Day fares range from Lm0.15 to Lm0.40 one way, depending on route and distance. Pay the driver when you get on, and he will give you a ticket; hold on to this for the duration of the journey, as you may need to present it to an inspector. Try to have some small change available for your ticket purchase – the driver is unlikely to give change of more than Lm1.

MAIN BUS ROUTES

From Valletta (except to Sliema & St Julian's)

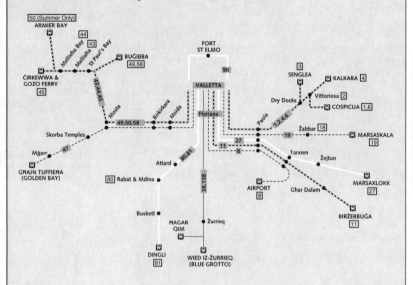

Direct Bus Routes To/From Sliema & Buġibba

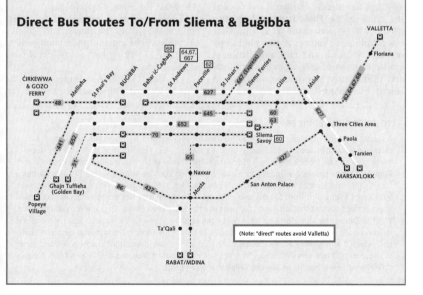

Note: "direct" routes avoid Valletta

TRANSPORT

TRANSPORT

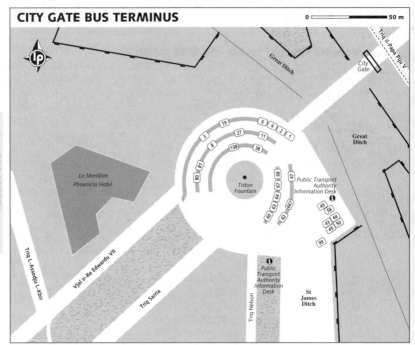

CITY GATE BUS TERMINUS

0 ▭▬▬▬▬▬ 50 m

Triq il-Papa Piju V

Great Ditch

City Gate

Great Ditch

Le Meridien Phoenicia Hotel

19
6 4 2 1
3
27
11
8
138
38
80 81
Triton Fountain
68
47
Public Transport Authority Information Desk ℹ
67
64
49
58
60
63
62
66
44
43 50
45
99

Triq L-Assedju L-Kbir

Vjal ir-Re Edwardu VII

Triq Sarria

Triq Nelson

ℹ
Public Transport Authority Information Desk

St James Ditch

The buses display their route numbers, but not their destinations, in the windscreen. You can find details of routes and fares at the office of the **Public Transport Association** (☎ 21 250 007/8/9; www.atp.com.mt) at City Gate bus terminus, or online. A free photocopy of route, schedule and fare information is available on most buses, from bus terminals and from tourist information offices; and colour bus maps (Lm0.35) are available from many bookshops and souvenir shops. Routes of interest to travellers are shown on the Main Bus Routes map (p181).

There is talk of relocating the city bus terminus away from the entrance to Valletta, but this will be a major undertaking and at the time of writing had not officially been commissioned.

On Gozo, all the bus routes except the No 25 Victoria–Mġarr service are circular,

TOURIST BUS SERVICES

A recent joint initiative of the Malta authorities for tourism and transport has seen the creation of two circular bus routes specifically to serve tourists. Bus No 505 (the North Route) departs every hour or two from 9.15am to 3.30pm from The Ferries in Sliema, picking up in Paceville and Buġibba-Qawra before continuing to places of interest such as Mdina, Rabat, Buskett Gardens, Dingli Cliffs and Mosta then returning to Sliema. Bus No 506 (the South Route) departs between 9am and 4.15pm, also from Sliema, and picks up in Paceville (but not Buġibba/Qawra) and takes in attractions such as the San Anton Gardens in Attard, Siġġiewi, Ħaġar Qim and Mnajdra temples, Wied iz-Zurreq (for the Blue Grotto), Marsaxlokk and the Three Cities. Tickets cost Lm2 and are valid on both routes all day (as well as other scheduled bus services), and passengers can alight and reboard at any stop along the route. Pick up a brochure detailing the schedules and stops of these tourist bus services at tourist offices or major hotels. You can buy tickets from the bus driver or at ticket booths in Sliema, Valletta or Qawra.

BEAUTIFUL BUSES & CLASSIC CARS

Malta's buses are a tourist attraction in themselves. Many of them are classic Bedfords, Thames, Leylands and AECs dating from the 1950s, '60s and '70s, brightly painted in a livery of yellow, white and orange; the Gozo buses have a more restrained colour scheme of grey, white and red. Although the old buses are undeniably picturesque, the downside is that they can also be noisy and uncomfortable, with clattering diesel engines and creaky-squeaky suspension that can rattle the fillings out of your teeth. *The Malta Buses* by Michael Cassar & Joseph Bonnici is an illustrated history of the island's celebrated public transport.

There are also hundreds of classic British cars still on the road, not because of any great enthusiasm for vintage vehicles, but because they are cheap and just seem to keep on going. Keen-eyed car enthusiasts can spot Ford Anglias, Ford Consuls, Cortina Mk1s, Triumph Heralds, Morris Minors, Hillman Minxes, Austin 1100s, old Bedford and Commer vans, and any number of Austin Minis, all in varying states of repair.

There are vintage trucks too. Many truck drivers decorate their vehicles with bright paint jobs, and adorn them with names like The Only One, Roy Rodgers, Buffalo Chief and Eskimo Prince.

starting and finishing at the Victoria Bus Terminal, off Triq Putirjal. The flat fare is Lm0.15. Services are less frequent than on Malta and are geared more to local needs than tourist requirements – buses are less frequent in the afternoon, and most stop running by early evening. Route numbers and destinations are clearly displayed on a notice board at the bus station in Victoria.

Bus Passes

The Public Transport Association (PTA) issues one-/three-/five-/seven-day bus passes costing Lm1.50/4/4.50/5.50, which give unlimited travel on Malta's buses between 5.30am and 11pm. They can be purchased from the PTA offices at City Gate bus terminus, Sliema ferry terminus and Buġibba terminus.

CAR & MOTORCYCLE

The Maltese love their cars. On weekends (Sunday in particular) they take to the road en masse, visiting friends and family or heading for the beach or a favourite picnic site. This means that there is often serious congestion on the roads around Valletta, Sliema and St Julian's. Friday and Saturday night in Paceville is one big traffic jam.

Distance isn't a problem – the longest distance on Malta is 27km and the widest point is around 15km. On Gozo the longest distance is about 14km, the widest is only 7km!

Driving Licence

All EU member states' driving licences are fully recognised throughout Europe. For those with a non-EU licence, an International Driving Permit (IDP) is a useful adjunct, especially if your home licence has no photo or is in a foreign language. Your local automobile association can issue an IDP, valid for one year, for a small fee. You must carry your home licence together with the IDP.

Fuel

The price of fuel is set by the government and at the time of research was Lm0.36 a litre for unleaded petrol. Petrol stations are generally open from 7am to 7pm Monday to Saturday; most are closed on Sunday and public holidays, but some larger stations have a self-service, cash-operated pump for filling up outside opening hours (Lm2 or Lm5 notes accepted).

Hire

Car rental rates in Malta are among the lowest in Europe, and hiring a car allows you to see a lot more of the island if your time is limited. If you hire a car on Malta you can take it over to Gozo on the ferry without a problem. However, rental rates on Gozo are lower and there's also the cost of a ferry ticket for the car to consider (Lm4 return).

Most of the car-hire companies have representatives at the airport, but rates vary so it is worth shopping around. Make sure you know what is included in the quoted rate – many of the local agencies quote very low rates that do not include full insurance against theft and collision damage.

Obviously rates will vary with season, length of rental period and the size and make of car (plus extras like air-con). Daily rates for the smallest vehicles start from around Lm6 a day (for rental of seven days or longer) in the low season, and the next size up starts at Lm8 per day.

The age limit for rental drivers is generally 21 to 70, but drivers between 21 and 25 may be asked to pay a supplement of up to Lm4 a day. You will need a valid driving licence that you have held for at least two years. Rental rates often include free delivery and collection, especially in the Valletta-Sliema-St Julian's area.

International agencies with offices in Malta include:

Avis (☎ 21 246 640; info@avis.com.mt)

Budget (☎ 21 241 517; www.budget.com.mt)

Europcar (☎ 21 388 516; europcarsales@alpinemalta.com)

Hertz (☎ 21 314 636/7; www.hertz.com.mt)

Holiday Autos (☎ 21 231 799; www.holidayautos .com .mt)

Thrifty (☎ 21 482 385; www.meligroup.com)

There are dozens of local car-hire agencies and many accommodation providers also offer car rental arrangements – it pays to ask when you're making a booking. The following have been recommended as being reliable; most will drop off and collect cars (usually for a small fee):

Billy's (☎ 21 523 676; www.billyscarhire.com; 113 Triq Ġorġ Borg Olivier, Mellieħa)

Mayjo Car Rentals (☎ 21 556 678; www.intersoftgozo .com/mayjo; Triq Fortunato Mizzi, Victoria, Gozo)

Wembleys (☎ 21 370 451/2; www.wembleys.net; Triq San Andrija, St Andrews)

Windsor Car Rentals (☎ 21 346 921; 10 Triq San Franġisk, Sliema)

Insurance

Car-hire companies offer CDW (collision damage waiver) and/or theft damage protection insurance with rental vehicles at extra cost (usually charged per day). Be sure to read the fine print and understand what you're covered for, and what excess charges you'll be up for in the case of an accident.

Parking

Parking can be a bit of a nightmare in the Sliema-St Julian's and Buġibba-Qawra areas. And don't even think about taking a car into Valletta – unless you're a resident,

you're not allowed to park within the city walls. Use the large underground car park near the City Gate bus terminus.

Local traffic police are swift and merciless in the imposition of Lm10 on-the-spot fines. Most main towns, tourist sites and beaches have a car park, with an attendant dressed in blue shirt and cap and usually wearing an official badge. These attendants will expect a tip of around Lm0.25 to Lm0.50 upon your departure.

Road Rules

Like the British, the Maltese drive on the left. Speed limits are 80km/h on highways and 50km/h in urban areas, but they are rarely observed. The wearing of seat belts is compulsory for the driver and front-seat passenger. Any accidents must be reported to the nearest police station (and to the rental company if the car is hired); don't move your vehicle until the police have arrived, otherwise your insurance may be nullified.

Road signs and regulations are pretty much the same as the rest of Europe, with one important difference – in Malta no-one seems to pay the least attention to any of the rules. Be prepared for drivers overtaking on the inside, ignoring traffic lights, refusing to give way at junctions and hanging on your rear bumper if they think you're going too slowly. All rental cars have registration numbers ending in K, so tourists can be spotted easily. Vehicles coming from your right are supposed to have right of way at roundabouts, but don't count on vehicles on your left observing this rule.

You should also be aware that many of the roads are in pitiful condition, with cracks and potholes, and there are very few road markings (it is hoped that EU funding will soon see improvements to these roads). In winter, minor roads are occasionally blocked by wash-outs or collapsed retaining walls after heavy rain. Signposting is variable – some minor sights are easy to find, while major towns remain elusive. Get yourself a good road map (see p169).

The maximum blood-alcohol concentration allowed in drivers in Malta is 0.08%.

FERRY
Malta–Gozo

Gozo Channel (www.gozochannel.com; Ċirkewwa ☎ 21 580 435; Mġarr ☎ 21 561 622) operates the regular

---

KARROZZIN

The *karrozzin* – a traditional horse-drawn carriage with seats for four passengers – has been in use in Malta since 1856. Many of the carriages are treasured family possessions passed down from father to son, and are cared for with obsessive pride. If you can manage to get up early enough, you can see the owners turn up for a day's work with the *karrozzin* on the back of a pick-up truck and the horse towed behind in a horse-box. With a quick buff of the leather and brass, they back the horse into the harness and they're all set.

You can pick up a *karrozzin* in Valletta at City Gate, Pjazza San Ġorġ and Fort St Elmo, at The Ferries in Sliema, and at Mdina's Main Gate. Haggle with the driver and be sure to agree on a fare before getting in. About Lm5 is average for a tour of the local sights.

---

ro-ro car ferry services between Malta and Gozo.

There is a ferry that departs at 1pm Monday to Friday from the Sa Maison wharf at Pieta Creek (below the Floriana fortifications) sailing to Mġarr. The crossing takes about 1¼ hours and this service is used predominantly by heavy commercial vehicles.

The main ferry service runs between Ċirkewwa (Malta) and Mġarr (Gozo), with crossings every 45 to 60 minutes from 6am to around 11pm (and every two hours throughout the night in the peak summer months from July to September). The journey takes 25 minutes, and the return fare is Lm1.75/0.50 per adult/child, Lm4 for a car, Lm0.50 for a bicycle.

Bus No 45 runs regularly between Valletta and Ċirkewwa (one way Lm0.20), and bus No 25 operates between Mġarr and Victoria on Gozo (Lm0.15).

To Comino

Comino Hotel (☎ 21 529 821; www.cominohotels.com), see p159, runs its own ferry service, with around seven crossings a day from Ċirkewwa on Malta (between 7.30am and 11.30pm) and Mġarr on Gozo (between 6.15am and 10pm). Arriving and departing hotel guests are given priority on the boats and their return fare is Lm2/1 per adult/child. The ferry can also be used by nonresidents of the hotel (at a return fare of Lm3.50/1.75 per adult/child). The boats do not run from November to March when the hotel is closed.

You can also make a day trip to the Blue Lagoon from tourist areas like Sliema and Buġibba on Malta, and Xlendi on Gozo. Shuttle services (not operated by the hotel) also operate from Ċirkewwa and Mġarr.

Valletta–Sliema

The **Marsamxetto ferry service** (☎ 21 338 981) crosses frequently between Valletta and Sliema. The crossing takes only about five minutes and there are departures every hour (every half-hour from 10am to 4pm), beginning at around 8am and finishing around 6pm. Ferries depart from Sliema on the hour and half-hour, and leave from Valletta at quarter past and quarter to the hour. The fare one way is Lm0.35.

HITCHING

Hitchhiking is very unusual in Malta and is generally frowned upon. Hitching is never entirely safe in any country in the world and we don't recommend it. Travellers who decide to hitch should understand that they are taking a small but potentially serious risk. People who do choose to hitch will be safer if they travel in pairs and let someone know where they are planning to go.

TAXI

Official Maltese taxis are white (usually Mercedes, with a taxi sign on top) and are fitted with meters, though these are rarely switched on; the government has set up a fare structure, but this is widely ignored.

Details of the fixed fares from the airport are available at the taxi desk in the arrivals hall, where you can pay in advance and hand a ticket to the driver. The fares are as follows:

From the airport to	Fare
Valletta/Floriana	Lm6
Three Cities area	Lm7
Mdina/Rabat	Lm7
Sliema/St Julian's area	Lm8
Buġibba/St Paul's Bay	Lm10

From the airport to	Fare
Golden Bay area	Lm10
Mellieħa	Lm12
Ċirkewwa	Lm13

For other journeys you will have to settle a fare with the driver before getting in – Maltese taxi drivers are not noted for their tourist-friendly qualities and many tourists have reported being ripped off. Ask your hotel reception what the rates should be for any trips you plan to undertake by taxi. There are taxi ranks at City Gate and outside the Grand Master's Palace in Valletta, and at bus stations and major hotels in the main tourist resorts.

As an alternative to the white taxis, black taxis (also usually Mercedes, but with no sign on top) are owned by private companies and usually offer cheaper rates. To order a taxi by phone, it's best to ask at your hotel reception, or try one of the following services:

Belmont Garage (Gozo) ☎ 21 556 962
Freephone Taxis ☎ 80 073 770
Wembley Motors ☎ 21 374 141

TOURS

A number of companies operate bus tours and they are highly competitive, so shop around the travel agencies. The tours will restrict you to the well-trampled tourist traps, but they can give you a good introduction to the islands nonetheless.

There are dozens of tours on offer, from half-day tours to the Blue Grotto or Valletta's Sunday market, to full-day trips to the Three Cities, Mosta and Mdina, and Gozo, or evening trips to take in festa celebrations. Tours cost from Lm4 to Lm10 and can be arranged through most hotels and travel agents. Your tour guide will expect a tip.

Captain Morgan Cruises (☎ 23 463 333; www .captainmorgan.com.mt) is the biggest tour operator in the Maltese Islands. The company offers a wide range of boat excursions. There is a popular tour of Grand Harbour, which departs five or six times daily from March to October and costs Lm6.25/4.95 per adult/child. There is also an all-day cruise right around Malta and Comino (six times a week from May to October, three times a week in March, April and

November), which will set you back around Lm14.95/9.95 (buffet lunch included). Other options include day trips to the Blue Lagoon on Comino (from Lm6.95/4.95), a sunset cruise (Lm18.95/9.95 including dinner), or a full-day sailing cruise on a catamaran (Lm23.95/14.95 including lunch). These trips depart from The Ferries area in Sliema. Captain Morgan also runs 'underwater safari' cruises (Lm4.95/3.95) out of Sliema and Buġibba, on boats with underwater viewing areas.

Captain Morgan can also arrange Jeep safaris around the more remote parts of Malta (Lm19.95/16.45 per adult/child) and Gozo (Lm21.95/18.65). These are full-day trips where you drive your own Jeep and follow the tour leader, who is in radio contact. Drivers must be over 21; lunch is included in the price, as is the Malta–Gozo return ferry ticket for Gozo tours. Book ahead as places are limited.

Alliance Cruises & Tours (☎ 21 332 165; www .alliancecruises.com) offers a programme of boat tours similar to Captain Morgan, also out of Sliema, with similar prices. A day trip around Malta and Comino leaves four times weekly and costs Lm8.95/5.95 per adult/child, while a harbour cruise costs Lm6.25/3 (also available of an evening for the same price).

Alliance also runs bus tours to Gozo (from Lm5.95/4.50 per adult/child), Valletta (from Lm3.95/2.95), Mdina (from Lm3.95/2.95), and the highlights of the south (Marsaxlokk, the prehistoric temples and the Blue Grotto, from Lm5.75/4.50). On most trips, the company allows you to choose a 'basic price', which includes transport and guide, or 'all inclusive', which includes transport and guide, admission fees to museums and shows (where applicable) and lunch.

Also offered by Alliance is a Jeep safari (Lm15.95/12.95 per adult/child) to out-of-the-way locations on Malta.

Excursions to Sicily

Virtu Ferries (☎ 21 318 854; www.virtuferries.com) runs high-speed passenger catamaran services to Pozzallo and Catania (see p178) that enable travellers to make a day trip to Sicily.

Tour itineraries vary depending on the season: daily from March to October the ferry leaves Valletta at 7am, arriving in

Pozzallo at 8.30am, where you join a coach that takes you on a guided tour to see the active volcano Mt Etna, and to visit the ancient Greco-Roman city of Taormina. The return ferry leaves Pozzallo at 9.30pm and arrives back in Valletta at 11pm.

From November to February the tour includes a ferry departing Valletta at 7am and arriving in Pozzallo at 8.30am. The guided tour takes in Mt Etna and the baroque city of Modica, before meeting the return ferry leaving Pozzallo at 7pm, arriving back in Malta at 8.30pm.

The cost of both tours is Lm37 (including taxes, excluding lunch). Transfers from your hotel to the port (and back again at the end of the tour) cost Lm2.75. You can book a trip through most hotels and travel agents in Malta.

YACHT

If you'd like to tour the Maltese Islands in class, you could consider chartering a yacht. **Captain Morgan Yacht Charter** (☎ 23 463 333; www.yachtcharter.com.mt) offers half-day, full-day or two-day (overnight) charters (with skipper provided) from Lm95, Lm160 and Lm320, respectively. Bareboat charter is also available to experienced sailors, from Lm1100 a week in low season (Lm1350 in July and August). **S & D Yachts** (☎ 21 331 515; www.sdyachts.com) offers similar services.

TRANSPORT

Health

CONTENTS

Travel health depends on your predeparture preparations, your daily health care while travelling and how you handle any medical problem that does develop. Health care in Malta is of a high standard and almost all health professionals will speak English.

BEFORE YOU GO

Prevention is the key to staying healthy while abroad. A little planning before departure, particularly for pre-existing illnesses, will save trouble later: see your dentist before a long trip; carry a spare pair of contact lenses and glasses, and take your optical prescription with you. Bring medications in their original, clearly labelled, containers. A signed and dated letter from your physician describing your medical conditions and medications, including generic names, is also a good idea. If carrying syringes or needles, be sure to have a physician's letter documenting their medical necessity.

INSURANCE

If you're an EU citizen, an E111 form, available from health centres or, in the UK, post offices, covers you for most medical care. E111 will not cover you for nonemergencies or emergency repatriation home.

Malta has reciprocal health agreements with Australia and the UK. Nationals of these countries, visiting Malta for no longer than one month, are entitled to free medical and hospital care.

If you do need health insurance, make sure you get a policy that covers you for the worst possible scenario, such as an accident requiring an emergency flight home. Find out in advance if your insurance plan will make payments directly to providers or reimburse you later for overseas health expenditure.

RECOMMENDED VACCINATIONS

The World Health Organization (WHO) recommends that all travellers should be covered for diphtheria, tetanus, measles, mumps, rubella and polio, as well as hepatitis B, regardless of their destination. Since most vaccines don't produce immunity until at least two weeks after they're given, visit a physician at least six weeks before departure.

ONLINE RESOURCES

The WHO's publication *International Travel and Health* is revised annually and is available online at www.who.int/ith/. Other useful websites include www.mdtravelhealth .com (travel health recommendations for every country; updated daily), www.fitfor travel.scot.nhs.uk (general travel advice for the layman), www.ageconcern.org.uk (advice on travel for the elderly) and www .mariestopes.org.uk (information on women's health and contraception).

FURTHER READING

Health Advice for Travellers (currently called the 'T6' leaflet) is an annually updated leaflet

---

ADVICE ONLINE

It's usually a good idea to consult your government's travel health website before departure, if one is available:

Australia www.dfat.gov.au/travel/
Canada www.travelhealth.gc.ca
UK www.doh.gov.uk/traveladvice
USA www.cdc.gov/travel/

by the Department of Health in the UK available free in post offices. It contains some general information, legally required and recommended vaccines for different countries, reciprocal health agreements and an E111 application form. Lonely Planet's *Travel with Children* includes advice on travel health for younger children. Other recommended references include *Traveller's Health* by Dr Richard Dawood (Oxford University Press) and *The Traveller's Good Health Guide* by Ted Lankester (Sheldon Press).

IN TRANSIT

DEEP VEIN THROMBOSIS (DVT)

Blood clots may form in the legs during flights, chiefly because of prolonged immobility. The longer the flight, the greater the risk. The chief symptom of DVT is swelling or pain of the foot, ankle, or calf, usually but not always on just one side. When a blood clot travels to the lungs, it may cause chest pain and breathing difficulties. Travellers with any of these symptoms should immediately seek medical attention.

To prevent the development of DVT on long flights you should walk about the cabin, contract the leg muscles while sitting, drink plenty of fluids and avoid alcohol and tobacco.

JET LAG & MOTION SICKNESS

To avoid jet lag (common when crossing more than five time zones) try drinking plenty of nonalcoholic fluids and eating light meals. Upon arrival, get exposure to natural sunlight and readjust your schedule (for meals, sleep and so on) as soon as possible.

Antihistamines such as dimenhydrinate (Dramamine) and meclizine (Antivert, Bonine) are usually the first choice for treating motion sickness. A herbal alternative is ginger.

IN MALTA

AVAILABILITY OF HEALTH CARE

Good health care is readily available in Malta. For minor self-limiting illnesses pharmacists can give valuable advice and sell over-the-counter medication. They can

also advise when more specialised help is required and point you in the right direction. There are pharmacies in most towns; these are generally open from 9am to 1pm and 4pm to 7pm Monday to Saturday. On Sundays and public holidays they open by roster in the morning – the local Sunday newspapers print details of the roster.

Malta's public general hospital is **St Luke's Hospital** (Map p86; ☎ 21 241 251, emergency ☎ 196; www.slh.gov.mt; Triq San Luqa, Gwardamanġa), near Pietà (southwest of Valletta) and accessible by bus No 75 from the capital. A large new teaching hospital is under construction near the University of Malta in Msida. Gozo has a smaller hospital: **Craig Hospital** (Map p142; ☎ 21 561 600; Triq l-Arċisqof Pietru Pace, Victoria). GP service is also available at a network of health centres (at Floriana, Gżira, Qormi, Paola, Cospicua, Mosta, Rabat and on Gozo).

The standard of dental care is usually good; however, it is sensible to have a dental check-up before a long trip.

TRAVELLER'S DIARRHOEA

Simple things like a change of water, food or climate can all cause stomach upsets. If you develop diarrhoea, be sure to drink plenty of fluids, preferably an oral rehydration solution (eg dioralyte). A few loose stools don't require treatment but, if you start having more than four or five stools a day, you should start taking an antibiotic (usually a quinolone drug) and an antidiarrhoeal agent (such as loperamide). If diarrhoea is bloody, persists for more than 72 hours or is accompanied by fever, shaking, chills or severe abdominal pain you should seek medical attention.

ENVIRONMENTAL HAZARDS
Heat Exhaustion & Heatstroke

Take care in the fierce heat of a Maltese summer. Heat exhaustion occurs following excessive fluid loss with inadequate replacement of fluids and salt. Symptoms include headache, dizziness and tiredness. Dehydration is already happening by the time you feel thirsty – aim to drink sufficient water to produce pale, diluted urine. To treat heat exhaustion, replace lost fluids by drinking water and/or fruit juice, and cool the body with cold water and fans. Treat salt loss with salty fluids such as soup or

HEALTH

Bovril, or add a little more table salt to foods than usual.

Heatstroke is much more serious, resulting in irrational and hyperactive behaviour, and eventually loss of consciousness and death. Rapid cooling by spraying the body with water and fanning is ideal. Emergency fluid and electrolyte replacement by intravenous drip is recommended.

Insect Bites & Stings

Mosquitoes are found in most parts of Europe; they may not carry malaria but can cause irritation and infected bites. Use a DEET-based insect repellent.

Bees and wasps cause real problems only to those with a severe allergy (anaphylaxis). If you have a severe allergy to bee or wasp stings carry an 'epipen' or similar adrenaline injection.

Sandflies are found around Mediterranean beaches. They usually cause only a nasty, itchy bite but can carry a rare skin disorder called cutaneous Leishmaniasis.

Bed bugs lead to very itchy lumpy bites. Spraying the mattress with crawling insect killer after changing bedding will get rid of them.

Scabies is caused by tiny mites that live in the skin, particularly between the fingers, and cause an intensely itchy rash. It is easily treated with lotion from a pharmacy; other members of the household also need treating to avoid spreading scabies between asymptomatic carriers.

Water

Malta's tap water is safe to drink but heavily chlorinated, so stick to the bottled variety if you don't like the taste. Any water in the countryside, whether from a stream or spring, is best left alone.

TRAVELLING WITH CHILDREN

If you are travelling with children you should know how to treat minor ailments and when to seek medical treatment. Make sure the children are up to date with routine vaccinations, and discuss possible travel vaccines well before departure as some vaccines are not suitable for children under a year old.

In hot moist climates any wound or break in the skin is likely to let in infection. The area should be cleaned and kept dry.

Remember to avoid contaminated food and water. If your child has vomiting or diarrhoea, lost fluid and salts must be replaced. It may be helpful to take rehydration powders for reconstituting with boiled water.

WOMEN'S HEALTH

Emotional stress, exhaustion and travelling through different time zones can all contribute to an upset in the menstrual pattern. If using oral contraceptives, remember some antibiotics, diarrhoea and vomiting can stop the pill from working and lead to the risk of pregnancy – remember to take condoms with you just in case. Time zones, gastrointestinal upsets and antibiotics do not affect injectable contraception.

Travelling during pregnancy is usually possible, but always consult your doctor before planning your trip. The most risky times for travel are during the first 12 weeks of pregnancy and after 30 weeks.

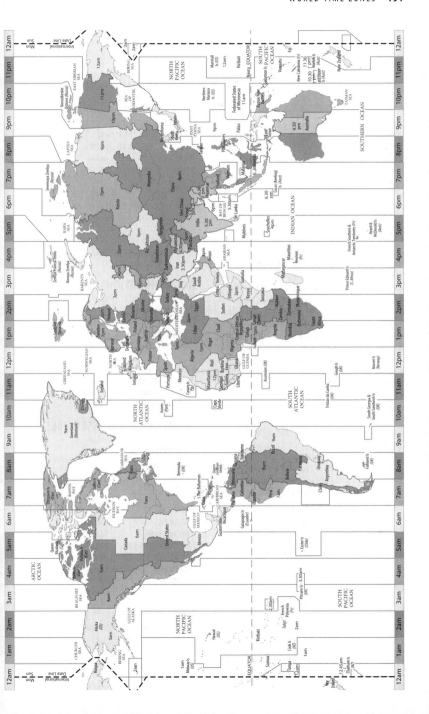

Language

CONTENTS

Malti – the native language of Malta – is a member of the Semitic language group, which also includes Arabic, Hebrew and Amharic. It's thought by some to be a direct descendant of the language spoken by the Phoenicians, but most linguists consider it to be related to the Arabic dialects of western North Africa. Malti is the only Semitic language that is written in a Latin script.

Both Malti and English are official languages in Malta, and almost everyone is bilingual. Travellers will have no trouble at all getting by in English at all times. However, it's always good to learn at least a few words of the native language, and the sections that follow will provide a basic introduction to Malti.

If you want to learn more about the language, look out for *Teach Yourself Maltese* by Joseph Aquilina or *Learn Maltese – Why Not?* by Joseph Vella. Lonely Planet's *Europe Phrasebook* has a useful Maltese section. A small range of pocket dictionaries and phrasebooks is available in bookshops in Malta. They are of variable quality and usefulness, so it's worth checking the content carefully before buying.

PRONUNCIATION

There are 29 letters in the Maltese alphabet. Individual letters in Malti aren't too diffcult to pronounce once you learn the rules, but putting them together to make any kind of sense is a major achievement. Most are pronounced as they are in English. The following list covers the letters that may cause a little confusion.

ċ	as the 'ch' in child
g	as in 'good'
ġ	'soft' as the 'j' in 'job'
għ	silent; lengthens the preceding or following vowel
h	silent, as in 'hour'
ħ	as the 'h' in 'hand'
j	as the 'y' in 'yellow'
ij	as the 'ai' in 'aisle'
ej	as the 'ay' in 'day'
q	a glottal stop; it's like the missing 't' in the Cockney pronunciation of 'bottle' (bo'ul)
x	as the 'sh' in 'shop'
z	as the 'ts' in 'bits'
ż	soft as in 'zero'

ACCOMMODATION

Do you have any rooms available?	Għad fadlilkom xi kmamar vojta?
Can you show me a room?	Tista' turini kamra?
How much is it?	Kemm hi?
I'd like a room ...	Nixtieq kamra ...
with one bed	b'sodda waħda
with two beds	b'żewġ sodod
with en suite	bil-kamra tal-banju

CONVERSATION & ESSENTIALS

Hello.	Merħba.
Good morning/day	Bonġu.
Good evening.	Bonswa.
Goodbye.	Saħħa.
Yes/No.	Iva/Le.
Please.	Jekk jogħġbok.
Thank you.	Grazzi.
Excuse me.	Skużani.
How are you?	Kif inti?
I'm fine, thank you.	Tajjed, grazzi.
Do you speak English?	Titkellem bl-ingliż?
What's your name?	X'ismek?
My name is ...	Jisimni ...
I love you.	Inħobbok.

DIRECTIONS

Where is a/the ...?	Fejn hu ...?
Go straight ahead.	Mur dritt.
Turn left.	Dur fuq ix-xellug.
Turn right.	Dur fuq il-lemin.
near	il-viċin
far	il-bogħod

LANGUAGE

SIGNS	
Miftuħ	Open
Magħluq	Closed
Dħul	Entrance
Ħrug	Exit
Vjalq	Avenue
Sqaq	Lane/Alley
Twaletta	Toilet
Rġiel	Men
Nisa	Women

NUMBERS

0	*xejn*
1	*wieħed*
2	*tnejn*
3	*tlieta*
4	*erbgħa*
5	*ħamsa*
6	*sitta*
7	*sebgħa*
8	*tmienja*
9	*disgħa*
10	*għaxra*
11	*ħdax*
12	*tnax*
13	*tlettax*
14	*erbatax*
15	*ħmistax*
16	*sittax*
17	*sbatax*
18	*tmintax*
19	*dsatax*
20	*għoxrin*
30	*tletin*
40	*erbgħin*
50	*ħamsin*
60	*sittin*
70	*sebgħin*
80	*tmienin*
90	*disgħin*
100	*mija*
1000	*elf*

SHOPPING & SERVICES

How much is it?	*Kemm?*
What time does it open/close?	*Fix'ħin jiftaħ/jagħlaq?*
... embassy	*ambaxxata ...*
bank	*bank*
chemist/pharmacy	*ispiżerija*
hotel	*hotel/il-lukanda*
market	*suq*

EMERGENCIES	
Help!	*Ajjut!*
Call a doctor!	*Qibgħad ghat-tabib!*
Police!	*Pulizija!*
I'm lost.	*Ninsab mitluf.*
ambulance	*ambulans*
hospital	*sptar*

post office	*posta*
public telephone	*telefon pubbliku*
shop	*ħanut*

TIME & DATES

What's the time?	*X'ħin hu?*
today	*illum*
tomorrow	*għada*
yesterday	*il-bieraħ*
morning	*fil-għodu*
afternoon	*wara nofs in-nhar*
Monday	*it-tnejn*
Tuesday	*it-tlieta*
Wednesday	*l-erbgħa*
Thursday	*il-hamis*
Friday	*il-gimgħa*
Saturday	*is-sibt*
Sunday	*il-ħadd*
January	*Jannar*
February	*Frar*
March	*Marzu*
April	*April*
May	*Mejju*
June	*Ġunju*
July	*Lulju*
August	*Awissu*
September	*Settembru*
October	*Ottubru*
November	*Novembru*
December	*Diċembru*

TRANSPORT

When does the boat leave/arrive?	*Meta jitlaq/jasal il-vapur?*
When does the bus leave/arrive?	*Meta titlaq/jasal il-karozza?*
I'd like to hire a car/bicycle.	*Nixtieq nikri karozza/rota.*
left luggage	*hallejt il-bagalji*
I'd like a ... ticket.	*Nixtieq biljett ...*
one-way	*'one-way'*
return	*'return'*

Glossary

See also the Language chapter (p192), for an introduction to the Maltese language and useful phrases, and the Food & Drink chapter (p53) for an explanation of Maltese specialities.

auberge – the residence of an individual langue of the Knights of St John

bajja – bay
bastion – a defensive work with two faces and two flanks, projecting from the line of the rampart
belt – city
bieb – gate

cavalier – a defensive work inside the main fortification, rising above the level of the main rampart to give covering fire
ċimiterju – cemetery
curtain – a stretch of rampart linking two bastions, with a parapet along the top

daħla – creek
dawret – bypass
demi-bastion – a half-bastion with only one face and one flank
dgħajsa – a traditional oar-powered boat

festa – feast day
fortizza – fort
foss – ditch

għajn – spring (of water)
għar – cave
ġnien – garden

kajjik – fishing boat
kappillan – parish priest
karrozzin – traditional horse-drawn carriage
kastell – castle

katidral – cathedral
kbira – big, main
knisja – church
kwartier – quarter, neighbourhood

langue – a division of the Knights of St John, based on nationality
luzzu – fishing boat

marsa – harbour
mdina – fortified town, citadel
mina – arch, gate
misraħ – square
mitħna – windmill
mużew – museum

palazzo – Italian term for palace or mansion
parroċċa – parish
passeggiata – evening stroll (Italian term)
pjazza – square
plajja – beach, seashore
pulizija – police

rabat – town outside the walls of a citadel
ramla – bay, beach
ras – point, headland

sur – bastion

telgħa – hill
torri – tower, castle
triq – street, road

vedette – a lookout point
vjal – avenue

wied – valley

xatt – wharf, marina

Behind the Scenes

THIS BOOK
The 1st edition of Lonely Planet's *Malta* was written by Neil Wilson. This edition was updated by Carolyn Bain.

THANKS from the Author
Carolyn Bain Many thanks to LP's Michala Green for sending me off to Malta, thereby allowing me to continue my LP-subsidised search for the perfect Mediterranean island. I'm also grateful to Neil Wilson for his work in putting together such a solid 1st edition of this book. His 1st-edition coverage, and his travel advice, helped make my job much more enjoyable.

Various locals, expats and tourists in Malta gave freely of their time, patiently answered my questions and kindly shared with me their local knowledge – I'm grateful to all of them, especially Tony at the tourist office in Valletta, Jean Paul at the YMCA, Charlie at Coronation Guesthouse and Joseph on Gozo. Thanks also to Charmaine Saliba for the chance to see Portomaso from a local's perspective, and for an excellent night out. And last but not least, warmest thanks to the fabulous Kelvin Adams for his company on much of this trip.

CREDITS
This title was commissioned and developed in Lonely Planet's London office by Michala Green. Cartography for this guide was developed by Mark Griffiths. Overseeing the project was project manager Rachel Imeson, managing editors Martin Heng and Stephanie Pearson and managing cartographers Mark Griffiths and Adrian Persoglia.

Editing was coordinated by Andrea Baster with able assistance from Barbara Delissen, Kate Evans, Charlotte Harrison, Carly Hall and David Andrew. Cartography was coordinated by Kim McDonald. Steven Cann was the prelayout designer, and Tamsin Wilson laid the book out with support from Adriana Mammarella and Kate McDonald. Annika Roojun designed the cover. The language content was coordinated by Quentin Frayne. Andrea Baster and Tamsin Wilson prepared the index.

THANKS from Lonely Planet
Thanks to the many travellers who used the last edition and wrote to us with helpful hints, useful advice and interesting anecdotes:
A Marcelo Amaya, FH Armstrong **B** Brendon Bailey, Geoff Bannister, Jacqui Belgrave, Florian Bertram, Michel & Clément Betout, Ellen Beunderman, Diana Binney, Jackie Bolger, Andre Bosmans, Phil & Tessa Bromley, Harry Broome, Danjel Bugeja, Emanuel Buttigieg **C** Chris Carabott Terry Casstevens, Thomas Christodoulides, Marie Clark, Jane Cooper, Michael Counsell, Polly Crabtree, Elena Crini, Gary Cullimore, Carrie Cunningham **D** Morton Davis, Louise Dixson, Liesbeth Dubois **E** Moray Easdale, Frank Edmondson, Jean Edmonson, Ralph F Ernst, Margaret Stewart Evans, Christopher Eyton **F** Mario Falzon, Victor Falzon, Bob Farrell, Stephen Farrugia, Angela Felgate, Kevin Finegan, Philippa Fleetwood, Nicky Francis, Andy Frost **G** Aleksandra Golbiowska, Ari Goldmann, Miguel Alvim Gonzalez, Harry Goovaarts, Mathew Gore, Deborah Gravrock, Kathryn Griffiths, Simon Grinter **H** Kate Hamilton, Andy & Vivien Hamnett, Dr J Handley, Joan Hawkins, Anna Heino, Ivor Hicks, Gavin Hodgson **I** Amy Ip **K** Tobias Kalchreuter, Margit Kastner, Manuel Kielmannsegge, Sytske Kimstra, Pauline van der Kleijn, Martti Koskenniemi, Peter Kosmider, Carole Krone **L** Karen Lamorey, Henry Lang, Bernice Lapoint, Anselmo Lastra, Marjon Lips,

---

THE LONELY PLANET STORY
The story begins with a classic travel adventure: Tony and Maureen Wheeler's 1972 journey across Europe and Asia to Australia. There was no useful information about the overland trail then, so Tony and Maureen published the first Lonely Planet guidebook to meet a growing need.

From a kitchen table, Lonely Planet has grown to become the largest independent travel publisher in the world, with offices in Melbourne (Australia), Oakland (USA), London (UK) and Paris (France).

Today Lonely Planet guidebooks cover the globe. There is an ever-growing list of books and information in a variety of media. Some things haven't changed. The main aim is still to make it possible for adventurous travellers to get out there – to explore and better understand the world.

At Lonely Planet we believe travellers can make a positive contribution to the countries they visit – if they respect their host communities and spend their money wisely.

Peter Little, Warren Littleton, Michael Low **M** Chris Manning, AN Mather, Kathryn McDonnell, Peter McSorley, Alan & Winifred Mealing, Joanne Micallef, Marianne Miller, Lars Molin, Birte Mueller-Heidelberg, Rob Muijsenberg **N** Mrs H Nelson, Steve Newcomer **O** Kim & Laura Overall, Dr Jenny CE Owen **P** Tom Palinkas, Rolf Palmberg, Katy Peters, Karen Pickering, Alexander Pieri **R** Kornelia Ring, Gillian Rowe, JAV Rose **S** John Sacco, David Sadler, Will Sam, Lil Sassen, Judith Schaniel, Karl Scharbert, Kate Schwarz, Janet & Geoffrey Stevens, Derek Stone **T** Zara Tai, Terence Tam, Dafne Ter-Sakarian, Russell Thompson, K Thomson, Michael Townend, Jessica Trenholme **V** Pierre Van Den Heuvel, Geert van der Heijden, DH Vedder, DV Vedder, Florens Versteegh **W** MF Ware, Bill Watson, Jennifer P Wilson, Joe Wojtowicz **Y** Imran Yusuf

ACKNOWLEDGMENTS

Many thanks to the following for the use of their content:

Globe on back cover © Mountain High Maps 1993 Digital Wisdom, Inc.

Index

INDEX

INDEX

MAP LEGEND

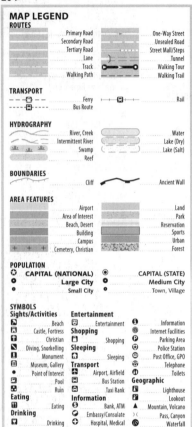

LONELY PLANET OFFICES

Australia
Head Office
Locked Bag 1, Footscray, Victoria 3011
☎ 03 8379 8000, fax 03 8379 8111
talk2us@lonelyplanet.com.au

USA
150 Linden St, Oakland, CA 94607
☎ 510 893 8555, toll free 800 275 8555
fax 510 893 8572, info@lonelyplanet.com

UK
72–82 Rosebery Ave,
Clerkenwell, London EC1R 4RW
☎ 020 7841 9000, fax 020 7841 9001
go@lonelyplanet.co.uk

Published by Lonely Planet Publications Pty Ltd
ABN 36 005 607 983

© Lonely Planet 2004

© photographers as indicated 2004

Cover photographs: Fishing boats, Marsaxlokk harbour, Rex Butcher/
Photolibrary.com (front); Mosta Dome, Eoin Clarke/Lonely Planet
Images (back). Many of the images in this guide are available for
licensing from Lonely Planet Images: www.lonelyplanetimages.com.